NEST OF SPIES

AMERICA'S JOURNEY TO DISASTER IN IRAN

By the same author

The Spirit of Allah: Khomeini and the Islamic Revolution
Holy Terror: The Inside Story of Islamic Terrorism

NEST OF SPIES

AMERICA'S JOURNEY TO DISASTER IN IRAN

AMIR TAHERI

PANTHEON BOOKS
NEW YORK

First American Edition

Copyright © 1988 by Amir Taheri

All rights reserved under International and Pan-American Copyright Conventions. Published in the United States by Pantheon Books, a division of Random House, Inc., New York, and simultaneously in Canada by Random House of Canada Limited, Toronto.

Originally published in Great Britain by Century Hutchinson Ltd., in 1988.

Library of Congresss Cataloging-in-Publication Data

Taheri, Amir.
  Nest of spies.

  Bibliography: p.
  Includes index.
  1. United States—Foreign relations—Iran.
2. Iran—Foreign relations—United States. I. Title.
E183.8.17T34 1989   327.73055   88-43240
ISBN 0-394-57566-0

Manufactured in the United States of America

Contents

If you make friends with people who ride elephants,
Build a house big enough for elephants.
Persian proverb

INTRODUCTION

Gun-toting children trampling the stars and stripes under foot. Bearded revolutionaries dancing around bonfires illuminated by burning effigies of Uncle Sam. A blindfolded US diplomat being presented to a mob on the verge of lynching delirium. Burned bodies of American soldiers strewn in the desert amid the wreckage of helicopters. An American pilot giving a live television interview while a terrorist presses a gun to his temple. The fearful expression of an American passenger whose fingers have been chopped off and thrown out of a jetliner by Muslim militants. The bullet-ridden body of an American diver tossed out of a hijacked aircraft. The charred corpses of scores of Marines murdered in their sleep by an explosion caused by a suicide squad. Coffins draped in American colours arriving in Washington from distant lands with strange names. The grim expression of frustrated American leaders. And the disdainful demeanour of dour-faced ayatollahs.

These are only some of the images associated in the American mind with the US experience in the Middle East in the 1980s. To them could be added other no less dramatic images offered by the Irangate saga: Colonel North's angelic face defending dark schemes in the name of patriotism. The angry expression of George Shultz and the cynical smile of William Casey. The professorial haughtiness of John Poindexter and the arrogant assertiveness of Arab and other Muslim arms smugglers and US adventurers who for some eighteen months took over the task of shaping American policy towards an important corner of the world.

During a decade of drama the American public was frequently reminded of the existence, somewhere in the world, of a reservoir of hatred and violence against the United States, whose volcanic eruptions seemed to defy logic. Each time the Americans thought that they had heard the last of that particular nightmare, it bounced back with the brutality of a boomerang.

The American experience of Islamic fundamentalism was, in a sense, even more frustrating that Vietnam had been half a generation earlier. In Vietnam the USA had fought a war, initially in the name of helping local patriots and democrats stop the spread of Soviet-backed Communism. In Vietnam one could recognize the two sides of the story and be for or against this or that policy. And from the mid-1960s onwards many Americans realized that the real war was not being fought in the swamps of Indochina but in the United States itself where the peace movement gradually captured the imagination of a whole generation and emerged as an irresistible force. Vietnam could be analysed and understood within the realm of common logic.

In the Middle East, however, the United States was not officially involved in a war and most Americans sincerely believed that they had no particular quarrel with anybody there. Receiving the coffins of the Marines killed in Beirut in 1983, President Reagan, attending a special ceremony in Washington, asked why that atrocity had been committed. The president's perplexity found many echoes throughout a shocked America. The Marines had been sent to Beirut at the invitation of the Lebanese authorities to help restore peace and prevent the massacre of Palestinians by their Maronite enemies. And yet they had been killed in their sleep without the slightest warning.

Some commentators pretended that the Americans were somehow, perhaps genetically, incapable of understanding why they were being murdered or abducted by people with whom they believed they had never quarrelled. Robert McFarlane, the former national security adviser, went even further and told a congressional hearing in February 1987 that most American politicians could not understand 'the peculiar politics' of the Middle East. Others simply asserted that the USA was in trouble in the Middle East because a group of mad mullahs were in a murderous mood. Such explanations, however, could only lead to greater confusion.

The situation became even more confused when Americans learned that President Reagan, the very man who had vowed never to make concessions to terrorists, had secretly sold arms to the mullahs in exchange for the release of three hostages in Beirut. More disappointing to many Americans was the fact that Israel, America's closest and most popular ally in the region, had played a crucial role in persuading President Reagan to seek a long-term association with the hated mullahs of Tehran.

Reagan's dramatic change of course in the summer of 1987 did not help the task of understanding America's problems either. The president had justified his secret deals with the mullahs by referring to the Soviet threat to Iran. But in July 1987 he ordered the US Navy to enter the Persian Gulf to bolster the Arab side against Iran while he issued an invitation to the Soviets to help bring peace to the region.

In the Irangate episode the sublime had been replaced by the ridiculous as a small group of plotters played at high strategy. The so-called reflagging exercise, which reversed the previous policy of seeking accommodation with Tehran, raised the ridiculous to the level of the sublime in a uniquely farcical though no less dangerous situation. In it the United States ran the risk of a major international conflict so that Kuwaiti oil could flow to Japan and Europe, enabling Iraq to earn enough money to buy arms from the Soviet Union with which to fight Iran, which, in turn, received American-made arms with help from Israel, Washington's closest ally in the Middle East.

The present book is an attempt to chart the route which, over more than four decades, took the United States to Irangate and beyond. It examines the reasons for the failure of presidents Roosevelt and Truman in their efforts to help Iran become a model of democratic development. It also shows how the seeds of the Islamic Revolution were unwittingly sown by policies pursued by the shah with support from six American presidents. Finally it relates and analyses the Irangate scandal and its consequences in the broader context of the American experience in the Middle East.

The American experience of Islamic fundamentalism has been the subject of long and impassioned debates for nearly a decade. Some people would not be convinced that America's humiliation in Iran was not simply due to President Carter's alleged softness and indecision. Others would not tire of blaming President Nixon for having supported the shah beyond all measure and against all reason. The debate is likely to continue as long as the Middle East remains in turmoil and the USA continues to appear confused and vulnerable. My purpose here is not to cross any polemical swords with the partisans of this or that ultimate theory about the American failure in Iran. I have tried to tell the story of America and of Americans in Iran as objectively as possible against the background of Islamic funda-mentalism as the dominant political force in the Middle East in the 1980s.

To do so I have drawn on the documents seized at the United States embassy in Tehran in 1979 and gradually published over the following years. The capture of the embassy provided the first opportunity since Trotsky, as External Affairs Commissar, began publishing secret diplomatic documents after the Bolshevik revolution, for a mass of confidential material of this type to be made public. Some of these documents were published in book form in fifty-eight volumes up to July 1987 and a selection of others was made available to researchers in Tehran. I have cross-checked most of these documents through some 150 personal interviews with people involved in Irano-American relations at various levels over some forty years. Records of the Iranian Foreign Ministry and the US Congress have also been consulted whenever neccessary. Personal experience of eighteen years in political journalism has further guided me in putting some of the events related in the book into proper perspective.

The documents seized at the embassy show that the United States knew much of what it needed to know for a proper understanding of Iran but failed to understand because of errors of judgement made by the leading decision makers. The common assumption that the American failure in Iran was principally due to lack of intelligence and even of ordinary information may be hard to dislodge. But the documents published so far show that this was not the case. They show that, while the Central Intelligence Agency (CIA) often missed the target, the diplomats dispatched to Iran frequently did a good job of gauging the mood of the country and offered generally sound advice. A major drawback for Irano-American relations was the relatively low level of interest that Congress had in the subject. Media interest in Iran was also sporadic and highly selective, reflecting and at the same time perpetuating a lack of interest on the part of the public. Even the dramatic events of 1979–81 did not succeed in persuading Congress and the media to change their basic attitude on this issue. Iran was a domain where the White House, the CIA and the Pentagon could play very high stakes without encountering the usual congressional and media hurdles that have marked American policy-making since the Second World War.

The embassy documents are interesting for a number of other reasons also. They reveal the techniques of superpower diplomacy first hand and on a day-to-day basis. Through them we learn about the areas of most concern to the United States in a country of crucial importance and the methods used for gathering and analysing information related to them. We also see the process through which field reports and analyses carried out at headquarters influence decision making. In some cases we see that the policy is in no way warranted by the facts on which it is supposedly based. The documents further illustrate rivalries between various sections of the United States government both in the field and at headquarters concerning projects and prerogatives. As a result of these rivalries, further complicated by personal jealousies, no major issue was ever decided one way or another for any appreciable length of time. In his testimony to the Senate Foreign Relations Committee in February 1987, Secretary of State George Shultz complained that nothing was ever decided in Washington. His point is amply illustrated by the documents seized at the Tehran embassy.

The first part of the present book takes us up to the Islamic Revolution and the hostages crisis that resulted from it. In the second part we focus on secret diplomacy and covert operations which provided the basic method the Reagan administration used in its attempts to influence events in the Islamic Republic. What became known as the Irangate or Iranscam scandal constituted only one part of a whole series of often unrelated and contradictory covert operations that the Reagan administration pursued with regard to Iran.

In relating the history of more than eight years of covert operations we come into contact with a host of colourful characters. These include amateur diplomats dreaming of making history with the help of 'the death merchants' and professional plotters who, working in the dark, never lose sight of opportunities for making personal profit. The behind-the-scenes drama enacted over more than eight years in Tehran, Washington, Jerusalem, London, Cairo and a dozen other cities reflected the realities of a secret world which obeyed few rules either of international conduct or of individual morality. It is in this broader context that the Irangate fiasco might be properly understood.

The present book also fills some of the important gaps left in the Irangate saga by the various official bodies which have dealt with it in the United States. In 1987 no fewer than nine separate inquiries were carried out on the subject. But all of them left out important pieces of the Irangate jigsaw puzzle for a variety of reasons. We have found these pieces and fitted them into their proper places in the hope of offering a complete picture.

Had it not been so sadly real, the Irangate scandal might have been taken as the quintessential American soap opera and even praised for the months of entertaining drama that it provided for the television-watching public. But the episode did long-term harm to relations between the United States and Iran in particular and the Muslim world in general. It showed the fragility of international life at times of systemic crises and the vulnerability of diplomatic relations to cowboy-style initiatives that quickly ran out of control. Irangate showed how easy it was for a superpower to stray off the beaten track of diplomatic practice and end up in the cloak-and-dagger universe of the Arabian Nights.

The United States, because of its system of government, which makes the setting and pursuing of precise and long-term foreign policy goals excessively difficult and at times even impossible, has often been tempted to have recourse to covert action in different parts of the world. Some policymakers in the USA even seem to believe that the only real alternative to covert action is the naked use of force in the pursuit of a more dynamic foreign policy. Thus the secret talks with the mullahs and the subsequent recourse to sabre-rattling in the Persian Gulf both reflected long-established traditions in American foreign policy.

The backdrop to the drama of duplicity that was Irangate was provided by the Gulf War, which entered its eighth year in 1987. The world's longest and costliest conflict since Vietnam, the Gulf War has claimed more than a million lives and wrecked the economies of both Iran and Iraq.

The story of the American experience in Iran, however, is not one of diplomatic failure only. It is also the story of a beautiful friendship that developed over more than a hundred years and brought immense benefits to both sides. It drew inspiration and strength from many shared dreams and countless personal contacts between the two peoples which often led to abiding loyalties on both sides. The fact that the relationship was, almost suddenly, transformed into one of bitter enmity in the 1980s surprised many on both sides who had looked forward to an everlasting friendship between the two countries. What went wrong? How did Iran, described by President Carter as a trusted and esteemed ally of the United States, become President Reagan's number one enemy? Is the United States alone responsible for what happened, as some Americans, apparently believing a new version of original sin, like to pretend? Or should one fix the blame solely on Iran, a nation whose independence and territorial integrity were saved by the United States but whose ingratitude knew no bounds?

These questions and many more must be discussed and answered by both sides as a means of putting their experience in perspective and learning the lessons of the past. Iran and the United States needed each other in the past and will need each other even more in the future. There is no reason why they should not look beyond the bitterness of the past nine years to the prospect of better relations in the coming decade. The Persian poet Hafez said:

> I break the cord of your friendship
> So that, when it is knotted again, I come closer to you.

BEAUTIFUL AMERICANS

Howard C. Baskerville had just turned twenty-one when the vagaries of fortune and his own quest for adventure took him to Iran[1] in 1909. A graduate of Princeton, Baskerville wanted to see the world and, chance permitting, do some good. He ended up in Tabriz, then Iran's second most populous city after the capital Tehran. There he became a teacher at the local school which had been set up and was run by American missionaries. He could not have chosen a more exciting time or place to be, for in those dramatic days Tabriz was the stronghold of constitutional revolutionaries who wanted to put an end to the shah's tyrannical rule and establish 'a government of the people, for the people'.

The shah, one Mohammad-Ali, was backed by the Russian Tsar and an army of ruthless Cossacks supported by tribal warriors who, fanaticized by mullahs, believed that constitutional government would spell the end of their religion – Islam. By the time Baskerville settled in Tabriz a civil war had become inevitable. The young teacher lost no time in deciding which side he would fight on and, eventually, die for.

The American presence in Tabriz consisted of a few dozen teachers and missionaries, who looked to the local consul for political guidance in those troubled times. Washington had opted for neutrality in the Iranian civil war; there was little of practical use that the United States could do to help, and, perhaps more importantly, it saw none of its interests served by taking sides in a bizarre, though no less bloody, conflict some six thousand miles away.

Baskerville, however, could not remain neutral. For a while he toyed with the idea of raising an international force of volunteers to help the anti-shah camp. But none of the Americans and Europeans present in the excited city were attracted to the idea of fighting. Most were looking for the first opportunity to leave. The fact that Baskerville had absolutely no military experience and did not know how to fire a musket did little to promote him as a promising general.

The young Princetonian was left with his pupils only. The boys, mostly aged between twelve and eighteen, were eager to fight and Baskerville enlisted them all in his little revolutionary army. Using old military manuals and some ingenuity, he succeeded in putting his fighting force on the confused map of Tabriz. In the process he was reprimanded by the US State Department and asked to resign his job with the mission board. He introduced the word 'militia' into the Persian language and began teaching the constitutionalists to use the type of guerrilla tactics that General George Washington had employed against the British.

Baskerville's military career lasted less than two weeks: he was killed in a suburb of Tabriz while leading an attack on a stronghold of the monarchist forces. The young revolutionary's death instantly turned him into a hero of the noble cause in a land distinguished by its cult of martyrs. Baskerville's funeral, marked by the closing of the local bazaars, was attended by thousands of armed constitutionalists and wailing women. As news of the young American's selfless heroism spread throughout Iran, it helped rally the anti-shah forces and served as a timely morale booster for the constitutionalists. Later Baskerville was to enter legend: he would, for example, be seen in dreams of the pious holding the reins of the white stallion ridden by the Hidden Imam, the Islamic Messiah whose return would fill the universe with justice and peace.

The shah's forces were eventually defeated and the constitutionalists gained control of the government in Tehran. They purged and reorganized the Russian-led Cossack force and had one of the leading ayatollahs of the day hanged as a traitor for his support of the now deposed monarch. They remembered the young American in Tabriz and named a street after him. They also began seeking ways and means of getting the United States interested in Iranian affairs as a force capable of counterbalancing the dual pressure exerted on Iran by the Tsar and the British Empire.

There was no reason for the United States or even for individual Americans to have become interested in Iran. The few Americans who came to visit the country in the 1820s found nothing but death and desolation. Iran had just emerged from its series of wars against the Tsars – wars that had cost her some of her richest regions in the Caucasus, unceremoniously annexed by St Petersburg. The once proud Persian Empire was a sad shadow of its former self. From 1824 onwards – that is to say, after the conclusion of a humiliating treaty with Russia – those among the Iranian elite who had not been completely wasted by corruption and cynicism began to think about a powerful but distant ally which could help the country adapt itself to

the modern world of gunboats, long-range artillery and industrial progress. Fatah-Ali Shah, the incompetent Qajar monarch, had tried to conclude an alliance with Napoleon during the latter's wars in Europe. The defeat of revolutionary France had, however, ended all hopes of a Franco-Iranian alliance. The first time the idea of looking to the United States for a potential ally was seriously raised seems to have been in the late 1820s when Abbas Mirza, the crown prince, heard a favourable account of life in the New World from a Turkish merchant.

The first Americans who came to Iran, however, looked nothing like people interested in entering 'the Great Game' on the side of a poverty-stricken and demoralized Persia. They were missionaries and do-gooders dedicated to improving the lives of Iran's Christian minority. The British had made it clear to the shah that they would not tolerate the presence of their American cousins in the southern regions of the country, which were considered to be part of Britain's sphere of influence. This British policy was further strengthened by the fact that the various missions did not wish to compete against one another. As a result, they tacitly agreed to 'divide' Iran into a number of zones each of which gradually emerged as the exclusive 'diocese' of one of the various Protestant churches. The Southern Baptist and Presbyterian missions, mostly active out of the unofficial 'British zone of influence', quickly fell under American domination. As a result the newcomers settled mostly in Azarbaijan, in the northwest of the country, or in the central regions of Tehran and Isfahan. They brought with them two of the first three printing presses in Iran and commissioned a Persian translation of the New Testament. They set up schools and opened clinics where people were treated regardless of their religious faith. The Iranians who came into contact with them were astonished by the selfless dedication of the strangers. The fact that most of the American missionaries scrupulously refrained from any attempt to convert Muslims to Christianity meant that their presence was not opposed by the mullahs. Many of the mullahs were, in fact, puzzled by the attitude of the American missionaries. 'They give everything they have and demand nothing in exchange,' one mullah commented.[2] The missionaries were loved by their fellow Christians in Iran and respected by almost everyone they had occasion to meet. They portrayed America as the land of the free: a country where equality reigned and accident of birth did not bestow any particular status on an individual. Many Muslim Iranians attended the mission schools and were introduced to such modern concepts as the rule of law, the intrinsic worth of the human individual, freedom of faith and of expression, the merits of disciplined method and, above all, the possibility of achieving happiness in this world. But what impressed the Iranians most was the way the Americans worked from dawn to dusk, tackling a variety of tasks from teaching to farming to sewing and carpentry. The missionaries and their wives were polyvalent self-helpers who combined industriousness with thrift.[3]

Between 1829, when the first group of American missionaries settled in Iran, and 1883, when the first United States diplomatic mission was established in Tehran, no more than a few thousand Iranians had come into contact with the representatives of the New World,[4] but a definite image of the United States as a land of freedom and justice had already taken shape in the minds of thinking Iranians. A decade later the American system of government was frequently considered as an ideal model by many of the Iranian reformers whose writings helped provoke the constitutional revolution.

Thus it was only natural that the constitutional government of 1909–12 should think of seeking support from the United States. Iranian democrats recognized the country's urgent need for financial, technical and military support. That support could not come from the traditional colonial powers, which knew that only a weak and backward Iran would obey their diktats. The constitutional leaders eventually contacted President William H. Taft's administration in Washington with the offer of friendship and cooperation. It is likely that Taft did not fully grasp Iran's strategic importance and was, in any case, reluctant to provoke a confrontation with both Britain and Russia over a country he could hardly locate on the map. Informed that the Iranian economy was on the verge of collapse, President Taft thought he could best respond to the appeal for help from Tehran by nominating a financial consultant. The man Taft recommended was one W. Morgan Shuster, a lawyer with some knowledge of economics and a background of service in Cuba and the Philippines. Tehran immediately agreed to take Shuster and offered him a three-year contract. The Iranian leaders wanted to get the United States involved in the development of the country and believed that Shuster, being recommended by the president himself, must be a man of influence with the administration.

Shuster may be considered as the precursor of numerous idealist-technocrats who tried to help remove the heavy hand of the Middle Ages from Iran's keel in the first seven decades of this century. But he was to be beaten into disappointment more quickly than most of his successors. Within a few weeks of his arrival in Tehran the dashing lawyer from Washington realized that his mission had little hope of success. Nevertheless, he fought on for a whole year until his dismissal was imposed on the Tehran government by the Russians. Shuster impressed the constitutional leaders and the Iranians with whom he worked. He told them that Iran did not have to live in slavery and could become a great and powerful nation again only if the old privileged elite curbed their appetites and stopped acting as the local bailiffs of plundering foreigners. He found the way the British and the Russians treated Iran to be 'uncivilized' and spared no effort to get the United States more actively interested in helping Iran's democratic government, but to no avail.[5]

Shuster's dismissal proved the first step in the defeat of the constitutional government and the reimposition of the shah through Russian force and British intrigue. The parliament was dissolved and the constitution, which limited the shah's powers, was violated although not formally abrogated. The Shuster experiment was dismissed as irrelevant and Americans were depicted as 'naive idealists who would never understand this country and this people'.[6] Shuster's year in Iran was, nevertheless, far from being totally wasted. He succeeded in reorganizing the treasury and establishing a system of tax collection and accounting that was to become part of the tradition of public finance management in the country. He also trained half a dozen Iranians who, nearly a generation later, were to create a full ministry of finance under Reza Shah.

Shuster left Iran almost at the same time as a new chapter was opening in the nation's history with the discovery of substantial oil reserves in the slopes of the Zagros range of mountains in the southwest. From then on oil was to become the key factor in shaping Iran's politics. Iran's value, until then limited to her geopolitical location, was dramatically increased as the country was now a source of energy. With abundant supplies of oil assured, the British, thanks to Winston Churchill, at that time First Lord of the Admiralty, decided to convert her navy from coal to petroleum in 1911. This meant that Iran would be certain of a continued flow of foreign currency in the form of a 16 per cent royalty offered it within the framework of the newly constituted Anglo-Persian Oil Company.[7]

The oil contract imposed on Iran by the British was anything but just. The company paid neither tax nor duties to the Iranian government but was subject to full income tax in Britain. Iranians were not allowed access to the company's accounts and production data and had no means of knowing how much oil was extracted and exported. Iranian oil was sold to the Royal Navy at a discount while the company refused to lower its prices for customers within Iran itself. Very quickly the British-controlled company began to develop its own political role, which at times was even at variance with policies set by the British government itself.

The First World War, which was to establish the United States as a major power, also resulted in a dramatic change in the international climate that concerned Iran. The Bolshevik revolution of 1917 knocked Russia out of 'the Great Game' and opened the way for a full domination of Iran by Great Britain. In 1919 the British attempted to impose a new treaty which would have turned Iran into a protectorate in all but name. In the aftermath of the war the Iranian leaders had tried hard to air their grievances in international forums but their efforts had been thwarted by the British. President Woodrow Wilson had supported an Iranian demand for participation in the Versailles peace conference and indicated a willingness to consider Tehran's claims on former Iranian territories annexed by Russia. But once again the British succeeded in persuading the United States to stay out of Iranian affairs. The Iranian team in Versailles had nevertheless managed to secure a hearing with American diplomats accompanying President Wilson to the conference. They found the Americans sympathetic to Iran's cause and saw this as confirmation of their belief that the United States was the only major power capable of using her influence on behalf of the 'victims of colonialism'.[8]

The newly established Soviet regime in Moscow attempted a dramatic comeback on the Iranian scene in 1921 with the signing of a treaty with the government in Tehran. The signing was preceded by a Soviet announcement foreswearing all the advantages secured in Iran by the Tsars and cancelling all Tehran's pending debts to Russian businesses and banks. In exchange the treaty committed Iran to neutrality against the Soviet Union: Iranian territory could not be used by a third power for aggression against her northern neighbour.

The British, worried about the outcome of Bolshevik efforts in Iran, encouraged the creation of a strong central government in Tehran. In 1921 they supported a putsch that forced the weakling Ahmad Shah Qajar to appoint Sayyed Ziaeddin Tabataba'i as prime minister. Tabataba'i, a fiery writer and effective orator, was genuinely convinced that only Britain could save Iran from being overwhelmed by the rising tide of Bolshevism. In the name of Persian nationalism he advocated the turning of Iran into a British protectorate in all but name. Within months of the success of the putsch the new war minister, one Brigadier Reza Khan, commander of the Cossack Division, had emerged as the cabinet's strongman. Tabataba'i was ousted soon afterwards and forced into exile in Palestine, then a British mandate territory. Reza Khan, who took the surname of Pahlavi ('heroic'), wasted no time: he persuaded the parliament to appoint him prime minister and then organized a gilt-edged exile for Ahmad Shah. By 1925 the Cossack officer was declared Shahanshah ('King of Kings') by the parliament: the Pahlavi dynasty was born. But a change of regime did not alter the Iranian equation. The threat from the north remained while the nation's economy continued to decline.

In 1922 the putsch leaders decided to employ a new American economic and financial adviser and Washington recommended Dr Arthur Millspaugh for the job. Millspaugh, a former professor of economics, was at the time special adviser to the State Department. This meant that his mission to Iran had greater official status than that of Shuster. There was one more difference between the two: Millspaugh brought with him a team of assistants and a number of research papers on various aspects of life in Iran. But all that did not give him a better chance of succeeding where Shuster had failed. Millspaugh spent five frustrating years in Iran, only to arrive at the same conclusion that Shuster had reached in only ten months: reform was a hopeless cause in the land of Cyrus the Great.

Nevertheless Millspaugh's mission was not wholly without success. He built on the structures created by Shuster and trained a number of Iranians capable of running a more or less coherent system of taxation. His mission also focused Iranian attention on the need to harness the country's oil revenues for the purpose of further economic development. It was, perhaps, thanks to Millspaugh's quiet coaxing that several American businessmen interested in oil came to Tehran for exploratory talks with Iranian officials. Their presence in the Iranian capital coincided with what was to be only the first of many ugly incidents in Irano-American relations.

In July 1924, while the oil talks were in progress, a Tehran mob attacked and seriously injured the American vice-consul, Robert Imbrie, accusing him of sacrilege for having attempted to photograph a religious procession. The injured Imbrie was transported to a hospital for treatment. But another mob, led by a group of mullahs crying, 'Allah Akbar' ('Allah is the Greatest'), attacked the hospital and fell upon Imbrie, beating him to death with bricks, stones and sticks. The killer mob then went through the streets of the capital with cries of 'The infidel is dead' and 'Islam has triumphed', creating a sense of hysteria in the poorer districts.

Many people in Tehran believed that the murder of Imbrie had been inspired by British agents, who were said to finance and control many mullahs and prayer leaders in the capital. According to this theory the murder was aimed at achieving two goals: to push Millspaugh out of Iran and to discourage American oil companies from venturing into what looked like a turbulent and barbarous land. Both these goals were to be achieved, but for entirely different reasons. Millspaugh left Iran in 1927 after prolonged quarrels with Reza Shah, who accused him of pretending to be 'the monarch of this land'. To Reza Shah all

Millspaugh had to do was to give advice to his superiors and leave the final decision to them. The American, however, had the zeal of a missionary and was wholly incapable of adopting the passive attitude of a professional technocrat. He saw Reza Shah as an arrogant upstart interested only in bolstering his own illusions of grandeur rather than seeking to improve the lives of Iran's poor and broken masses.

In the stormy sessions he had with the king Millspaugh strongly argued for modernization and industrialization as the only means of saving Iran from poverty and foreign domination. His advice was not totally without effect, and Reza Shah, predisposed to bring Iran into the twentieth century, became the architect of his nation's first, albeit incoherent, attempt at industrialization. He also decided to send a number of young Iranians to the West to study modern sciences. Most chose Germany and France, where they enrolled at prestigious universities, but a few also made their way to the United States.

Millspaugh's departure did not mean an end to Irano-American relations. A number of Iranian merchants secured agency rights with major American companies and from 1930 onwards imports from the United States formed a growing part of Iran's foreign trade. In 1935 and 1936 two separate incidents led to the first diplomatic crisis between Tehran and Washington. The first concerned the arrest of Ghaffar Jalal, the Iranian minister plenipotentiary in the United States, on a charge of speeding through Elkton, a village in Maryland, in November 1935. Jalal was released after paying a fine and establishing his diplomatic immunity. He was received by Secretary of State Cordell Hull, who apologized about the incident while insisting, in a light-hearted tone, that diplomatic immunity did not mean one could break traffic rules. The incident was reported to Tehran by the vengeful plenipotentiary as a deliberate insult to the King of Kings by a representative of an upstart state whose history of less than two hundred years bore no comparison to that of the Persian Empire, which had been created five centuries before the Christian era.

The second incident followed hard on the heels of the first. A number of American newspapers began publishing anti-Reza Shah stories in which they claimed that the founder of the Pahlavi dynasty had been a stable boy at the British embassy in Tehran and that, by implication, he had been put on the throne by Great Britain. The press allegations reached Tehran, where rumour-mongers compounded their effects by spreading a variety of other stories about the shah in which he was variously depicted as a Jew, a Zoroastrian or a secret convert to Christianity. A strong protest note from Tehran to Washington brought a bland and delayed response from the State Department explaining the American government's inability to curb press freedom. Worse still, the note went on to say that it was no insult to describe someone as a self-made man in a country where many people rose from the ranks thanks to their intelligence and hard work.

The note could not but anger Reza Shah, who was at the same time patiently cultivating the fiction that he was a descendant of Iran's ancient kings and that God had destined him to become the saviour of his nation. Iranian diplomats were withdrawn from Washington and relations between the two countries were frozen, although no formal break was announced. An attempt at improving ties was made towards the end of 1938 but the freeze ordered by the shah remained in effect until Iran was engulfed in the flames of the Second World War.

The virtual removal of the United States from the Iranian scene strengthened the hand of those among the shah's advisers who argued for an alliance with Nazi Germany as a means of protecting Iran from both Britain and communist Russia. Hitler was quick to realize Iran's geographical importance both as a source of oil for Britain and as a country with the second longest frontier with the Soviet Union. By 1940 thousands of Germans were working in Iran and hundreds of Iranians were attending German universities and technical colleges. Hitler had declared Iran to be the original homeland of the Aryans and Berlin Radio broadcast a Persian programme which offered a daily dose of propaganda concerning the reshaping of the 'Jewish-infested world' by the 'Aryan nations of the East and of the West'. German agents in Iran had established contact with tribal groups and created an operational plan for sabotage in the oilfields. The rapid eastwards progress of German forces soon after the invasion of Russia by Hitler greatly encouraged Reza Shah in his dream of an 'Aryan axis' between Tehran and Berlin. But in August 1941 the Allies invaded Iran and the shah's 120,000-strong army disappeared like 'snow in summer'.[9] The King of Kings was forced to abdicate and left the country aboard a British steamer, which took him first to Bombay, then to Mauritius and finally to South Africa, where he died an exile in 1944.

Although Iran was quickly declared one of the Allies, her treatment by the British and Soviet forces of occupation could not have been harsher. Worse still, they made it abundantly clear that they had no intention of leaving Iran even after the war had come to an end. Once again the beleaguered Iranian leaders, who found themselves caught between Anglo-Russian pressures on the one hand and mounting economic and social problems on the other, began to look to the third major member of the anti-Hitler alliance, the United States, for help. It was under pressure from Washington that London and Moscow finally agreed to sign a treaty with Iran under which Allied forces were to be withdrawn within six months of the war's end.

The signing of the treaty did not end Iran's fears for the future and there were abundant reasons why Iranian leaders suspected the true intentions of the two traditional colonial powers. The Soviets were openly working for the creation of independent 'republics' in the northwestern provinces of Azarbaijan and Kurdistan. The British, for their part, created the Khuzestan Wellbeing Party with the aim of detaching the oil-rich regions of the country if and when Iran began to fall apart.[10] They also revived their special relationship with Bakhtiari tribal chiefs and put many of them on a special secret payroll. The Soviets organized, financed and, through hand-picked militants, led the Tudeh (Masses) Party and the Azarbaijan Democratic Sect as their political arms. The British worked through the traditional network they had among the mullahs. Both sides spent great sums of money on bribing politicians, financing newspapers favourable to their cause and buying the allegiance of local notables.

In 1943 the United States created the Persian Gulf Command as part of a scheme to send food and arms to the Soviet Union. The command, which symbolized American power in a region that was to become vital to US interests many years later, meant that Washington now had to be taken into account in any consideration of Iran's future. In December of the same year President Franklin D. Roosevelt came to Tehran for a conference with the British prime minister, Sir Winston Churchill, and his Soviet counterpart, Joseph Stalin.

While in Tehran both Churchill and Roosevelt refused to call on the new shah, who had succeeded his father in August 1941, at the royal palace. The shah, then aged only twenty-four, had to come to the British embassy for the meetings, and Roosevelt kept the shah waiting for what seemed like an eternity before receiving him. Only Stalin had the courtesy to go to the shah's palace. The shah was to remember those meetings with a great deal of resentment. He felt humiliated by both Roosevelt and Churchill, and yet he remained convinced that it was in his meeting with Roosevelt that he persuaded the American leader that the Allies should open a new front against Germany. That belief became part of the mythology the shah created in order to persuade himself that he was something of a military genius.[11]

The Tehran Declaration that followed the tripartite conference was a major boost to Iranian morale. Virtually written by General Patrick Hurey, Roosevelt's adviser on the Middle East, the declaration guaranteed Iranian independence and territorial integrity in the postwar period. It made the United States directly involved in ensuring respect for the terms of the agreement.

One immediate result of the Tehran Conference was the expansion of American diplomatic and intelligence presence in Iran. The Office of Strategic Services (OSS), which was later to be developed into the Central Intelligence Agency (CIA), had been present in Iran from 1941 onwards. Its agents travelled throughout the country and sent alarming reports to Washington. They complained about British and Russian policies in Iran and indirectly promoted the idea of the United States as a counterbalancing force in the country. Their conclusions were supported by both General Hurley and Louis Dreyfus, the American minister in Tehran, who was eventually to be dismissed under pressure from London. The State Department had inadvertently sent some of Dreyfus's critical reports on British behaviour in Iran to the Foreign Office in London as part of a routine account to a trusted ally. Dreyfus did a great deal to maintain the image of the United States as a well-meaning power caring for the weak and the poor. The clinic built in south Tehran with charity funds collected by Dreyfus's wife Grace was to become a symbol of American goodwill in practice.

While much of Iran's problems were rightly blamed on British and Soviet policies, which Dreyfus at one point described as 'barbarous', the State Department in Washington was not totally unaware of other reasons for the country's backwardness and misery. One extensive report prepared in 1942 graphically described the corrupt domination of the country by a minority of feudal barons, mullahs and bazaaris who opposed all reform and any attempt to distribute the nation's income more fairly. It also recommended that American experts be dispatched to Iran once again, and in greater numbers, to help put the country on a course of reform. The enthusiasm that General Hurley and Ambassador Dreyfus felt for an 'Iran project' soon spread to Cordell Hull, the Secretary of State. And Hull, in turn, persuaded President Roosevelt that Iran could become a model for poor and backward countries saved thanks to American help.[12] In January 1943 the first group of seventy-five American experts arrived in Tehran to advise the Iranian government in various fields. The best-known among them was Millspaugh, who was appointed director-general at the Ministry of Finance. His task was to modernize the system of budgeting, tax collection and control of public expenditure.

Other American experts looked after the customs office, the central bank and the office of government monopolies and helped reorganize the urban police and the gendarmerie. Their combined efforts did much to curb a soaring inflation, which had provoked bread riots in Tehran in 1942, and to improve security in the capital and on the major provincial roads. Most of them, including Millspaugh, however, had to leave shortly after the end of the war as Soviet propaganda against the presence of 'American imperialists' began to hit Iran. The presence of a local pool of American-educated Iranians was a great help to the advisory mission of the war years. Most of these Iranians had attended the American Mission College in Tehran, which, beginning as a humble school, had developed into the country's finest centre of secondary education under the leadership of one Dr Jordan, who was to become a figure of legend revered by his pupils.[13]

Throughout the years of occupation the future of Iranian oil remained at the centre of the country's political preoccupations. The British were determined to maintain the status quo which served their narrow interests magnificently. The Russians, however, insisted that they too should have a share in Iranian oil. They pressed the Tehran government to grant them exploration rights in the Iranian part of the Caspian Sea as well as in provinces bordering the USSR. The prime minister, Mohammad Sa'ed, who had served as ambassador to Moscow and knew the Russians well, used every delaying tactic he could think of. In the end he was forced to ask the parliament to pass a law which forbade the government from negotiating any oil deals with foreign powers until after the end of the war and the departure of foreign troops from Iran.

The Americans, who until 1944 had ignored various warnings that Stalin was already thinking of his postwar empire, began to show some concern over Moscow's intrigues in Iran. Roosevelt had naively hoped to turn Iran into a model of tripartite cooperation in the rebuilding of the postwar world. His successor, Harry S. Truman, had no such illusions, however. In 1945 Averell Harriman, the US ambassador to Moscow, reported the existence of a well-prepared plan aimed at enabling the Soviet Union to annex virtually all territories occupied by the Red Army during the war. One of the key prizes in this new version of 'the Great Game' was the badly shaken and unstable Iran of the 1940s.

The Soviet plan for detaching Azarbaijan from Iran was a joint venture bringing together the MVD, the Soviet secret service and the precursor of the KGB, the Soviet Azarbaijani Communist Party and the Red Army commanders in northern Iran. In overall command of the project was Jaafar Baqer Zadeh (alias Baqerov), a companion of Lenin and chief of the Azarbaijani Communist Party in Baku. Two MVD agents, Arkadi A. Krasnykh and Jaafar Pishevari, were picked by Baqerov as commanders in the field. The latter had been born in Iran and thus claimed to speak in the name of Azarbaijani 'nationalism'. The contact man for the two operatives and Baqerov was Mirza Ebrahim Zadeh (alias Ibrahimov) whose official title was 'Deputy President of the Presidium of the Azarbaijan Soviet Socialist Republic'. The Kurdish part of the operation was less directly controlled by the Soviets, mainly because the proud Kurds would not take orders from Russians.

The last of the American troops left Iran on 1 January 1946 in accordance with the tripartite agreement of 1942. British forces of occupation soon followed and were out of Iran by March. The Russians, for their part, showed no sign of wanting to leave. Instead they intensified their propaganda on the theme of dividing Iran into its ethnic component parts. The message was clear: Stalin would settle for nothing less than a full southward expansion of his empire. Both Harriman and George Kennan, the State Department's sovietologist, were persuaded that the Tehran government would fall without strong support from Washington. The extension of Soviet power to the Persian Gulf could put American oil interests in the Arabian Peninsula in jeopardy, they argued. The loss of Iran to Soviet domination would, in time, threaten the other 'weak dominos' in the region, notably Turkey, Washington was told. But it was probably Churchill more than anyone else who in the end persuaded Truman that the West was entering a period of 'cold war' against Russia and that Stalin's ambitions in Iran should be resisted by force if necessary.

The fact that the United States enjoyed a monopoly of nuclear weapons at the time gave Truman a strong hand to play against Stalin. Urged by the Iranian ambassador to the newly created United Nations, Hossein 'Ala, to intervene, the United States came out with a series of strong warnings to the Soviet Union. It was assumed at the time that Washington even envisaged the use of the atomic bomb to prevent Moscow from dismembering and dominating Iran. The Azarbaijan episode was the first of several dramatic episodes in which the USA showed its commitment to the preservation of Iranian independence and territorial integrity. There is no doubt that this commitment was a morale booster to Iranian leaders and an effective diplomatic weapon against Stalin.

In subsequent years, however, some Americans began to exaggerate the role played by the United States in pushing Soviet troops out of Iran in May 1946. One or two adventurers-turned-writers even claimed that they had 'saved' Iran simply by happening to be in Tehran at the time. The 'miracle of Azarbaijan', as the withdrawal of the Red Army from Iran came to be known to Iranians, was, more than any other factor, a result of the astute strategy of Ahmad Qavam, the elder statesman who became prime minister to save the situation. Until the arrival of Reza Shah on the scene Iran's hundred or so leading families had been divided into russophiles and anglophiles. Qavam's family had often belonged to the first category. Thus Moscow was reassured when the Old Fox, whose half-brother Vosuq ad-Dowleh had been known for his support for Russian interests in Iran, came up with a plan to meet most of Stalin's basic demands. Qavam invited three

Soviet-sponsored Tudeh politicians to join his cabinet as ministers, while the russophile Prince Mozaffar Firuz became deputy premier and chief government spokesman. The move had the double advantage of dividing the local communists and tempting Moscow into contemplating the prospect of dominating the whole of Iran without the use of force and without provoking an international crisis that could lead to a confrontation with Washington.

Qavam visited Moscow and held lengthy talks with Stalin. He managed to convince the field-marshal that Russia's best interests lay in a quick withdrawal of troops from Iran, a move which, he led Stalin to believe, would lead to the granting of oil and other concessions to the USSR. Using the Persian technique of *ketman* ('secretiveness'), Qavam even went so far as to ask the United Nations Security Council to disregard Iran's earlier pleas for urgent action as negotiations between Tehran and Moscow continued. He also called in the US ambassador, George V. Allen, and told him that it was no longer necessary for Washington to prepare for confrontation with Stalin as Moscow had agreed to treat the Azarbaijan issue as a domestic Iranian problem. Qavam played his pro-Soviet role so consummately that even the shah suspected him of having sold out to the Russians.[14]

Once the Russians had agreed to the terms of the deal Qavam lost no time in revealing his true intentions. He promptly sacked his Tudeh ministers and marshalled his supporters in the Majlis to throw out his own proposal for granting oil concessions to the Soviet Union. He also invited the United States to come to Iran's support by providing financial and military aid. The small US military mission, which had been set up largely to help reorganize Iran's armed forces, which had disbanded as a result of the Allied invasion, was quickly enlarged and in October 1946 the US joint chiefs-of-staff testified in writing that the protection of Iran's independence and territorial integrity was of strategic importance to the United States. Thus for the first time Iran became an object of US-Soviet rivalry in the context of the Cold War.

But Qavam was not to be justly rewarded for his services. The shah dismissed him as prime minister and the Old Fox stayed out of office until his death in 1960.[15] In the meantime he suffered internal exile and the confiscation of most of his personal property.

The shah was anxious to supervise personally the development of relations with the United States as his regime's foreign protector. At the same time he began dreaming up grandiose plans for the creation of a large army which would be strong enough to offer him security against his domestic enemies and future Soviet military pressure. He had already quarrelled with Millspaugh on the subject of the army. The shah had pressed for budget allocations with a view to raising an army of 150,000. The American financial adviser had insisted that Iran could afford no more than 30,000 soldiers. In 1947 the shah brought the subject up with the Americans and received a cool response. The State Department was of the opinion that Iran would collapse under the weight of so disproportionately large an army.

By the time the shah paid his first visit to Washington in 1949 the United States had already emerged as the rising power on the horizon so far as the Iranian ruling elite was concerned. During the war years the number of Iranians attending American mission schools or going to the United States itself for further education had increased dramatically. In 1943 the defunct Persian-American Society, created by the archaeologist Arthur Upham Pope in 1925, was revived under a new name: the Iran–America Relations Society. It grouped a number of very influential Iranians such as Issa Saddiq, several times education minister, Hossein 'Ala, who was to become prime minister, Abol-Hassan Ebtehaj, who became the founder of Iran's Plan Organization, and the Saleh brothers, who were to serve in a number of high official positions. On the American side, Dr Boyce, a veteran missionary, represented the old-style Americans whose interest in Iran had been confined to cultural and humanitarian fields – those Americans who could be described as 'beautiful' because they loved Iran for her own sake and genuinely wanted to help improve the lives of her suffering people. A new and different type of American was, however, represented in the society by people like Colonel Norman Swartzkopf, of the military advisory mission, and Donald N. Wilber, an OSS operative who had for years presented himself as an archaeologist and who was later to become a CIA agent in Iran. Wilber became the society's secretary and used that position to establish personal relations with a number of influential Iranians. During the war years Wilber had helped create a network of agents in Iran and impressed his superiors by the sheer volume of reports he prepared on all aspects of the turbulent situation in the country.[16]

Had it not been for his exaggerated expectations, the shah's state visit to Washington, which was followed by a private visit to New York, where he addressed the United Nations, would have been a complete success. The young monarch made a favourable impression on President Truman and won much acclaim from the American press which saw him as a modernizing leader determined to bring democracy and progress to Iran.[17] Only Secretary of State Dean Acheson proved immune to the shah's charms. He saw the Iranian leader as 'a very impractical young man' who 'fancies himself as a great military leader'.[18] Acheson gave the shah a lecture on the necessity of reform and social justice as the best means of combating communism. The shah hated the secretary of state's arguments and interpreted them as signs of American naivety and of the Democratic Party's 'imbecilic belief that American ideals could be applied throughout the world, regardless of local conditions'.[19] The interview with Acheson persuaded the shah that he should look for friends among American Republicans. The experience of the following thirty years was to prove him right.

The shah returned home from his Washington visit convinced of his stature as a world leader but with practically empty hands. The Americans were prepared to help Iran with a limited military training scheme, plus gifts of food and pharmaceuticals. Soft loans could also be arranged for Iran through the World Bank and other aid agencies. Beyond that, the shah was told, his country should look to better management of its oil resources as a means of financing development projects. While Truman did not want a confrontation with the British over Iran's oil, Acheson was persuaded that concessions were both inevitable and necessary. The secretary of state believed that only nationalist governments capable of proving their true independence would be able to blunt the edge of Moscow's anti-imperialist propaganda in Asia and the Middle East.

Many nationalist politicians in Iran and in other Muslim countries of the Middle East shared Acheson's belief and looked to the United States for support in what they saw as a war on two fronts: against the corrupt ruling classes at home and against Soviet-sponsored communism in the region as a whole. With what now looks like unpardonable naivety on their part, these politicians believed that the United States would support all attempts at democratization in the Middle East simply because of her own democratic convictions. They saw the USA as a disinterested power which, because of her own wealth and economic strength, did not have to exploit other nations in the way the traditional big powers of Europe had done throughout the nineteenth century.

The newly created Iran Party, which emerged in 1946 from a merger of the Iran Club with other smaller groups, was determined to play the American card against both the British and the Russians. The party enjoyed the tacit support of Dr Mohammad Mossadeq, a highly respected parliamentary leader who was to lead the oil nationalization movement a few years later. The party's leader, Allahyar Saleh, a graduate of Dr Jordan's missionary school, was in contact with the US embassy in Tehran and was to remain convinced of American good intentions until the end of his long and eventful life in 1981.[20]

America as a land of wonderful opportunities and wonderful people was a favourite topic with a number of Iranian poets. Some, like

Bahram Ashna in the *Nowbahar* magazine, wrote about it in romantic terms: 'America is the only country in history that owes its very existence to respect for individual freedom and dignity. . . . There you are somebody even though you may be nobody in particular.'[21] Others, like Fereidun Tavalali, adopted a satirical tone when writing of that distant land of beautiful people they had never seen with their own eyes.[22] The very mention of the word America (pronounced 'Amrika') aroused high expectations among most literate Iranians.

SATANIC LIQUID

Between 1908, when oil was first discovered in Iran, and 1950 dozens of American businessmen, researchers and technicians linked to the petroleum industry visited the country. They all observed two golden rules during their stay in Iran: not to criticize the Anglo-Iranian Oil Company and not to talk to the local press. Both rules were to be broken in January 1950 when a group of American oilmen arrived in Tehran for what was described as an exploratory visit. The visit came hot on the heels of the shah's talks with President Truman and Secretary of State Acheson in Washington, where both men had urged him to use Iran's oil revenues for the purpose of developing the nation's economy.

The American visitors now invited a number of Tehran journalists to what turned out to be a lecture on the state of the international oil industry. Without ever mentioning Anglo-Iranian, they made it abundantly clear that the British concern was plundering Iran's natural wealth. They reported that American oil companies had already concluded fifty-fifty agreements with oil-producing nations such as Venezuela, implying that Iran too should seek such a deal.[1]

This ploy was seen by Anglo-Iranian's bosses, who often acted independently of the British government, as a bid by American oil concerns to secure a share of the cake in Iran. Anglo-Iranian was determined to resist such a move and it used its influence to force the shah to appoint a veteran anglophile, Ali Mansur, as prime minister. Mansur, an ineffectual and corrupt politician, was the last person to face up to the growing anti-British movement. All he could do was speed up the negotiations which had begun a year earlier between Anglo-Iranian and Tehran government officials. The USA had urged Britain to offer Iran a fifty-fifty deal, partly, perhaps, in the hope that greater Iranian control of the oil industry might open up new opportunities for American companies. But Anglo-Iranian was incapable of gauging the rising mood of xenophobia in the country

and believed it could continue to control the situation through its network of agents as well as through the fat bribes it paid to mullahs, politicians, press barons and other influential figures. The Foreign Office in London, meanwhile, asked the United States to stop any aid to Iran for the time being in the hope of forcing the Iranian parliament to approve a new agreement on oil. Angered by the British attitude, Washington not only gave the green light for aid to flow again but also began sounding the shah about the possibility of replacing Mansur.

The shah had long believed that only the army could set things right. It was therefore not surprising when, in June 1950, he chose as his prime minister Brigadier-General Haj-Ali Razm-Ara, the chief-of-staff of the armed forces and the man who had led Iranian troops during the Azarbaijan campaign against Moscow-backed secessionists in 1947. Razm-Ara was instantly persuaded that his appointment had been the result of advice from Washington and began spreading the rumour that he now represented a new force in Iranian politics. At first glance the new prime minister looked like the kind of model politician who Acheson believed could do the trick in countries like Iran. A self-made man, Razm-Ara was known for his personal integrity, his taste for hard work and his intense dislike of futile ceremonies. He lived the simple life of a soldier and blamed both Britain and Russia for Iran's defeat and decline. A teetotaller and non-smoker, he stood out in a political class where addiction to opium, love of wine and dislike of work were deeply entrenched habits.

Razm-Ara, despite his undoubted qualities, turned out to be a poor political leader. Inflexible and tough in a country where almost all life consisted of soft compromises, he antagonized the political elite within a few weeks. Worse still, he had no concrete policies to offer. All he had was a great deal of goodwill, but that was not enough to get the economy off the ground and keep Tehran's hungry lumpen-proletariat quiet in that year's harsh winter. Parliament disliked Razm-Ara for a variety of reasons and would not lift a finger to help him. It also rejected a draft bill providing for a new accord with Anglo-Iranian which offered Iran minor concessions.

The United States did much to bolster Razm-Ara's administration. The American embassy in Tehran was upgraded to first class and military aid and food donations increased throughout the year. But what was done was far less than what was needed and certainly much less than what Razm-Ara expected. The US ambassador, Henry Grady, a strong believer in Razm-Ara's ability to pull through, bombarded the State Department with requests for more aid for Iran but received little encouragement. He was convinced that British pressure was responsible for Washington's reticence in giving

Razm-Ara wholehearted support at a critical moment.[2] Such differences of opinion and of appreciation between the embassy and the State Department were to become more frequent in later years, leading to much confusion on all sides.[3]

The British successfully portrayed Razm-Ara as an ambitious military dictator who dreamed of deposing the shah and declaring himself president of a new republic. They also claimed that the prime minister favoured a policy of non-alignment for Iran along the lines then being promoted by the Indian prime minister, Jawaharlal Nehru. The campaign of character assassination aimed against Razm-Ara reached fever pitch in February 1951 when the announcement of a fifty-fifty agreement between an American oil concern and the Saudi Arabian government forced London to present Tehran with the offer of a similar deal. Razm-Ara was prepared to accept the offer but he had already been marked for assassination by the Fedayeen of Islam, a fanatical religious group suspected of maintaining close links with Anglo-Iranian. Razm-Ara was gunned down on 7 March 1951 by one Khalil Tahmassebi, who took his orders from Mojtaba Mirlowhi, a former employee of Anglo-Iranian who had adopted the code name of Mohammad Nawab-Safavi.[4] The murder of the prime minister was hailed by the partisans of oil nationalization as a warning to all those politicians who might have believed that a compromise with the Angle-Iranian was in Iran's best interests. At the same time, however, some Iranians saw in Razm-Ara's death a warning from the Anglo-Iranian that attempts at playing the American card would simply not be tolerated.[5] The liberal-nationalist movement saw the Fedayeen of Islam, the group that had carried out Razm-Ara's murder, as a dubious organization manipulated by British agents.[6].

Razm-Ara's murder did not end agitation against Anglo-Iranian, however, and seven weeks later the parliament in Tehran passed a bill nationalizing all the country's oil resources. The man who had drafted the bill and led its passage through parliament, Mohammad Mossadeq, was invited by the shah to form a new government. The shah had tried to prevent Mossadeq's nomination as prime minister but had failed because of pressure from the Majlis. Thus relations between the shah and his new prime minister were far from cordial right from the start. The shah might have regarded Razm-Ara's removal from the scene as an opportunity for reasserting his own authority, but Mossadeq's emergence as a popular prime minister with a strong personality and oversize ego quickly dashed the shah's hopes of gaining direct control over Iran's destiny.

The oil nationalization bill which became law on 2 May after receiving the royal assent was the brainchild of Mossadeq. But the

shah, determined to move with the nationalist tide, quickly claimed it as his own. In later years the shah was to reminisce that, despite initial misgivings about Mossadeq, he had not imagined that he would have 'such big problems' with the old politician.

That the United States wanted Mossadeq to succeed was demonstrated by the increase in American aid from $500,000 in 1950 to nearly $24 million two years later. The Iranian leaders, including the shah himself, continued to press Washington for more aid without, however, improving Iran's absorption capacities. The seven-year development plan, worked out by a group of American-trained technocrats, set lofty goals. But the infrastructure and trained personnel needed for achieving them were singularly lacking. Iran was not even capable of making use of a soft loan negotiated with Exim Bank thanks to State Department support. The technical backwardness of the nation's educated elite and the careless attitude of many managers towards investment options was to be demonstrated by what was to be known as the Karkheh scandal. A dam constructed at a cost of nearly $2 million on the river Karkheh in the southwestern province of Khuzestan turned out to be a disaster because it irrigated lands which turned out to have salt deposits; the salt thus washed down the gently sloping plain destroyed good farmland.

Despite such failures the Iranians resented Washington's insistence on employing American managers to run most of the aid projects. Iran, an ally of the United States in the Second World War, had not been included in the Marshall Plan and received less than one tenth of what was offered to Turkey and Greece in American aid. This created some resentment although it is clear that Iran could not have absorbed a stronger dose of financial aid without provoking further inflation at the time.

In addition to subsidies to the Tehran government, the United States also financed and managed a number of smaller projects aimed at the direct improvement of life in the more neglected parts of the country. These projects were grouped under the Point Four scheme which from 1951 onwards became an important instrument in developing bilateral relations. William Warne, who headed the project from 1951 until the end of the decade, quickly became an influential figure in the country. Point Four was involved in a variety of operations ranging from sanitary water supplies for villages to textile mills and road-building ventures. It employed scores of young educated Iranians and financed the further training of some of them in various American universities. A good percentage of Iran's managers and leaders in the 1960s and 1970s were graduates of Point Four projects, among them Jamshid Amuzegar, who was to become finance minister and then

prime minister, Abdul-Reza Ansari, who served as provincial
governor-general and interior minister, and Ardeshir Zahedi, the
shah's son-in-law, who later became foreign minister. Point Four's
American agronomists achieved wonders in raising wheat output in
various provinces in addition to introducing new seeds and new
pesticides. David Lilienthal, the man who had masterminded the
Tennessee Valley Project in the United States, was invited to visit Iran
and saw the southwestern province of Khuzestan as an ideal place for a
similar venture. His dreams of building dams on the river Karun, the
only navigable waterway in the country, were to be realized in the
1960s and 1970s. The emphasis was, all along, on improving the
country's agricultural economy in the hope that, once Iran was in a
position to feed its own population, it would be able to use its oil
revenues for industrial development projects.

The shah and Mossadeq worked together for a while: they both
wanted to see Iran free of foreign influence. But their relations were
soon to become sour over the question of the means needed to achieve
their common goal. Mossadeq believed that the expulsion of the
British had to be considered as the nation's top priority. Everything
else would then follow, he argued. The shah, on the other hand, was
persuaded that as long as Iran remained militarily weak and
economically backward it would not be able to win in a straight duel
against Britain, and that an openly anti-West policy could only pave
the way for the expansion of Soviet influence in the country. He was
worried about Mossadeq's policy of turning a blind eye to the re-
emergence of the Tudeh Party, this time hiding behind a number of
front organizations, in the name of democratic freedom. Tudeh,
benefiting from generous Soviet subsidies, quickly established itself as
the best-organized political structure in the country. It published five
dailies and two weeklies in Tehran with a total readership of over one
million. By 1952 the party was reported to have over 25,000 card-
carrying members and at least four times as many sympathizers in the
capital alone. Tudeh militants also dominated most trade unions,
especially in the oil industry, where a charismatic union leader, Ali
Omid, had emerged as a power to be reckoned with.

While the shah pressed for the strengthening of the armed forces as a
bulwark against communism, Mossadeq remained convinced that
only open debate and full freedom of political activity would
ultimately defeat Tudeh. The charismatic prime minister was, at the
same time, the prisoner of the image he had created for himself: he was
the darling of xenophobic mobs and would not risk antagonizing his
supporters. Standing firm against the British had won him popular
support and now he found himself incapable of compromise.

The Truman administration, sincerely hoping for a settlement that would meet most of Iran's demands, offered to mediate. Averell Harriman was chosen by Acheson as the troubleshooter. He visited both London and Tehran and held lengthy discussions with British and Iranian leaders as well as with the directors of Anglo-Iranian. It was at Harriman's home that Acheson warned the British ambassador to Washington, Sir Oliver Franks, in July 1951 that the United States would not stand idly by if British troops invaded Iran. The United States had also promised to help Iran with the technical assistance needed to get the newly nationalized oil industry back into full operation.

The British, however, began to think that no deal would be possible so long as Mossadeq remained in power. The destruction of his government became an important foreign-policy aim in London. There is evidence that much of this intransigence was dictated to the British government by the directors of Anglo-Iranian. They wanted to make an example of Mossadeq so that no one else in the British-dominated Middle East would dream of challenging the old imperial power. With all negotiations between the two sides suspended, the British put their forces on the alert in Iraq and dispatched the gunboats *Mauritius* and *Wild Goose* to the Persian Gulf to intimidate the Iranians. The move only served further to inflame passions in Iran, making it even harder for Mossadeq to contemplate any way out of the crisis.

The attitude of the Soviets to Mossadeq had remained cool bordering on hostile right from the start. But by the end of 1952 Moscow began to ponder a different strategy: Mossadeq would be supported by Tudeh in his bid to eliminate British influence from Iran so that pro-communist officers could, at the first opportunity, stage a *coup d'état* and, in turn, get rid of the old man. Unknown to the shah, who bore the title of the Commander-in-Chief of the Armed Forces, Tudeh had successfully infiltrated the army and enjoyed the support and loyalty of more than six hundred army officers, including two brigadiers-general, and hundreds of NCOs.[7] Meanwhile the MVD had revived an earlier plan for the annexation of Azarbaijan by smuggling into Iran hundreds of its agents who, having been recruited from the Asian members of the Soviet Communist Party, spoke Persian and Turkic. With its control of the oilfields through Tudeh-led trade unions and its assets within the army, Moscow could, when the time came, seize power in Tehran. Would the United States risk a Third World War to counter such a move? The question was debated in Moscow where the general consensus was that Washington would not go beyond diplomatic protests.

The first stage of the plan consisted of helping Mossadeq force the shah either to abdicate or to leave the country. Mossadeq would then be persuaded to declare a republic with himself staying on as prime minister. The Soviet secret services had even thought of who should become the first president of the People's Republic of Iranstan. For a while their candidate was one Abol-Qassem Lahuti, a cashiered Iranian gendarmerie officer who had distinguished himself in 1922 by seizing control of Tabriz for a few weeks and creating an ephemeral 'socialist state' there. After his defeat at the hands of Persian Cossack troops, Lahuti and some of his companions had fled to the USSR, where they ended up in the Persian-speaking Soviet Republic of Tadzhikistan. There Lahuti was enlisted as an agent of the Soviet secret services and assigned to a special propaganda section working on Iran. A man of many talents, Lahuti pursued his youthful love of poetry by writing a number of dramatic odes in praise of Lenin, the Red Flag, Stalin and Revolution. That the Soviets had better things in mind for Lahuti became apparent from 1950 onwards when tens of thousands of copies of his selected poems were shipped into Iran and distributed throughout the country. Full-colour portraits of Lahuti, with the red flag and the hammer and sickle in the background, were also available in various sizes to whoever cared to ask for one. Two radio stations broadcasting in Persian – from Baku in Soviet Azarbaijan and Stalin-Abad in Tadzhikistan – also made a point of building up Lahuti's reputation as a man who had met and known Lenin and thus, by implication, been blessed by the father of the revolution.

The first stage of Tudeh's plans seemed within grasp when, in February 1952, the shah, quarrelling with Mossadeq over who should control the Ministry of Defence, threatened to leave the country. He agreed to stay after a huge demonstration, organized by Tehran's mullahs, took place in front of the royal palace.

Meanwhile the mood in Washington had changed dramatically with the change of administration. The new Republican government of President Dwight D. Eisenhower quickly adopted a more militant anti-communist stance. Both Truman and Acheson had believed that it was sufficient for Asian leaders to be non-communist to merit the support of the United States. Eisenhower and his secretary of state, John Foster Dulles, insisted, however, that such leaders must be actively anti-communist and, more specifically, anti-Soviet before they could expect any help from Washington. Dulles all but discarded Acheson's more sophisticated view of the postwar world in favour of his own Manichaean vision in which the United States represented Good against the forces of Evil led by the USSR. It did not take Dulles long to develop his famous 'quarantine the aggressor' doctrine – a doctrine which substantially increased Iran's geostrategic importance in so far as she shared more than 2500 kilometres of border with the USSR. Where Truman and Acheson had argued for reforming change in the underdeveloped world as the best means of keeping communism at bay, Eisenhower and Dulles put the emphasis on the need for stability. The new administration was prepared to back almost any government provided it could prove its anti-communist credentials. The Cold War that had begun during Truman's tenure in the White House was now the established reality of big power relations and Dulles was determined to fight it on all fronts. The debacle in China, the war in Korea and the ongoing crisis in Central Europe contributed to a change of mood in the United States, where a nationwide witchhunt, led by the notorious Senator Joseph McCarthy, took the Cold War deep into the lives of many American families. The 'reds under the bed' syndrome led to a realignment of Washington's more balanced policy towards Iran with Britain's dogged intransigence.

One of the first steps taken by the new administration was to strengthen what was euphemistically called 'an intelligence presence' in Iran. The OSS had given way to the new Central Intelligence Agency (CIA) under Truman and a number of agents had been active all along in Iran. The CIA's new director Allen Dulles, brother of the secretary of state, was determined to go much farther. He saw his agency as a partner in both the shaping and the execution of American foreign policy in countries of special geostrategic importance. His easier access to the White House plus his own activism were to establish covert operations as an important component of US foreign policy for nearly two decades. Before the end of 1953 the CIA was actively present on the Iranian scene with the aim of frustrating Soviet schemes and supporting Mossadeq's increasingly isolated government. The CIA managed to launch a successful campaign of character assassination against Lahuti. The unseen exiled poet was depicted as an enemy of Islam who would organize a system of wife-sharing as soon as he came to power. The CIA paid professional versifiers to forge poems ostensibly written by Lahuti advocating the elimination of Islam, free sex and equal rights for women. But the campaign did not stop there. A CIA team went one step further and carried out an operation based on Lahuti's alleged death. The operation was so successful that even Radio Moscow announced the poet's death while Tudeh organized a mass funeral in Tehran. When it subsequently became clear to the Russians that their man in far away Stalin-Abad had not died it was too late to deny the news; such a denial would have destroyed the credibility of both Moscow Radio and the Tudeh Party.[8] Tudeh soon began promoting another literary-cum-political figure, Ali-Akbar Dehkhoda, as the future head of a 'people's Iranstan'.[9]

Though concerned about Soviet intrigues in Iran, the Eisenhower administration continued the Truman–Acheson policy of support for Mossadeq well into 1953. The special Iran taskforce created at the CIA headquarters at Langley, near Washington DC, was not asked to contemplate a game plan without Mossadeq until the June of that year.[10] Talks concerning an exceptional $10 million US loan to tide over the Mossadeq government in the difficult months ahead were never formally broken off.

Three factors were to change the situation. The first was Mossadeq's own intransigence: all he could do was to say no to all proposals for a settlement. The second was the change of emphasis in Washington from the promotion of social reform in Iran to the combating of communist influence there. Finally, the British Conservatives, now back in power under Churchill, were better able to influence the Eisenhower administration. The old bond of friendship between the two men and their shared vision of an 'iron curtain' about to cut off Iran and its oil resources from the Western world led to growing cooperation between Washington and London. Gradually, the United States rallied to Britain's strong anti-Mossadeq stance.

The American change of heart was hardly a result of CIA analyses of the situation in Iran. On the contrary, the CIA agents in Iran soon began to understand the new mood in Washington and tailored their reports to confirm the views of their new bosses. Until the last days of the Truman administration intelligence reports from Iran had made a point of urging strong support for Mossadeq as the leader of a popular, nationalistic and anti-communist movement. These reports sharply contradicted British assessments of the situation. But from the spring of 1953 onwards the two major Western powers began to see Iran in more or less the same light. This quickly led to a coordination of their policies. What this meant in practice was that the British, although diplomatically excluded from Iran after a break in formal relations, were back in the lead. They had one objective: the elimination of Mossadeq. And the United States was to help realize that goal by providing technical and financial support.

The events of August 1953 that led to the fall of Mossadeq have since been the subject of numerous wild accounts. The CIA has for years presented them as a master coup in order to justify its use of covert operations as the surest means of attaining US goals in peripheral countries. Some former CIA agents, adventurers by temperament, have even put themselves forward as men who 'saved' Iran. But a closer examination of the mass of evidence now available proves that the CIA and its former agents deliberately exaggerated their role in those events and that this tactic was, ironically but perfectly understandably, also used by anti-American elements throughout the so-called Third World as a means of castigating 'Yankee imperialism'. But before entering this particular controversy we should recall the sequence of events.

Frustrated by what he saw as American reticence, Mossadeq began talks with the USSR in the spring of 1953 while promoting his policy of 'negative balance', which meant Iranian neutrality in the Cold War. The move antagonized Mossadeq's clerical supporters as well as some of his closest aides such as Hossein Makki and Mozaffar Baqa'i. That gave the anglophiles, who had not vanished into thin air, an opportunity to regroup with the help of several leading ayatollahs and senior politicians. The idea was to force Mossadeq to resign after a vote of no confidence in the unicameral parliament. But the prime minister moved first by disbanding parliament after a referendum in which Tudeh ran most of the show for him. Mossadeq's opponents then contemplated the traditional Persian tactic of marching on the capital with a tribal army. But Iran had already changed and there was no longer any tribal force strong enough to make such a move. The only option left was a military operation to dislodge Mossadeq and replace him with a new prime minister. The scenario was worked out by the British in consultation with Princess Ashraf, the shah's twin sister, who had been forced into exile by Mossadeq and now used her Swiss villa as headquarters for a counter-revolution. The next move was to secure American support. This was done by the British prime minister, Sir Winston Churchill himself. Washington, however, did not want to be seen to be directly involved. Tudeh was already accusing the United States of colonial intervention in Iran and the US embassy in Tehran, as well as its consulates in several other cities, had been attacked by mobs in an earlier crisis during which Mossadeq had left the premiership for a few days.[11]

In January 1953 Mossadeq announced that his special powers, which in practice made him a dictator acting in violation of the constitution, had been extended for a further twelve months. The move meant that he could no longer expect Washington to support him as the democratically chosen leader of a legal government facing a communist threat.

The British plan to overthrow Mossadeq required the shah's close cooperation. And it was in that connection that the United States played a crucial role. Kermit (Kim) Roosevelt was dispatched to Tehran for a secret rendezvous with the shah. The message he was to pass on to the monarch was simple: Washington would support the dismissal of Mossadeq and his replacement by a new prime minister willing and able to resume negotiations with Britain over the future of Iranian oil.

Despite later claims by some of the peripheral actors in what was to develop into a sordid drama of cynical intrigue, the shah was certainly not briefed about the details of what the CIA taskforce in Washington had codenamed Operation Ajax. All he had to do was to sign a decree dismissing Mossadeq and appointing in his place Major General Fazl-Allah Zahedi, who had once served as interior minister in one of Mossadeq's cabinets. Zahedi's name as the future saviour of Iran had been suggested to the CIA station in Tehran by Ebrahim Kajehnuri, a veteran politician and part-time psychiatrist who ardently believed that only an alliance with the United States would end Iran's domination by the British.[12] His choice of Zahedi was not accidental. For the general, who then headed the Retired Officers Club, was known for his anti-British sentiments – sentiments which had led to his imprisonment by the Allied forces in 1941 and his subsequent exile to Palestine, then under British mandate. Neither Zahedi nor his mentor Khajehnuri were aware of the British role in the operation and believed that they were acting with US support only.

On 16 August the shah duly signed a *firman* ('edict') terminating Mossadeq's mission as prime minister, while another *firman* invited Zahedi to form a new cabinet. The *firman* dismissing Mossadeq was taken to the prime minister's personal residence on Khakh Avenue, in central Tehran, by one Colonel Nemat-Allah Nasiri, then commander of the Imperial Guard. Informed of Nasiri's mission, Mossadeq refused to receive him and ordered his arrest. Minutes later an order for Zahedi's arrest was also issued, forcing the general to go into hiding. On hearing news of the unexpected turn of events, the shah, then awaiting developments in the Caspian resort town of Ramsar, hastily left the country aboard an aircraft which took him first to Baghdad and then to Rome. His queen, Soraya, went with him. It was subsequently claimed that the shah's departure from Iran had been part of an overall plan. But the haste in which the monarch left and the fact that no preparations had been made in Baghdad or Rome to receive him underline the impromptu nature of the royal exit. The shah, as several events were to prove in the future, was simply not a man for a season of crises; his natural instinct was to leave, allowing events to unfold without him.

With Nasiri arrested and the shah out of the country, the CIA plotters in Tehran quickly concluded that their mission had failed. They went into hiding. Kermit Roosevelt himself was so scared in his hiding place, a safe house belonging to one of Zahedi's friends, that he hid himself behind the huge stove in the reception room whenever the doorbell rang.[13]

At the US embassy only two diplomats had been informed of the coming operation, albeit without learning of the details. Ambassador Loy Henderson was ordered to Beirut pending clarification of the situation. When he learned that the plot had failed he quickly returned to Tehran and met Mossadeq, promising him more understanding from the USA on the subject of aid for Iran. It was clear that the CIA station and the embassy, as well as their headquarters in Washington DC, were convinced that Mossadeq had won yet another round.

But this was to prove a double-barrelled coup and it was only three days later that the second barrel went off in the shape of large pro-shah demonstrations. These demonstrations had in part been organized by British agents as well as pro-shah elements who were increasingly concerned about Mossadeq's speedy drift towards Tudeh. Grand Ayatollah Abol-Qassem Kashani, one of Tehran's leading religious personalities, for example, played a key role in bringing the lumpen elements of south Tehran onto the streets in support of the shah. Many demonstrators carried the pictures both of the shah and of the ayatollah. One of the many legends concerning the events of 19 August is that they were largely led by one Shaaban Jaafari, nicknamed Bimokh ('brainless'), who had grouped around him dozens of local tough guys in south Tehran. But Jaafari was, in fact, in prison at the time and was released only after Mossadeq had been overthrown and Zahedi sworn in as prime minister. The tough guys, known as *jahels* or 'ignorant ones', who led the march of the poor on Tehran were, in fact, led by one Tayyeb Haj-Reza'i, who was to be hanged a decade later for his support of Ayatollah Ruhollah Khomeini.[14] In those days, however, Iran's religious leaders advised the faithful to back the shah against Mossadeq.

The Americans in Tehran were startled at the dramatic reversal of the shah's fortunes and did not confirm Mossadeq's defeat until that afternoon, several hours after the battle had already been won by royalist mobs in the streets. The CIA agents and some of the embassy personnel, who only the night before had been ordered to prepare to leave the country lest they fall into Tudeh hands, were now told to unpack their suitcases and stay on. But even then few of them ventured to contact the various government departments in Tehran to find out exactly what had happened. In the evening however, Henderson received Ardeshir Zahedi, the general's twenty-five-year-old son, who had served as liaison officer between his father and the various groups involved in planning and executing the revolt. Zahedi told Henderson:

'We have won, it is now your turn to help us solve our problems.'[15]

Now, according to the yarns woven by the CIA on the one hand and anti-shah elements on the other, the entire August uprising had been an American enterprise whose success was solely due to CIA money and intrigue. Kim Roosevelt was, as expected, the first to see himself as the genius who had given the United States its first major victory in the Cold War. But Miles Copeland too was determined to make his own claim to a place in history.[16] Donald Wilber, the old CIA hand in Tehran, went even further and claimed that 'events happened exactly as I had planned them to happen'.[17]

Let us first deal with the question of the so-called 'whirlwind of dollars' that the CIA supposedly brought to Tehran. All records show that the budget earmarked for the entire Operation Ajax did not exceed $1 million.[18] Of this, just over $100,000 was put at the disposal of a group of four plotters charged with the task of mobilizing the south Tehrani crowds. They were the two Rashidian brothers, both known as veteran British agents, Mrs Malekeh Etezadi, who supervised some of south Tehran's houses of ill repute, and Hojat al-Islam Shamseddin Qanatabadi, a mullah turned politician. According to the shah himself, no more than $75,000 of the money earmarked for the purpose was actually distributed in south Tehran.[19] It was almost natural that at least a quarter of the money in question should disappear in the form of commission. The remaining $900,000 of the total budget remained unspent because the CIA believed that the game had been lost until the very last moment. It was later presented to the Zahedi government as a gift. According to some rumours, the general and his close associates pocketed the money themselves, but these charges have been strongly denied by the general's son.

The CIA, by all accounts, was a junior partner in what was a British plot against Mossadeq. But, even then, what actually happened was not the successful conclusion of a conspiracy but a genuine popular uprising provoked by economic hardship, political fear and religious prejudice against the communist movement. The plotters were, in fact, pushing an open door. It was no accident that Mossadeq, who was put on trial and sentenced to a brief term in prison which he never served, at no point blamed the Americans for what had happened. In his lengthy defence, which was read at the trial, he blamed the British as well as plotters in the armed forces and south Tehran mobsters.[20] Mossadeq's supporters remained in contact with the CIA until 1979 and continued to believe that the United States would one day come round to supporting them as a democratic alternative to the shah's regime. Soon after the overthrow of Mossadeq, his grandson, the lawyer Hedayat-Allah Matin-Daftari, received a scholarship to spend a year in Washington learning about the workings of the American Congress.[21] Had there been any question of his grandfather having been a victim of the CIA at the time he would almost certainly not have accepted such an invitation. Most of Mossadeq's closest associates had no doubt that the August uprising, which they described as a *coup d'etat*, had resulted from British intrigues. To them the United States remained a long-term ally. It was, therefore, not surprising that prominent Mossadeqists chose the United States as their place of exile both under the shah and after his overthrow by Ayatollah Khomeini in 1979. The strategy of Mossadeqists in the National Front was, in fact, based on the vain hope that Washington would one day abandon the shah and support their bid for power.

Roy Melbourne, the embassy's number two at the time of the anti-Mossadeq rising, was the first to recognize that the British-American plot had failed and that what happened three days later was a genuine movement of support for the shah. He told Henderson that the pro-shah demonstrations he had seen in Tehran had been the most genuine he had witnessed in his two years in the Iranian capital. Henderson agreed with Melbourne's assessment but commented rather cynically that they could 'certainly not tell that to the department'.[22] Nearly eight hours of newsreel made on that hectic day in the Iranian capital show a city teeming with popular anger against Mossadeq and his Tudeh allies.[23] The crowds seen in the streets of Tehran are so large and so diverse that any suggestion that they were confined to rented mobs is preposterous. Tudeh commentators were later to recognize the fact that the pro-shah movement had drawn upon the vast reservoir of the poor and the downtrodden in south Tehran. The Tudeh party, which immediately went underground, began blaming the CIA for the events only after 1961 when the agency itself began leaking stories about its 'triumph' in Iran. The reason for the agency's decision was probably a desire to reduce the effects of the Bay of Pigs fiasco, which put the CIA under the spotlight and forced President John Kennedy to order a rethinking of its role and structure. The wildly exaggerated importance given to the CIA's part in the Tehran events of 1953 was nevertheless to become almost a cliché for many 'Iranologists' who, for a variety of reasons, hated the shah and all he stood for. They pointed to the fact that General Zahedi's new government immediately received help from Washington as an indication that the CIA had brought him to power in a *coup d'état*.

One important question which was to be debated for more than a quarter of a century concerned Tudeh's strange passivity in the face of the pro-shah uprising. The Moscow-backed party was, at the time, a very well-structured and strong organization with many 'submarines'[24] in the armed forces. It could have easily brought onto the streets of the capital as many as 50,000 supporters. In the absence of anything resembling a credible police and intelligence force at the time, Tudeh might have made its bid for power even after Zahedi's arrival at the prime minister's office. But the party and its many front organizations made absolutely no move. Why? At least two reasons should be considered. First, the party's rigid decision-making process, based on the Leninist concept of democratic centralism, which in practice means the domination of the party by a small group of individuals, prevented any quick response to rapidly unfolding events. The party's work was rendered still more complicated by the fact that its operational chief, Nureddin Kianuri, only took orders from the local MVD station commander, who, for some unexplained reason, could not be reached on that fateful day.[25] But even had Kianuri succeeded in contacting his Russian controller in time there would have been no guarantee that the Soviets would have given the green light for any Tudeh takeover bid in Tehran at that time. 'Socialist' planning would not have been flexible enough to allow the Russians to make a quick countermove. The second reason for Tudeh's inaction was that it could not move against the very people it claimed to represent. The vanguard of the crowd that attacked Mossadeq's home was provided by workers from the Tehran cigarette factory, considered a Tudeh stronghold until then.[26]

The British had begun thinking of using covert action against Mossadeq as early as 1951 when Churchill returned to 10 Downing Street. The appointment as Soviet ambassador to Tehran of Anatoli Lavrentiev, the man who was said to have organized the takeover of Czechoslovakia by the communists, was seen by the new British foreign secretary, Anthony Eden, as a sign of imminent danger. He was convinced that Moscow had a secret agenda for Iran and insisted that the West should work out its own response to the challenge. It was on that basis that Kim Roosevelt was called to London for consultations. The British needed American support to counter 'a common threat to the Alliance'. Allen Dulles, then deputy director of the CIA, was immediately enthusiastic about the British scheme. But his boss, General Walter Bedell Smith, opposed any American involvement; he was persuaded that neither Truman nor Acheson would approve such an enterprise. Allen Dulles had to await the advent of the Eisenhower administration before he could commit the United States to supporting the British policy in Iran. It was not until 22 June 1953 that the decision to launch a covert action in Iran was taken at the office of John Foster Dulles, the new secretary of state. The secretary for defence, Charles Wilson, Allen Dulles, Kermit Roosevelt, Robert

Bowie, who headed the State Department's policy planning staff, and Ambassador Henderson attended the meeting.[27]

By the time that meeting took place the British had already put into effect a good part of their overall plan to weaken Mossadeq's government. It is possible to say that they set in motion a series of events that would have continued with or without support from the United States. The strength of their plan resulted from the fact that it made effective use of Mossadeq's growing isolation and reflected popular sentiments towards the shah. But most of the main characters in the unfolding drama had reasons of their own for opposing Mossadeq and could not have known of any British or American involvement at the time. Grand Ayatollah Kashani, for example, could not have been accused of having any friendly sentiments towards the British, who had imprisoned his father in Mesopotamia in the 1920s and sent him himself into exile in mandated Palestine in the 1940s. The anti-Mossadeq bandwagon had begun rolling on its own when first the British and then the Americans jumped on it. Without Mossadeq's own mistakes, Tudeh's paralysis and widespread popular discontent against the government, no amount of foreign money and force and intrigue would have been able to restore the fugitive shah to the Peacock Throne.[28]

The extravagant claims made by the CIA about Operation Ajax in later years were to have disastrous effects for future relations between Iran and the United States. They also did irreparable damage to the position of the very man the CIA pretended to have supported. For from the 1960s onwards the legitimacy of the shah's regime began to be increasingly questioned as CIA leaks, magnified by opponents of the monarchy as well as Soviet propaganda, claimed that the monarch owed his restoration to a few American super-spies. The fact that the CIA had failed in Cuba and made a mess of things in Guatemala was to be covered by its claims of success in Iran.

Besides casting doubt on the shah's legitimacy, the CIA claims about Operation Ajax helped create an anti-American sentiment that had not previously existed in Iran. The literate classes were deeply hurt by outlandish pretensions of a few suspicious characters concerning the rewriting of Iran's history. The vision of America as a land of democracy, liberalism and the rule of law was gradually replaced by one of a new-style colonialist power. CIA's self-promotion with regard to Iran provided a golden bonanza for Soviet propagandists, who never tired of attacking the shah as the 'CIA's station master in Tehran'.[29] False claims concerning Operation Ajax did more damage to the image of the United States in Iran in the 1960s than all the communist propaganda of the two preceding decades had done.

Nothing was ever to be the same again in Irano-American relations.

Amateurs of the rewriting of history with the help of 'ifs' and 'buts' have speculated about the possible course of events had Mossadeq not been overthrown by street crowds in the August of 1953. Some have claimed that without that 'historic event' Iran would have been swallowed by the USSR.[30] The shah himself was certainly convinced of that. But there is no evidence that Moscow and its local agents in Iran were in any position to attempt a direct takeover of the country at that time. To be sure, the MVD had its contingency plans and its secret structure well entrenched inside Iran. But Tudeh support was still limited to Tehran and a few other major cities. More importantly, the religious leaders, whose overwhelming position among the popular masses was to be dramatically illustrated by the Islamic Revolution of 1979, could have ordered the massacre of Tudeh activists and leaders by declaring *jihad* ('holy war') on communism. Grand Ayatollah Mohammad-Hossein Borujerdi, who supported the shah, was at the time in a position to mobilize millions of people with a simple edict issued from his office in the holy city of Qom.

Internal Soviet politics also precluded an immediate takeover bid by Moscow's men in Iran. Stalin's death had left the vast Bolshevik empire in a state of shock. The old dictator's successor, the ineffectual Gheorghie Malenkov, had great difficulty in establishing his authority, while a bitter power struggle raged between the notorious police chief Lavrenti Beria and the CPSU's rising star Nikolai S. Khrushchev. Tension in Central Europe over Berlin and Austria, the war in Korea and American nuclear superiority were other factors in dissuading Moscow from seeking an adventure in Iran at the time.

There is no doubt that Mossadeq was a hero of Iranian nationalism and played a crucial role in giving Iran that initial *crise de conscience* that every nation needs before it can assert its own specific identity in the modern world. A great leader in opposition, Mossadeq was an incompetent and muddled prime minister. He knew how to demolish but not how to construct. He was incorruptible, which was admirable, but incapable of compromise, which, in politics, is dangerous. He did not create divisions among the Iranian people as a whole, but the urban elite was to remain permanently divided over his record and the reasons for his fall. That division benefited the reactionary religious forces, who saw Mossadeq and the shah as the two sides of the same coin. He never became anti-American and continued to believe that the United States was still the only major power capable of making a positive contribution to the reshaping of the world in favour of those nations which had long suffered from European imperialism.

The super-spies who some years later went around claiming medals

for their supposedly heroic role in Operation Ajax deserved no such rewards. Unknowingly, they did a great disservice both to Iran and to the United States. Discovering the real rhythm and tempo of events is an art the importance of which in shaping policy cannot be over-emphasized. Those who, because of greed for glory or simply out of crude activism, wish to speed things up, so to speak, are not necessarily best qualified to offer advice. A successful policy is one that takes into account not only immediate results but also the longer-term implications of every move. Seen in that light Operation Ajax was a disaster; it created a slur nothing could whitewash.[31]

The immediate aftermath of the shah's restoration proved a disappointment to the new Iranian leaders. Zahedi had expected the United States to loosen its purse-strings so that the new government could broaden its popular base through a number of economic measures. But the Eisenhower administration, still strongly influenced by the British, who had apparently convinced Dulles that they understood the Persians better than anyone else, began to use aid as a means of forcing Zahedi into an early settlement of the oil dispute. Instead of the $250 million it had asked for in military and economic aid, the new government received a total of $51 million. The policy produced the desired effect and a new oil agreement was quickly worked out between Iran and Anglo-Iranian with American mediation. Iran began exporting oil again in the autumn of 1954. Under the new agreement the National Iranian Oil Company (NIOC) retained the title to all oil found in the country. Thus the principle of nationalization, so dear to Mossadeq, was respected. But the actual task of exploration, production and marketing was left to two management/operations companies owned by foreign oil companies. The British received a 40 per cent share, with Shell securing a 14 per cent stake. The five American majors received 8 per cent each, while the remaining 6 per cent went to the French oil company CFP. Iran's income from oil sales was to be 12.5 per cent of the posted price – a substantial improvement. More importantly, the new consortium of oil companies agreed to a steady increase in output and exports in consultation with NIOC.

The shah's most urgent aim after his return from his brief exile in Baghdad and Rome was to establish his own authority as the main source of power in the country. He did not like Zahedi, who nevertheless was a loyal monarchist to the end. The general had a strong personality and his own direct line to the Americans. Further, the shah knew that he owed his restoration, at least in part, to Zahedi and his friends. And the shah hated nothing more than feeling obligated to others. Before long he dismissed Zahedi and sent him to

Geneva as ambassador to the European headquarters of the United Nations. Zahedi knew that he had, in fact, been sent into exile but accepted the shah's decision without question and remained in Switzerland until his death.

THE LAND WHERE HAPPINESS WAS INVENTED

By 1956 the United States was firmly established as the principal foreign power capable of influencing the course of Iranian politics. The British, their presence restored after the settlement of the oil dispute, regained some of their former prestige and revived many of their contacts, especially in the provinces. They remained active and in 1955 even succeeded in drawing Iran into a regional defence system with Iraq, Britain's main base in the Middle East at the time, as a pivotal member. Known as the Baghdad Pact, the defence grouping also included Turkey and Britain itself as full members. The United States was apprehensive about the scheme and advised the shah not to commit himself too hastily. But this advice was conveniently ignored, an indication that the shah did not consider himself indebted enough to Washington to follow US policy in every instance. Instead he offered to sign a separate defence agreement with the United States. That was to come three years later. The US Secretary of State John Foster Dulles believed that Iran should not join a formal military alliance with the West so soon after 'its troubles'. He was also concerned that the inclusion of Iran into a Western-sponsored alliance might have an adverse effect on the forthcoming summit between President Eisenhower and the Soviet leader Nikita Khrushchev.[1]

The shah, however, was anxious to get the Western powers formally committed to the defence of Iran as quickly as possible. He often recalled that Iran had been neutral in both world wars and yet had fallen a victim to aggression on both occasions. He believed that non-alignment was a 'deadly course' for Iran because of her lengthy borders with the USSR. The Americans were aware of Iran's efforts to secure a place in a defence pact underwritten by the West. Iranian negotiators pointed out that two of Iran's neighbours, Turkey and Pakistan, were already linked with the Western powers through NATO and the Southeast Asian Treaty Organisation (SEATO) while

Iraq enjoyed a special relationship with Britain. Iran felt 'alone and exposed so close to the Soviet Union'.[2]

The Eisenhower administration ended up accepting the Baghdad Pact as a *fait accompli* and eventually even adopted it as part of its own policy for creating a *cordon sanitaire* around the USSR. But it was only after the *coup d'état* in Iraq in 1958 that the US agreed to a formal link in what was left of the alliance.[3] The creation of the Baghdad Pact marked the restoration of British influence in the region, but as far as Iran was concerned Britain could in no way compete with the United States where it mattered most: the provision of military assistance and economic aid.

Between 1953 and 1956 the United States pumped into Iran more than $400 million – a figure that exceeded the total Iranian revenue from exports of crude oil in that period. By 1956 the largest US aid project in the world was under way in Iran with over three hundred Americans busy helping build roads, schools and clinics and, above all, putting the Iranian army, gendarmerie and police into some shape. By the end of the 1950s the United States had provided Iran with more than $1000 million in aid. That figure was lower than those for neighbouring Turkey and even communist Yugoslavia, which also received US assistance, but it was large enough to give Iran's moribund economy a new lease of life until growing oil revenues made US assistance unnecessary from the mid-1960s onwards. Because almost exactly half the aid given by the United States was spent on the military, Washington was inevitably suspected of aiming at strengthening the shah's personal power base. Everyone knew that Iran's armed forces were far from prepared to face any external threat and that their main function was the suppression of internal dissent.

The third major power interested in Iran, the USSR, saw itself virtually excluded after the fall of Mossadeq. The newly created SAVAK, set up with help from the CIA as well as the Israeli intelligence service, Mossad, made its debut by dismantling practically the whole of the Tudeh and MVD underground networks in the country.[4] The imprisonment of thousands of Tudeh and pro-Mossadeq activists and the execution of twenty-three communist army officers and nine Fedayeen of Islam terrorists between 1953 and 1956 represented the first major wave of political repression that had hit Iran since the 1930s. The systematic censorship imposed on the press, the banning of all political parties and associations, the restrictions imposed on trade union activity and the general atmosphere of fear that gradually set in were all seen as direct results of American support for a new tough policy in Tehran.

The positive side of the American presence was all but ignored for two reasons. First, many of the development projects set up with US assistance were implemented in remote provinces such as Sistan and Baluchistan and the Persian Gulf coast, which played virtually no role in national politics. Second, they benefited for the most part very poor peasants who exerted little influence on public opinion as a whole. The urban middle class, which, at that time and until the seizure of power by Ayatollah Ruhollah Khomeini in 1979, dominated the political debate in Iran, saw in the United States little more than a foreign power determined to prop up an increasingly oppressive state apparatus.

Despite pro-Tudeh and pro-Mossadeq misgivings about the growing American presence and influence in Iran, the United States' image as a whole remained fairly positive until the early 1960s. Between 1953 and 1963 more than 30,000 Iranians were educated in the United States, as 'Amrika' replaced Western Europe as the desired objective for further education for the children of middle-class Iranians. More importantly, a growing proportion of the young Iranians who studied in the United States were children of fairly modest families. An American education had become accessible to them either because many of them worked and paid their way while studying there or because the government offered a growing number of scholarships to those who preferred studying in the New World rather than in Europe. As the years went on the securing of an American education became established as an important means of upward social mobility in urban Iran.

Between 1953 and 1963 urban Iran thirsted for more knowledge about the United States. American films and music appealed to growing audiences, including those in the villages, where mobile audio-visual units became a feature of life and a very welcome diversion from a dull routine. Many of the Hollywood filmstars became household names and several popular magazines offering stories and pictures of the marvellous universe of cinema were launched. The first blue jeans made their appearance in Iran around 1958: one of the first to wear them at weekends was Abol-Hassan Ebtehaj, who headed the Plan Organization. And in 1956 the first hamburger and hot dog shop was opened in Istanbul Avenue, offering a meal for less than 3 cents. Other aspects of American culture were not neglected either. By the end of the 1950s many of the major works of the leading American writers and poets were translated into Persian and published in Tehran. Preference was given to contemporary writers such as Ernest Hemingway, William Faulkner, John Dos Passos, Sinclair Lewis, Erskine Caldwell and Howard Fast, who became best-sellers.[5] The local press, meanwhile, dramatically increased its coverage of American political and cultural life with the help of the Associated Press and United Press International, which set up fairly active Tehran bureaus in 1958. Franklin Publications, a company benefiting from US subsidies, launched the first pocketbooks in Persian and, in turn, contributed to strengthening the American cultural presence in Iran. Some of the books sold in excess of 10,000 copies, a figure which, compared with previous best-sellers, hovering around 2000 copies, represented a dramatic improvement.

In spite of all that activity most Iranians still did not have a definite vision of the United States, especially when it came to politics. The shah and his closest advisers certainly believed that Americans were well intentioned but naive. To many Iranians in urban areas 'Amrika' was the land where the notion of happiness had been invented for the first time. Since many Iranians were deeply convinced that man had been created by God mainly to be punished in this world so that he would appreciate the next, they were persuaded that the American way of life was contrary to nature. A satirical version of this theory was presented in the popular comedy *Berim Amrika* (*Let's Go to America*) which dominated the Iranian theatre stage for more than four years and attracted record audiences. The comedy related the story of a middle-class Tehrani family's emigration to the United States and the troubles it had to face once established in that 'land of careless happiness, boundless freedom and endless repose'.[6] A less flattering picture of America was imagined by Hossein Madani, the satirist whose *Small in New York* related the adventures of a south Tehrani tough guy in a Manhattan the author had never visited and knew only through films, comic strips and detective stories.

The ostensible aim of *Let's Go to America* was to discourage Iranians from seeking a way of life that was supposed to be totally alien to their own traditions. But what happened in reality contradicted the play's contention, for the decade 1953–63 was marked by the first major wave of Iranian emigration to the United States. Iranians had never been keen emigrants and had played no part in the great waves of migration that marked the period from 1850 to 1950. In 1953 the number of Iranians who had opted for American citizenship and settled in the United States did not exceed 100; by 1965, however, this had risen to more than three thousand.[7] Ironically many of the emigrants were pro-Mossadeq or pro-Tudeh families who began to feel life in an Iran dominated by a growingly oppressive regime intolerable.[8] In a sense, therefore, they were political or economic refugees. Some of these emigrants were to return to Iran during the Islamic Revolution of 1978–79 to claim positions of leadership as a new wave of Iranian emigrants left for the United States.[9]

The 1952 *coup d'état* which toppled the monarchy in Egypt introduced a new factor in the Middle East equation in the shape of militant Arab nationalism.[10] Colonel Gamal Abdul-Nasser's gradual drift towards Moscow and the 1956 Suez crisis heightened a mood of insecurity in the region that could not leave Iran indifferent. Having adopted the Dulles view according to which every upheaval in the region was the direct or indirect result of Soviet scheming the shah was convinced that Moscow would in future use surrogates for the purpose of expanding its influence through intimidation or the direct use of force. Very quickly Nasser became the shah's most hated foreign enemy.

The shah saw part of his policy of getting America directly involved in the defence of pro-Western regimes in the region realized when Washington announced the so-called Eisenhower Doctrine in 1957. This committed the United States to the defence of Middle Eastern states facing communist-sponsored aggression. The doctrine was put to the test in 1958 when Eisenhower sent the US Marines to Lebanon in a move aimed at supporting the Christian minority in that country. It was also in 1958 that the British-sponsored monarchy in Iraq was overthrown in a military *coup d'état* led by a maverick brigadier general who was instantly seen as an agent of Moscow by Tehran and Washington.[11]

The shah had all along wanted a formal military commitment by the United States to come to his assistance in time of need. He was to get much of what he wanted in 1958 and 1959. The Baghdad Pact, which collapsed after the new revolutionary regime in Iraq denounced it, was quickly replaced by the Central Treaty Organization (CENTO), which grouped together Iran, Turkey, Pakistan and Britain as full members. The United States joined as an associate member with an active presence in the treaty's military division. Eisenhower and his new secretary of state, Christian Herter, had at first favoured the creation of an Islamic Pact of which Saudi Arabia would also be a member. The shah was enthusiastic about the idea despite his refusal to consider Saudi Arabia as an equal partner. But the scheme fell through for two reasons: the Saudis, worried about Nasser's national-istic propaganda and also reluctant to be associated with Shi'ite Iran, refused to play;[12] and Turkey objected to the idea on the grounds that it might be construed as a betrayal of Atatürk's heritage of secularism by the majority of the people in urban areas.

In 1959 a bilateral mutual defence agreement was signed between Tehran and Washington. The shah now had what he had wanted all along: a formal US commitment to the survival of his regime. In December of the same year Eisenhower paid a state visit to Tehran, the first American president to do so. The welcome Eisenhower received in Tehran contrasted sharply with his Japanese experience a few days earlier when protesting students in Tokyo had prevented his visit from taking place. The shah saw himself as a privileged ally of the United States and believed he would get virtually all he asked for. He was to be disappointed.

It was not until 1960 that the shah began to develop an adequate grasp of the way the American political system worked. Until then he saw the United States as a 'normal' big power capable of developing and applying long-term policies based on self-interest. In 1956, for example, the shah had great difficulty understanding how the US Congress could impose an oil import quota that could destroy Iran's sinking economy while the State Department and the White House pressed for urgent aid to Iran precisely to avoid such an outcome. He also did not understand why his offer to build up Iran's forces so that they could defend the country without putting any American lives at risk should be rejected by the US military, who insisted that of the sixteen divisions needed to defend Iran the shah should only provide ten with the rest being promised by Washington.[13] One thing he was persuaded of was that the American Democrats and Republicans, despite the common perception of them as variations on the same theme, really did differ in their conception and execution of foreign policy. Over the years he came to despise the Democrats as 'people who provoke wars, while Republicans always end them'.[14]

He did not forget how Truman and Acheson never missed an opportunity of telling him that Iran needed social reform and that he should develop a system of taxing the rich and improving the lives of the poor. These themes were not totally absent from Irano-American negotiations during the Eisenhower years and Herter was specially outspoken in his demand for a package of reforms to accompany the improvement of Iran's defence capabilities. But such sentiments, when aired by the Republicans, somehow rang hollow in the shah's ears. He took them to be attempts at keeping up a ritual. What was essential was that Washington should eventually accede to most of his demands without waiting for progress in the field of socioeconomic reform. The shah firmly believed that he had established a personal friendship with Eisenhower. 'We are both soldiers,' he liked to say. 'We understand each other and know that without strong defences there is nothing.'[15]

An important segment of Iranian society which began to feel concerned about growing American influence in the 1950s and 1960s consisted of the mullahs and the bazaaris, who saw the steady introduction of certain aspects of Western life as a direct challenge to Islam. The brutal murder of an American technician and his wife by bandits in Baluchistan in 1958 might have been the result of an accident, but some mullahs saw in it a rejection of 'a heathen way of life by true believers'.[16] The activities of American missionaries, mostly from the Baptist Church, also caused much resentment. Unlike the earlier missionaries, who had scrupulously refrained from proselytizing, the new generation of 'cross-worshippers', as the mullahs called all Christians, became active in converting Muslims, even in the villages. The fact that the missionaries also cooperated with the Baha'is at a local level made matters worse as far as Muslim zealots were concerned.[17] And when Iran extended *de facto* recognition to Israel in 1960, after years of illicit relations, the mullahs saw the move as the result of American pressure on the shah.

The establishment of ties with Israel also provided Nasser with the excuse he had long been looking for to sever diplomatic ties with Iran. The Egyptian leader then moved to establish links with some of the more fanatical mullahs but failed because his proto-Marxist vocabulary and his crackdown on the Muslim Brotherhood in Egypt rendered him as suspect on religious grounds as the shah. Ironically, Iran's left-leaning intellectuals, who might have found Nasser's message attractive because it condemned the shah, were not yet prepared to see Israel as an enemy and 'an agent of US imperialism in the Middle East'. To many of them, including some who had strong Islamic convictions, Israel was a socialist society in which the noble ideas of monotheistic faith were being put into practice.[18] It was only after the 1967 war that this favourable image of Israel gave way to one that depicted the Jewish state as an arrogant and aggressive power bent on territorial expansion and domination.

Throughout the 1950s the US embassy as well as the CIA station in Tehran maintained regular contact with Mossadeqist personalities such as Mehdi Bazargan and Allahyar Saleh.[19] Some old contacts, provided the embassy with regular and valuable information and analyses on various developments within the opposition groups.[20] But as time went on such contacts lost their importance and the embassy and the CIA began to prefer information and analyses prepared by SAVAK to what their own tested sources had to offer.[21] This was in part the result of growing confidence in the shah's regime but also reflected American impatience with those of the anti-shah opposition who, while describing themselves as 'nationalists' opposed to foreign intervention in Iran, insisted that Washington should dictate the policies of the Iranian government as a means of achieving social and political reform.[22] It is often said that the United States should have listened to both sides of the story in Iran, meaning that such a method would have produced a more accurate understanding of developments in the country. But what appears reasonable in the context of conventional wisdom is not necessarily the best course of action. The fact is that the two sides in question were both on the same side. The shah and his middle-class opponents, who claimed the heritage of Mossadeq, shared the same interests and the same *Weltanschauung*. Each side believed it could give Iran a better deal, and both believed that the United States should, in the end, foot the bill. The United States was not in contact with the shah's real opponents – that is to say the mullahs, the communists and, from 1965 onwards, the urban guerrillas – until very late in the day. The United States was left with information that was hardly ever disinterested. In later years SAVAK would use the CIA's sources within the opposition groups for the purpose of either planting stories or discrediting the sources by providing false information.[23]

Just as the shah had concluded that he could work better with the Republican Party, his Mossadeqist opponents were convinced that any future Democratic administration would favour their cause. Their chance to put this theory into practice came with the successful campaign and the subsequent election of John Kennedy as president of the United States. Even before Kennedy had entered the White House the Mossadeqists in Tehran began to regroup. One of their leaders even went so far as to send a cable to the Democratic nominee in which it was claimed that the 'entire Iranian nation prayed for your victory'.[24]

Although Kennedy did not begin to show an interest in Iran until 1961, the shah's opponents did not wait that long. They began by organizing a mass rally in Tehran and encouraged protest moves by Iranian students abroad.[25] One of the student leaders, Sadegh Ghotbzadeh, succeeded in meeting the president's brother, Robert F. Kennedy, who served as attorney-general, in Washington in 1961. Bobby Kennedy was apparently moved by Ghotbzadeh's account of how bad things were in Iran and how the United States could, by a mere change of tactics, achieve dramatic improvements.[26] The shah's Mossadeqist opponents succeeded in attracting the support of many influential people in the US administration, Congress and the media, and an informal anti-shah lobby gradually came into being in Washington. This made it even more difficult for US policy-makers to obtain balanced and reliable views concerning internal developments in Iran. The Mossadeqists virtually saw themselves as the Iranian representatives of the US Democratic Party and accused the shah of having financed Richard Nixon's campaign against Kennedy in 1960.[27]

What persuaded Kennedy to take an active interest in Iran had nothing to do with the views of Bobby and his Mossadeqist friends, although the president's brother became a *bête noire* of the shah.[28] It was Khrushchev who, during his summit meeting with the new American president in 1961, inadvertently sounded the alarm on Iran. The Soviet leader described Iran as a 'rotten plum' about to fall and insisted that Moscow would not have anything to do with the shah's inevitable downfall although he was sure the West would blame the USSR when that happened.

Kennedy wasted no time and asked the State Department to prepare a detailed critique of US policy in Iran and present suggestions for future action. The paper that resulted was almost a rewrite of the policy that had been followed under the Truman administration. Iran, it suggested, should cut its military expenditure and devote more resources to economic development. The shah was to be persuaded to reduce the number of his soldiers from 250,000 in 1961 to just over 150,000 by 1965. In return the United States would renew its support for Iranian independence and territorial integrity against any communist-sponsored attack. Further, new financial incentives would be provided for the more buoyant sectors of the Iranian economy. The shah was informed of the plan both through US officials in Tehran and during talks with Kennedy in Washington. He saw the whole thing as gross intervention in Iran's domestic affairs but decided to go along all the same. He was persuaded that any reticence on his part might mean a withdrawal of US support at a time Iran was not strong enough to stand on its own feet.

To meet the exigencies of this new situation the shah appointed Ali Amini as prime minister. Amini had served in almost every cabinet between 1951 and 1961. In addition, he had spent some time as ambassador to Washington where he had, according to his friends, become a 'close friend' of Senator John Kennedy, as he then was, in 1955–58. Although there is no evidence to support the belief that Amini was imposed as prime minister on the shah, this was what almost everyone believed at the time. Amini himself fed the myth that he was Kennedy's chosen saviour of Iran as a means of enhancing his own status *vis-à-vis* the monarch. The shah, on the other hand, spread rumours about Amini's 'loyal services' to the Americans in order to cultivate his own image as a true nationalist.[29] What was almost certainly little more than a myth was gradually established as fact and even the CIA began referring to Amini as 'one of our boys'.[30]

One of the more immediate effects of the cool spell in relations between the shah and the White House was an order to the CIA to expand its independent network of sources in Iran. The agency began by dispatching some of its older hands to Tehran and also recruited a number of agents from among Iranian students in the United States. Tipped off about this new activity, probably by Mossad, SAVAK counterattacked by forcing some of the newly acquired CIA agents into playing a double role. Some of these double agents were to rise in the SAVAK hierarchy; one of them, Mansur Rafizadeh, recruited by the CIA in 1962, became head of SAVAK's activities in New York in the 1970s.[31]

The CIA's new attitude had yet another unexpected result. SAVAK's director, Lieutenant General Teymour Bakhtiar, concluded that the Americans were planning to get rid of the shah in favour of some of their National Front contacts and began to see himself as an attractive alternative to both the shah and the Mossadeqists. An ambitious man, Bakhtiar had earlier even asked the CIA director Allen Dulles to support his bid for power. Dulles had promptly informed the shah of Bakhtiar's strange request in 1959. But the SAVAK chief was not removed until some eighteen months later; during that period, however, a close watch was kept on him by the shah's loyal agents within the secret police. In 1962 Bakhtiar was determined to sabotage Amini's new cabinet and, with the help of National Front activists managed to turn a student demonstration at Tehran University into a major crisis. The ambitious former SAVAK boss was quickly cashiered and forced into exile.[32]

The shah eventually succeeded in winning Kennedy's respect, though not his friendship, and US policy towards Iran largely reverted to the pattern established in the last years of the Eisenhower administration. But the brief chill in relations in 1961–62 was not quickly forgotten by the shah, who would not easily forgive either. In private conversation he referred to his experience with Kennedy as '*un accident de parcours*' and declared that one of his major goals was to avoid its repetition. Kennedy's assassination was clearly welcomed in the royal entourage, which lost no time in establishing close personal relations with the Johnson administration.

The unrest fomented by the mullahs in 1962 and 1964 revealed the depth of religious hostility towards the shah's policies of Westernization. The mullahs, led by Ayatollah Ruhollah Khomeini, objected to three specific moves on the part of the shah: the distribution of land among the peasants, the granting of electoral rights to women and, last but not least, the provision of limited-immunity rights to some of the US servicemen attached to the military-aid mission in Iran. This last measure was a standard clause that the United States included in all its military cooperation agreements. But Khomeini and his supporters saw this as 'capitulation' to the wishes of a 'cross-worshipping state'.[33]

The troubles caused by Khomeinist agitation were quickly forgotten in Washington, where the shah's new ambassador, Hushang Ansary, and his wife Maryam became personal friends of the president and his wife Ladybird. To a United States already sinking deeper and deeper in the Indo-Chinese quagmire, Iran under the shah appeared a stable and valuable ally. Suggestions that anything might be amiss with the situation there were quickly dismissed at the White House. Both the State Department and the CIA expressed concern about rising opposition to the shah and the possibility of an entente between the Mossadeqists and the pro-Khomeini zealots. But such an eventuality seemed extremely remote at the time despite several excellent and almost prophetic accounts arguing the contrary.[34]

The close personal relations between the shah and President Johnson and the growing supply of American arms to Iran did not, however, mean that all was well between the two governments. A number of US policy choices surprised and disturbed the shah. The Johnson administration recognized the Egyptian-sponsored republic in Yemen, while Saudi Arabia and Iran, both allies of the United States, supported the royalist tribes of the north. And in 1965, when India attacked Pakistan, the United States promptly banned all military sales to its Pakistani allies, interpreting the CENTO accords in the most cavalier fashion. The shah did all he could to buttress the Pakistani defences and the crisis quickly subsided. It seemed strange to him that the United States should have effectively decided to help India, a close friend of the USSR in Asia. He also considered US food grants and cash gifts for Egypt and Syria, both of which pursued pro-Soviet policies, to be incomprehensible.

In addition to his growing attention to Iran's immediate geopolitical habitat, the shah came under new influences. He developed a close personal relationship with the French president, General Charles de Gaulle. It was de Gaulle more than anyone else who persuaded the shah to improve Iran's relations with the USSR. The shah had taken some timid steps in that direction as early as 1959. But it was only in 1965 that he visited Moscow and also received the Soviet president, Leonid Brezhnev, in Tehran.[35] Direct contact with Soviet leaders persuaded the shah that the USSR was not necessarily a source of aggression against Iran. The *rapprochement* with Moscow was accepted by Washington as a welcome development that would relieve some of the pressure on Iran.

One private American who achieved a growing influence on the shah's thinking concerning foreign affairs in those days was Richard M. Nixon, the former vice-president and the unsuccessful Republican candidate in the 1960 presidential election. Nixon had visited Tehran during his vice-presidency and declared himself an admirer of the Iranian monarch. In the 1960 elections the shah, according to many accounts, contributed to the Nixon campaign.[36] But what mattered most was the genuine sympathy the two men felt for each other. Nixon was not forgotten even after the defeat he suffered against Edmond Pat Brown in California's gubernatorial election. The shah invited him to visit Tehran and treated him like a head of state. A private meeting with Nixon remained an important part of the shah's programme whenever he visited the United States. The two men also corresponded on a fairly regular basis and kept in contact through mutual friends or lengthy telephone conversations. Nixon supported the shah's new policy of expanding Iran's relations while insisting on privileged ties with the United States.[37]

The period 1960–65 also saw a steady increase in Israeli influence in Tehran. The Israelis had worked hard to win the shah's confidence. Mossad provided regular and reliable reports on Arab states hostile to Iran and also kept an eye on the shah's domestic opponents. Israeli experts, including one Lieutenant Colonel Moshe Levi, helped train some of SAVAK's best officers and also played a central role in the so-called Trident Project which linked Mossad with SAVAK and the Turkish security service TSS (later renamed MIT).[38] The Israelis were also well placed with some of the shah's leftist opposition. In 1966, for example, they used their contacts with Khalil Maleki, the leader of the Socialist Third Force Party, to prevent the creation of a united front against the shah which would have included Khomeini's supporters.[39]

By the end of the 1960s Iran was already in possession of an impressive arsenal of American-made weapons: F4 Phantom fighters, C130 transport aircraft, M47 tanks, M16 rifles, anti-tank missile-launchers, long-range artillery pieces and the first stage of a machine-gun assembly plant. The White House, the Pentagon and the State Department colluded in finding legal loopholes and a variety of devices with which to block any possible congressional opposition to the arms-for-Iran scheme. In addition soft loans and easy credit terms were arranged for almost all the deals made. The influential defence industry lobby had discovered Iran as an increasingly attractive customer and in turn helped make the administration's policy a success.

That the shah was seen as a special ally was illustrated by the fact that no global detailed analysis of the American aid programme in Iran was ever demanded. The United States had spent more than $1000 million in Iran in just over a decade – a substantial sum in those pre-inflation days – and everyone openly assumed that a good part of that had either been wasted due to faulty project design and mismanagement or simply siphoned off by corrupt local officials. And yet that dossier was quietly closed and buried with a minimum of ceremony.

No longer needing cash from the United States, the shah promptly launched his new 'Independent National Policy' as a slogan that heralded small but significant adjustments in the direction of Iranian diplomacy. The 1967 Arab-Israeli war had dealt Nasser, one of the shah's bitterest foes, a blow from which he was not to recover, while Syria, another of Iran's regional enemies at the time, was in a state of shock after the loss of the Golan Heights. As for Iraq, which also preoccupied the shah with her aggressive gestures, the Kurdish rebels, led by Mullah Mostafa Barzani, were to neutralize Baghdad's radical energies for more than six years.

On the eve of the 1968 presidential election in the United States the shah was a very happy man: everything was going his way both at home and abroad. His opponents inside the country had been silenced by internecine feuds and lack of credible projects, the Soviets were beginning to court him and the Arab nationalists were defeated and disheartened. The US political elite, for its part, was taking the shah's White Revolution seriously as a model of economic and social development for Third World countries. The result of the presidential election in November 1968 was to make the shah an even happier man: one of his closest friends was to occupy the White House for at least the next four years.

COLOSSUS WITH A FOOT OF CLAY

The tomb of Cyrus the Great, the Achaemenid king who founded the Persian Empire more than five centuries before the birth of Christ, is situated in the remote village of Pasargadae in the Plain of Morghab, dominated by the rugged crests of the Zagros, some 800 kilometres south of Tehran. Over centuries of oblivion, history simply forgot both the village and the king who was buried there. The nomads who roamed the plain hardly ever took notice of the modest edifice, while the local peasants continued to chip at the monuments around the tomb, dismantling them brick by brick and using the proceeds of their pillage for the purpose of building mediocre huts for themselves. By the middle of the nineteenth century, when European archaeologists began to visit Pasargadae, nothing but the tomb itself remained of the once proud imperial city. That the tomb itself was not destroyed was largely due to a lucky rumour according to which the edifice contained the remains of a mythological king who could turn offenders into ashes.

The discovery of Iran's pre-Islamic past in the reign of Reza Shah (1925–41) did not lead to any dramatic improvement in Pasargadae's status as a forgotten village half in ruins. That picture of majestic desolation was still intact when, on one unusually warm October afternoon in 1971, the shah, flanked by his overdecorated generals, stood in front of the Achaemenid tomb to read a eulogy which began thus: 'Lie in peace, Cyrus! For we are awake!' The ceremony at Pasargadae was the highlight of a series of parties the shah gave at Persepolis and its surrounding region, with some five hundred foreign dignitaries, kings, princes and princesses, presidents, premiers and ministers from sixty countries attending. The party was supposed to mark the twenty-fifth centenary of the foundation of the Persian Empire. But that was no more than an excuse; that particular centenary had come and gone in 1941 when Iran was under the Allied occupation. What the shah was, in fact, celebrating, was, as he put it in

private, 'the rebirth of the Persian Empire: Iran's return to the forefront of the human experience.'[1]

The shah was not happy about President Richard Nixon's decision to miss the party.[2] After all, even the Soviets had sent their head of state, Nikolai Podgorny. Nixon and more specially his wife Pat had sincerely wanted to attend but were persuaded to change their minds because of the adverse publicity the Persepolis party had attracted before it took place. Security considerations might have also played a part in keeping Nixon away from the shah's party, which, by a curious coincidence, also marked His Imperial Majesty's fifty-second birthday. Apart from that small contretemps, the shah had every reason to be pleased with himself.

With hindsight the Persepolis party, which, despite some of its more extravagant aspects, did not cost more than $4 million, marked the summit of the shah's power and prestige.[3] There were times in the years that followed when the shah appeared far more powerful, and Iran was certainly far stronger in 1979, when the shah left the country, than at any other time in her contemporary history. But in 1971 the shah still held his most important asset, an asset which he had lost by 1979: the confidence of his people in his leadership. His reform programme at home was bearing fruit, while growing oil revenues permitted his government to avoid the classic guns-or-butter dilemma, enabling the shah to press on with the expansion of his armed forces. As far as foreign policy was concerned, the shah felt that he had established exactly the kind of relations he had always wanted with the United States: unlimited access to American weaponry without undue meddling by Washington in Iranian affairs.

As early as 1965, when the Americans imposed a brief arms embargo on Pakistan, one of their allies in the region, the shah was convinced that the United States would not necessarily honour all its treaty obligations towards Iran. The 'strange and complicated system of government in the United States' would prevent any president from making the necessary moves at the right time, he believed.[4] An America haunted by the nightmare of Vietnam from 1968 onwards would not risk getting involved in another major war in defence of a remote and trouble-ridden ally. It was on the basis of this analysis, strongly shared by his closest advisers, that the shah began working on the concept that was eventually reflected in the Nixon Doctrine in 1969. And in 1972 President Nixon presented the shah with a formal pledge to supply Iran with whatever weapons it wanted 'with the exception of nuclear arms'.[5] Thus in a single blow the United States gave up its say in the arming of Iran, a right it had earned during more than thirty years of military cooperation with Iran. In later years Iran was even to order arms that the US forces had not yet acquired for themselves.

One man who played a crucial role in helping the shah get what he wanted was Henry Kissinger, who served as Nixon's national security adviser. Kissinger had worked for the Rockefellers, who had been close friends of the shah for more than three decades. But it was not out of the pure sentiment of friendship that Kissinger shared the shah's analysis. The adviser first established his credentials with the shah by torpedoing a Pentagon report on Iran which expressed serious reservations about the shah's military build-up in 1969. By the time he became secretary of state in 1973 Kissinger was fully convinced that the United States could not act as a global gendarme and that it should help its regional friends to defend themselves either collectively or individually. The Nixon Doctrine, also known as the Guam Declaration, was designed to serve precisely that purpose and Iran was to become its first 'beneficiary'. In later years Kissinger and the shah became close friends and together examined a number of scenarios for the defence of the West. These included the creation of a 'trident' alliance, grouping together Australia, Iran and South Africa for the purpose of countering Soviet and surrogate activities in the Indian Ocean region.[6]

The immediate effect of the new Nixon–Kissinger policy was that the shah soon found himself short of money in spite of an appreciable increase in Iran's oil revenues between 1968 and 1972. This forced Iran to join hardline states within the Organization of Petroleum Exporting Countries (OPEC) in calling for a sharp increase in the price of crude oil. And once oil prices rose, as they did, especially after the 1973 Arab-Israeli war, which was also accompanied by the interruption of Arab oil exports to the United States and a number of other countries 'allied to Israel', American arms manufacturers counterattacked by increasing steeply the price of their own lethal wares. This leapfrogging was to be a source of friction in an otherwise remarkably smooth and friendly relationship. The unintended effect was that crude oil became costly enough to justify the development of marginal oil reserves such as those of the North Sea, while giving the impetus to an energy-saving campaign that helped the West reduce its consumption by some 15 per cent in less than a decade. But it also meant the beginning of a long recession from which the industrialized world continued to suffer even in the 1980s.

Nixon's first secretary of state, William Rogers, had tried to continue relations with Tehran on more traditional lines. During a visit to Tehran in 1969, he had even made it abundantly clear that the United States would not underwrite any of the shah's regional plans unless they proved to be 'reasonable and conducive to peace'.[7] The shah had not been pleased by that stance and welcomed Rogers's replacement by Kissinger, whom he saw as 'a formidable brain, probably the most intelligent American ever'.[8] Rogers was not, however, to lose the shah's favour and later handled the Pahlavi Foundation interests in the United States through his law firm.[9]

Reassured about American support, the shah immediately began to apply his energies to the solving of some of Iran's major problems in the region. The most important of these was the dispute with Iraq over who should own and administer the Shatt al-Arab border estuary. A treaty signed by Iran and Iraq in 1936 had given Baghdad almost exclusive sovereignty over the Shatt. Iran had signed that treaty reluctantly under British pressure and was constantly looking for an opportunity to amend it. In 1969 Iran announced the unilateral abrogation of the treaty and sent in her navy to escort merchant ships bearing the Iranian flag through the estuary. Iraq instantly ordered full mobilization and for a few hours there was every chance of a head-on confrontation between the two neighbours. The Iraqis solicited support from the USSR but were advised to restrain themselves. They therefore limited their reaction to verbal attacks on Iran and the expulsion of some 70,000 Shi'ites from their holy cities in southern Mesopotamia.

Nevertheless, the episode was to have lasting effects. The Iraqi leaders, certain that the shah had firmly allied himself with Washington, urged Moscow to sign a treaty of friendship and cooperation with Iraq. This was done in 1972 and included clauses that could be interpreted as meaning a Soviet commitment to defend Iraq's independence and territorial integrity. For the first time the two super-powers were dragged into a new theatre of confrontation without precisely wanting it or having analysed its full consequences. Iran was to settle its dispute with Iraq with the signing of the so-called Algiers Accord in 1975. But the seeds of a much greater conflict had already been sown.[10]

Having forced Iraq into acquiescence over the situation in the Shatt al-Arab, the shah focused his attention on the problem of the continental-shelf demarcation between Iran and the Arab states which occupied the western coasts of the Persian Gulf. By 1975 Iran had concluded a series of continental-shelf accords with Saudi Arabia, the United Arab Emirates, Bahrain, Qatar and Oman.[11] At the same time Iran settled a number of minor border disputes with the USSR and Pakistan.

Next on the shah's agenda after the 'chastisement of Iraq' was the future of relations with Afghanistan. Iraq was expected to be bogged down in its domestic problems, especially with the Kurds, for the foreseeable future. Support for the Iraqi Kurdish rebellion, led by the charismatic Mullah Mostafa Barzani, alias the Red Mullah, began in 1968 with a $400,000 investment from SAVAK. But by 1970 Barzani was being supported by the United States and Israel as well. A tripartite committee of SAVAK, CIA and Mossad experts organized and supervised the channelling of arms to Barzani's forces and, at the same time, exercised overall political control in consultation with the royal court in Tehran. Barzani and his sons Idriss and Messaoud became frequent visitors to Tehran, Tel Aviv and Washington, where they used Iranian passports and a variety of pseudonyms and disguises. The shah could have financed the entire Kurdish operation in Iraq without any outside help, but he insisted that the United States should also make a contribution. He told Barzani that it was essential to get Americans financially involved since if 'they put down their money they are unlikely to just walk away'.[12]

While the Kurdish rebellion was no more than a contributory factor in getting both the United States and the USSR involved in Iraq's domestic affairs, the shah's Afghan project paved the way for a more important superpower conflict in the 1980s. Iran and Afghanistan had long quarrelled over the sharing of the waters of the Hirmand river which the Afghans claimed as entirely their own. In 1971 the shah ordered his government to settle the Hirmand dispute and to work out a plan for establishing 'the closest possible relations' with Kabul. Afghanistan was to become something of an obsession with the shah. In private conversations the shah lamented the fact that Iran was 'a lonely nation'. He referred to the European Common Market, the Arab League, the various Latin American and African unity organizations, and concluded that Iran, because of its 'racial and cultural uniqueness', was all alone – a nation with no relatives in the world. This perception of Iran's situation gave Afghanistan a special place in the shah's dreams of a renascent Iran which would once again become a world power. Afghanistan had been an important part of the Persian Empire for centuries and some 45 per cent of the Afghans, especially in the cities, were Persian-speakers by birth.[13] Therefore, if Iran were to follow the world trend towards bigger groupings of nations, it was to Afghanistan that she had to turn in the first place.

The Afghans, for their part, had always been suspicious of Iranian intentions and feared an eventual takeover by their larger and wealthier neighbour. But, thanks to patient diplomacy, hard work and the systematic bribing of scores of influential Afghans between 1971 and 1975, the shah succeeded in changing Kabul's attitude towards relations with Iran. By 1974 secret committees in Tehran and Kabul were working on plans for the creation of a federation that would tie Iran and Afghanistan together in a number of crucial economic and commercial fields. The shah pumped more than $1000 million into the Afghan economy. Hundreds of scholarships were offered to Afghan students for the first time. And, also for the first time, the Afghan authorities removed most restrictions on the sale of Iranian newspapers and books and the showing of Iranian films and television programmes in Afghanistan. Inexpensive group tours, secretly subsidized by the Iranian government, took a growing number of Iranian tourists to Afghanistan. The Afghan prime minister, Mohammad Mouusa Shafiq, made no secret of his hopes that Iran and Afghanistan would, one day, share their destinies.[14]

Iran's growing activism in Afghanistan alarmed the Soviets, who believed that the shah wanted to woo the Afghan leaders into an indirect alliance with the United States. Moscow, making use of its strong position within the Soviet-trained Afghan officers corps, reacted by staging a coup in 1973. The king, Mohammad Zahir Shah, was overthrown and replaced by his cousin, the ambitious and megalomaniac Prince Mohammad Daoud, who declared a republic.[15] Daoud had made himself a reputation as a neutralist during an earlier term as prime minister in the 1950s. The Soviets trusted him. But soon it became obvious that Daoud too had found Iranian money and promises of other advantages to come irresistible. The wooing of Afghanistan away from the USSR was also assisted by Saudi Arabia which, in a rare exception to the rule, coordinated its policy with that of Iran. Large contracts were signed between Iran and Afghanistan for the exploitation of the Hajigak iron ore reserves, the natural gas deposits of the north and the waters of Hirmand. Iranian technicians began to replace some Soviet experts in a number of fields. High-level official visits betrween Tehran and Kabul multiplied, causing more consternation in the Kremlin. Five years later the Soviets reacted by organizing a second *coup d'état*, this time seizing control through the two communist parties they had financed in Afghanistan for years.[16] The stage was set for the Afghan civil war and the eventual Soviet invasion of the country in 1979. The Nixon administration unwittingly contributed to the creation of a new flashpoint in that troubled part of the world by underwriting the shah's *tous-azimut* activism.[17]

The direct communist takeover in Kabul came as a shock to the shah and Iranian forces were put in a state of alert.[18] Did the shah envisage a military response? It is difficult to know at this stage, but plans for the seizure of the Afghan city of Herat had already been prepared by the Iranian army in 1973. It is possible that the United States cautioned

the shah against any rash military action to counter the Soviet move
in Afghanistan.

The emergence of Iran as a regional power, or 'superpower of the
region' as the shah would have it, was supported by the Nixon
administration as a means of ensuring stability in the Persian Gulf.
With hindsight it seems astonishing that US policymakers did not
realize that a powerful and dominant Iran with its own goals of
grandeur would soon be seen as an imponderable in the fragile
balance and would ultimately become a generator of instability. The
shah began flexing his newly acquired muscles as early as 1969, when
the Iranian navy was ordered to destroy oil installations set up by
Occidental, a small American oil company, on an atoll in the Persian
Gulf claimed by Iran but occupied by Saudi Arabia. The Saudis, also
enjoying special relations with the USA, took the matter to
Washington. They were advised by Kissinger to make a deal with the
shah. The atoll was handed over to Iran and instantly renamed Farsi
('the Persian'). In exchange Iran agreed to let the Saudis have another
atoll, which was baptized al-Arabi ('the Arab'). Two years later, on
the day the British formally ended their military protection of the
former Trucial States, Iran regained control of three strategic islands
in the Strait of Hormuz at the entrance to the Persian Gulf.[19] Before
that SAVAK agents had played an active, though not a central, role
in organizing a *coup d'état* in the sultanate of Oman against the
obscurantist Sultan Sa'id Ben-Teymour.[20] The USA was no doubt
consulted on both occasions.

The shah's new policy towards the Arabs was not, however,
limited to such hostile moves. In the 1973 Arab-Israeli war, Iran,
while refusing to join the oil boycott asked for by the Arabs, helped
Egypt by sending large amounts of free oil, food, medicine and field
hospitals. The USSR was allowed to rush in supplies to Syria through
an 'airbridge' that spanned the Iranian air space.[21] Iran also used her
newly acquired C130 Hercules transport aircraft to transfer some
units of the Saudi army to Jordan. Iran went on to intensify her
support of the Arab cause in regard to Palestine in the United
Nations.

What the Israelis saw as the shah's new pro-Arab attitude was in
reality no more than posturing. Iran's deep suspicion of the Arabs did
not evaporate overnight despite a determined campaign by Ardeshir
Zahedi, who became foreign minister in 1967, to change the Iranian
image in the Arab world. In 1968 Zahedi played a key role in
arranging the first Islamic summit conference, which was held in
Rabat, the capital of Morocco, to discuss the future of Jerusalem.
Later the young foreign minister negotiated the relinquishment of

Iran's historic claims to sovereignty over the Bahrain archipelago despite what he described as 'intense heartache'.

The policy of *rapprochement* with the Arabs continued after Zahedi's dismissal in 1971, and even such radical states as South Yemen, Libya and Syria were not left out. Hafez al-Assad, the Syrian president, visited Tehran and was granted a loan of $157 million as a sign of Iranian goodwill. An exchange of ambassadors took place with Libya, which, as a member of OPEC, had special importance in the eyes of the Iranian leaders.

Special relations were established with Morocco, Tunisia and Jordan. An Iranian military mission, consisting of more than four hundred technicians and experts, was established in Morocco in 1975 and later played a role in training special units to fight the guerrilla war in the Sahara, annexed by King Hassan after the 'Green March' in the desert. Morocco also received some $200 million in Iranian aid with which to modernize its armed forces and build a hydroelectric complex on the Oued-Zerroud river.

Tunisia's share of Iranian aid did not exceed $45 million, in exchange for which President Habib Bourguiba offered the Iranian navy visiting facilities in the Mediterranean. Tunisia also agreed to allow Iran to build a powerful radio transmitter on Tunisian territory to beam Persian, Arabic, English and French programmes to North Africa, Western Europe and the Eastern Mediterranean.

Jordan was rewarded for its friendship with aid totalling $85 million, some of which was spent on improving the lives of Palestinian refugees in the Hashemite kingdom.

Iran's rapidly growing revenues from oil gave the shah an additional means for projecting power and influence in his region and beyond. Between 1968 and 1978 Iran earned more than $100,000 million from oil exports. More than 10 per cent of that was used in the form of loans or outright gifts to friendly countries. The United Kingdom received some $1,200 million in loans. France had its share through the $1000 million Iran invested in a uranium-enrichment plant. In West Germany Iran purchased substantial shares in Krupps and Benz as a means of saving them from financial difficulties. A further $1000 million went to India, where Iran helped construct an oil refinery at Madras and developed iron ore deposits in southern India. Neighbouring Pakistan, for its part, received $750 million. Pursuing his dream of attaining a direct role in world oil markets, the shah also invested in oil refineries at Pussan in South Korea and Sasolburg in South Africa. He also made a bid for the American millionaire Armand Hammer's oil company and planned to penetrate the Western European markets by investing in an oil refinery in Liège in Belgium and by purchasing three hundred petrol stations in Italy, Switzerland and Austria.

Not all Iran's foreign aid and investments were used through normal commercial and economic channels and for legitimate purposes. Part of the 'special supplementary funds' at the disposal of the prime minister, amounting to some $100 million a year in the 1970s, as well as part of the SAVAK budget, were spent on covert activities in countries as far apart as Senegal in West Africa and Bangladesh. More than seven hundred 'key personalities' in some thirty countries were on the secret Iranian payroll from 1975 onwards. Among them were politicians in several Arab states as well as in Pakistan, India, Bangladesh and several African countries. Also included in the list were 'influential people' in the West: American and European politicians, journalists, academics and diplomats. Even foreign security services were not spared.[22] One director of the French intelligence service, for example, received a monthly gift of $10,000 in exchange for occasional confidential reports on the latest French and other European thinking on the shah.[23] Iranian money was also used to foment trouble in a number of countries. Iraq, for example, was the victim of no fewer than three unsuccessful coup attempts in addition to the Kurdish rebellion financed by Tehran. The Syrian Muslim Brotherhood, opposed to the Ba'athist regime of Damascus, also received financial aid from SAVAK, as did several leading Shi'ite and Maronite personalities in Lebanon.[24]

The shah was determined to project Iran's new military power wherever possible. Thanks to American pressure, he received invitations from the United Nations for Iranian troops to serve in international peace-keeping missions in Vietnam, the Golan Heights and southern Lebanon. Iranian military missions were also established in Yemen, the Sudan, Somalia, Zaïre and Lesotho, while SAVAK 'experts' helped train intelligence officers in Morocco, Tunisia, Jordan and Pakistan. Elaborate SAVAK offices were established in New York, Washington, Paris, London, Hamburg, Geneva, Rome and a number of other international centres. In 1977 Iran had some 4000 officers and men on duty in eighteen countries.[25]

The most dramatic illustration of the shah's new military power came in the form of Iranian intervention in the war in the southwestern Omani province of Dhufar. There a Marxist rebel movement had been in operation since 1969 with support from South Yemen, China and the USSR. Chinese support for the rebels ceased in 1971 as a result of the Iranian *rapprochement* with Beijing (Peking). The following year Iran dispatched a small unit to help the sultan's British-led army. By 1975 the number of Iranian troops in Oman had topped 5000, representing a major force compared to the sultan's own 18,000-strong army of Baluchi and Pakistani mercenaries with British and Canadian officers and NCOs. Iran's intervention in the Dhufar war was seen by Moscow as an indirect challenge by Washington. As a result the Soviets began thinking about bringing Cuban troops from Ethiopia to face the shah's forces in Oman. Possible Cuban intervention was also discussed in October 1975 when the Iranians bombarded the South Yemeni port of Hauf from sea and air. The Soviets did not make use of their Cuban option after Tehran gave assurances that there would be no more direct attacks on South Yemen, which had a treaty of friendship with Moscow.[26]

The fact that the shah used his American-supplied weapons pretty well as he chose was illustrated by his transfer of arms and materiel to Pakistan in the 1971 clash with India and to Turkey during the Cyprus crisis of 1974 which led to the Turkish invasion of the island. On both occasions the Pentagon made feeble attempts at drawing the shah's attention to the special conditions attached to the sale of US arms to foreign countries. But these were no more than minor irritants in an increasingly close relationship. An administration which had begun by approving a single master contract for the supply of $2100 million's worth of arms to Iran was not to be deterred by details and legal niceties. That contract was the single largest of its kind ever signed between the United States and a foreign country for the sale of arms.[27]

In May 1972 President Nixon, on his way home from Moscow, where he had held a particularly successful summit conference with the Soviet leader Leonid Brezhnev, paid a state visit to Tehran to underline the shah's special place in Washington's global strategy. He showered lavish praise on the shah and promised Iran virtually unlimited support in her efforts to police the Persian Gulf and ensure regional peace and stability.

The president's open-ended commitment to the shah did not please everyone in Washington. The defence secretary, Melvin Laird, had opposed the provision of technical personnel in the numbers the shah wanted and also refused to give his consent to the sale of aircraft that had not yet become operational with the US services at home. Laird had further expressed concern that through Iran the Soviets might be able to get some of the advanced weapons and the technology that went with them.[28]

Some members of the political team at the US embassy were apparently anxious that the president should hear the views of some of the shah's more moderate opponents during Nixon's visit to Tehran. This was to be arranged through a chance encounter at the Iran-America Society, where the president was to make a brief visit. But the idea, if it ever seriously came up, was not implemented and Nixon did not see any of the shah's local critics.[29] The president and more specially his national security adviser did not wish to hear bad news about the shah. Even the fact that a plot to murder the president by throwing a bomb at his motorcade shortly after his arrival in Tehran had been discovered did not seem to disturb Kissinger and his boss.[30] The plot had been called off at the last moment, apparently after Khomeini opposed its execution from his exile in Najaf in Iraq.[31]

Nixon's visit to Tehran was hailed by the official media as a recognition of the shah's personal prestige in world affairs. 'The highest of the world's leaders come to our capital to pay tribute to our wise and beloved King of Kings,' said the state-owned radio in a commentary.[32]

Gradually the shah emerged as a spokesman for OPEC and, using Iran's position as the world's largest exporter of crude oil after Saudi Arabia, began to demand a greater say for himself in the world's councils. Kissinger and Nixon continued to support the shah in spite of the fact that Iran's oil policy was so obviously opposed to the one Washington wanted OPEC to pursue. Curbing oil prices was one of the basic objectives of US policy in Iran as set out in several State Department papers between 1973 and 1976.[33]

One member of the Nixon administration who dared speak his mind was the treasury secretary, William Simon, who, pointing the finger at the shah as the man most responsible for the frequent rises in the price of crude oil, called the monarch 'nuts'. The remark provoked anti-imperialist attacks on the United States by the official media in Tehran and made Simon *persona non grata* in Iran. Nixon personally apologized to the shah for Simon's disrespect and agreed that the treasury secretary should be left out of the Irano-American Economic Cooperation Commission. Nixon suggested Kissinger as co-chairman of the commission, and the shah agreed. On the Iranian side Hushang Ansary, minister of the economy at the time, served as co-chairman. Simon's idea of using arms sales as a means of restraining the shah over oil prices was rejected by Kissinger and quickly forgotten. The assistant secretary of state for the Middle East, Joseph Sisco, was an early convert to the shah's views and policies concerning the region and went out of his way to make sure that Iran received everything she asked for from the United States.

By cultivating his personal friendship with Nixon the shah gradually deluded himself into thinking that the United States would not take any major foreign policy decisions without consulting him. In other words, he felt that he had secured a say in the shaping of the policies of the West's superpower. Some other leaders also shared the shah's belief in his own special influence in Washington. Morocco's King Hassan, King Hussein of Jordan, Pakistan's Zulfiqar Ali Bhutto and, from 1973 onwards, President Muhammad Anwar Sadat of Egypt all used the shah as an influential channel of communication with Washington. The special relationship that the Nixon administration fostered with Iran was deeply resented by Washington's other staunch ally in the Persian Gulf – Saudi Arabia. It was to offset Saudi misgivings that Kissinger later developed the so-called 'two pillar' policy under which Iran and Saudi Arabia were jointly to assure the security of the Persian Gulf. The Saudis did, indeed, receive huge quantities of US-made weapons, but it was obvious that they did not enjoy the same status as Iran in Washington. King Faisal's militant stance against Israel and his funding of some of the Palestinian guerrilla organizations prevented Saudi Arabia from being seen as an ally for all seasons. The shah used what he privately described as his 'Washington card' for the purpose of enticing Egypt to consider a full reversal of her alliances. He played a crucial role in bringing Sadat and the United States closer together in a process that eventually led to the so-called Camp David accords between Israel and Egypt. Iran also played a key part in persuading Somalia to break with Moscow and join the Western bloc. The shah was further instrumental in securing US military support for the Moroccan war effort in the Sahara.[34]

The 'special relationship' both Nixon and the shah spoke of did not, however, mean any greater leverage by the United States on Iranian policy-making. On the contrary, it is possible to argue that American influence on Iran was somewhat reduced between 1968 and 1976. The Iranian pattern of voting in the United Nations changed, moving away from the US camp on such issues as the Middle East conflict, South Africa, Vietnam and the future of undersea resources. Iran also became an increasingly vocal member of the so-called Group of 77 countries which called for a radical reform of the world economic system. When the United States made the sale of some $10,000 million's worth of nuclear power generators to Iran conditional to stiff security checks and regular inspection by American personnel, the shah simply stopped all negotiations and asked his officials to buy what he wanted from West Germany and France. The fact that the shah diversified Iran's source of arms to include Britain, France, Italy, Switzerland and Brazil must also be seen as an indication that he did not want to be totally dependent on the United States in so vital a domain. Iran's plans for the development of fighter-bombers in two separate projects with India and Israel also marked the shah's desire for greater independence.[35]

Nixon's fall from power in 1974 dealt a serious psychological blow to the shah, who was convinced that the United States was entering a prolonged period of decline.[36] The fact that Kissinger was retained as secretary of state reassured him up to a point. And soon he succeeded in establishing very close personal relations with Nixon's successor, President Gerald Ford. The Ford administration also had another attraction from the shah's point of view: it included as vice-president one of the monarch's oldest and closest friends, Nelson Rockefeller. Together, Rockefeller and Kissinger succeeded in convincing the shah that Nixon's enforced retirement would not undermine Washington's 'special relationship' with Tehran. In the years that followed Kissinger had to fight hard to keep that promise, for the shah's pursuit of grandeur combined with increasingly frequent reports about alleged abuses of human rights in Iran attracted more and more attention.

The debate was soon extended to the administration itself where Defence Secretary James Schlesinger, echoing reservations previously aired by General George Brown, then chairman of the joint chiefs-of-staff, insisted that the shah should abandon at least part of his plans for purchasing seemingly endless quantities of modern and sophisticated weapons which his armed forces found difficult to use and to maintain. Directed by Schlesinger, the Pentagon prepared a report critical of the arms aspect of Washington's Iran policy and also warned of socioeconomic difficulties for the shah's regime if a change of course was not implemented. The report was presented to the State Department and the National Security Council (NSC) for comment and revision in 1975. When it emerged from there to be presented to President Ford it had been so amended as to amount to a fresh endorsement of the long-established Kissinger policy towards the shah. The Iranian monarch was determined to hang himself and his American friends obliged by selling him the rope. Even Congress, which in those post-Vietnam days was striving after control of foreign policy, did not succeed in getting the better of the tenacious Dr K. 'Kissinger will have all of them for breakfast,' the shah once said in 1976 with reference to his critics in the US Congress.[37]

Nevertheless, in August 1976 the Senate Foreign Relations Committee succeeded in putting out a very critical report on US policy in Iran, concluding that Washington risked being dragged into a regional war on the side of the shah. But even then Kissinger was undaunted. A few days after the report was published, attracting unusual media attention, the secretary of state flew to Tehran to reassure the shah. He concluded his talks with the shah with a ringing endorsement of the monarch's 'wise and farsighted leader-ship' at a press conference in which he also announced that the sale of American arms to Iran would continue at the pace His Majesty desired at least until 1980.

Kissinger's audience with the shah had been less warm than usual and the monarch had 'lost his temper' about 'those amateur politicians who do not understand the realities of this world'.[38] He had also reminded Kissinger that Iran was spending her own money and risking the lives of her own soldiers to defend the West's interests as well as pursuing her own goals. 'We are not beggars asking for alms,' he told Kissinger. 'We have pulled ourselves through, thanks to our own efforts.'[39] It was to cool down His Majesty's temper that Kissinger speeded up the approval of the sale of 160 F16 fighters to Iran at a cost of $3300 million. This reinforced an earlier 'personal note' from President Ford to the shah in which the American leader emphasized 'the very great importance' he attached to 'the special relationship we enjoy with Iran.'[40] That brief but categoric message was to be borne in mind by all members of the administration when working on issues related to ties with the shah.

The 'special relationship' to which President Ford made reference was not limited to the arming of the shah. From 1973 onwards Iran became one of the most important markets for American goods outside Western Europe and Japan. The Joint Economic Commission approved a trade protocol that envisaged the purchase of some $55,000 million's worth of American goods and services by Iran between 1977 and 1982. The protocol, signed by Kissinger and Ansary, was justly hailed as the most ambitious trade accord ever concluded in history. Needless to say, it was not fully implemented as Iran was swept out of the deal by the Islamic Revolution of 1979.

All through his long reign and until the 1970s the shah had remained a cautious and conservative politician especially in regard to Iran's foreign relations. While vehemently rejecting any suggestion of foreign influence in Iran, in practice he had based his policy on the full recognition of the dangers involved in provoking any of the big powers whose interests lay in maintaining a regional balance so that none of them would have a distinct advantage over the others. The shah remembered that Britain and Russia had effectively divided Iran into two zones of influence in 1907. He ostensibly rejected that partition as 'a shameful act of surrender' on the part of Iranian politicians at the time. In practice, however, he respected that partition and reflected it in his overall policies. He had in his mind an imaginary line running from east to west south of the central Iranian city of Isfahan. He would not allow Western powers, especially the United States, to have any major investment or economic presence to the north of that line. In exchange the Soviets and their allies were completely shut out of the provinces to the south of the imaginary line. Iran launched a number of important joint ventures with the USSR and Soviet-block countries representing thousands of millions of dollars in investment. The iron and steel complex at Riz-Lenjan, the machine tools industry at Arak, the tractor manufacturing centre at Tabriz, the Asfrayen industrial city, the rosewater distilleries of Kashan and caviar fisheries on the Caspian were all projects carried out with Eastern Bloc financial and technical participation. All these enterprises were situated in regions north of the shah's imaginary line.

It was because he did not want Western companies to operate in those parts of the country which he considered to be 'too sensitive' from Moscow's point of view that the shah prevented the exploitation of oil resources found by an Italian group near the holy city of Qom in the 1950s. Later he also ordered oil prospecting to be halted in the Garmi region of the Moghan Plain on the Irano-Soviet border. Western companies were asked not to bid for projects related to the gas reservoirs at Sarakhs on the border with the USSR. And Western diplomats and journalists were not allowed to venture into such areas as Qezel-Qeshlaq, Khoda-Afarin and Atrak where Irano-Soviet hydroelectric units operated. On the other hand, Soviet and East Bloc concerns were systematically kept out of all activities to the south of Isfahan. The 1907 partition accord was respected in practice, leaving the Soviets with no reason to fear that Iran might become a base of aggression against them.

The shah no doubt had always wanted to change that situation so that he could exercise Iran's full sovereignty and independence in whatever way he deemed fit. By 1975 he felt strong enough to erase that imaginary line which had always appeared to him as a limit imposed on the nation's autonomy and a permanent attack on Iranian dignity and pride. He cautiously began to dismantle it by allowing Western interests to move northwards while joint ventures with Eastern Bloc countries began to be moved south.

It was as part of his new policy to make 1907 a dead part of history that he allowed the United States to install two listening posts near the Soviet border to monitor missile tests carried out by the USSR. The project, although later vehemently criticized by Moscow, was originally devised with tacit Soviet approval as a means of monitoring the Strategic Arms Limitation Talks (SALT) accords between the two superpowers. In changing his traditional policy towards the big powers the shah provoked strong resentment on the part of the Soviets. They saw Iran emerging as a regional military power determined to counter Soviet influence in Afghanistan, the Indian subcontinent and the Horn of Africa.

As early as 1971 the Soviets had given their approval to the training of Iranian urban guerrillas in Cuba, North Korea and South Yemen as well as in Palestinian camps in Lebanon. In 1973 two guerrilla 'schools' were set up exclusively for Iranian militants at Hadhramaut in South Yemen with the German Democratic Republic and Cuba providing most of the instructors. The People's Mujahedeen of Iran Organization, an Islamic-Marxist group, and the People's Fedayeen Guerrillas both maintained their headquarters in Aden where KGB officers took most of the important decisions. Guerrillas trained in South Yemen and Lebanon were later responsible for the murder of six American military officers, including one brigadier general, and an attempted kidnapping of the US ambassador in Tehran, Douglas MacArthur III.[41] Soviet-inspired anti-American propaganda also started from 1972 onwards to warn the Iranian people of the consequences of 'neo-colonialism'.

Soviet alarm about what they saw as the shah's attempt to alter 'the realities of the region' with support from Washington reached fever pitch in 1973–74 when Moscow became convinced that Iran planned to play the Chinese card against the USSR. The shah had looked to China as a regional superpower capable of counterbalancing Soviet influence in Asia as early as 1970. By 1972 almost anybody who was somebody in the Iranian hierarchy had visited the People's Republic. Princess Ashraf, Empress Farah, Prime Minister Amir Abbas Hoveyda and scores of other officials had all returned from Beijing impressed with China's socioeconomic progress and rising military power. The Foreign Ministry, however, did not share these views and warned against provoking the Soviets by getting too close to the Chinese. 'China,' a confidential report told the shah, 'is unlikely to become a major power before the year 2000.'[42] But the shah thought otherwise. He dispatched as ambassador to Beijing the former foreign minister Abbas Aram, a seasoned diplomat, to underline the special import-ance Tehran attached to Iran's new ties with the People's Republic. A stream of Chinese dignitaries began to visit Tehran, among them Li Xiannien[43] and Deng Xiaoping. The shah's very last foreign guest in Tehran was to be the Chinese Communist Party leader, Hua Kou-feng, who came to the Iranian capital in 1978, shortly before monarchy was overthrown.

The Soviet leadership was visibly divided on how to react to what Andrei Gromyko, then foreign minister, saw as 'an adventurist policy' on the part of the shah.[44] Gromyko and Premier Aleksei Kosygin urged tough measures against the shah, while Leonid Brezhnev, the first secretary of the Communist Party of the Soviet Union (CPSU) and Nikolai Podgorny, who served as president, were not so sure. By 1976, however, Gromyko had won the debate and Moscow began to regard the shah as an element of instability, threatening the security of the USSR. What Gromyko feared most was the emergence of a Cairo–Tehran–Islamabad–Beijing axis backed by Washington. Such an axis would have posed an immediate threat to Moscow's allies in North Africa, the Middle East and Southern Asia.[45] Worse still, Gromyko could envisage the day when China and Iran, which respectively shared the first and second longest borders of the USSR, would realize Dulles's dream of imposing a 'quarantine on the aggressor'.

The Chinese for their part lost no opportunity to poison Irano-Soviet relations. In 1974, for example, the *People's Daily* published a lengthy article dealing with what it termed 'Russian imperialism'. In it the writers recalled that the Tsar had annexed large chunks of Iranian territory in the nineteenth century, just as they had nibbled at China itself. They concluded by saying that Iran was now becoming strong enough to recall her 'usurped territorial rights' and would, in future, be able to 'drive the foreign occupant out'.[46] Parts of the provocative article were read on Tehran Radio in a review of the international press. Moscow's reaction was swift and further publication of the Chinese article in Tehran was stopped.

UGLY AMERICANS

Early in 1976 some of Tehran's newspapers carried a story about a double murder in Isfahan: a jealous husband had sprayed the bodies of his wife and her lover with bullets from a machine gun. The story was interesting not only because it was the first time a machine gun had been used for committing private murder in Iran but also because all the personages involved in the triangular drama were Americans. One important detail immediately caught the attention of the public: both the wronged husband and the imprudent lover had served in Vietnam as 'military technicians'. The story was quickly hushed out of the newspapers because of pressure from SAVAK, but it managed to focus attention on the presence in Iran of many thousands of US servicemen who were making a second career in Iran after the debacle of Vietnam.

The Iranian press had, from 1968 onwards, paid special attention to the situation in Indo-China, in the process demonstrating un-mistakable sympathy for the Viet-Cong cause in defiance of the government's wholehearted support of the American position in Southeast Asia. Reports of alleged atrocities committed by US troops in Vietnam and Cambodia received prominence and helped create a new image of America as a cruel power using its overwhelming might against small but heroic peoples. The many thousands of Iranian students in the United States and the estimated 300,000 Iranians who visited that country each year were also affected by the growing mood of anger about the Vietnam War in the United States itself. The older generation of Iranian intellectuals opposed to the shah in the 1950s resented the role the United States had played in overthrowing Mossadeq. The new generation began to dislike the United States because of what it saw as Washington's support for corrupt and dictatorial regimes in the Third World. The television, often using footage purchased from the American networks, depicted the USA as an arsonist, a mass murderer and a hedonistic beast ready to destroy whole countries in a mad rage.

This new image of America took some time to filter down to other
levels of society. But by 1970 teachers at secondary schools frequently
chose the war in Vietnam as a subject in composition classes. With
hindsight, it seems almost incredible that the United States did
virtually nothing to put its side of the story and try to modify some of
the more negative aspects of its new image. One likely explanation for
this strange passivity may be the fact that the United States was already
persuaded that all it needed in Iran was the shah's friendship. The fact
that Iran was growing into a fairly sophisticated modern society with a
dynamic intellectual elite which did not share all the shah's views and
dreams was ignored in Washington. Suffering from centuries of
xenophobia, Iranians did not lose much time in viewing the growing
physical presence of America in their country with apprehension. 'Iran
is the next Vietnam' became the warcry of the increasingly active
urban terrorist groups and their sympathizers among Iranian students
both at home and abroad.

Until the 1970s most urban Iranians had a very positive view of the
United States. The Americans they had met or seen at work had, until
then, been mostly teachers, builders, technicians, aid officers and
Peace Corps men and women. The majority of new-wave Americans,
whose number rose to over 50,000 by 1978, were equally honest,
decent people who had come to Iran to help the country achieve its
economic and military goals. But the fact that large numbers of them
were military personnel who appeared in their uniforms in public was
resented.[1] Also resented was the fact that the new wave brought with it
a disturbingly large number of unscrupulous merchants, fixers,
influence peddlers, layabouts, adventurers, smugglers of antiques and
of drugs, and at times even characters linked with the American
Mafia.[2]

Many of the Americans lived in secluded areas and spoke no
Persian. Almost all of them seemed to have more money than they
were judged to deserve. The triple salaries, tax-free shopping and six-
week-long holidays offered to many of the Americans working in Iran,
created envy and resentment among the people who worked with
them. In parts of Tehran, Isfahan and Shiraz the presence of large
numbers of foreigners prepared to pay four or five times the going rate
for the best houses and flats pushed urban rents through the roof,
angering the very middle class who ought to have appreciated
American friendship with Iran. The fact that most Westerners in Iran
were wrongly believed to be Americans gave rise to the belief that a
full-scale takeover of Iran by American businesses and government
departments was under way.[3] Most Americans kept to themselves,
avoiding Iranians as much as possible, apparently in accordance with

instructions from their firms or the government departments that employed them. And those who did seek Iranian contacts always looked upwards, trying to forge links with the wealthier and more influential natives. For many of them this meant entering a world more sophisticated than theirs, in which they appeared gauche, naive or outright uncivilized.

To the less fortunate urban masses the strangers 'brought in by the shah'[4] were representatives of an alien and threatening faith. The relaxed way in which these strangers dressed, their love of liquor, their noisy parties, their car and motorcycle races and their ostentatious opulence could not but arouse envy, resentment, mistrust and anger over the years.

It was not only the United States which ignored the need for putting its case to public opinion in Iran. The shah too came to believe that all he needed was the continuation of unlimited support from Washington. He took the Iranian people, for whose wellbeing and future grandeur he sincerely strived, for granted. By 1976 none of the basic reasons for which governments everywhere need the support of their peoples were present in the shah's calculations. He did not need his people for their votes in a general election. He was there by divine right, and parliamentary elections, organized every four years, were little more than ritualistic exercises in futility. His government did not need the people for their financial contribution to the national budget either. The shah's government derived more than 95 per cent of the money it needed from oil exports and a variety of state monopolies. Further, the shah even gave the impression that he did not need the people to work; the type of work which he considered essential for making Iran into a powerful nation state could be done by the estimated one million foreigners who were employed in practically all walks of life, including agriculture. Wherever shortage of manpower was signalled the shah gave the green light for importing as many foreigners as necessary to do the job.[5] Finally, it seemed that the shah did not need the Iranian people to fight in defence of the country either; that task too could be handled by foreign technicians and the increasingly sophisticated war machines that the imperial government purchased principally from the United States. The shah made no secret of his fears that the average Iranian might not want to die in a prolonged war with no prospect of an early victory or peace. He based his strategy on deterring any would-be aggressor through overwhelming superiority in arms combined with the American insurance policy he thought he had.[6]

By 1974 and after the so-called oil shock, resulting from the virtual quadrupling of OPEC prices, had exposed some of the weaknesses of the leading Western economies, the shah became convinced that the leadership of the West had become 'too soft' and that more vigorous leaders such as himself should assume greater responsibility in facing the challenge of communism on a global scale.

Gradually, the shah lost interest in the domestic affairs of his kingdom and applied his energies to seeking solutions to international problems. He saw Iran's own problems as details that could be handled by lesser mortals. He abandoned his long-established practice of travelling throughout the country to ensure direct contact with the people. Instead, he multipled state visits abroad. And when at home he was constantly seen in the company of foreign dignitaries.

It was to assist him in meeting his new global responsibilities that the shah ordered the creation of a think-tank in 1976. Kissinger became a key member of the group which was supposed to hold an annual two-day conference at the shah's seaside palace at Nowshahr at the Caspian. The group's conference in September 1977 was to be its second and last.[7]

By 1977, almost on the eve of the Islamic Revolution, the USA had become Iran's principal trading partner for the first time in the history of a long friendship. Some 25 per cent of all of Iran's imports from the industrialized countries came from the United States, compared to West Germany's 22 per cent and Japan's 18 per cent. Iran purchased nearly 3 per cent of all manufactured goods that the USA exported. In the case of the aircraft industry in the USA, Iran's share was 8 per cent of all exports.[8] More than 500 American companies, including 150 of the largest, were trading with Iran and many more were fighting to secure a share of the Iranian market.

A confidential report prepared by the State Department's Office of the Inspector Genral in September 1976 had this to say:

> Iran is a vital element in the US Middle Eastern policy and a very considerable factor in the US posture vis-a-vis the USSR. The country occupies a position of exceptional strategic importance by virtue of its location, oil resources and political influence. The US has sought to follow a policy towards Iran aimed at the constitution of a stable, responsible and friendly country which would (a) offer the US strategic military facilities and (b) play a constructive regional role including the limitation of Soviet influence in the area. This policy has been, on the whole, very successful.[9]

The report also expressed some concern about the possibility of Iran becoming too strong and too self-reliant systematically to take into account American interests. It stated that the United States would, in any case, need Iran for four reasons: monitoring facilities to make sure the Soviets do not violate SALT agreements; overflight rights so that US aircraft could have access to the Indian Ocean; making sure that oil continued to flow to the United States and other Western countries; a share in Iran's import market.[10]

The report did mention some of the reservations expressed in the USA about the wisdom of so close a link with the shah. It said:

> Iran is a monarchy ruled by an autocratic, dynamic shah who personally makes all the critical decisions in Iran and controls all aspects of the country's economic and political life. There is no effective internal challenge to his leadership. There are many progressive aspects of the shah's policies, and his achievements in modernizing the country and improving the conditions of most Iranians during his reign have been substantial. Nevertheless, many Americans – officials, Congressmen and public opinion leaders – deplore the shah's authoritarian regime and his policies, in particular the relatively low regard for human rights in the political sphere and the shah's role in keeping oil prices high. The idea of a 'special' relationship with Iran based on US military support is also distasteful or repugnant to many. There is concern that US arms sales policy will lead to a conflagration rather than stability in the area.[11]

The outgoing Ford administration, which had ordered the report, had no time to consider doing anything about it. And the report was to provide the basis for President Jimmy Carter's ambivalent policy towards the shah. Its cold, detached tone contrasted sharply with earlier American diplomatic literature on Iran. It showed that the USA had abandoned its traditional concern for improving the lives of the people of Iran – a concern which had originally persuaded Roosevelt to make an initial commitment to helping Iran break out of medieval poverty and backwardness. There was no mention of any interest in seeing any development towards greater public participation in decision making in Iran.

By limiting US interest in Iran to geopolitical and commercial areas only, Kissinger in a sense destroyed all chance of Washington being able to influence developments in Iran at a critical moment. He also put his mark on a period in Irano-American relations that witnessed exceptional cynicism on both sides in the name of the 'special relationship'. That period made Iran more profitable to the United States in cash terms and the United States more important to the shah as a source of weapons. But it also dealt serious blows to the genuine friendship that had taken shape between the two nations since the nineteenth century. Kissinger's policy also meant that the United States was, over the years, practically shut out of Iran's domestic developments precisely at a time when economic growth and mass education were creating a genuine broad-based constituency likely to support a serious programme of democratization on a step-by-step basis.

The drift towards what was to become known as 'shahdulation' as the only form of diplomatic reporting on Iran likely to attract attention in Washington, began during the Johnson administration. William G. Miller, a second secretary at the Tehran embassy, for example, was encouraged to return home in 1966 after he had been spotted contacting some of the shah's liberal opponents.[12] His reports were nevertheless excellent, although they were to be ridiculed by some of his successors who saw no sign of what Miller described as a burgeoning mood of anti-Americanism. In 1963 Miller reported that Khomeini was 'an important national figure' and recommended that the shah should 'treat him with caution'.[13] The shah, of course, did exactly the opposite and first imprisoned and then exiled the troublesome ayatollah. Miller saw Khomeini as 'the only man capable of leading a vast coalition against the shah and even to win support from the intelligentsia.'[14]

In later years such daring reports either would not be prepared at all or would never get far within the bureaucracy. Undue curiosity on the part of diplomats in Tehran could land them in trouble. Max McCarthy, a former Congressman who came to Tehran as press attaché in the 1970s, was soon singled out as a potential enemy by SAVAK simply because he went around asking direct questions about the rationale behind the Iranian defence build-up and persistent rumours about the royal family's growing corruption. The Ministry of Information even advised local editors to avoid McCarthy because he might be 'working for the Soviets [sic]'.[15]

One major difficulty in understanding what was going on in Iran was that few of the high-ranking members of the embassy knew Persian. This made even an assessment of what the Persian press had to say extremely difficult because the subtle hints, the meanings between the lines and a whole coded language which the regular readers understood were lost in translation. Lack of Persian also made contact with all types of people difficult if not impossible, gradually limiting the embassy's relations to individuals and groups within the middle and upper classes only. Where embassy members spoke Persian they often obtained remarkable results. Michael Metrinko, a consul in Tabriz in 1978, for example, had managed to develop a network of friends and acquaintances which extended into almost all classes of Azarbaijani society. These relations helped save his life and the lives of seven other Westerners who sought his protection during the chaotic days of the revolution that followed the fall of the shah's last premier in Tehran.[16]

Many of the diplomats that served at the Tehran embassy were either en route to other, to them, more challenging posts or simply awaiting retirement. Working in Iran was no challenge as everyone assumed that the country was on a steady course and that her leaders enjoyed close personal relations with their counterparts in the United States. In practice all the US diplomats in Tehran had to do was to keep themselves informed about Iran's progress and to congratulate the shah. Because Iran policy was set at the highest level in Washington what was left was only a matter of execution. Tehran was a place to relax in or to get bored to tears in while waiting for more exciting days elsewhere. The imperial capital had a very busy and varied social life for a Third World country. It was therefore possible to let oneself be carried away on a wave of endless parties and receptions punctuated by hunting trips, skiing weekends and desert trekking adventures.

The key staff of the embassy attended a weekly session dealing with Iran's domestic problems. These sessions were to be held almost daily as the revolution built up to its crescendo. But accounts of many of these meetings, published as part of the documents seized at the embassy in November 1979 by revolutionary students, show that they resembled a formal high mass in which the staff saw the ambassador and were seen by him. Accounts show that much time was devoted to gossip, especially related to court circles, and relatively minor issues received unusually great attention. Unable to probe and chart the profound currents of Iranian society, the participants spent time discussing visits of dignitaries, the latest rumours concerning changes in the Iranian bureaucracy and matters of routine logistics and administration concerning the mission. Some of the reports reflected the growing tendency of the mission to prefer colourful gossip to hard-nosed analysis. For example, Parviz Raji, for years an influential private secretary to the prime minister and later Iran's ambassador to London, was described only as 'a clever "graduate" of Princess Ashraf's stable of young men'.[17]

Nevertheless flashes of insight were not totally absent. The embassy was certainly aware of the presence of a strong undercurrent of religious dissent likely to affect the future of Iran. In one report we read:

> Fanatical Muslim clergy constitute a latent opposition which no longer has major political influence but retains sufficient following to slow down many government programs. . . . For the past decade these forces have been fighting a losing rearguard action against the growing tide of secular economic development. Should unforeseen developments (the shah's death, military disaster, severe recession) lead other segments of the population to challenge the government, the Muslim clergy could, undoubtedly, drum up a modest, perhaps (depending on the issue) substantial following in the streets.[18]

The report went on to conclude: 'Since the US is closely associated in their minds with the shah's reforming regime, and the clergy has always opposed foreign influence, the US could come under severe political attack in the event of revived religious nationalism.'[19]

The embassy was also aware of the serious charges of corruption against some members of the shah's own family. One report said: 'Several members of the Royal Family are thought to be, in varying degrees, corrupt, immoral and largely uninterested in Iran and the Iranian people.' The report went on to cite the example of a prince who stole several precious archaeological objects found in a famous dig northwest of Tehran and sold them in Europe.

Most members of the embassy genuinely wished Iran well and hoped that in time the regime would come to modify some of its harsher aspects and allow normal political evolution to take its course. Such evolution, they hoped, would remove the threat of a revolution led by Muslim fundamentalists.[20]

Those diplomats who tried to go beyond doing a merely routine job found themselves confronted with a labyrinthine system designed to confuse and confound. Their sentiments were reflected in one report:

> No outsider can fully understand the Iranian decision-making process. For a Westerner used to analysing institutional structures in a government, the highly personal system of government under the shah presents a complexity which can be highly frustrating. For one thing it is extremely hard to get facts about anything going on within the high councils of the Government of Iran. . . .[21]

Although 'shah-watching' was considered an important task of the embassy in Tehran, the results of the exercise were often unsatisfactory. Once again a taste for juicy gossip and rumours of scandal prevailed over the urge to look for more serious information. Rumours that the shah was having an affair with a young woman – described by salon gossipmongers in Tehran as 'the golden girl' – were raised and discussed at the embassy. But no attention was paid to serious reports that the shah might have cancer. The United States had built its entire strategy in Iran on one man, and that man was suffering from a fatal disease. The embassy first learned of this in 1976 when Austrian papers mentioned it, but no further investigation was made. Later one of the embassy's Iranian sources reported that the monarch was in declining health. But the subject was mentioned only in passing at one of the staff meetings and never pursued. It was not until October 1978, when the shah's strange performance in the face of a growing challenge to his rule had become all too apparent, that the embassy received a detailed questionnaire from the CIA in Washington concerning the shah's state of health.[22]

What could be described as the Kissinger style of diplomacy led, over a period of eight years, to a sharp reduction in the contribution of American missions abroad to the making of foreign policy. Kissinger clearly believed that diplomacy was too important a matter to be left to diplomats. He expressed admiration for the efficiency and discipline of the US bureaucracy but saw it as no more than an instrument for implementing decisions made by a very restricted circle. His was high diplomacy of the type practised by nineteenth-century European statesmen at a time when rulers made and unmade history while their peoples played the role of extras. As far as Iran was concerned, the new style differed sharply from the tradition set by US diplomacy since Roosevelt. Documents seized at the Tehran embassy show that the mission had been in contact with no fewer than 5000 Iranian sources from all walks of life until the late 1960s. But many of these sources and contacts were later lost as Washington began to limit its interest to the shah and a dozen or so other dignitaries in the land. Members of the mission were gradually led to understand that they should not report what they saw but rather should see what Washington wanted them to report. Kissinger and the shah were playing for high stakes, and lesser mortals were not allowed to cut in.

The embassy remained understaffed right to the end while other major powers interested in Iran – especially the USSR – more than trebled the number of their diplomats in Tehran between 1965 and 1978. The post of the US ambassador in Tehran was also somewhat downgraded. Armin B. Meyer, who had served as ambassador to Iran during the Johnson administration, was posted to Tokyo and replaced by Joseph Farland, who had been a contributor to Nixon's presidential campaign. Farland, an easygoing, pleasant man was nevertheless seldom at home with what was going on in Iran. The appointment of former CIA director Richard Helms as Farland's successor did nothing to enhance the status of the embassy. The move was seen as part of a plot by Nixon and the shah to turn Tehran into the CIA's main base outside the United States. The truth, however, is that Helms's appointment resulted from considerations of domestic politics rather than any geostrategic calculation on Nixon's part. Helms had refused to use the agency as part of the president's plan to cover up the Watergate scandal and clearly could no longer work with Nixon in Washington. It was Helms himself who asked to be sent to Tehran because he believed Iran to be 'an important country passing through a fascinating phase of its history'.[23]

Although Helms and his dynamic number two, Jack Miklos, revitalized the embassy, the mould created during the previous years could not be broken. The shah and his close aides felt flattered that Helms had been named ambassador to Tehran. The subject was brought up with Prime Minister Hoveyda by the Soviet ambassador, Vladimir Erofeev, at a party at the Swedish embassy in Tehran. Erofeev referred to Helms's appointment and asked the premier: 'Why is it that the Americans have sent their number-one spy to Tehran, Excellency?' Hoveyda's reply was quick: 'Because they are our friends and do not send us their lowly spies like some others do.'[24] Helms, who had attended the same Swiss school, Le Rosey, as the shah and his mysterious confidant, General Hossein Fardoust, established close friendly relations with the monarch and came to share most of Iran's objectives. The shah's opponents quickly concluded that the CIA had, in fact, taken control of the entire American presence in Iran. And because they saw SAVAK as no more than the Iranian chapter of the CIA, they began increasingly to blame the USA for the rising wave of repression that marked the period 1971–76.

During that time Iran suffered a genuine problem of terrorism. Marxist urban guerrillas were responsible for no fewer than 713 acts of violence which claimed nearly two hundred lives.[25] SAVAK had virtually no experience in dealing with the problem and turned to the CIA and Mossad for help. They obliged by offering some training as well as the loan of equipment. When one of the most active leaders of the urban guerrillas, Hamid Ashraf, was finally gunned down after escaping the police net on three occasions, it was rumoured that CIA agents had directly helped SAVAK in the operation. Ashraf was something of a hero to the young guerrillas and was soon to become a figure of legend. There is no evidence of direct CIA involvement in his eventual death in a gunbattle in Tehran, although the agency did provide the telephone-tapping equipment which helped trace his movements.[26]

It was to avenge Ashraf's death that his comrades seized the American ambassador to Afghanistan, Adolph Dubs, in Kabul in February 1979 and murdered him when Soviet and Afghan security agents tried to rescue him by storming the hotel room where he was being held.[27] Two US Air Force colonels, Shaffer and Turner, as well as Brigadier General Price, were also killed by members of Ashraf's group in 1975. Another victim of the terrorists was Hassan Hosnan, a US embassy interpreter who was, perhaps mistakenly, identified as a contact man between the CIA and the section of SAVAK dealing with the terrorists.

The terrorist problem which Iran faced in the 1970s was only partly due to Soviet provocation. The absence of any means of vocalizing and channelling dissent left many young men and women with little choice but to have recourse to violence to express their opposition to a regime they hated for a variety of reasons. But both the shah and the United

States believed that the terrorist problem was no more than an aspect of East–West rivalry in Iran. As a result the shah could not think of a better response than greater repression, and Washington endorsed his choice. Worse still, neither the shah nor the United States even bothered to probe for the deeper causes of the phenomenon. Embassy documents show that reports sent to Washington on the subject often reproduced accounts given by SAVAK and the analysis made by the government.

One sign of growing resentment against the United States was the success achieved by a pamphlet entitled *Heir to Colonialism*.[28] In it the writer, a paediatrician by profession, argued that the United States had emerged as heir to British colonialism in many parts of the world, especially in the Middle East. The pamphlet, written in a chaotic style, offered a hotchpotch of selected facts and rumoured allegations in order to portray the United States as the new 'colonial enemy'. It attracted attention from SAVAK and was put on the black list. It was rumoured that Nixon himself had telephoned the shah in the middle of the night to ask him to stop the pamphlet. Clandestine editions were hastily prepared and *Heir to Colonialism* sold more than 50,000 copies and attracted at least ten times as many readers.

Fashionable anti-Americanism of the type often encountered in some chic circles in Paris had always had its advocates in Tehran also. But from the end of the 1960s a new and more militant form of anti-Americanism rapidly developed into an attitude if not a full-blown ideology. The incorrigible amateurs of a monistic view of history began to claim that the United States alone was responsible for all Iran's ills, indeed for all the problems of entire humanity. This was to border on the ridiculous when Khomeini declared in 1979 that the 'Great US Satan has dominated our country for the past 2500 years'.[29] But many people believed another of Khomeini's wild claims, that the United States had a secret plan to establish colonies near various major Iranian cities. The first of these was to be a satellite city north of Isfahan where some 1700 American employees of Bell Helicopter and more than 6500 of their dependants lived in what from 1976 onwards, had become a chunk of the United States on Iranian territory.[30] Because ordinary Iranians were prevented from even driving through the new city, rumours concerning life there gained wide currency. Mullahs addressing semi-clandestine gatherings of the faithful claimed that 'cross-worshippers' had already gained a foothold in the land of Islam and had established a new version of Sodom and Gomorroh near Isfahan.[31] The truth, however, was that the 'American paradise' near Isfahan was a dull replica of many of the soulless suburbs found in the United States and offered little worth getting excited about.

The CIA, which had, until the 1960s, concentrated on keeping an eye on the shah's domestic opponents, was by 1970 either convinced that this was no longer necessary or ordered to devote its resources to monitoring and, whenever possible, countering Soviet activities throughout Western Asia. The agency began trying to recruit Iranians and foreigners with access to the diplomatic service, foreign businesses operating in Iran and joint-venture enterprises with the USSR and Soviet bloc countries. The agency's operations in the Persian Gulf region were directed from Tehran with substations in Dubai, Bahrain, Abu Dhabi and Kuwait.[32] But a good part of the CIA's energies in Iran was spent on competing with the US Defence Intelligence Agency (DIA) and the US Air Force for the control of the two monitoring stations set up in northern Iran. The station at Kabkan was to be expanded as part of a larger plan codenamed Ibex. The system, which was to be constructed by Rockwell International at a cost of $500 million, was to offer a comprehensive surveillance of military activities in the USSR to a depth of 1500 kilometres along 2500 kilometres of border.[33]

Although there was no evidence that Iran would draw any direct benefit from Ibex, the shah was prepared to go ahead with it in the face of stiff opposition from Moscow. The project was, however, soon beset by technical difficulties, financial complications and rumours of corruption. Towards the end of 1976 the Ford administration decided to postpone the project until after the presidential election. The murder of three American technicians working on the project was no doubt a factor in Ford's decision. The murder was claimed by the Fedayeen Guerrillas. The shah had enthusiastically supported Ibex to the end because he saw in it yet another means of making himself indispensable to the United States. A few months after Ibex was abandoned he began pressing Washington for the sale of Airborne Warning and Command System (AWACS) units, citing as his strongest argument the fact that the system in question could be used to guide US bombers to Soviet targets in the event of a major conflict. Congress, after initial hesitation, bought the argument and gave its approval to the deal in 1977, but the shah was overthrown before the system could be supplied to Iran.

Rumours of corruption were not limited to the Ibex project. Between 1968 and 1978 the shah purchased more than $30,000 millions worth of weapons and technical backup, mostly from the United States, Britain, West Germany, France and Italy. The original purchase of F4 fighters from the USA was almost certainly accompanied by a generous kickback from the American companies involved to the then commander of the Iranian Air Force, General Mohammad Khatam, a brother-in-law of the shah. It was to silence widespread criticism among air force officers regarding Khatam's 'open habit of taking bribes' that the shah replaced him as the man in charge of weapons procurement. The task was entrusted to General Hassan Toufanian, who presided over the largest international transactions concerning military hardware ever recorded in history. Toufanian himself was seldom the object of accusations of corruption, but a number of civilian middlemen, some of them closely linked with the shah, continued to appear as brokers in deals which involved fat bribes. The shah, however, blamed American companies for spreading corruption in Iran. His claims were partly borne out when senate investigators in Washington found out that two American firms, Grumman and Northrop-Page, had paid a total of $26.1 million in baksheesh to middlemen claiming to represent Iran. The shah protested and forced the two companies to pay back the sums involved in the form of spare parts and services. Toufanian used the occasion to lash out against 'thieves and plunderers', without naming anyone in particular,[34] but he was at the same time unable to offer information on claims by three American companies – Westinghouse, Textron and Northrop – to have paid a total of $4.2 million to three Iranian middlemen.

The Americans who had worked on aid projects in Iran between 1943 and 1968 had built themselves a reputation for financial incorruptibility. The Americans of the 1970s, however, were a different breed. Prime Minister Hoveyda described some of them as 'vultures' and claimed that they practised a deliberate policy of spreading corruption in the Iranian bureaucracy.

The more expensive hotels in Tehran and Isfahan were often full of American high-pressure salesmen, former diplomats turned business-men and retired officers seeking a second career as arms brokers. Admiral Thomas Moorer became a consultant for a firm repairing Iranian naval vessels only three months after he retired as chairman of the joint chiefs-of-staff. Major General Harold Price, Major General Harvey Jablonsky, Captain R. S. Harward and Richard R. Hallock, who had served as special assistant to Defence Secretary James Schlesinger, all came to Iran in connection with a variety of arms contracts. General Richard Secord, deputy commander of the American military assistance mission in Iran until 1979, wanted to continue that tradition after the revolution.[35] Many of the other eight hundred officers making up the mission, which was the largest of its kind in the world, emulated the more senior ones and after retirement returned to work in Iran or, in some cases, simply applied for early retirement to be able to take up better-paid jobs with the shah's armed forces.

By 1975 Iran had become a salesman's paradise. Premier Hoveyda complained that after having drafted the largest budget in Iran's history – the seventh largest in the non-communist world – he still had $150 million he did not know how to spend. Government departments were criticized for not being able to spend budgets which had more than quadrupled in just three years. 'Those who don't have the guts to spend money better look for other jobs,' the prime minister told his ministers only half in jest. Thousands of Americans poured into Iran to help spend the petrodollars. In the process they portrayed the American people as a race totally devoted to money – 'a tribe that worships gold' one Iranian poet called them.[36] They were the ugly Americans, living ostentatious lives, getting drunk more often than was good for them, offering slipshod goods and mediocre services, and constantly looking for more opportunities for making still more, largely unearned, money.

The shah attached great importance to his image in the United States. The task of looking after that was entrusted in part to his dynamic ambassador to Washington, Ardeshir Zahedi, and to a network of personal friends the monarch had made over the years. Zahedi, a tireless socializer, turned the Iranian embassy in Washington into a popular rendezvous for high-ranking politicians, senior officials and influential journalists and business people. The ambassador maintained close ties with a number of senators, notably Robert C. Byrd (D. West Virgina), the majority leader, and Charles Percy (R. Illinois), both of whom had Iranian sons-in-law. Senators Jacob Javits, Barry Goldwater, John Tower, Birch Bayh, Lloyd Bentsen, Claibourne Pell, Abraham Ribicoff and Frank Church were also close to the ambassador. Javits's wife Marion received an annual salary of $67,500 to promote a campaign on behalf of Iranian Airlines in New York.[37] Many of the diplomats who had once served in Iran kept their contacts with the Iranian government after retirement. Ambassador Armin Meyer was involved in a Ferdowsi University project, while Ambassador Helms set up a consultancy in Washington DC. He named his firm Safeer, which means 'ambassador' in Persian, and would have had good business from Iran had not the Islamic Revolution swept the shah away.

Many prominent Americans visited Iran as guests of the shah or the government even though they had no official business. Among them were Mrs Ladybird Johnson, the widow of the former president, the wife and daughters of former President Nixon, and Ronald and Nancy Reagan, who came to Tehran in May 1978 when the Islamic Revolution was already in full swing. The future president of the United States was received by the shah and was guest of honour at a party offered by Zahedi's sister Homa at her Hessarak home. Before that the Reagans had spent a few days as Zahedi's house guests at the Iranian embassy in Washington. They were not the only stars to visit Tehran. Frank Sinatra, Elizabeth Taylor, Gregory Peck, Farah Fawcett, Lee Majors, Candice Bergen and many others also visited the imperial capital and enjoyed the hospitality of Tehrani high society.

A report by an adviser to Empress Farah concerning the growing importance of academics in American life persuaded the shah to loosen his purse strings for donations to a number of universities in the United States.[38] An $11 million contract for exchange students and teachers linked Georgetown University to Ferdowsi in Mashhad. Columbia received over $360,000 to set up a social welfare school in northern Iran, and Harvard, which was already involved in other projects in Iran, received $400,000 for planning a postgraduate school in Mazandaran. The Massachusetts Institute of Technology was linked with the Tehran Business School through a number of contracts and the Stanford Research Institute cooperated with the Tehran Institute for International Political and Economic Studies. At the same time the fees paid by thousands of Iranian students in the United States helped a number of American universities through especially difficult years.

The shah also encouraged the holding of international conferences and academic seminars in Iran. In 1974 the Aspen Institute organized a week-long conference at Persepolis which was attended by the empress and the prime minister. Aspen later 'elected' Empress Farah as vice-president. Aspen's original benefactor, the oil tycoon Robert Anderson of ARCO, became a close friend of the shah and even purchased substantial plots of land in north Iran with a view to developing an agro-industrial complex in partnership with the shah's half-brother Prince Abdul-Reza.[39]

The shah failed to grasp the sociopolitical changes that transformed American society in the post-Vietnam years and believed that all he had to do was to maintain his network of influential friends and make sure that Washington became increasingly dependent on him in the Persian Gulf and the Indian Ocean. As already noted, the Rockefellers figured prominently among the shah's friends. It was, therefore, not surprising that the shah chose Chase Manhattan to handle the banking services needed to process much of Iran's huge oil revenues.[40]

In August 1976, less than three months before the American presidential election, the shah appointed a small committee to contemplate the country's prospects as a regional power. He told them that only one factor would remain constant: Iran's special relationship with the United States, which he believed would continue well into the

1990s. And by then, he hoped, Iran would be strong enough militarily to be accepted and respected as a regional power on its own terms. He dismissed a suggestion that the Democratic candidate, Jimmy Carter, who was already being perceived as a politician hostile to Iran, might win the election. Zahedi had assured the shah that Ford would stay in the White House at least until 1980.

With the possible exception of Edward Kennedy, whom the shah disliked with unusual intensity, Jimmy Carter was the last person the monarch cared to see in the White House. Early in his campaign Carter had attacked the shah because of alleged violations of human rights in Iran. When Carter's election became a distinct possibility the shah decided to forestall any possible pressure from a new Democratic administration in Washington by ordering a series of reforms aimed at improving conditions in Iranian prisons and allowing some limited expressions of dissent; this soon became known as 'the policy of opening the political space'. He also ordered a crackdown on 'corrupt officials' and threatened some members of the royal family with 'harsh measures' if they did not limit their dubious commercial activities.[41] At the same time, however, he made it clear that he was prepared for a head-on collision with any US administration which thought of dictating his choice of weapons.[42]

He also repeated his earlier tactic of anticipating what he thought would please a Democratic administration in Washington by firing Premier Hoveyda. He appointed as prime minister Jamshid Amouzegar, who had for years represented Iran in the OPEC ministerial councils as minister of finance and then of interior. Amouzegar was rumoured to be popular in Washington and his selection as premier was seen as a gesture of goodwill towards Carter from the shah. Needless to say, none of these rumours could be substantiated and there was no evidence that Amouzegar enjoyed any special status in the eyes of the US government.

What with hindsight seems astonishing is the almost total absence of meaningful dialogue between Tehran and Washington on a number of vital issues. The shah's opponents saw him as a sort of American bailiff in Iran. But at least from 1968 onwards the United States went out of its way to avoid any discussion of domestic Iranian issues with the shah. As a result the shah's perception of what the United States wanted to see in Iran was often based on pure imagination or rumour. This absence of dialogue was to become an important handicap to the two allies in facing the challenge of the Islamic Revolution in 1978–79.[43] It is now known that President Carter had absolutely no intention of taking any risks with the special relationship and was not even prepared to raise the question of human rights with the shah when the two met in Tehran in December 1977. It was the shah himself who brought up the subject and insisted that Iran was determined to continue her new policy of liberalization. The fact that Carter and his wife spent the New Year's Eve as guests of the shah and the empress was instantly seen as a sign that there was no longer any danger of Irano-US relations entering a zone of turbulence as they had done in the early phase of the Kennedy administration.

Nevertheless the shah did not like Carter. 'Those frozen blue eyes,' he commented after meeting the new president. 'Somehow there are no feelings in them at all.'[44] Carter and his wife Rosalynne, however, seemed to have been charmed by the royal couple. But personal likes and dislikes were of only incidental importance at that stage in Iran-US relations. The US commitment to Iran had become so strong and so complex over the previous two decades that no president could have stopped it or altered its course significantly in a short period of time. Had Carter considered a change of policy in regard to Iran a priority, which he did not, he would still have needed at least two to three years before he could devise a new policy, sell it to Congress and assemble the means to implement it. Within a few months of entering the White House Carter was convinced that the Nixon Doctrine remained the most realistic option in the Persian Gulf. And the full weight of the shah lobby in Washington was exercised to convince Carter that Iran represented the most successful example of that doctrine in practice.

The Tehran visit during which Carter became the first president to spend the New Year out of the United States did not persuade everyone that all was still well between Tehran and Washington. In politics perceptions are often more important than facts. And in countries like Iran where notions, once established, are difficult to dislodge, the US Democratic Party continued to be regarded by the shah's opponents as a natural ally of the Iranian opposition. A number of anti-shah personalities began preparing themselves for what they expected would be dramatic changes in US policy towards Iran as early as the summer of 1976 before Carter had even won the Democratic nomination.[45] Several opposition groups, notably the Iran Nation's Party and the Radical Movement, announced the resumption of their activities on the day Carter arrived in Tehran on 31 December 1976 for a state visit. Both parties, as well as the renascent Mossadeqist National Front, dispatched lengthy letters to Carter in Tehran.[46] Other opponents of the shah also acted on the basis of what they imagined the new US administration would do in Iran.

Some of the better-organized opposition groups, notably the Marxist-Leninist Fedayeen Guerrillas, were determined to exploit what they saw as a weakening of Irano-US ties as a result of Carter's election to force the regime into making hasty concessions. In a lengthy analysis of the situation which they published in December 1977 they claimed that Carter was 'bound to pressure the shah to wear a liberal mask' as a means of 'saving the hated US imperialism from eventual defeat in Iran'.[47]

A series of strange episodes gave credence to that belief. The daily *Ettelaat* began serializing Carter's book *Why Not the Best* before the presidential election. This was seen as an oblique way of showing displeasure at the shah's policies. Once elected, Carter did not reply to a congratulatory cable from the shah for nearly two weeks. This was perhaps due to bureaucratic delays on both sides. But Tehran opposition circles saw it as a clear anti-shah signal from the new president. A few weeks after Carter's election the United States Information Agency in Tehran published a few hundred copies of a speech made by Secretary of State Cyrus Vance on human rights. The speech was reprinted by mysterious groups and distributed in thousands of copies with the heading 'Even US recognizes the shah's savagery'.[48] SAVAK believed this to be the work of the Tudeh Party and the KGB in Tehran. Khomeini's supporters also began to think of the 'new possibilites' that the expected rift between Tehran and Washington might offer. Ibrahim Yazdi, an Iranian-born American citizen representing the ayatollah in the United States, wrote to him in Najaf in Iraq that 'the shah's friends in Washington are out. . . . It is time to act.'[49]

From the first days of the Carter presidency the shah's pro-American opponents began contacting the US embassy in Tehran. Some members of the embassy staff were reluctant to take the risk of meeting them but were apparently reassured by the Iranian government itself. The shah had ordered 'liberalization' and there was no reason why former opponents, now reduced to irrelevance, should not have a drink with American diplomats or entertain them at their homes. These contacts, at first dismissed by the shah as another example of his opponents' desperation, were soon to assume some political significance as the word got round that the United States was sounding out Mossadeqist politicians.

Both opponents and supporters of the shah also remembered the strange scenes they had witnessed on television during the state visit paid by the shah and the empress to Washington soon after Carter's election. The White House welcoming ceremony had been seriously disturbed by violent demonstrations against the shah which forced the police to use teargas, as a result of which everyone – including the shah, the president and the empress – had to reach for their handkerchiefs. The whole episode had been televised live in Iran, and to most average Iranians the incident looked like a plot by Carter to humiliate the King of Kings. To Iranians unfamiliar with details of American law and the sanctity of the First Amendment it seemed inconceivable that the shah's opponents could have got so close to the White House without collusion on the part of the US police. It is almost certain that the shah himself was of the same opinion and believed Carter was playing a double game towards him. Millions of Iranians saw their shah crying in front of television cameras. 'The Washington tears', as the incident came to be called, dealt a damaging blow to the monarch's prestige at home: he had shown serious cracks in his armour. He had been revealed to be just a man, like any other, and that, in a culture where the king had an almost divine status, was not an enviable state to be in.

6

FORT PERSEPOLIS

The complex of redbrick buildings that housed the United States embassy in Tehran was situated at the end of Takht Jamshid Avenue in a part of the capital that had maintained something of a village atmosphere up to the 1960s. When the embassy was first set up in the 1940s, Takht Jamshid had just been made into a street, paved with cobblestones, passing through vast plots of unbuilt-on land on both sides. The choice of the site was probably due to commercial and other non-political considerations, but many Iranians saw it as a sign that the United States was different from other big powers. That the United States had chosen to stay out of Ferdowsi Avenue, where all major embassies – the Soviet, the British, the German and others – were situated was seen as a deliberate political choice: America wanted to keep its distance from the big powers that had caused Iran so much hardship over some 150 years. The simple design and modest functionality of the US embassy buildings also contrasted with the pompous architecture of other big-power embassies, which were surrounded by brick walls 3–4 metres high. In contrast the American compound was not walled in but was surrounded only by low wooden fences which allowed passers-by a good glimpse of the well-kept flower gardens inside.[1]

Over the years the quiet embassy on the fringes became an important power house in a rising Iran that made its alliance with the United States the cornerstone of its foreign policy. By 1978 the embassy had become a symbol of suffering and an object of hate to many of the militant opposition groups who wanted to overthrow the shah so that they could build their own dream society. By then the Islamic Revolution was well on its way to an unexpected victory.

The embassy had at first paid little attention to repeated signs that the shah's regime was in deep trouble. Because it had over the years lost most of its sources within the opposition groups, it was not in a position to check the veracity of the analyses offered it by SAVAK and other governmental organs. Some dissidents had taken the initiative of contacting the embassy and the CIA as early as the summer of 1976.[2] And the head of the Israeli mission in Tehran, David Turgman, had also begun to introduce some opponents of the shah to US diplomats in 1977.[3] But these contacts remained sporadic and essentially aimless. The embassy did not know what to look for or where. The thought that the shah might be on his way out was so unthinkable that it did not cross anybody's mind until it was too late. No one wanted to take the risk of becoming an object of ridicule by predicting that a ruler who had worked with eight US presidents during thirty-seven years might soon become a fugitive from his own land.

Between 1955 and 1978 the embassy had on a few occasions tried to think the unthinkable and prepared reports on what might happen if the shah were no longer there. But none of the imaginary scenarios included the possibility of an Islamic revolution and the end of the monarchy.

Analysts both at the embassy and in Washington took their clues from a number of simple beliefs that had ossified into clichés since the Second World War. They assumed, for example, that economic development would inevitably lead to social and political progress, which, provided it was not hijacked by Marxist revolutionaries, could only produce a multiparty system of democracy. Without admitting it, they also shared Marx's central belief that the economic infrastructure determines the political superstructure in society. Thus it was assumed that the undoubted economic development that Iran experienced under the shah could only lead to political progress as well. In this respect both Moscow and Washington made exactly the same mistake about Iran, albeit with different outcomes in mind. The Soviets began playing a key role in Iran's industrialization from 1965 onwards. They were accused by the Chinese as well as by many Iranian Leninists of helping consolidate the shah's regime. For their part they argued that industrialization would lead to the emergence of a proletariat in Iran, which in turn would provide the socialist revolution with the vanguard class it needed. Therefore the shah had to be supported, even to the point of being armed. Washington for its part believed that Iran's economic development would lead to the emergence of a middle class, which would then build a parliamentary democracy in Iran. Again, the shah had to be supported in the performance of his historic mission.

There was one big difference, however, in the respective attitudes of the Soviets and the Americans towards the shah. The Soviets did not want the shah to change as long as he did not directly threaten the military balance in the region. All the shah had to do was play his own role; history would take care of the rest. The Americans, on the other hand, had begun by pressing the shah to act against himself, to play the role of a liberal president, to be an un-shah. Kissinger understood the futility of such efforts but made the much bigger mistake of encouraging the shah to change in another direction: to cease being the shah of the Iranian people and begin acting as if he were the ruler of the world.

Both Moscow and Washington examined the possibility of a revolution in Iran at different times between 1945 and 1975. Both assumed that if and when such an event occurred, which both became persuaded would not happen this side of the year 2000, Iran would have a progressive revolution. Neither side imagined a reactionary revolution – one that did not promise progress towards any golden future but advocated a return to a bleak but pure past. Both Washington and Moscow were convinced that the shah's policy of modernization would end the influence of the Muslim clergy in Iran. A US embassy report written in 1970 suggested this would happen in ten years' time.[4] The shah fell just one year short of that prediction when he was overthrown in 1979.

Few Iranologists took seriously the resurgence of religious senti-ments which began as early as 1971. Between 1968 and 1978 more mosques were built in Iran than in the preceding two centuries.[5] The number of Iranians going to Mecca for Haj pilgrimage rose from 12,000 in 1967 to more than 100,000 a decade later. In the same period the number of theological students also more than quadrupled, while more than 60,000 new mullahs entered the market for religious services.[6] Private donations to the ayatollahs increased more than seventy times to reach the estimated figure of $250 million in 1978.[7] The new religious vogue affected all classes of society: the shah's sister, Princess Fatemeh, and the empress's mother, Farideh Diba, joined the Mecca pilgrims. And high-society ladies competed with one another by throwing sumptuous religious parties in which turbaned mullahs sermoned wealthy matrons and glamorous debutantes dressed in French *haute couture* clothes.

Some anti-shah Iranologists, especially in the United States, believed that the main source of tension in Iran was a desire on the part of the middle class for more freedom. But the main revolutionary forces in the country – the mullahs and the Leninists – had no time for what they respectively saw as 'the cross-worshippers' way of life' and 'decadent bourgeois democracy'. The mullahs wanted to restrict the social and legal freedoms that Iran had won for her people since the 1906 constitutional revolution, and the left was determined to destroy the entire socioeconomic structure of the country by force if necessary.

Even the first shockwaves of the revolution did not jolt the embassy out of its comfortable views. It continued to believe that former Mossadeqists would play a leading role in the unfolding drama. The Mossadeqists who took the initiative and contacted the embassy interpreted the new American interest in them as a sure sign that Washington wanted to help them win a chunk of power under the shah. Some of them even spread the rumour that Carter himself had contacted them with a view to forming a coalition government. Every word uttered by US diplomats was seized upon as a signal from Washington and wildly interpreted far beyond its original context. In October 1978, for example, the political counsellor, George Lambrakis, suggested to a liberal opponent of the shah that opposition groups ought to organize themselves with a view to fighting a general election. He also mentioned the fact that the shah would have to prepare the ground for his being succeeded by the crown prince at some unspecified date in the future.[8] These remarks were taken to mean that Carter had ordered the shah to organize a general election, in which his opponents would win a majority, and then abdicate in favour of his son.[9]

The shah saw contacts between the embassy and his opponents as a sign of American intrigue against him. Like his Mossadeqist opponents, he was convinced that the USA had a crucial role to play in shaping the outcome of what was, by the end of 1977, an unstoppable challenge to his rule. Sharing the mistaken belief that people are unlikely to revolt against progress and in favour of fewer freedoms rather than more, the shah doggedly stuck to his 'liberalization' policy and offered more and more concessions to sections of society that had not asked for them. All that, he thought, would please the Carter administration. And it was in some frustration that he dispatched one of his aides, Amir-Khosrow Afshar, to Washington in the summer of 1978 to ask the Americans 'what they exactly want from us'.[10] Afshar had a long session with Secretary of State Vance, who did not see why the shah seemed so worried. 'The real question is what the shah wants from us,' Vance told Afshar. The secretary of state's reply was sincere but the shah saw it as another sign of American bad faith. He was sure Carter was plotting against him.

The year 1978 was marked by almost continuous acts of violence by the Leninist groups, provoking violence in return from the police. But far more disturbing was the ever-growing number of people who took to the streets to chant anti-shah slogans and to call for the return of the exiled Ayatollah Khomeini. The imposition of martial law first in Isfahan, where a mob had tried to lynch an American employee of Bell Helicopter after he had gone berserk and fired on demonstrators, and then in Tehran and twenty-three other cities did not end the revolt.[11] A visit in May by Nelson Rockefeller to the shah, who was vacationing on Kish Island in the Persian Gulf, went a long way towards reassuring the monarch of continued support from 'real America'.[12] It was after that meeting that the shah ordered a crackdown on demonstrators against the regime. But he soon reverted to his former policy of appeasement after interpreting signals from the Carter administration to mean that a tough policy would not be welcome in Washington.

At least until the end of 1978 no one at the embassy or in Washington wanted the shah to go or thought his regime doomed. And yet there were unmistakable indications that the Pahlavis could not weather that particular storm. Some of the oldest and most trusted sources told the embassy that the shah had to leave the country before a compromise could be worked out with the revolutionary mullahs.[13] In July 1978 the US consulate in Tehran reported that it was issuing an average of 600–700 non-immigrant visas a week.[14] This was an unmistakable sign of a growing lack of confidence in the shah's future on the part of the very classes of society that might under other circumstances have supported him. Yet another indication was furnished by Central Bank figures which showed that individual Iranians were sending a total of more than $1000 million out of the country every month.[15] Many people sold their factories, shops and even homes and withdrew their bank deposits as a precautionary measure. The fact that more than 30,000 people were listed by the bank as having sent out various sums of money – from $1000 to more than $100 million – showed that the flight of capital did not involve a few rich families only.

Even earlier than that the consul in Tabriz had reported a conversation with the Armenian patriarch of the city that merited far more attention than it received. The patriarch, Diyair Panossian, told the consul that the shah would not survive the current agitation. More importantly, he said he was advising the Armenians to leave Iran because the country would no longer be safe for them after the establishment of an Islamic regime.[16] The fact that Armenians, who had lived in Iran for some 2200 years, were now worried about the future should have been taken as a measure of the gravity of the situation. It was not.

The US embassy was not even moved by some of the most dramatic episodes of the anti-shah revolt. In August 1978 Khomeinist militants set fire to a packed cinema in the southern city of Abadan after having locked the doors from the outside. More than six hundred people were burned alive. A month later a group of militants provoked an army unit trying to impose the martial law in Tehran into firing on a crowd.

More than 120 people, including many women and children, were killed. By then Khomeini and the revolutionary mullahs who worked on his behalf were well established as the real leaders of the revolt. And yet the embassy continued to persist in its strange belief that the key to the problem rested with the isolated Mossadeqists. Even as late as September 1978 Ambassador William Sullivan, who had spent the preceding two months on home leave in the United States, saw what he termed 'the disturbances' as an indication of a desire for more freedom by the urban classes and was convinced that the shah's policy of 'liberalization', which in practice meant putting his former officials in prison and allowing his sworn enemies ample scope for agitation, should continue.[17] That view was also supported by the State Department in Washington, where several high officials, including Assistant Secretary of State Pat Derrian and the department's spokesman Hodding Carter III, believed that the shah had to atone for his 'past guilts' and allow 'democratic forces' to express themselves in Iran.[18] Worse still, the anti-shah lobby at the State Department succeeded in blocking the sale of teargas and riot-control devices to Iran.[19] The shah had never envisaged street riots against his rule despite Iran's long-established tradition of violent street politics. As a result the country lacked the means and the experts needed to control the crowds and avoid bloodshed. The ban imposed by the State Department was lifted later in the year and the shah received the teargas canisters he had ordered. But by that time the game was up and His Imperial Majesty was preparing to leave the country. The teargas supplies were later used by the Khomeini government against its own opponents in the spring of 1979.

Not everyone agreed with Sullivan and the State Department that the shah should not take off his kid gloves. In an implicit criticism of the administration's insistence on human rights and the development of political institutions in Iran, the political counsellor reported that it was futile to speak in such terms in the Iranian context.[20] The national security adviser, Zbigniew Brzezinski, was also convinced, as early as July 1978, that the shah should be given strong support so that he could adopt a two-pronged policy of crushing those who wanted to overthrow him but, at the same time, giving full concessions to those who only asked for a share in power. The adviser's views were reported to the shah by Ambassador Zahedi, who began spending most of his time in revolt-stricken Tehran.

Despite repeated attempts by the revolutionary mullahs to open up a channel with Washington from the summer of 1978 onwards, the embassy refused to show any encouraging signs. Two potentially good contacts with leading ayatollahs were summarily dismissed by embassy officials on two separate occasions.[21] Judging by the documents seized at the mission, the diplomats spent more time with busybodies and adventurers than with people capable of offering them insight into what the mullahs really wanted from their revolution.

As the shah's downfall approached, the invasion of the embassy by amateur politicians and self-styled political soothsayers assumed almost farcical proportions. An American citizen, George Nathanson, described in an embassy report as 'an adventurer', became a frequent visitor to the political section. He claimed to represent General Hossein Fardoust, who ostensibly demanded American support for a plan to save Iran by putting the shah's son on the throne.[22] Later the same Nathanson returned with a friend, Gregory Lima, an American journalist who had lived in Iran for more than twenty years, and claimed that the two of them had a plan to save the country provided Washington backed them.[23] Nathanson returned a third time to ask the embassy to get Lima a job as publicity manager to the prime minister.[24] A former Iranian employee of the embassy, Adnan Mazarei, had his own magic formula for saving the situation: the United States should help him create a 'humanist movement' that would convince the people that violence was bad and democracy was good.[25] Yet another would-be saviour, this time met by the ambassador himself, was Rahim Saffari, who wanted US support for his socialist Unity Alliance.[26]

People with original ideas to save Iran also came from abroad. Siavash Dahesh, a businessman from Dallas, Texas, flew into Tehran with a project to 'send the mullahs back to the mosques'. Referring to the clergy, Dahesh told the embassy: 'Just give us a sign and we shall wipe out these monkeys in twenty-four hours.'[27] Khosrow Eqbal, another wellwisher, came up with a plan in which he would go to Paris and meet Khomeini, then in exile there, and try to knock some sense into his head. The embassy was enthusiastic about the idea and Eqbal made the trip. But once in France, Eqbal was told to join the rest of the crowd, some 3000, and pray behind Khomeini. He came back and said he was disappointed.[28] Bahram Chubin, a former National Iranian Oil Company aide, was given no fewer than nine hours in which to explain his plans for stopping the revolution. He had organized his friends into a group called G28 and advocated a series of acts of derring-do. To establish his credentials as a well-informed man he told his audience that the orchid which the former Premier Hoveyda always wore in his buttonhole hid a tiny microphone.[29]

Getting in touch with the Americans became a favourite sport in Tehran's pseudo-political circles. The embassy's military attaché was lured into a meeting with the retired rear-admiral Ahmad Madani by his landlord.[30] The landlord was persuaded that Madani was the man to save Iran and wanted his tenant to secure American support for his project. Abbas Amir-Entezam, a pro-American politician working with the Khomeinists, urged the embassy to support the nomination of one General Bakhshi Azar as the shah's defence minister as a step towards a compromise.[31] Karim Sanjabi, the old Mossadeqist leader, also had a magic recipe: Washington should help him become prime minister.[32]

What is difficult to explain is the fact that the embassy seldom thought of using the diplomatic cliché about non-intervention in the internal affairs of a friendly country. This led visitors to the embassy to believe that the United States was indeed, as Khomeini and Radio Moscow charged, directly involved in every aspect of Iran's domestic politics. This attitude was to have grave consequences. Mehdi Bazargan, who was to become Khomeini's first prime minister, kept in touch with the embassy through his son-in-law Mohammad Tavassoli. It was through Tavassoli that he asked the embassy to prevent the army from firing on demonstrators.[33] The embassy did not tell Tavassoli that this was none of their business, which it certainly was not. As a result, when the army resumed firing on riotous mobs, the word was spread that orders to massacre the people had come directly from Washington. Some of the sessions organized by the embassy bordered on the farcical. A group of bazaar merchants, for example, offered three embassy officials their own formulas for stopping the revolution and protecting US interests in Iran. One of the bright ideas was that the United States should force all customers of Iranian crude oil to purchase an equal value of Persian carpets in order to help the traditional sector of the economy represented by the bazaars.[34]

The embassy was swamped with useless information and no system of filtering was installed until the very end. As a result the more sober reports from the embassy's own staff and consular personnel in the provinces did not receive the attention needed. The confusion at the embassy was exported to Washington, where President Carter pursued his own Middle East agenda, at the centre of which were his efforts to bring about formal peace between Egypt and Israel. The shah's troubles featured fairly low on the president's list of priorities until it was too late.

Few people realized that the United States had no Iran policy and was even incapable of reacting to events at a time and in a manner likely to influence their course in the direction of a compromise solution to Iran's problems. The Carter administration, for example, strongly supported the imposition of martial law by the shah but at the same time insisted that no force should be used against those who broke the rules. Brzezinski insisted that the shah should stand firm, but the State Department urged the monarch not to imprison his opponents and to offer more concessions to revolutionaries. Some prominent Americans, notably Senate majority leader Robert Byrd and Assistant Secretary of State Alfred Atherton visited Tehran to show support for the shah. In Washington, however, other high-ranking officials and politicians openly called for the shah's over-throw. Once again perceptions proved more important than facts and the shah's supporters began to abandon him in the belief that Washington had also written him off. The fact that personalities known for their special relationship with the United States or wrongly perceived as such were among the first to take their money and leave the country only reinforced the view that the United States had told its favourites to get out before it was too late.[35]

The Israeli mission also contributed to the mood of pessimism among the shah's supporters. Israel had for long been unhappy with what it wrongly saw as a tilt in Iran's foreign policy in favour of the Arabs. With the gathering storm of revolution the Israelis began to set in motion a plan they had prepared over many years: to encourage as many of Iran's 75,000 Jews as possible to emigrate to Israel. Ambassador Sullivan referred to the plan in a special report in 1978. He said Israel was keen to get Iranian Jews to settle in Israel especially because they were mostly middle class, wealthy and well educated and would become 'profitable immigrants'.[36] The Israeli mission's alarm-ist view that Iran was lost and that the Jews should get out contributed to the general malaise and became a self-fulfilling prophecy. A representative of French Jewry, however, visited Iran only two months before the fall of the shah and reported that most Iranian Jews preferred to stay in Iran regardless of the troubles ahead.[37]

The embassy's troubles were not confined to dealing with the multiplying number of saviours of Iran. As the economy ground to a halt many American businesses active in Iran faced the prospect of losing their money. Some American businessmen and technicians had to escape from various provinces to Tehran because they were no longer able to pay their employees. Others were not so lucky and were held hostage or threatened with lynching. Trouble even spread to Kabkan where the main listening post monitoring Soviet missile tests was situated. The workers there simply shut off the machines and held their American bosses hostage for a few days. A special team of officers was dispatched with a bagful of ready cash to cool things down and free the hostages.[38] As many American businessmen left the country others arrived. The new arrivals openly admitted that they specialized in 'making a fast buck where there is trouble'.[39] They offered rich Iranians exile homes in California and Florida as well as ranches in Arizona and New Mexico and 'a chunk of the Great American West' in Colorado. One particularly sharp estate agent from California came to sell the shah a ranch and plagued embassy officials with persistent demands for an audience with 'His Highness'.[40]

As the situation worsened and the middle class either fled abroad or kept to themselves for fear of suffering physical violence at the hands of Khomeini's 'partisans of Allah' – who were armed with daggers, saw chains, meat choppers and bottles of vitriol – the stage was set for the left to direct the rage of the feverish mobs against the United States. Towards the end of November 1978 acts of intimidation and violence against Americans began, and then continued after the fall of the monarchy on 11 February 1979. But even so there was no evidence that the revolution as such was anti-American. The Mossadeqists were more genuinely pro-American than the shah had ever been. And the mullahs, once they had established direct contact with the embassy from December 1978 onwards, saw no reason to antagonize the United States, a powerful potential ally in facing the communist threat.[41]

Washington's last attempt at saving the situation came in January 1979 when the shah asked Shapour Bakhtiar, a turncoat member of the largely mythical National Front, to try to put together a cabinet of transition. The shah had begun urging his allies to let him leave the country as early as August 1978. Both Washington and London eventually agreed. The shah was later to claim, from exile, that he had been forced to leave the country by the United States.[42] But those who saw him often in those days and had occasion to converse with him at some length bear testimony to the fact that the decision to leave Iran was entirely his own. He was a heartbroken man and felt betrayed by a people he had loved and worked for with so much dedication. He was also very ill with cancer, which was to end his life a year later. Further, he was not the bloodthirsty tyrant that his enemies claimed. He could not order his troops to massacre his own people. 'What is the good of reigning at the crest of a wave of blood?' he demanded in September 1978.[43] Did he also want to let history teach the Iranians a lesson? The question must be posed because the monarch himself hinted at such a sentiment on a number of occasions. Iranian myths made much of the unity of the shah and the people and warned that any betrayal of one by the other would plunge the country into seven years of violence, darkness and death. The shah wanted that mythological prophecy to come true yet again; he was persuaded that the nation had betrayed him out of ignorance and ingratitude. He left the country on 16

January 1979 an hour after his last prime minister had won a confidence debate in parliament.

It is possible to suggest that it was from that date that the USA began assuming or, at least, pretending to assume more or less direct responsibility for the success of an Iranian government which existed at that time in name only. This was a dramatic development in US policy in Iran and neither the administration in Washington nor the embassy in Tehran had fully thought out the possible consequences or prepared for them. The shah's tergiversations had created a vacuum, and the United States allowed itself to be sucked into it not knowing this was a chasm leading to an infernal universe of chaos no one could fathom.

The myth that the Carter administration abandoned or betrayed the shah was created by hardline monarchists in Iran and conservatives in the United States. The truth, however, is that, if there was betrayal in what was a long and repeatedly tested friendship, it came during the Nixon–Kissinger era.

The embassy began advocating a 'foreign holiday' for the shah long after everyone else had written the monarch off. Sullivan, in a report dated 3 December 1978, raised the issue for the first time. In the same report he noted that his British, French and German colleagues had long before concluded that the shah was finished.[44] Sullivan, who had frequent meetings with the shah between September and December 1978, must have been aware of the monarch's deteriorating health.[45] But at no point was he prepared to contemplate a future for Iran without the shah – until the monarch himself refused to assume his responsibilities. To think of an Iran without the shah was to think the unthinkable. And yet this was precisely what a lengthy and well-argued study had already done in 1977. The study, prepared at the embassy over a number of months, included among its recommendations the following: 'As long as the shah is in power we should maintain our relations with other social groups so that we can identify those who may come to power after the shah.'[46] The same study had warned that the shah was bound to try to become more independent of the United States while increasing US dependence on his own regime. The study analysed the various pillars of the shah's power and found them for the most part fragile and unreliable. SAVAK, for example was described as 'overestimated and inefficient'.[47]

One feature of the embassy's working life over the year was the surprising laxity of rules with regard to what follow-up work was required. Reports were prepared, read and discussed and then simply shelved, soon to be forgotten. This was specially true in the case of studies dealing with long-term social and political issues. As a bureaucratic machine dealing with day-to-day tasks, the embassy often functioned reasonably well, but when it came to planning for contingencies, the system somehow failed. This was perhaps partly because the embassy had been goaded into concentrating on dealing with concrete matters only, leaving broader concepts and abstractions to the brains back in Washington.

In most cases the people who knew the country best were not those who took the decisions affecting relations. Washington would, in any case, look with some suspicion on sophisticated reports coming from far-away missions which could not pretend to know everything the mandarins back home knew. Washington's attention could best be caught by short, anecdotal reports. For example, in October 1978 the embassy reported that the shah might be fatally ill. Ambassador Sullivan himself could not have failed to notice, during his long audiences at the palace, that the monarch had lost at least a quarter of his weight and took a variety of pills even while receiving foreign dignitaries. But what eventually persuaded Washington to take seriously reports of the shah's illness was an account of a royal audience given by an American businessman. David Scot, the president of Allis Chalmers, met the shah in November 1978 and found him a pale shadow of himself. Scot was surprised when the shah, who was normally haughty and proud, embraced him at the end of the audience and, with eyes full of tears, asked: 'Why is this happening to me?'[48] Scot's report of the strange meeting was relayed to Washington by the embassy and everyone began getting worried.

One sure way of catching Washington's attention was to bring in the Russians and their allies. Rumours concerning corruption in the royal family, for example, had for years been circulating in Tehran and the embassy frequently reported them, at times with documentary support. But Washington began showing genuine interest in the subject only after learning of two specific cases. One concerned a fat bribe paid by the Soviet airline, Aeroflot, to a brother-in-law of the shah in order to secure a licence for scheduled commercial flights to and from Tehran.[49] The other consisted of a cash gift made to one of the shah's half-brothers by the Rumanian president, Nicolae Ceausescu, in exchange for a contract to build a tractor assembly plant in Tabriz.[50] Bringing in the Russians and brandishing the communist menace was frequently used by the shah as well as by his opponents as a means of dictating a specific course of action to the United States. The last head of SAVAK, General Nasser Moqadam, for example, managed to convince Robert R. Bowie, a deputy director of the CIA, in December 1978 that Iran's troubles were a result of communist agitation.[51] By that time, however, even the proverbial schoolboy knew that Iran was experiencing an Islamic revolution led by the mullahs. At almost exactly the same time the embassy was reporting that the role of the left in general and of communists in particular was at best marginal in the unfolding revolt.[52]

Once the shah left the country the United States concentrated its efforts on preserving the Iranian armed forces, which faced total disintegration as a result of direct confrontation with the ever-growing crowds in the streets. The army had manifested almost incredible discipline in the face of months of psychological warfare against it. Despite repeated appeals by Khomeini and a persistent campaign by the mullahs as well as by leftist militants throughout the country, the number of deserters from the army remained negligible.[53] The embassy was concerned about the possibility that some of the more adventurous generals might attempt a *coup d'état* as a means of saving the situation.

One of the many myths that have persisted in regard to the shah's army concerns the control that the United States supposedly exercised over the Iranian military. Some of the shah's enemies have even claimed that Iran's army was, in fact, under direct American command. Nothing could be farther from the truth. The Iranian military was not allowed any contact with foreigners outside strictly official business. They could attend social functions organized by foreigners only with the prior approval of their commanders. And in the case of officers of brigadier general's rank or higher, the approval had to come from the shah himself.

At least three separate intelligence organizations performed the task of watching the army officers with a view to detecting any undue contact with non-Iranians. The slightest suspicion would be followed by instant expulsion or early retirement from the armed forces. One of the themes that the shah himself constantly hammered at meetings with his generals concerned the United States' 'unreliability' as an ally.[54] The shah's last chief-of-staff recalls how the USA dissociated itself from Iran every time the shah made a military move in the pursuit of his regional objectives.[55] In 1969, for example, Washington privately warned the shah that it would suspend arms supplies and other assistance to Iran if the shah's forces opened fire first against the Iraqis in the Shatt al-Arab dispute.[56]

The United States could have exercised some influence within the Iranian armed forces as long as Iran was a recipient of aid and Washington retained the initative in deciding what type of weapons to be supplied. But that situation changed with Nixon's presidential decision in 1972.[57] The shah saw the decision as marking a new era in relations with the USA and most Iranian officers shared that view. The

fact that the United States was prepared to provide Iran with all the technicians the shah needed, sometimes at the cost of leaving certain US units dangerously depleted, was seen by Iranian officers as a sign that the real power was in Tehran and not in Washington.[58] Iranian officers also took pride in the fact that Washington seemed ready to supply Iran with weapons which even the US armed forces had not yet acquired.[59]

The shah's policy of divide and rule, which was applied to both civilian leaders and military commanders, also made it difficult for the armed forces to act in unison on any project without approval from His Imperial Majesty. High-ranking commanders were not allowed to socialize or foster personal friendships. The chief-of-staff was, in practice, no more than the shah's military secretary. Further, because Iran's army had never played a political role, it was eminently unsuited to dealing with the complex issues of a revolution. The top brass of the armed forces mustered enough courage to get together in an informal way from September 1978 onwards. Their rendezvous was Ambassador Zahedi's Hessarak home in the mountains of north Tehran.

As the shah gradually sank and faded because of his illness and indecision, Zahedi began to look like the strongman who could offer the army the political direction it needed. General Mohammad Yamin-Afshar, the Imperial Guards' commander, and Major General Manuchehr Khosrowdad, commander of the Airborne Paratroopers, were the most active members of the informal group.

With the shah's prior approval, Khosrowdad had fostered a friendship with Brigadier General Richard Secord of the US military assistance mission in Iran. As a result Secord accompanied Khosrowdad to Hessarak on a number of occasions for informal talks with other commanders. It was suggested at the time that Secord had encouraged Khosrowdad and others to consider 'more energetic action' against 'troublemakers'.[60] But Khosrowdad did not need any encouragement; he was sizzling with a passion to 'crush the revolt' until 16 January 1979, the day the shah left. From then on the dashing general was dispirited and even urged a compromise with the mullahs in the hope of saving the army from disintegration.

It is possible that the machinery for exchanging information between the embassy, the CIA station and the military mission in Tehran did not function satisfactorily, for views concerning possible moves from the armed forces differed sharply. It was to obtain a first-hand appreciation of the situation that President Carter dispatched NATO's deputy commander, General Robert C. Huyser, to Tehran early in December 1978. Huyser, who had previously visited Iran on a

number of occasions, broke with tradition by not informing the shah
of his presence in the Iranian capital. The general also stayed away
from the embassy and operated semi-clandestinely under Secord's
protection.

Huyser's presence in Tehran, however, did not remain a secret and
Moscow Radio began attacking him as 'deputy ambassador'[61] and
claimed that his mission to Tehran consisted of preparing a putsch
with the aim of stopping the revolution. The truth was exactly the
opposite: Huyser was ordered by President Carter to discourage any
attempt by the military to undermine Bakhtiar's authority. Washington, in fact, had given Bakhtiar an insurance policy and Husyer was in
Tehran to symbolize it. The presidential envoy succeeded in sowing
enough dissension among the Iranian commanders and creating a
sufficient degree of confusion concerning Washington's true intentions in Iran to render any serious attempt at making a military
move virtually impossible.[62] Even General Gholam-Ali Badreh'i, the
new commander of the ground forces, abandoned his plan of seeking a
direct dialogue with the embassy with a view to discussing a possible
coup d'état.[63]

The Hessarak group disbanded immediately after Zahedi himself
also left the country. The various generals certainly thought about a
variety of desperate actions but failed to develop a coherent strategy.
General Yamin-Afshar had prepared a plan for arresting Khomeini
and putting him on trial soon after the ayatollah's return. The air force
commander, General Gholam-Reza Rabi'i, talked of shooting
Khomeini's plane down before it could land in Tehran.[64]

The State Department, determined to win the bet it had made on
Bakhtiar, was not quite reassured by Huyser's report that the Iranian
commanders would not make a move. The department asked
Iranologist Richard Cottam, who knew Bakhtiar personally, to visit
Tehran. In January 1979 Cottam reported that a coup d'état was being
planned. He also gave what he thought were details of the alleged
plot.[65] Minutes of the secret meetings of the Iranian High Command,
however, show that there was absolutely no basis for Cottam's report
except the wild rumours that circulated in Mossadeqist circles in
Tehran. Far from wanting to overthrow Bakhtiar, who had in any case
failed to exercise the function of prime minister in anything but name,
the generals were afraid that he might resign, leaving them alone in
charge of an ungovernable country.[66] The chief-of-staff, General
Abbas Qarabaghi, even tendered his resignation to Bakhtiar on or
around 20 January but was persuaded by Huyser to stay on.[67] Many
of the commanders were preparing to get out of the country as fast as
possible, taking their cue from the country's three most senior

generals, who had already fled to France and the United States.[68]

The State Department, the Pentagon, the CIA, the NSC and the embassy all had their own scenarios for the way the crisis in Iran would end. The CIA was, until the very last moment, convinced that the shah would pull through. In an analysis circulated barely three months before the shah left the country it forecast that 'the shah will be there for the foreseeable future'.[69] A staff report prepared by the House of Representatives almost at the same time offered the same opinion. The State Department, for its part, was anxious to find the silver lining in the Iranian cloud. The liberal lobby within the department had always opposed US support for the shah and was now anxious to show that the monarch's 'brutal autocracy' would be replaced by a government likely to offer Iran a more acceptable political life. The embassy was not so sure, although key officials there also began looking for moderates likely to temper the excesses of the revolution.

The end came in a way no one had imagined. The army commanders simply declared their 'neutrality' in what they described as 'a conflict among various political groups'.[70] Then they all went into hiding or began looking for someone who would agree to arrest them. The generals were by then convinced that, with discipline in most units already undermined by desertions and acts of disobedience, they would not be able to make much of an impression on the situation. A series of armed attacks by Leninist and Islamic guerrilla groups on police stations, army barracks and gendarmerie posts also underlined the fact that the shah's military machine was not even able to defend itself. The *coup de grace* came when a group of air force technicians staged a revolt in a base east of Tehran and took an oath of allegiance to the Islamic revolution in front of a huge portrait of Khomeini. A unit of the Imperial Guards was quickly dispatched to the scene with orders to crush the rebellion. In the battle that ensued the air force technicians, joined by some cadets, were supported by Marxist-Leninist guerrillas. The unit of the Imperial Guard won that battle but lost the political war. Soon afterwards many of its members, following in the footsteps of their commanders, went into hiding or returned to their native villages. The prime minister and most of his ministers, who had not even succeeded in penetrating the buildings of the ministries assigned to them, went underground and soon fled to Europe.

Khomeini, who had returned to a tumultuous welcome on 1 February 1979, was now the master of Tehran and the whole country. A week before the shah's last cabinet melted away, Khomeini had asked Mehdi Bazargan to form a new government. Bazargan took formal charge of the country on 11 February 1979. The embassy was reassured: Bazargan was known for his strong anti-communism and genuine desire to maintain close ties with the United States. Several months earlier he had established regular contact with the embassy through two of his closest aides, Mohammad Tavassoli and Abbas Amir-Entezam.

Washington was visibly anxious to hear good news from Iran and the embassy did its best to supply it. The fall of the shah had been greeted as a triumph for democracy and human rights by much of the American media and the Carter administration saw no harm in presenting it as a positive result of the president's campaign for human rights. The time when the United States supported dictators and violators of human rights out of callous self-interest was past: today the shah was gone and tomorrow Anastasio Somoza, another dictator facing a revolution, would go. Neither the embassy nor analysts in the State Department saw any reason why Khomeini's revolution should adopt an anti-American stance. The influence of the Marxists on the leadership of the revolution appeared minimal. Many in Washington could not imagine anyone being anti-American without being a communist.

Another reason for Washington's optimism was the presence in the higher echelons of the new revolutionary power of many people linked with the United States in one way or another. Several members of Bazargan's cabinet, including the then all-powerful deputy premier, Ibrahim Yazdi, were naturalized Americans. The new minister of agriculture, for his part, had applied to emigrate to the United States a few months before the revolution triumphed.[71] More importantly, the revolution had at no point advanced any anti-American slogans.

President Carter, obviously shocked by the failure of the so-called intelligence community to foresee any of Iran's strange events, asked the State Department and the NSC to enlist a number of leading Iranologists in an effort to forecast the likely course of future policies of the revolutionary government. Most responses were reassuring. Professor Cottam said in his report that the new regime's foreign policy would be 'Islamic messianic in theory only. In practice it will not seek Islamic goals in other countries. Already Iran has carefully avoided taking up the cause of the Shia minorities in Iraq and Lebanon.'[72] This report was circulated only five weeks after the seizure of power by Khomeini and exactly at the time when a campaign for the 'liberation' of Shi'ites in Bahrain was in full swing, while Hojat al-Islam Mohammad Montazeri was sending arms and money to Shi'ites in Lebanon. As for Iraq, Tehran Radio had already launched its attacks on 'the heathen regime' of Baghdad and was calling for an Islamic revolution there.

Another Iranologist, Marvin Zonis, believed that the future belonged to liberal, Westernized intellectuals. He thought, for example, that Hedayat-Allah Matin-Daftari, a grandson of Mossadeq who had been in contact with the embassy for years, would become 'very important'.[73]

This should not be seen as an argument against seeking the views of academics prior to the shaping of foreign policy. Both professors Cottam and Zonis had been studious and often accurate observers of the Iranian scene for over twenty years. But their skill lay in discerning longer-term trends and not giving on-the-spot advice about a rapidly changing situation. They were not consulted when they should have been and were now asked for advice when they should not have been.

The difficulty of understanding the new situation in Iran was recognized by the embassy. In an excellent report by Charles Naas, the embassy's counsellor, one reads: 'Analysing basic problems in the middle of a revolution is like building skyscrapers on quicksand.'[74] Naas also warned about hasty conclusions about Khomeini and wrote: 'Those who know Khomeini, even his more modernized associates, say he is virtually paranoid about the US.'[75] He further noted that anti-American sentiments were being systematically built up to the point that even holders of American Express cards were being accused of working for the CIA.[76]

Washington, however, continued to ignore such warnings. A report sent from the State Department to the embassy said: 'State Department policy seems now to accept Khomeini as a useful anti-Soviet force. Khomeini's assumption of power is, for the long run, not viewed as a bad development after all.'[77] This view was partly prompted by a paper prepared by the Center for International Studies of the Massachusetts Institute of Technology, which said:

> The Iranian revolution has highlighted one of the principal religious and political developments of our time: the revival of Islamic fundamentalism, from Indonesia to Morocco and from Turkey to Central Africa. In the short run it will cause more problems to the West. In the long run, however, it may be more dangerous to the Soviet Union in Muslim Central Asia.[78]

That paper encouraged the illusion that the Khomeinist tide would soon turn against Moscow.

The tendency to look for good news where there was none was symbolized by Washington's constant search for moderates among the new leaders. The fact that revolutions are never made by moderates was conveniently ignored as experts fantasized about the chances of their favourite heroes coming out on top. The frontiers of farce were left behind when one study suggested that Yazdi, an Iranian-born pharmacist from Houston, Texas, would emerge as the future Reza Khan to 'control the country after Khomeini's death'.[79] The theory that Iran was passing through a period of 'dual power' and that the 'moderates' and pro-American 'Westernizers' would eventually prevail remained popular in the face of real developments that contradicted it. Some people never accepted the 'dual power' theory in the first place. The economic counsellor, Andrew Sens, tore that theory into pieces in a daring report which apparently received little attention in Washington.[80]

Most American observers saw the tip of the iceberg that was revealed by the fall of the shah. They saw American-educated Trotskyites and sundry other revolutionaries, often dressing themselves up as Palestinian guerrillas and speaking with Texan or Californian accents, seizing control of the remnants of the imperial state. The fact that so many American-educated Iranians were involved in the revolution's earlier stages was also noticed by middle-class Iranians who began the growing campaign of rumours about Khomeini's 'secret links' with the CIA. One embassy report mentioned these strange rumours: 'In sub-rosa talk even Khomeini has been linked to CIA/USA in many conversations. The long personal ties of such leaders as Yazdi, Entezam and Ghotbzadeh, not to mention a host of other less well-known provincial revolutionary leaders, to the USA only adds fuel to this particular fire.'[81]

The embassy did not come into direct and systematic contact with hardcore Khomeinists until the very end. As a result the revolution's middle-class fellow-travellers were taken as the real makers of history. The Tabriz consul offered a tragicomic portrait of them in these terms:

> Despite all of their accusations, however, the personal commitment felt by a vast number of Iranians to the USA seems not to be decreasing. After the most vituperative attack on the pro-shah or pro-Revolution stance of the US it is almost absurdly typical for the attacker to inquire about visa possibilities, or to proudly mention his many relatives presently in California. It almost seems impossible for Iranians to believe that Americans might have reasons to be negative in their feelings towards them. After all, when they have erased the last traces of American influence in Iran, the revolutionaries still fully intend to study or retire in the USA.[82]

A post-mortem seminar organized on Vance's orders in Washington in July 1979 was not sparing in its conclusions: 'The State Department has never understood Iran, culturally, religiously or economically. It had only meagre clues to the depth of the Iranian dissatisfaction. . . . The few reports hinting at severe problems were suppressed.'[83] Strangely enough, however, this dramatic judgement, no doubt widely exaggerated, led to no concrete action. Rather than improving the system of information gathering and analysis at the embassy in

Tehran, the department recalled most of the more experienced diplomats stationed there and failed to build up the staff to its full strength for several months.

Determined not to allow reality to stand in the way of its dream of turning the Islamic Revolution into an ally in an anti-Soviet crusade, Washington systematically ignored the propaganda campaign conducted by the Tudeh Party and other pro-Moscow groups. None of these groups was numerically or organizationally strong enough to make a bid for power or even a small share in it. They were revolutionaries, to be sure, but they knew that this was not their revolution. As a result they decided to concentrate their energies on drawing a wedge between the Islamic Revolution and the United States. In a lengthy analysis dated 20 February 1979, the Tudeh Party central committee argued that 'the main contradiction in Iran today is between the people and American Imperialism. . . . Internal class struggle must be set aside until Imperialism is driven out of the country.'[84] Tudeh was to pursue that suicidal strategy to the bitter end.[85]

The embassy, judging by the documents seized there, did not have access to information regarding the Iranian left with the exception of the Trotskyites, most of whom had spent years in the United States and who were almost certainly infiltrated by the FBI and the CIA. Some reports make brief mention of 'Soviet agitation' but do not probe deeper.[86] One report speaks of a clandestine radio transmitter installed by the Soviets somewhere in the Tehran region to broadcast anti-American programmes.[87] The embassy was not aware of the deep infiltration of the media by pro-Moscow militants and felt reassured by the presence of the pro-American Ghotbzadeh at the head of the state-owned radio and television networks.

Soon after Khomeini seized power a number of incidents indicated the steady deterioration of the situation with regard to the future of relations between Tehran and Washington. Only three days after the fall of the shah's regime a band of Leninist guerrillas attacked the US embassy compound, killed an Iranian employee and wounded a Marine guard. The attackers also seized 109 hostages, including Ambassador Sullivan and most of his key aides. The drama lasted no more than two hours and Khomeinist forces saved the situation. Five days later the embassy invited all non-diplomatic American citizens to leave Iran because it could no longer guarantee their safety. A few days later two American air force officers were arrested at Mehrabad Airport by Khomeinist gunmen and were only allowed to go free after an Iranian air force colonel, who was a member of the People's Mujahedeen Organization, interceded on their behalf. But not all the

Mujahedeen were favourably disposed towards the USA. The organization's second-in-command, Mohammad-Reza Saadati, was in
regular contact with the KGB in Tehran and was later caught handing
to a Soviet agent a list of CIA contacts in Iran which he had apparently
stolen during a raid on the headquarters of SAVAK.[88]

A series of measures aimed against the United States were also
adopted by the new government. On 21 February it was announced
that the USA would no longer be allowed access to the Kabkan and
Behshahr listening stations in northern Iran. In May the revolutionary
government refused the nomination of Walter Cutler as the new US
ambassador to Tehran.[89] It also announced the cancellation of some
$12,000 million's worth of orders for American-made arms which
had been placed by the shah.[90] A few days later the 1947 Arms
Cooperation (Iran-United States) Act was formally repealed, ending
more than thirty years of military cooperation between the two
countries.

These measures, accompanied by repeated attacks on US consulates
in Tabriz, Isfahan and Shiraz, as well as the Iran-America Society
buildings in Tehran and Shiraz, failed to dampen Washington's
optimism, however. In September, for example, Henry Precht, who
headed the Iran desk at the State Department, wrote to Bruce Laingen,
the chargé d'affaires, that revolutionary Iran should be encouraged to
play a role in preserving world peace. The United States, Precht
argued, should tell the Iranians that they could assume control of the
listening posts installed to monitor the SALT agreements. 'We must
show our sincerity,' he suggested.[91]

The assumption that all that one needed to do was convince the new
regime of Washington's good intentions led, at times, to very original
suggestions. In August 1979, for example, the embassy suggested that
Fulbright grants be offered to two *talabehs* (Shi'ite students of
theology, mullahs-to-be) from the holy city of Qom to go to the United
States for courses in divinity. In exchange, the embassy plan
continued, American theological students should be encouraged to
attend the Faizieh Seminary in Qom.[92]

Trying to make sense of what was happening in Iran and seeking a
working relationship with the new regime would have been difficult
under the best of circumstances. But the peculiarities of the American
political system were to render the task virtually hopeless. To
Khomeini, who based his entire strategy on a Manichaean view of
existence, any suggestion that the United States might be critical of
certain aspects of the new regime's policy while supporting it as a
whole seemed an impossible proposition. The ayatollah could not
believe that the US Senate, the House of Representatives, the White

House, the Pentagon, the NSC, the CIA, the State Department, the embassy in Tehran and, last but not least, the media could each have their own policies and attitudes towards his holy Islamic Revolution. Thus he saw a US Senate resolution condemning political executions without trial in Iran as a sign that Washington was preparing the ground for sinister moves against his regime, which he regarded as the reflection of Allah's will on earth. 'These Americans,' he asked Deputy Premier Amir-Entezam in the spring of 1979, 'are they for us or against us?'[93]

The embassy was instructed to do whatever possible to achieve three objectives: to prevent a rupture of relations; to revive joint projects wherever possible; and to prevent the Soviets from gaining undue advantages in a chaotic situation.[94] The embassy and the CIA station in Tehran were also charged with the task of creating a new and more credible network of sources and agents. Many of the tested sources had fled the country, while some of the agents had lost their positions and contacts. George Cave, who had worked at the CIA station in Tehran until the revolution, was sent back in April 1979 to try to recruit new informers and contacts. He established close personal relations with Deputy Premier Amir-Entezam, Foreign Minister Ibrahim Yazdi and Defence Minister Mostafa Chamran.[95] He also approved the recruitment of some former SAVAK agents as well as members of the Second Bureau of the Armed Forces, which dealt with counter-espionage.

Not all the CIA's emissaries were as successful as Cave. Another recruitment officer went to Tehran after consulting Khosrow Qashqa'i, a long-time source of the agency, about new potential 'assets'. Qashqa'i recommended one Abol-Hassan Bani-Sadr, then considered to be one of three men with access to the ayatollah. The officer used a fake passport in the name of William Foster. He used as cover Carvers Associates, a firm with CIA links. He met Bani-Sadr three to five times and offered to employ him as an economics consultant for a salary of $1000 a month.[96]

The United States also needed to buy as much time as possible in order to make sure that all its nonessential personnel were out of the country together with the more sensitive military materiel supplied to Iran. A Colonel Charles W. Scott, for example, came to Tehran as the head of a mission to pick up the listening devices and other sensitive equipment relating to the abortive Ibex project.[97] The Iranians were later to accuse the US military of having sabotaged the air force's computer system, creating chaos in inventories, but there is no evidence to suggest any US involvement. It is possible that the sabotage was carried out by leftist guerrillas and their sympathizers among air force technicians.

When years of almost total reliance on SAVAK for information on Iran's domestic politics came to an abrupt end, the CIA found itself facing the prospect of either losing out to the much better entrenched KGB or expanding its network as quickly as possible. Obviously the second option was chosen with results that were not always happy. The agency tracked one of its former Iranian agents to Oslo and pressed him to create an Iran antenna in Paris. But the agent, who had for years used a women's magazine as a cover, refused to play, apparently fearing for his safety.[98] In Paris the agency contacted the former publisher of the Persian version of *Playboy* magazine, who had at the time converted to Islam and worked as the President of 'Muslims in France Association'.[99] But here too the agency proved unlucky as the new recruit turned out to be 'a professional liar interested only in money'.[100] A third contact in Paris was one Kenize Murad, an Indian-born reporter with the weekly *Nouvel Observateur*, who visited Tehran several times and maintained generally good contact with some of the revolutionary figures there.[101] The search for new 'sources' on Iran led the CIA into the quagmire of exile Middle Eastern politics in Paris. A Lebanese fixer, identified under the code-name 'Slippery', persuaded the agency to pay him unspecified sums in exchange for introducing a number of individuals who claimed to have access to Iran's new leaders. A Tunisian serving as the Kuwaiti cultural attaché in France, the publisher of an Arab magazine in Paris and several individuals with no clearly defined sources of income were put on the agency's payroll for several months.[102]

Thirsting for information about events throughout the country, the embassy used the visa as a weapon to recruit some occasional informants. As the number of visa applications grew dramatically the embassy's potential choice of informants also expanded. But very soon word got round that offering information could accelerate the process of obtaining a visa. As a result many people began inventing very interesting pieces of information. The experiment was a failure and the visa section was subsequently closed.

The CIA was apparently anxious to draw support from some of the allied intelligence networks in Iran, especially the British, and on occasions offered to exchange information with them. The British were, for example, informed of Cave's success in setting up the Amir-Entezam contact group.[103] Amir-Etnezam was later appointed as Khomeini's ambassador to Stockholm. Was this because he was already suspected of maintaining 'special relations' with the Americans? Or was it because Premier Bazargan wanted to continue the dialogue with Washington through Amir-Entezam from a neutral capital? In his trial in Tehran the unfortunate Amir-Entezam supported the second hypothesis.[104]

The agency realized that the chaotic situation created by the revolution and the fact that the new rulers of Iran had virtually no experience of running a complex society provided ideal conditions for infiltration at most levels of government as well as the private sector. Subsequent events showed that the KGB had reached precisely the same conclusions and tried to profit from the situation.[105] The Soviets played up two major propaganda themes. The first was that the revolution had not yet been completed. This theme proved extremely successful for a variety of reasons. Khomeini's revolution had succeeded far too quickly for many latter-day revolutionaries to prove their zeal and establish their credentials. In fact, many people had become revolutionaries after Khomeini had already seized power. They were looking for a means of enhancing their position within the hierarchy of 'sacrifices for the revolution'. For the revolution to continue it was essential to find an adversary against whom it could fight. The USA was an excellent candidate for such a role. It was a superpower, an ally of the fallen shah and the mecca of the Iranian middle class. The second theme of propaganda chosen by the Soviets concerned alleged threats to the achievements of the revolution. Here KGB psychological warfare experts excelled themselves by creating Iranian versions of Kolchak and Denikin.

Their main bogeyman was General Mostafa Palizban, who was reported to be raising a counter-revolutionary army with help from the United States in western Iran. Forged edicts supposedly promulgated by Palizban in which the general had supposedly sentenced revolutionaries to death were widely circulated as his phantom army continued its imaginary attacks on government offices and gendarmerie posts in remote regions. In reality, however, Palizban was already in San Jose, California, and had opened an ice-cream parlour where he himself served at the counter. The general's attempt at staging a revolt had lasted only a few days with the help of Jaaf tribesmen. Rumours were also spread about alleged plans by Vice-Admiral Madani, the navy commander and governor of Khuzestan, to march on Tehran in a putsch and put 'genuine revolutionaries' to death. Few people stopped to ask how could a naval force invade Tehran which was over 1000 kilometres inland.

The American attitude throughout the crucial months of the summer and autumn of 1979 seemed to confirm the worst fears of the mullahs. To be sure, the political counsellor remained in contact with two of Khomeini's closest aides, ayatollahs Beheshti and Ardabili, but it was clear that Washington supported middle-class, liberal elements in a power struggle which opposed them to the mullahs. The Pentagon's decision in October to resume exports of military materiel and spare parts to Iran was seen as just another sign that the USA was hoping to buttress its own friends in Tehran. Earlier, a meeting between Bazargan and President Carter's national security advisor, Brzezinski in Algiers and a session of 'amicable' discussions between Foreign Minister Ibrahim Yazdi and US Secretary of State Cyrus Vance had been interpreted by the mullahs as further signs of Washington's siding with those who had no real claim on the revolution. The US policy of backing the Bazargan faction was presented by KGB propaganda as a first step towards restoring the shah to his throne.

Documents seized at the embassy, as well as other accounts of developments in those crucial months, however, show no sign that the United States was pursuing a coherent policy aimed at well-defined objectives. Washington was in fact essentially reacting to events it did not fully understand and was trying to save the family silver so to speak. Its attempts at fostering close relations with Bazargan and helping his cabinet somehow to get along were certainly not part of a plot to restore the shah. Nor was the massive recruitment of new sources and informants, which was undoubtedly carried out by the CIA as well as the embassy itself, necessarily aimed against the revolution. Documents available show that the main purpose of this policy was to counter the growth of Soviet influence.

Throughout those uncertain months, when history hesitated between a course of chaotic reform and a deep plunge into the unknown, the atmosphere at the embassy and around it continued to grow heavier. Diplomats began to feel increasingly isolated as the compound began to look like Fort Apache on the eve of an assault. Some people began to refer to the embassy as 'Fort Persepolis', after the name of the street in which the embassy compound and most of its annexes were situated.[106]

7

THE LONGEST SIEGE

Right from the start of what he knew would be permanent exile, one sombre January day in 1979, the broken shah was determined to make his way to the United States where he hoped to spend the few remaining days of his life. His choice of the USA as a home-from-home was not due to any preference for the American way of life, which, in private conversations, he often described as 'fascinating but chaotic'. He was convinced that the United States was the only country where he would be effectively protected from assassination attempts. The shah had spent much of his life as ruling monarch fearing assassination.[1] He had many enemies, no doubt, but he believed two of them were capable of making an attempt on his life: the KGB and the Palestine Liberation Organization. Only the United States could protect him against such enemies, he thought. He was also concerned about the safety of his children, who were all studying in the USA at the time, and wished to be with them.

Some of the shah's close American friends, notably Henry Kissinger and David Rockefeller, had urged him to go to the United States right away. Another friend, Ambassador Walter Annenberg, had even offered his California estate to the shah as a temporary residence pending the purchase of a permanent home for the royal family. The move to bring the shah to the United States was blocked on 25 January 1979 by President Carter with support from Secretary of State Vance, who strongly opposed the continuance of any special relations with the fallen monarch and his relatives. Vance did not always win. The State Department was, for example, defeated in its attempts to prevent Princess Ashraf from obtaining an American visa. David Rockefeller's attorney, William Jackson, helped the princess beat Vance's stratagems.[2]

Both the embassy in Tehran and the State Department in Washington were fully aware of the possible consequences of admitting the shah into the United States. Bruce Laingen, the chargé d'affaires in

Tehran, who spent some time in Washington in September, pointed out that the new relationship the USA was trying to build with the Bazargan moderates would not survive any major upsets. Henry Precht, head of the Iran desk at the department, was more specific and wrote: 'Should the shah come to the US it would be a disaster for Iran–US relations, for the Western position in the region, and would create a severe security problem for our personnel in Tehran and US Government officials in Washington.'[3] He was not sure that 'we would be able to maintain the embassy in Tehran' and also mentioned 'the probability of PLO-assisted kidnapping of the shah' during his stay in the United States.[4]

The campaign launched by Kissinger and Rockefeller to help the shah find the exile home he wanted has been portrayed by some commentators as an example of sacrificing national interest to considerations of a personal nature. But the Kissinger–Rockefeller stance did not stem solely from their understandable desire to repay an old and often generous friend. They were equally concerned about the consequences of a policy of totally rejecting the shah on the USA's image in other countries where Washington maintained special relations with those in power. The fate of the shah had shocked many of the pro-American rulers in the Middle East and North Africa. Some of them believed that Carter had abandoned or even betrayed the shah.

This feeling of betrayal was also found among many members of the fallen regime, especially the military, whose cooperation was deemed essential for rebuilding American influence in Iran. Between January and October 1979 the CIA approached many former or still active army and navy officers to enlist their support in what was presented as a campaign to 'save Iran from Communism'. But many of those contacted refused to cooperate and pointed to the treatment of the shah by the USA as a sign that Washington could not be trusted as a friend. One high-ranking Iranian naval officer told the CIA director, Admiral Stansfield Turner, that he could not take any 'American guarantees' seriously because he could never hope to be closer to Washington than the shah had been, adding 'and yet see what you are doing to him'.[5]

Kissinger was also concerned that giving in to Khomeini's pressure on the shah might be seen by the ayatollah as a sign of weakness on the part of the United States and thus mark the beginning of a long campaign of Islamic blackmail of Washington. The shah was just an excuse, Kissinger apparently believed, and the ayatollah could use any of a wide variety of other issues to threaten the United States in whatever way he wanted. Was a clash between the United States and the ayatollah inevitable or was it solely provoked by the eventual admission of the shah to the USA? The debate has been going on for some nine years and may continue for many more. With hindsight, however, one thing seems almost certain: had the shah gone to the United States in the very first days of the revolution the matter might have caused far less damage than it eventually did. The reasons for this contention are many. By the time President Carter finally rallied to the Kissinger–Rockefeller stance in October, other factors likely to put Irano-US relations off course had already built up in Tehran – factors which had not been present ten months earlier. The president took the right decision at the wrong time.

The fantastic idea of fostering a long-term friendship with Khomeini as a means of an eventual anti-communist alliance had its own supporters within the administration and among the academics around it. As a born-again Christian, President Carter felt he could understand some of the ayatollah's religious enthusiasm. Some commentators even went so far as to see in Khomeini a 'neo-conservative' with a 'moralistic approach to politics' and a 'monet-arist' platform on economics.[6] The CIA described the ayatollah as 'a philosopher king' and underlined the possibility of turning the Islamic Revolution into an anti-Soviet and even anti-Arab movement.[7]

It was from such a standpoint that the CIA began supplying the Bazargan government with detailed information concerning Soviet activities aimed at fomenting tribal uprisings among the Kurdish and Turkoman minorities in Iran. The new regime was impressed when the CIA supplied a whole dossier on illegal overflying activities by Soviet aircraft in Iranian air space. The dossier showed that the Soviets had been flying at a height of 4000 feet only on a number of occasions, violating an accord that set the limit at 21,000 feet en route to the Persian Gulf. The CIA also showed that on at least one occasion the Soviets had airlifted supplies to Kurdish rebels in western Iran.[8]

The new ministers, who had spent years as revolutionary conspir-ators, were naturally inclined towards the notorious theory of conspiracy and believed that international life consisted essentially of a series of plots. They loved the 'secret' information the CIA fed to them and asked for more. The agency obliged, concluding that intelligence would be an important weapon in forging special relations with the new rulers in Tehran. It provided information on a secret visit to Iranian Kurdistan by George Habash, the leader of the leftist People's Front for the Liberation of Palestine (PFLP), during which he had met rebel leaders and provided them with financial help.[9] Habash was involved in a wider plan, backed separately by Libya and Iraq, to encourage subversive activities in Iran, notably among Kurdish and

Arab-speaking minorities. The information provided by the CIA on
these activities helped the new Islamic regime deal with the threat at an
early stage.[10]

As part of a confidence-building programme the CIA also offered to
help Amir-Entezam and his group produce an international newspaper in Europe with the aim of presenting the 'true image' of the
Islamic Revolution to the West. George Cave, the agency's case officer
for the so-called modernists within the new regime, supported the
scheme. Nasser Minachi, who had maintained close contact with the
embassy for a long time before the revolution, was to supervise the
project from his position as minister of Islamic guidance.[11] The man
picked to get the project going in Switzerland was Simon Farzami, an
old agency source who used as his cover the post of Tehran stringer for
the British newspaper, the *Daily Telegraph*.[12]

The agency, working closely with Mossad agents in Iran, also
succeeded in drawing the attention of the new leaders to the threat
posed by PLO elements in Tehran and the provinces. The PLO played
an important role in training Iranians for terrorist activities before the
revolution and now wanted a share of victory. Yasser Arafat, the PLO
chairman, went around pretending that the Islamic Revolution in Iran
was in fact an offshoot of the Palestinian movement. His 'ambassador'
in Tehran, Hani al-Hassan, installed in the building previously
occupied by the Israeli mission, spent most of his time whipping up
anti-American sentiment. Although Saudi Arabia, a close ally of the
USA, financed the Palestinian presence in Iran, both Arafat and al-
Hassan were determined to steer the new revolutionary regime
towards closer ties with Moscow. Some local Arab rulers in the region
came to believe that Arafat was really the man to see in connection
with the Iranian revolution. They were not alone in falling for the PLO
chief's clever posturing. The Austrian chancellor, Bruno Kreisky, also
believed that Arafat was influential in Tehran. Kreisky even asked
Arafat to intercede with Khomeini to allow Iranian Jews to emigrate –
presumably to Israel.[13] It was only later, when Arafat was declared
persona non grata by the mullahs and his 'embassy' placed in virtual
quarantine, that the PLO chief's game was fully exposed.

Retiring Ambassador Sullivan had on a number of occasions
expressed doubts about the ability of the Bazargan–Yazdi tandem to
outlast the year.[14] Laingen echoed the same sentiment as late as 9
October when he predicted that 'a strong current' was sure to push the
ineffectual premier out of power.[15] Vance, however, was not convinced and when he met Yazdi in New York two days later talked to
him as if the two were engaged in a routine negotiations under
perfectly normal conditions.[16] Vance's assurances that the United

States wanted the best of relations with Islamic Iran rang hollow in view of other developments. The Iranians could not understand why Washington could not quash court rulings brought in Texas and New York under which millions of dollars worth of Iranian assets were frozen as a result of suits filed by individuals and private companies.[17] Nor could they believe that senators Gary Hart (D. Colorado) and Frank Church (D. Idaho), both influential members of the president's own party, were simply expressing personal opinions when they called for a US military presence in the Persian Gulf.[18] Matters were not helped by a statement made by the newly appointed commander of NATO, General Bernard Rogers, who, in introducing the Rapid Intervention Force, said that it had come into being as a result of developments in Iran.[19]

Three more issues contributed to the rising tension provoked by Iranian suspicions about Washington's true intentions. A leaflet entitled *America's Secret Plan* and probably prepared by the KGB was distributed in Tehran by mysterious groups as 'proof of Washington's evil designs against our revolution'. The plan, supposedly worked out by the American Islamologist Bernard Lewis, aimed at carving up Iran and the rest of the Middle East into mini-states representing the various ethnic and religious groups in the region.[20] The second issue concerned the resumption of the Persian programme of Voice of America. The programme had been discontinued several years before the revolution as part of a budget-cutting plan. By September 1979, however, VOA was offering two hours of programmes in Persian. British Foreign Secretary David Owen had urged the Omani government to allow VOA to use relay facilities for its Persian programme in the island of Massirah. The new broadcast was an instant success. VOA offered a full programme of Persian music, banned inside Iran by Khomeini, as well as a fairly objective news bulletin. The fact that many of the most popular Iranian radio and television personalities of the pre-revolutionary era now worked for VOA increased its appeal.[21]

Finally the new revolutionary government was angered by an American decision to close temporarily the embassy's visa section. This was seen as a hostile move calculated to show that Washington did not wish its formerly close ties with Iran to continue.[22]

The 'strong current' Laingen had warned about was in search of an outlet towards the end of October when Carter decided to allow the shah to enter the United States. Once the decision was made, in the face of serious objections from both the State Department and the embassy, Precht was dispatched to Tehran to sell the idea to the new regime. The mission was designed to fail: Precht, not convinced that the president had made the right decision, sounded pretty unconvincing. More importantly, once in Tehran he did not even try to talk to the Khomeinist mullahs, who at the time controlled the masses. Precht negotiated with Bazargan and Yazdi, men unlikely to contemplate the seizure of hostages and equally unable to prevent such an event from taking place.

The shah arrived in New York on the night of 22 October 1979, and was immediately admitted into the New York Hospital–Cornell Medical Center. The move provoked no initial reaction from Tehran and the president began to think that he had made the right decision. But matters were not allowed to rest there. The shah, installed in his hospital bed, began to receive a string of visitors, including several of his former ministers and generals, in addition to the inevitable Kissinger and Rockefeller. His stay in New York topped the prime-time news bulletins and a few days later Barbara Walters of ABC Television News pulled off a scoop by interviewing the sick shah. The mullahs had patiently spread the rumour that the shah, after leaving Iran, had undergone plastic surgery to change his facial features and did not plan to surface ever again. Now, with the shah once more in international limelight, the men of Allah were proved to have lied to the faithful.

The mullahs were preparing nationwide demonstrations to mark the sixteenth anniversy of Khomeini's exile to Turkey and were determined to use the occasion for a show of force. On 1 November, nine days after the shah's arrival in New York, Khomeini called on Islamic students to protest against the fallen monarch's presence in the United States. Two days later the Iranian Foreign Ministry put out a mildly worded protest. As yet, however, there seemed to be no immediate threat to the embassy and no steps were taken to destroy or otherwise secure more sensitive documents.

On 4 November a group of militant students under the influence of one Habib-Allah Payman, a dentist with links with the PLO, gathered in front of the embassy as part of a march that was to take them to several parts of the capital. Very soon, however, they found out that they could enter the embassy compound without encountering any serious resistance and did so, initially to stage a sit-in. Many of the militants had been students in various American colleges, where they had learned the sit-in tactic, and at first did not mean to go any further. Once inside the embassy compound all control was apparently lost and many of the students must have surprised even themselves when they announced that they would stay in the building, holding everyone there hostage, until the shah was returned to Iran with his wealth which they later estimated to be over $56,000 million.[23] By the end of the day some hundred American diplomats and Iranian employees of

The Good Old Days: President Richard Nixon, flanked by the shah and Empress Farah, poses for pictures during a state visit to Tehran in 1972. The shah's eldest son, Crown Prince Reza, is on the right (*M. Norcia, Sygma*)

(Below left) Champion of Nationalism: Dr Mohammad Mossadeq, leader of the oil nationalisation movement in Iran, at his estate west of Tehran. Mossadeq was overthrown in a military putsch backed by the United States in 1953 (*Associated Press*)

(Below centre) Trusted Friend: Henry Kissinger, who served as Secretary of State under presidents Nixon and Ford, became one of the shah's closest advisers in the 1970s. Kissinger was a member of a commission the shah set up to 'save the West' in 1976 (*William C. Allen, John Hillelson Agency*)

(Below right) On an Island of Stability: The shah with President Jimmy Carter during the latter's state visit to Tehran in 1976. Carter called Iran an 'island of stability in a sea of turmoil' (*John Hillelson Agency*)

The Return of the Avenger: Ayatollah Ruhollah Khomeini is greeted by delirious crowds at Tehran Airport on his return home after an exile of more than fifteen years in February 1979. Ten days after his return, Khomeini was master of revolutionary Iran (*Patrick Zachmann, Magnum*)

Conquering the 'Nest of Spies': Khomeinist militants burn an American flag on the roof of the captured embassy compound in Tehran in November 1979 (*Associated Press*)

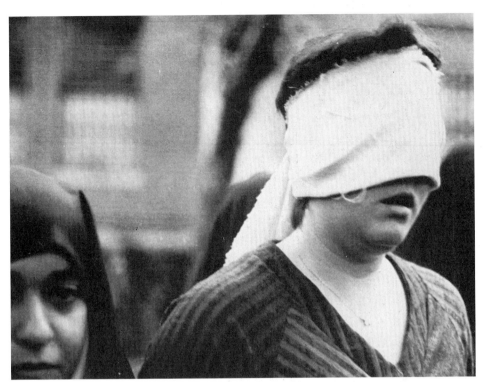

Marked for Execution: A woman diplomat held hostage is paraded blindfold in front of the embassy compound in Tehran in 1979. The Khomeinist kidnappers threatened to execute the hostages as spies (*Popperfoto*)

Secret Documents: A Khomeinist militant holds up one of the many confidential documents seized at the American embassy in Tehran. The militants referred to the embassy as the 'Nest of Spies' and 'Den of Espionage' (*Associated Press*)

THE U.S.A
EMBASSY HAS
BEEN A DEN OF
ESPIONAGE

Disaster in the Desert: Charred corpses of American commandos and the remains of two helicopters and an aircraft involved in a collision are scattered in the Iranian desert near Tabas. This was all that was left of Carter's rescue mission aimed at liberating the hostages in Tehran in April 1980 (*Popperfoto*)

(*Below left*) *The President must Hang*: A Khomeinist militant acts as President Carter at a hanging ceremony at the U.S. Embassy in Tehran. The show was part of festivities throughout Iran marking the first anniversary of the seizure of the embassy (*Popperfoto*)

(*Below right*) *Death to the Ayatollah*: An American protestor hangs a mask of Ayatollah Khomeini during a demonstration in New York in 1980 (*Associated Press*)

(*Above left*) *Direct Line to Tel Aviv*: Islamic Prime Minister Mir-Hossein Mussavi-Khamaneh'i. He initiated direct contacts with Israel and then with the United States from 1983 onwards (*Associated Press*)

(*Above right*) *International Arms Dealer*: Jaacov Nimrodi, the Iranian-born Israeli businessman, played a key role in supplying the Islamic forces with arms and equipment in the war against Iraq (*Milner, Sygma*)

(*Below left*) *Secretary of State for One Day*: Iranian-born American businessman Albert Hakim (left) listens to his lawyer during a congressional hearing in Washington in 1987. Hakim handled secret talks with Khomeini's envoys and promised them that the U.S. would declare war on the USSR if Moscow attacked Iran (*Associated Press*)

(*Below right*) *North American Hero*: Lt. Colonel Oliver North during a congressional hearing in Washington in 1987. President Reagan called the former National Security aide 'an American hero' (*Alain Tannenbaum, Sygma*)

(*Above left*) *Traveller to Tehran*: Former National Security Adviser Robert McFarlane takes the oath at a congressional hearing in Washington in 1987. He led the secret American mission to Tehran in May 1986 (*Sygma*)

(*Above right*) *Playing at Strategy*: Vice-Admiral John Poindexter approved secret arms sales to Iran as part of a deal involving the release of American hostages held by Khomeinist militants in Lebanon (*A. Grace, Sygma*)

(*Below left*) *He put up the Money*: Saudi financier Adnan Khashoggi helped Iran and Israel clinch a series of arms deals with the United States by providing 'bridging loans' through secret Swiss bank accounts (*Associated Press*)

(*Below right*) *The 'Can-Do' General*: Retired US Air Force General Richard Secord at a congressional hearing in Washington in 1987. Secord handled negotiations with the Speaker of the Islamic Majlis, Hashemi-Rafsanjani (*Jean-Louis Atlan, Sygma*)

Assessing the Damage: President Ronald Reagan comments on the report by the Tower Commission concerning secret arms sales to the Islamic Republic. Commission members are also present. From left to right: former Secretary of State Edmond Muskie, former Senator John Tower (Commission Chairman) and retired Air Force General Brent Scowcroft. The Commission completed its work in Washington in February 1987 (*Mathieson, Sygma*)

A Gift from Reagan: A Khomeinist militant holds up the copy of the Bible autographed by President Ronald Reagan and sent to Tehran as a gift for Ayatollah Khomeini. Islamic Majlis Speaker Hashemi Rafsanjani (left) is also present at this press conference in Tehran in January 1987 (*Sygma*)

(*Above*) *Travellers to Paradise*: Islamic 'volunteers for martyrdom' take time off to pose for cameras in the Persian Gulf in July 1987. They had trained to act as kamikazes operating from light speed-boats capable of waging a marine guerrilla war against the US Navy (*Gamma/Frank Spooner*)

(*Left*) *Running the Gauntlet*: The US Navy escorts Kuwaiti oil and gas tankers through the Persian Gulf in defiance of warnings from Ayatollah Khomeini to turn the waterway into 'an ocean of American blood' in 1987 (*Associated Press*)

(*Below*) *Taking on 'The Great Satan'*: Islamic Revolutionary-Guard sailors patrolling the Persian Gulf in August 1987 (*Gamma/Frank Spooner*)

the embassy had become hostages. Laingen and two of his colleagues escaped because they happened to be at the Foreign Ministry at the time but they became hostages there.

Was the takeover of the embassy an accident or was it a carefully planned move by revolutionary radicals to force a formal break with Washington? The question was to be debated for many years. All the evidence shows that no prepared plan was involved, although some communist provocateurs were present among the students.[24] Iran's own turmoil, coupled with persistent confusions concerning policy and methods in Washington, had made this type of 'accident' inevitable. Sooner or later it or something like it had to happen to remove the logjam in the revolutionary process.

Khomeini could, of course, have ordered the drama to end on the first day. But such a move would have undermined his prestige as a radical revolutionary. He could not afford to allow anyone to appear more anti-American than he. The following day he endorsed the move and dispatched his son Ahmad from Qom to congratulate the students on their 'splendid Islamic act'. Ahmad, who had never been known for his keen intelligence, confused the situation further by asking the government to cooperate with the students. The government's response came a few hours later in the form of collective resignation. The country was left without a government and what became 'the second breath of the revolution' began.

Because he could not find any of his closest aides in time, the ayatollah, then residing in Qom, chose a young mullah to serve as prayer leader at the occupied embassy. The mullah, Hojat al-Islam Mohammad Mussavi-Khoiniha, was soon presented as a seasoned KGB agent by some American writers. He was, in fact, an ardent Khomeinist with strong anti-communist credentials.[25]

The seizure of the embassy set off a series of events that for the most part engineered themselves. The attackers, who called themselves Muslim Students Following the Imam's Line, had embarked on their adventure only as a means of protest. Very soon, however, they found other post-factum justifications for their act. They claimed that the United States was plotting to overthrow the revolution and that a meeting between Brzezinski and Bazargan in Algiers on 1 November, with Yazdi also present, had been part of the plot. A few days later, encouraged by the unprecedented television coverage given them in the United States while they also dominated the scene in Iran, they enlarged the scope of their ambitions and declared that they wanted to bring the United States down to its knees. Khomeini went with them all the way, dubbing the USA as the 'Great Satan' and launching his famous slogan: 'America cannot do a damn thing!'[26]

The militants released all the non-American hostages plus all the Black and almost all the female members of the mission within a few days. But they kept fifty hostages, while a further three diplomats remained captive at the Foreign Ministry building. The occupied embassy became the centre of attraction for all the frustrated revolutionaries who were convinced that they were on a divine mission to change the history of the world.[27] Every day thousands of people demonstrated in front of the compound, which became a place of pilgrimage for revolutionaries from the four corners of the land. Some mullahs told their congregations that a visit to the occupied US embassy held as much merit as a pilgrimmage to Mecca.[28]

The radical mullahs now felt confident enough to make their final bid for exclusive control of the government. Nevertheless, using the traditional tactic of *howsaleh*, which means 'taking no risks until the likely pattern of events has become clear', the mullahs allowed all the key cabinet posts to be occupied by technocrats. The mullahs feared an energetic reaction from the United States and, as usual, did not wish to find themselves exposed in the front line. It was only when they realized that the Carter administration was indeed unable or unwilling to retaliate in a decisive manner that the mullahs eventually pushed the technocrats out and exerted full control.

The seizure of the embassy meant that the radicals gained access to a veritable treasury of secret and confidential documents covering some thirty years of Iranian history. Some of the documents had been shredded or powdered, in the heat of the invasion, by the more alert members of the staff. But enough had survived to give the students the ammunition they needed for their daily propaganda. Over the next eight years the students developed their own techniques for re-assembling the shredded documents. But even evidence that the embassy had been engaged in the most routine of diplomatic tasks was seen by the students as proof that Washington had plotted against Iran and Islam for several decades. They dubbed the embassy 'the Nest of Spies' and announced they would try the hostages for espionage. Some technocrats who, because of their familiarity with the modern world, ought to have known better, echoed these sentiments out of pure opportunism.[29]

By the end of November it had become apparent to all those who wanted to know that radical mullahs, inspired by Khomeini but led on a day-to-day basis by Ayatollah Mohammad Hussein Beheshti, had won the power struggle within the revolution. And yet President Carter still searched for moderates with whom he could make a deal. Such colourful, though lightweight, politicians as Sadeq Ghotbzadeh, who became foreign minister for a while, and Abol-Hassan Bani-Sadr, who even rose to become Khomeini's first president of the Islamic Republic, were looked upon by Washington as serious future partners for the USA in Iran. Beheshti and the radical mullahs had played no direct role in organizing the embassy takeover,[30] but they used the incident for two purposes: to push their rivals out of positions of power and to send a signal to Washington to recognize Beheshti as Iran's veritable strongman. It took Carter nearly six months to understand that signal and to begin dealing directly with the Beheshti–Khomeini faction. By that time the occupied embassy had become an important institution of the revolutionary state and not even Khomeini himself could have ordered the unconditional release of the hostages.

Although President Carter had been repeatedly warned about the possibility of the embassy being invaded and occupied by militants, he had ordered no contingency plans to be prepared. When the drama began he was taken by surprise and forced to improvise as events unfolded. As a result he never regained the initiative and allowed much of his policy to be dictated by what the mullahs did in Tehran. Carter's first reaction was to treat the matter as a diplomatic incident and to use the routine stick-and-carrot method. A host of goodwill envoys, ranging from Ramsey Clark, a former attorney-general, to Black priests and several Irish and other European international busybodies were dispatched to Tehran to help solve the problem. The visitors provided the Tehran militants with material for their propaganda: the 'Great Satan' was begging to be forgiven. Some self-styled saviours offered their services and were instantly encouraged by the White House to do what they could. An Egyptian and a French journalist, a local representative of the Ford Motor Corporation, the pro-PLO clergyman, Hilarion Capucci, a former Canadian girlfriend of Ghotbzadeh and several cosmopolitan adventurers also tried their diplomatic talents on behalf of the United States.

Some of the middlemen, hungry for publicity or motivated by prospects of financial gain, gave the impression that they had the USA feeding from their hand and pretended that Washington would concede virtually anything the Tehran blackmailers asked for.[31] One or two of them tried to bribe some of the students and to recruit informers among the group on behalf of the CIA. Together, these middlemen portrayed the USA as a weak and at the same time devious power which could be neutralized as long as the hostages were not released. The net effect of their efforts was to raise the political value of the hostages. The fifty-three captive diplomats came to represent an insurance policy for the Islamic Revolution: the United States would make no move to destabilize Khomeini as long as the drama continued.

The stick part of the Carter strategy, which was put together on a day-to-day basis, was presented by the halting of supplies of military materiel to Iran on 8 November and the freezing of Iranian assets in American banks some time later. The president also tried to show anger by issuing an order that all the estimated 50,000 Iranian students then in the USA should be re-registered so that those found to have violated immigration regulations could be expelled. The fact that the majority of those affected had no love to spare for Khomeini and his Islamic revolution must have appeared unimportant to the president.

While there is no doubt that the plight of the hostages was a source of great pain for President Carter, it is possible to suggest that his failure fully to understand the situation and to mobilize US resources in the most effective way were key factors in prolonging the drama, which in the end lasted 444 days. Right from the start Carter made entirely his own a problem that was of more urgency to the Iranians. He felt personally responsible for the wellbeing and the eventual safe release of fifty-three human beings in a situation he did not control and could hardly influence in a positive way. At the same time, however, he continued to be haunted by the classic fear of all US administrations over some thirty years: the takeover of Iran by Soviet-sponsored communism. And yet the most dangerous mistake in dealing with a political-hostage situation is to try to pursue a variety of objectives at the same time.

Any attempt to explain the multiple reasons which might have led to the seizure of hostages – and at times explanation easily becomes justification – entails the risk of pushing the existential reality of the hostages themselves into the background. A person or an authority who wants to have its hostages released cannot, deep inside its own conscience, share any of the excuses advanced by the captors or even give the impression of doing so. The kidnapping of people is first a crime, and thus a police matter while it is going on. It is only afterwards that it becomes a subject for social, political and psychological inquiry and speculation. Securing the release of the hostages must be the sole, exclusive objective, or at least must be perceived to be as such by the kidnappers. The Carter administration, however, was tempted by other objectives as well: turning the hostages drama into a vote-catching device for the president's re-election, helping the moderates in Tehran to oust the mullahs, and, as already noted, preventing the Soviets from advancing in Iran.

By keeping the limelight on the hostages crisis, the president turned it into a double-edged sword in electoral terms. As for the objective of supporting the moderates in Tehran, the small chance that such a project might have had in other circumstances was destroyed when Washington linked it directly to the fate of the hostages. People like Ghotbzadeh and Bani-Sadr could have hardly consolidated their own power base even with strong support from the USA in the best of conditions. Carter's experience with other moderates – ranging from Bakhtiar to Bazargan – had already proved that. Now to ask Bani-Sadr and Ghotbzadeh to beat the mullahs while also securing the release of the hostages was a task fit only for Superman. The objective of preventing Iran from tilting towards Moscow was redundant since the mullahs of Qom and the commissars of the Kremlin hated one another more than they hated the United States.

Had the president limited his objectives in Iran to the release of the hostages only, he would have had no choice but to go directly to the mullahs and ask for their terms. From a logistics point of view this was quite feasible. Both the embassy and the CIA had been in contact with Beheshti and Ardabili, two of the key figures involved, between the autumn of 1978 and the summer of 1979. Both men were ready to play provided Washington first recognized them as the new masters of Iran and then accepted their basic conditions. These conditions would have been very harsh, especially in electoral terms, for President Carter. Translated into simple language, the mullahs set three conditions. First, they should be allowed to hang on to the hostages for a while longer and even carry out a few more anti-American acts in the region, together with continued propaganda against the United States, as a means of forestalling any accusations of having sold out to Washington. Second, the USA should offer the mullahs support in such fields as armaments, intelligence and crucial technical services without asking for any favours in return. Third, the USA should recognize the Khomeinist revolution as the predominant force in the region and allow it to wage and win its own campaign against its rivals and enemies, who might happen to be allies of Washington.

To be sure, Carter was not prepared to pay such a price to ensure the early release of the hostages. As a result, choosing an early release as the vital immediate objective was a mistake. On occasions, and largely because of misrepresentation by intermediaries, the president gave the impression that he was ready to deal on terms set by the mullahs. But at no point did he consider that option seriously. He had two other options: (a) to consider the crisis as a misfortune which would only be resolved with the passage of time and (b) to mobilize US resources to threaten the very existence of the mullarchy so that Khomeini would be prepared to release the hostages in exchange for the safety of his own regime.

The president considered and tried both options, albeit in a half-hearted manner. He was conscious of the tremendous problems involved in both cases. The strategy of waiting the crisis out had little chance of success in a society dominated by media constantly in search of the marvellous, the dramatic and the exceptional. The president's silence and apparent inaction would have been construed as a sign of faint-heartedness or an abdication of responsibility.[32]

The second option was equally problematic. The United States did have some intelligence and influence assets in Iran, but there was little they could do beyond limited psychological warfare. Using military force against the mullahs was also difficult with unpredictable results. In January 1980 the president ordered the assembly of a strong naval force within reach of Iran.[33] But this show of force did not have the effect it might have had in an ordinary diplomatic context. The mullahs knew that the United States could not conquer Iran and send its troops into Tehran. And that was all that mattered to them. They used the same tactic against Carter that they had used against the shah: provoking him into brandishing enough force to make the mullahs look like heroes without, however, really trying to put them out of action. The mullahs had deliberately provoked clashes between the shah's troops and demonstrators, especially children and adolescents, in order to manufacture the martyrs they needed. Now they were praying that Carter would make the same mistake. The US administration eventually came round to approving the use of a military option – but only in the form of an attempt to rescue the hostages. While Carter hoped that his stick-and-carrot strategy would convince Tehran that a deal over the hostages was preferable to a long crisis, the radical mullahs soon realized that they too had lost control of events. Even the eventual expulsion of the shah from the United States could not change the atmosphere in Tehran.[34] Both sides continued with their posturing nevertheless.

One man determined to benefit from the situation to advance his own personal plans was Kurt Waldheim, the United Nations' secretary-general, who was approaching the end of his second term and already dreamed of a third one. Waldheim knew his re-election would be almost certain if he were to achieve the impossible and bring out the hostages. He flew to Tehran on 1 January 1980 amid unprecedented media attention. But within hours of his arrival Waldheim began to feel concerned about his own safety. The mullahs published photos of the secretary-general bowing to and kissing the hand of Princess Ashraf. They called for him to be arrested and put on trial for his 'crimes against humanity', meaning his cordial relations with the royal family.[35] Waldheim went out of his way to rescue a few crumbs while in Tehran and even appeared to agree to the convening of an international tribunal to investigate 'the crimes of the US in Iran'.[36] But he was told he could not see Khomeini and should not even mention the possibility of meeting at least some of the hostages. He was taken to tour a graveyard where his fate hung in the balance for some time as Ghotbzadeh's bodyguards tried to dislodge a group of revolutionaries who wanted to arrest him. The secretary-general was badly shaken; he was 'trembling like a leaf in the autumn wind', according to one of his bodyguards present at the time.[37]

Waldheim was obviously glad to be back in New York – 'especially alive', as he noted.

The Carter administration's difficulties in understanding the adversary persisted. The seizure of power in Afghanistan by KGB agents in Kabul on 27 December 1979 had been seen by Washington as an event that might encourage the mullahs in Tehran to mend their relationship with the United States.[38] After all, the Soviets had, with a single dramatic blow, extended their border with Iran by a further 1300 kilometres. Shouldn't the mullahs be worried? The question was answered in the affirmative by State Department specialists. And some three weeks later the department's spokesman, Hodding Carter III, proposed a joint Tehran–Washington response to what he termed 'the Soviet aggression in Afghanistan'. He also declared that the United States was prepared to meet Iran's 'security requirements', provided the hostages were released. This was a clear signal that arms shipments to Tehran could be resumed quickly. What the administration did not know was that the mullahs, like the quintessential poker player, concentrated only on one subject, considered to be of vital importance, to the exclusion of all others at any given time. They could not have cared less about Afghanistan or a Soviet threat to Iran's security in the medium term. Anything beyond the here-and-now fell outside their realm; Allah would take care of medium- and long-term problems. All that interested them was to win the battle they were waging for control of the state machinery in Iran. They knew that any concessions on the hostages would harm their prospects in what mattered to them above all else. The mullahs had their own agenda and it did not coincide with that pursued by President Carter.[39]

The president then appeared to try a different tactic. On 20 January he told Americans that they should think of the short-term and long-term interests of the country first and only then be concerned about the safety and even the lives of the hostages. Two days later he took the same argument further. He told Congress that the United States had no basic quarrel with Iran and once again suggested joint action to counter the Soviet presence in Afghanistan. What is interesting is that the president truly meant what he said and saw no reason why Iran and the United States should not become friends again. What he forgot to take into account, however, was the nature of the Khomeinist regime. The United States certainly did not have any reason to quarrel with Iran as a nation state: the interests of the two hardly ever clashed and were often complementary. But the Khomeinist regime did not think in terms of what suited Iran's interests best. It was, and was to remain, a pan-Islamic movement determined to establish its own rule over all the Muslim countries and then throughout the globe.[40] Leaving aside the wave of executions and the imprisonment of tens of thousands of innocent people inside Iran itself – matters that should have been seen as a cause for quarrel by a president who championed human rights – the Khomeinist movement had many other causes for quarrel with the United States when it came to their respective world views.

President Carter, by linking the fate of the hostages to his plans for joint action with Tehran against Moscow's presence in Afghanistan, made sure that he would succeed in neither field. The mullahs saw him as a weak leader vulnerable to pressure, while the Soviets did their best to block every one of his moves to end the hostages crisis through diplomatic efforts.[41] The Carter administration continued to threaten economic sanctions and even military intervention on a number of occasions. But every time it ended up offering more concessions to the mullahs. In February President Carter gave in to what he had resisted until then and approved the formation of an international commission to investigate the role of the USA in Iran. The mullahs called it 'the crimes of the US inquiry'. Its architect was the incorrigible Waldheim, who seemed to have learned little from his Iranian experience. The five-man commission of half-diplomats half-busybodies travelled to Tehran, played its part in the television shows assigned to it by the mullahs – which included a tacit admission that the USA had been responsible for crimes against humanity in Iran – and was then sent packing, having achieved nothing at all.[42]

During their stay in Tehran the commission members were taken to a strange happening, stage-managed by the mullahs, at Tehran Hilton's Royal Ballroom, renamed the Hall of Islam. There the commissioners saw a steady stream of handicapped people coming to the rostrum, or being wheeled there, to claim that they had had their legs or arms amputated or their eyes taken out of their sockets by 'US torturers'. None of the testimonies was genuine and the participants were all ordinary disabled people brought to play their part in advancing the cause of Islam.[43] But millions of Iranians who saw the show on television came to believe that the USA had indeed committed crimes in Iran and that this was now admitted by an international commission appointed by the secretary-general of the United Nations and endorsed by President Carter himself. Imaginary crimes were thus used for the purpose of justifying a real crime, that of holding fifty-three people captive and daily subjected to psychological torture and physical hardship.

The daring exploit of six American diplomats who had escaped the embassy kidnappers and managed to leave Iran with help from the Canadian embassy in Tehran was made public on 29 January 1980. This represented the first bit of good news the American public had had on Iran for months. The six, who had been hiding in the Canadian embassy since 4 November 1979, left Iran on Canadian diplomatic passports. The incident served further to inflame the anger of the militant students and their mullah mentors. But it also attracted attention in Washington to the possibility of a rescue mission for the fifty-three captives in Tehran. Supporters of quiet diplomacy, however, continued to prevail for a while longer. The trouble was that the diplomatic efforts, especially those made by the White House, which spent a disproportionate part of its time and energy on the subject of the hostages, continued to be aimed at people without any real influence in Iran. Secretary of State Vance, for example, accepted a suggestion by Bani-Sadr, who had been sworn in as president on 4 February, that the US Congress should investigate past policies in Iran and 'apologize' to 'our martyr-bearing Muslim people'.[44] Bani-Sadr used this as a personal victory and as a means of enhancing his own position in the ongoing power struggle in Tehran – he was the man who could 'make the Great Satan crawl and beg to be pardoned'.[45] The trouble, however, was that he could not deliver on his own since the hostage holders regarded him as an enemy and were already in possession of documents on the CIA's attempt to recruit him in 1979.[46] The radical mullahs saw the US gesture, which came in the form of a letter from Carter to Bani-Sadr, as just another attempt by Washington to deny the Shi'ite clergy the fruits of their victory in Iran.

The contents of Carter's letter were released in Tehran and Washington in almost conflicting terms. The Washington version presented a tough, no-nonsense president, who was ready to make a deal but who would not hesitate to fight as well if necessary. The Tehran version, on the other hand, was apologetic. The administration, it said, had just inherited the policy on Iran from its predecessors and was now anxious to make amends and looked forward to close relations with the revolutionary regime.

The Tehran version was received with anger and surprise by the American public, who continued to reject any idea of apologizing to the mullahs in order to secure the release of the hostages. The White

House was more or less forced to deny any knowledge of the letter, the 'original' of which was, nevertheless, produced in Tehran. Was it a forgery? Perhaps. The likeliest explanation is that one of the inter-mediaries involved in the negotiations simply stole a few sheets of paper with the presidential heading and wrote on them what he thought the American government's position ought to be.

The intermediaries in question were collectively known as the 'French Connection' because the group included several French lawyers. But the most influential figures involved were a former teacher of Bani-Sadr in Paris and an Argentine businessman who had once served as the dictator Juan Peron's chauffeur. Their original aim was to help Bani-Sadr consolidate his position by solving the problem of the hostages and securing US support. But very soon they realized that Bani-Sadr was not likely to make much impression on the kidnappers and began looking for other interlocutors in Tehran.

Considerations of US domestic policies, especially the forthcoming Democratic party primaries, however, dictated a tougher line to President Carter. On 7 April the president announced a series of measures against Iran starting with a formal break in relations. The package also included an economic embargo against Iran, an invent-ory of Iranian assets in the United States with a view to inviting private law suits, and the cancellation of all entry visas for Iranians. Once again these measures proved largely futile because they did not hurt the real culprits – the militant students and the radical mullahs who managed them. The net effect of the measures was a further erosion of the position of the very moderates whom Carter had originally hoped to support and deal with. By that time, however, the president had already decided to approve a military mission to rescue the hostages. The administration was divided over the issue. Vance tendered his resignation but agreed that the official announcement should be made only after the rescue mission was completed.[47] His objection to the plan was not solely due to moral considerations. The secretary was concerned that the mission might endanger the lives of an estimated 230 American citizens who were still in Iran and free.[48] He also believed that the attempt could provoke the Soviets and create complications in Washington's relations with allies in the Persian Gulf.

The operation was entrusted to Delta Force, an elite unit trained for coping with unusual situations. USS Nimitz was used as the base from which the force, using eight helicopters and two C130 Hercules transport aircraft, took off on the night of 25 April. Just under two hundred men, including ninety commandos, were involved in the team. The airborne flotilla flew on a northwesterly course over the

Gulf of Oman and entered Iranian airspace to the east of the Jask Peninsula and, crossing over more than 1000 kilometres of almost lunar landscape, arrived at a spot marked out as Desert One. This was an emergency landing site which had been built near the desert oasis city of Tabas a few years earlier to airlift supplies to earthquake-stricken families.

From Tabas the commando unit was to fly a further 300 kilometres to land at a site near Garmsar, some 70 kilometres southeast of Tehran. There the team would unload and the helicopters would be flown to a safe place where they would be guarded by friendly Iranian commandos wearing Iranian uniforms. The American commandos would spend the day recuperating in a car repair hangar and would then be driven to Tehran in five trucks after nightfall. Within one hour they would be positioned at Amjadieh Stadium just opposite the embassy on Roosevelt Avenue. From there a small unit would go to the Foreign Ministry some 4 kilometres away to rescue Laingen and his two fellow captives. The bulk of the force, however, would launch the operation at the embassy compound itself: the militant guards, estimated at around eighty, would be overpowered and the hostages transferred to Amjadieh where they would be airlifted by helicopter to Tabas and then taken out of the country aboard the C130 planes. A squadron of fighters, also taking off from USS *Nimitz*, would provide air cover. The final and most dangerous part of the operation was to last barely 130 minutes.

The Iranian team which was to cooperate with the rescue mission consisted of four air force officers who had trained in San Antonio, Texas, and twenty-five cashiered members of the Imperial Guard who believed they were recruited for an anti-Khomeini operation which was to serve as a prelude to a *coup d'état*. The four air force officers were to be taken out of Iran and to the United States at the same time as the hostages. But only one was eventually to make his way out; the three others remained and were later executed for their part in an abortive coup attempt.[49]

The rescue mission itself, meanwhile, met with disaster. Once in Tabas the mission commander realized that three of the helicopters had suffered technical disability as a result of sandstorms in the desert. To make matters worse, one of the helicopters collided with one of the C130s. The explosion caused by the collision killed eight members of the mission. President Carter, in direct telephone contact with the mission commander, Colonel Charles Beckwith, terminated all operations and ordered the force back home. The unexpected arrival at Desert One of a busload of Iranian pilgrims travelling to the holy city of Mashhad complicated matters further, forcing the commander to order a hasty withdrawal, leaving behind the charred bodies of his fallen troops.

This was President Carter's last chance to order a rescue operation before his party's convention where he had to fight to win renomination. The shortening of the nights and the harsh summer of the region soon made further secret military operations difficult. In any case, the hostages were better guarded and, as the militants claimed, were even dispatched to Caspian coast towns near the Soviet border. This meant that any future airborne rescue mission could be detected by radar, creating the risk of intervention by Soviet fighters.

The failure of the mission was hailed by the mullahs as a great victory for Islam and the re-enactment of a tale in the Holy Qur'an about an early war between the Christians and the Muslims in which the former were put to the rout by the intervention of fighting birds sent by Allah. Khomeini was hailed as 'the Breaker of Idols, the Humbler of the Great Satan'. He sent one of his closest friends, Ayatollah Sadeq Khalkhali, to Desert One to pray on the site of the American debacle. Khalkhali did even better and pretended that nine Americans, and not eight as President Carter had announced, had perished. This was to show that another Muslim tale, in which nine emissaries of the Byzantine emperor were burned to death before being able to harm the Prophet Muhammad, had come true once again. The ayatollah stuck to his story and nine coffins were later handed over to the International Red Cross for transfer to the United States – one of them was empty.

The failure of the Tabas mission left Carter with virtually no policy regarding the hostages and the future of US relations with Iran. The vacuum thus created was to be filled in two ways. First, the French Connection group returned and persuaded the president to enter into secret negotiations with the Beheshti faction, casting off the beleaguered Bani-Sadr, who was eventually dismissed by Khomeini and forced into exile. Hamilton Jordan, the White House chief-of-staff, handled the American side of the secret negotiations. Jordan had previously been involved in a secret meeting with Ghotbzadeh in Paris at the time the controversial politician still served as Khomeini's foreign minister.[50] Jordan seemed to enjoy his new role and liked the cloak-and-dagger atmosphere in which the secret talks were conducted. He made secret trips to Paris where he used a wig, false beard and a cane to hide his identity.[51] Beheshti's representative at the talks was Hassan Ibrahim Habibi, a French-educated sociologist. Jordan managed to convince the radical mullahs that the Carter administration now recognized them as the real masters of Iran and was prepared to deal with them. Once this was done, formal negotiations, also conducted in secret, began. Assistant Secretary of State Warren Christopher represented the US side while Tehran was represented by Sadeq Tabataba'i, brother-in-law of Khomeini's son Ahmad.

Khomeini had transferred responsibility for solving the problem to the newly elected Islamic Majlis, which was dominated by the Beheshti faction. By September 1980 there was no obvious reason why the ordeal of the hostages should continue. The radical mullahs had drawn all the benefit they wanted from the crisis. It had helped them marginalize their rivals, dominate the parliament and appoint a prime minister of their choice. Further, the mullahs had humiliated the United States and established their revolution as the only movement capable of standing up to Washington in the Middle East. They did not need the Iranian assets that Carter had frozen in the United States – oil revenues were still very high in those days – but they knew that an agreement on the issue would boost their prestige in Iran and throughout the Muslim world.

Nevertheless, the mullahs remained true to their tradition of *tafseed*, which means trying to draw maximum profit from any situation. They were informed that Carter's chances of re-election were diminishing and that the president would, out of desperation, offer even more concessions. The architect of this delaying tactic was the cabinet's strongman, Behzad Nabavi, who insisted that Carter should be humiliated right to the end. The hostages were in the end released some twenty minutes after Ronald Reagan had been sworn in as Carter's successor at the White House on 20 January 1981. Reagan's tough talk during the campaign and his assertion that he would not hesitate to order the bombing of Tehran and Qom may have also been factors in the mullahs' decision to offer a sign of goodwill to the new administration at the outset.

The mullahs succeeded in forcing Carter to play the game their way: they dragged him into secret negotiations, often conducted by dubious intermediaries in an unhealthy atmosphere, and forced him to abandon his lofty principles of never making concessions to 'terrorists'. After Tabas, Carter's re-education continued as the president gave the go-ahead for covert operations against the Khomeini regime. Deeply hurt by the all-too-evident ill will and duplicity of the mullahs, who delighted in humiliating him, Carter had openly warned that even the release of the hostages would not wipe the slate clean between the United States and the Islamic Republic. Was Carter thinking about some form of revenge? There is no evidence to back such a suggestion. The president was nevertheless determined to make life as difficult for the mullahs as possible. He achieved this in part through the complex rules that were attached to the release of Iranian assets, a process that began in December 1980 and was not yet fully completed in 1988.[52]

8

BUSINESSMEN WITH NOBLE INTENTIONS

The safe return of the fifty-two hostages from Tehran appeared, to most Americans, as the end of an ordeal they could not wait to relegate to oblivion.[1] The 'who lost Iran?' controversy, which had played a part in the presidential election, was left to the specialists and to special interests. The new Republican administration of President Ronald Reagan saw no reason why it should keep alive an explosive issue that had contributed to Carter's downfall. Nevertheless it was no secret that the new administration and the Republican Party in general were convinced that Carter had played a crucial role in hastening the fall of the shah – one of the oldest and most loyal friends of the United States. By its failure to act in time and decisively to back the shah and by giving confusing signals that encouraged the shah's opponents and disheartened his supporters, Carter had paved the way for Khomeini's victory and all that followed – thus argued the more sanguine of the former president's critics.

The shah's death in Cairo in July 1980 had provided some of the senior Republicans with an occasion to show their strong disapproval of the way Carter had treated the fallen monarch.[2] Former presidents Richard Nixon and Gerald Ford attended the shah's 'state funeral' organized by Egypt's President Muhammad Anwar Sadat, then a popular figure in the United States because of his historic peacemaking with Israel. The Carter administration had disapproved of the move and had even advised some of the shah's former generals, who had already established contact with the CIA, not to attend the Cairo funeral. The shah was dead and buried, the agency told the generals and if you wish to play a future role in Iran you ought to keep your distance from him.[3] To be fair the attitude of the Carter administration towards the shah's funeral was largely dictated by considerations for the safety of the American hostages still held in Tehran. Further, the funeral came only three months after the abortive rescue mission that had ended in disaster in the Iranian desert. Carter did not wish to provoke further anger among the mullahs in Tehran by appearing to honour the late shah.

Pro-shah elements in Iran had prayed for Carter's defeat in the American presidential election in the hope that his rival, Reagan, would help them get rid of the ayatollah. The more pious among them sacrificed sheep and lit candles in holy shrines so that the Republican candidate would win. A dervish magician was commissioned to spend forty days in seclusion, praying for Reagan's victory in the holy city of Mashhad. He was later to be executed on Khomeini's orders as an enemy not of the American Democratic Party but of Allah Himself.[4]

The rallying of pro-shah forces inside and outside Iran was not, however, limited to ritual sacrifices for Reagan. In July 1980 royalist officers, especially from the air force, made what became a disastrous attempt at staging a *coup d'état*. The plan was for a commando unit to seize control of the Shahrokhi air base west of Tehran, enabling the group to capture the eighteen F4 fighters stationed there. Some of the fighters would then be flown over Tehran, less than six minutes' time away, to bomb Khomeini's residence in the hope of killing the ayatollah. This would be the signal to other units positioned in the capital to seize the radio and television stations and to arrest the leading mullahs and their associates. The next move would consist of a march on central Tehran by thousands of tough guys from the southern districts of the capital.

The plotters had organized themselves in a secret group called Neqab ('the Mask') and were led by two officers known for their courage and dedication: Major General Reza Mahdioun from the air force and Brigadier General Ayat Mohaqeqi from the ground forces. Liaison was assured by Colonel Bani Ameri, while an oil engineer, Ali Qadessi, headed the political support group.[5] The mystery man in the plan was one Manuchehr Suzani, who worked for an Irano-Israeli shipping company, Starline.[6] Suzani was put in charge of the operation's finances in the sense that, because of his connections with professional moneychangers on the black market, he could convert currency sent from Europe into Iranian money to be spent in Tehran. Part of the money in question, some $6 million, came from Shapour Bakhtiar, the shah's last prime minister, who had fled into exile and established himself in a Paris suburb. Where had the rest come from? There are different versions. The most probable source was the royal family. There are also suggestions that it was Baghdad which supplied the cash in question. Bakhtiar himself has said that the money came from a number of 'businessmen with noble intentions'. The phrase was to become part of the exiled Iranians' political jargon and soon came to serve as a euphemism for a CIA connection.

At any rate the 'Mask' plot was quickly discovered and stopped before it could get off the ground. More than three hundred people were arrested and some eighty of them were later executed on Khomeini's orders. The executions were followed by a fresh purge of the armed forces, weakening them even further only weeks before Iraq invaded Iran. A few of those involved escaped into exile. Suzani was one of them. Wild accusations then began to be hurled in all directions. Some fingers were pointed at Suzani. Had he informed the Israelis of the plot? Suzani had been in touch with Mossad in Tehran for years. But why should he do so and why should the Israelis tell Khomeini? Another hypothesis was that Suzani informed one of his partners in the shipping company and the latter, in turn, told British intelligence, which passed on the information to Khomeini. The partner in question was known for his British connections and was a dual Irano- British national. Still another theory was that Mossad told the CIA, which told Khomeini as a means of convincing the ayatollah that Washington was not only not plotting against the Islamic regime but was even ready to help provided the hostages' issue was resolved. This theory seemed a bit farfetched, especially in view of the fact that some of those involved in the plot had provided the backbone of the failed rescue mission organized by President Carter. Why would Washington want to see its friends fall into the hands of the ayatollah? The KGB was also accused. It was pointed out that Nureddin Kianuri, the Tudeh Party leader and a key KGB figure in Tehran, had his one and only audience with Khomeini two days before the 'Mask' plot was discovered.

Suzani featured prominently in most accounts of why the plot failed. Suzani, however, blamed Bakhtiar, who supposedly boasted to the Iraqis about his 'imminent coup in Tehran' in order to strengthen his hand in negotiations concerning Baghdad's financial support to his cause.[7] At any rate Bakhtiar did not seem to suspect Suzani at the time and it was Suzani who was put in charge of organizing the flight of many of Bakhtiar's colleagues and friends from Iran.[8] Qadessi, the political brain behind the plot, claimed that Bakhtiar was contacted so that he could secure future diplomatic support from the United States to counter any Soviet move against a new anti-Khomeini regime.[9] Bakhtiar, however, claimed that he had masterminded the plot and that it failed because of 'treason by some elements'.[10]

The plot, although it failed lamentably, heartened the royalists, who staged several demonstrations in Tehran and other major cities. Hoping against all reason, they still expected the Carter administration to come to their support. Abroad, a series of marches and memorial services were organized to mark the shah's death.

The CIA established contact with General Gholam-Ali Oveissi through an Iranian agent, Mansur Rafizadeh, in December 1979.[11] Oveissi, who had been martial law administrator in Tehran in the summer of 1978, was at the time seen as a strongman likely to lead some form of military action against the mullahs. Initial financial support for him was provided by Empress Farah and Princess Ashraf, but much of this, amounting to some $2.5 million, was siphoned away by middlemen who seized the opportunity of buying themselves luxury villas in southern California. Oveissi was then approached by the Iraqis, who provided him with $18 million.[12] Once again, however, much of this disappeared in the form of 'commission' to the Iraqi officials involved and some of the Iranian adventurers who gathered around the general. The Iraqis also helped Bakhtiar, providing an initial $11.5 million.[13] In August 1980 Bakhtiar and Oveissi made separate visits to Baghdad. Both were told to try to win support from Washington. They both told the Iraqi leader, Saddam Hussein, that Khomeini's regime was shaky and would fall provided a push was given from the outside.[14]

The scenario worked out in Baghdad envisaged a quick Iraqi military victory over Iran followed by the formation of a 'provisional national government' headed by Bakhtiar in the southwestern Iranian city of Ahvaz.[15] Iraq would thus capture parts of the Iranian province of Khuzestan, leaving Khomeini to fight it out against his domestic opponents. Iraqi-backed Kurds, led by Abdul-Rahman Qassemlou, would seize control of the Iranian Kurdistan, while simultaneous revolts would also be staged by Baluchi tribesmen and communist guerillas in the Gorgan Plain, which was inhabited by Turkomans.

Washington was certainly fully aware of these plans but did nothing to stop them beyond advising both Oveissi and Bakhtiar to disengage themselves from Baghdad if and when Iraq invaded Iran.[16] It is possible to argue that Carter could not have guessed at the time that Iraq's adventure would lead to one of the longest and bloodiest wars in contemporary history, threatening the balance of power in a crucially sensitive region. Further, Washington's influence in Baghdad at the time was minimal. Nevertheless, the administration was certainly guilty of taking the whole matter rather light-heartedly. It is even possible that part of the administration welcomed the Iraqi invasion as an added pressure on the ayatollah, forcing him to release the hostages. Carter's obsession with the problem of the hostages arguably prevented him from appreciating the gravity of the Iraqi adventure and moving in time, perhaps in concert with European and Arab allies, to stop it.

The Soviets, who enjoyed a strong position in Baghdad at the time, did not move either.[17] Perhaps they too believed that the Khomeini regime was fragile and that its fall would enhance the position of their own supporters in a chaotic situation in Iran.

As a matter of basic policy, the Carter administration systematically discouraged covert operations against Iran, with the exception of routine intelligence work, which was done with the help of British, Israeli, West German and South Korean services. At the same time, however, it did not succeed in developing a coherent view of the post-revolution situation not only in Iran but throughout West Asia and the Middle East as a whole – a situation which was further complicated by the Soviet intervention in Afghanistan and the Arab boycott of Egypt because of the Camp David accords with Israel. Carter dismissed Khomeini's exiled opponents as irrelevant and as caricatures of the White Russians before them.[18] Carter's views were more than confirmed by the disarray among the exiles and the high percentage of professional adventurers who posed as their spokesmen. The hare-brained schemes which some of the exiles presented in the hope of securing US support did not help their cause either.[19]

The Reagan administration, on the other hand, had no qualms about making full use of covert action as a necessary and legitimate means of pursuing political goals abroad. Some of Reagan's advisers also believed that the fall of the shah had been largely engineered by the Soviets and that Carter had played into Moscow's hand by ignoring the East–West aspect of the crisis in Iran.[20] The thought of the Soviets sweeping down to the Persian Gulf and thus threatening nearly 70 per cent of the crude oil imported by the West remained a constant nightmare of the Reagan administration.

The CIA, under its new director, William Casey, a close friend of the new president, had to build up its Iranian assets from scratch. It had no means of directly influencing developments in Iran beyond a short-wave transmitter provided by Egypt for a daily half-hour broadcast in Persian beamed to Iran. The broadcast, which identified itself as Radio Vatan (Motherland Radio), was generally aimed at warning Iranians about Moscow's 'evil intentions' and inviting them to maintain close ties with the West as a means of preventing their country from being swallowed up by 'the successors of the Tsars'.

During the period when the Carter administration avoided any meaningful dialogue with anti-Khomeini exiles, except for the purpose of gathering information, contact with the Iranian opposition groups abroad was ensured by a number of American businessmen, senators and congressmen who were convinced that the president's policy would end up with Soviet domination of the region. One man who played a key role in boosting the morale of the exiles and encouraging them to get organized in time to benefit from changes in Washington was Raymond Mason, an old friend and admirer of the late shah. He succeeded in persuading many former officials to get together and to renew contacts inside Iran and lay the foundations for future cooperation with a United States that was expected to become active once again. Senator Barry Goldwater (R. Arizona), who later chaired the Senate's Intelligence Committee, was less successful. He received five former ministers of the shah in his suite at the Plaza Athene Hotel in Paris during a 1980 visit and blasted them for not having fought to prevent Khomeini from seizing power.[21] 'The American senator had not even bothered to get properly dressed and received us in his silk dressing gown,' said one of those present. 'We were disappointed because he was obviously unable to understand what had happened in Iran.'[22]

Another intermediary was retired Rear Admiral Max Morris, also a firm believer that the United States was duty-bound to help Iran get rid of Khomeini. It was Morris who eventually put Bakhtiar in contact with the Reagan NSC.[23]

The Carter administration had often toyed with the idea of making a deal with at least one of the factions which together formed the Khomeini coalition. It was with this view that Cyrus Hashemi, an Iranian businessman close to the mullahs, had been allowed to use his office in New York City's Grace Building for the purpose of obtaining arms and materiel for the Islamic Republic. Strictly speaking Hashemi's activities were illegal. The Carter administration had imposed an arms embargo on both Iran and Iraq and the Reagan administration did not reverse that. The Reagan administration, however, rejected any idea of coming to terms with the mullahs and hoped for their eventual overthrow. Hashemi's office was closed and he himself forced to flee the United States despite efforts by his lawyer, the former Republican attorney-general, Elliot Richardson, to show that Hashemi was not involved in any illegal activities.[24]

The main difficulty the new administration faced in its hope of one day being able to destabilize the Khomeini regime was the absence of a credible alternative to the ayatollah.

It was with the aim of creating a moderate, broad-based alternative to the Khomeini regime, as a springboard for future action in Iran, that the CIA encouraged the creation of a 'council of coordination' in Paris in the spring of 1981. Oveissi remained a key member together with the leaders of several political parties and groups in exile. Bakhtiar was left out for two reasons: Washington saw him as too closely linked with Baghdad at a time when the United States still believed that Iraq was a virtual satellite of Moscow, and some of the nationalist politicians objected to Bakhtiar's 'collaboration with the Iraqi enemy'.[25] Contact between the group and Washington was assured by Ali Sayfpour Fatemi, alias Shahin, a former professor of economics at the University of Akron, Ohio, who had been close to Robert Kennedy in the 1960s.[26] Limited financial support, in the form of seed money, was provided by the agency in the hope that the group would raise more funds among Iranian exiles.[27] It is quite possible that, with the exception of Oveissi, the members of the group were unaware of the exact nature of relations with the agency at that time.

The group failed to get off the ground and its attempts to turn Grand Ayatollah Kazem Shariatmadari, then in the holy city of Qom, into a focus of opposition to Khomeini did not go beyond salon talks.[28] Another scenario based on mobilizing support from the Tehran bazaar in the name of a former member of the Mossadeq government was also unsuccessful because the politician in question demanded 'personal guarantees from President Reagan' before he would even consider playing a part.

In the summer of 1981 the monarchists created some excitement by hijacking one of six French-built gunboats on their way to Iran from the port of Cherbourg in Normandy. The operation was led by a former commander of the Iranian navy under the shah, Rear Admiral Mir-Kamaleddin Mir-Habib-Allahi. Shaking off the French patrol boats which immediately began to chase them, the pirates took the boat *Tabarzin* (*Hatchet*) on a long trip to Rabat, the Moroccan capital, where the shah's son then resided. The young crown prince, declaring that he would condone no act which harmed Iran's military position in the war against Iraq, ordered the pirates to return to France and hand over the gunboat to French authorities for transfer to Iran. This was done and the monarchists were able to show Washington that they should not be written off too quickly.

The cause of the Iranian monarchists was also defended by President Sadat, King Hussein of Jordan and King Hassan of Morocco. The Saudis, on the other hand, remained hostile to the Pahlavis until 1982, while the Iraqis were angered by the young shah's nationalist attitude to the Gulf War.[29]

The shah's son, living in a modest villa on Rabat's seaside, attracted the sympathy and affection of many of his late father's friends and supporters. Former US presidents Nixon and Ford met him in his villa Tamara during their visits to Rabat. King Hassan encouraged many of his foreign guests to call on the prince, known to his supporters as 'the young shah'. US Secretary of State Alexander Haig, Attorney-General William Clark, the United States Information Agency (USIA) director Charles Wick, a close friend of President Reagan, and, finally, the CIA director William Casey all called on the young shah. Another visitor was Henry Kissinger, who remained a trusted adviser despite his stated reservations about the chances of a restoration in Iran.

As early as 1980 some of the friends of the royal family had sounded out Saudi Arabia about the possibility of securing financial support for the young shah's cause. The Saudis had made it plain that they would not back any anti-Khomeini group unless such a move was recommended either by the Iraqis or by Washington. It was in response to an Iraqi suggestion that the Saudis agreed to receive several Iranian opposition figures, notably Bakhtiar. They later contributed the sum of $5.5 million to Bakhtiar's operations after the transaction had been approved by Washington in the form of a verbal message delivered to the Saudi ambassador in the United States by a foreign policy aide to Vice-President George Bush. [30] The transfer of the funds was arranged through Ali Shaybani, a Saudi businessman who had previously rendered a similar service to another anti-Khomeini group inside Iran.[31] The Saudis had pinned their hopes on developments inside Iran itself and believed that former Premier Mehdi Bazargan and his principal aide, Ibrahim Yazdi, could play a role in ending direct rule by the mullahs. The Saudis maintained contact with the Bazargan party through a Lebanese journalist, who was a frequent visitor to Tehran, and also by occasional meetings in Switzerland and Belgium.

In their search for a charismatic personality capable of being built up against Khomeini, the White House and the NSC also sounded out Rear Admiral Ahmad Madani, who had just fled abroad with the help of Bakhtiar and Suzani. It was on American advice that the Saudi Crown Prince Abdullah received Madani in Geneva during a private visit in the summer of 1982. Madani had previously arranged for some seed money to be made available to him through personal connections with wealthy Bahrainis. Now the Saudi crown prince, persuaded that Madani was Washington's choice, signed a $4.2 million cheque for the rear admiral's campaign. But no sooner had the money been received than a couple of 'businessmen with noble intentions' called on the exiled rear admiral to tell him how to spend part of it. The two pretended to be 'in direct contact' with the White House and established their credentials by giving Madani details of his own meeting with Abdullah. They explained that the US government was unable to put its hand into its own kitty because of 'legal complications' and that Saudi resources had to be used instead. The two men urged Madani to invest in encouraging tribal uprisings against Khomeini in the provinces of Kurdistan, Fars and Baluchistan.[32] Madani agreed provided that he retained his own freedom of action. Over the next two years he spent most of the money made available to him on raising tribal armies in Iran's peripheral provinces. The Qashqa'i clan in Fars, the Qazi clan in Kurdistan and a number of Baluchi chiefs living in exile in Pakistan received a total of over $3 million in the two years that followed but made absolutely no move. The money had been provided for the purchase of arms and supplies for tribal warriors reportedly ready to raise the standard of revolt. But a disappointed Madani was to find out that there were no such warriors and not a single penny had been spent on fighting Khomeini: he had financed a ghost army whose chiefs resided on the French Riviera and in southern California.[33]

By 1982 the business of opposing Khomeini from abroad had developed into a prosperous industry employing several thousand people in Western Europe, the United States, various Middle Eastern countries and Turkey. The main source of finance for this industry remained Iraq, which spent an estimated $150 million between 1979 and 1982. A part of this, maybe as much as 30 per cent, never reached the Iranian exiles and was pocketed by Iraqi and other Arab intermediaries in Europe. In the same period the Saudis put in a relatively modest $12 million. Of this, $5 million was earmarked for the young shah's supporters and was channelled through the Moroccan court after Washington told Riyadh that this was a good idea. The Moroccan intermediaries kept half the Saudi donation in lieu of payment for the cost of hosting the shah's son and his entourage as well as building a sumptuous villa for him on the outskirts of Rabat. The young shah never lived in the villa and soon left Morocco for the United States. The rest of the Saudi money also quickly disappeared when two of the late shah's former advisers managed to persuade the staff of the new shah to invest in a plan of revolt in Tehran. The two advisers claimed they could mobilize up to a million people to march in favour of the monarchy in the Iranian capital on the birthday anniversary of the late shah. That date came and went and nothing happened and the two men simply disappeared into thin air with the money.[34]

The exiled opposition invested in maintaining three clandestine radio stations broadcasting in Persian. Two of them, Radio Iran and the Voice of Iran, operated from Baghdad and reflected the view of the supporters of Oveissi and of Bakhtiar respectively. A third radio station belonged to the monarchists and was run by the former director of the Iranian Football Association, Kambiz Atabay, who also handled some of the money that Empress Farah invested in oppositional activities.[35] The various opposition groups also published weekly or monthly bulletins and organized occasional gatherings in Paris. The French capital served as the nerve centre for exile activities.

This was strongly encouraged by the French socialist government which came into power in 1981 as a means of helping Iraq and investing in what they believed could be the future government of Iran.

Washington kept an eye on the exiles' activities and generally encouraged them without, however, getting directly involved until 1983. The Soviets also showed interest by dispatching Victor Louis, their globe-trotting 'journalist', to take the measure of some of the leaders in Paris.[36] It is also possible that Moscow received additional information on exile Iranian activities through the Indian services. One of India's ambassadors in West Europe remained in close touch with some of the exile leaders until 1983.

In its first two years the Reagan administration, unable to devise a long-term policy on Iran, remained a peripheral player, mostly reacting to developments and gradually being sucked into the absurd world of sterile intrigues. With the State Department practically neutralized and left to play for meagre gains in the form of broader Islamic smiles at The Hague joint commission, where representatives of the two sides haggled over the settlement of financial claims, the CIA and the NSC made Iran policy their own preserve. The State Department had managed to make at least one point stick: Washington should do nothing that might contribute to Iran's defeat by Iraq. The architect of that policy had been Alexander Haig, who was strongly influenced by the Israeli analysis of the situation in the Persian Gulf which pointed out Iran's geopolitical importance for the West while emphasizing Iraq's close ties with Moscow as a permanent threat to Western interests.

The Reagan administration had therefore turned a blind eye to supplies of arms and materiel to Iran by various allies. Turkey became a major channel for arms exports to Iran, who also maintained a seventy-five-man military mission in London charged with arms procurement. By 1983, however, the situation had changed. Haig was gone, replaced by George Shultz, who was more sympathetic to the views of the Saudis for whom a Khomeinist Iran menaced the whole region. At the same time it had become evident that Iraq would have no chance of defeating Iran; rather, it was Baghdad that faced defeat. A third factor that helped change the administration's attitude was the growing militancy of Khomeinist elements in the Gulf and Lebanon, where they began directly threatening US interests. The ayatollah was by then convinced that Reagan, despite his tough talk during the presidential campaign, was as vulnerable to acts of terrorism as Carter had been.

Early in 1983 the president signed a secret CIA 'finding' authorizing support for covert activities against the Khomeini regime. A finding is a device designed to enable the president to engage his own responsibility for secret operations in certain exceptional circumstances. The Findings Law was passed by Congress in 1974 as a compromise in the wake of the Vietnam and Watergate upheavals which led to rivalry between Congress and the president over the formulation of foreign policy in an atmosphere of general dislike for covert operations. The Act enabled the president to withhold information from Congress for a reasonable length of time but insisted that he must obey precise rules in authorizing any secret operations. The finding on Iran gave the CIA leave to help with the creation of a moderate political force capable of providing an alternative to the ayatollah's regime and bringing the Gulf war to an end.[37]

The phrase 'moderate alternative' excluded the People's Mujahedeen, a leftist Islamic group whose leader, Massoud Rajavi, had fled into exile together with Bani-Sadr in 1981. The agency approached Bani-Sadr with a view to persuading him to distance himself from the Mujahedeen. The agent, who used the name William Foster, informed the dismissed president that a number of 'businessmen with noble intentions' were prepared to finance him provided he broke with the Mujahedeen.[38] The break came a year later when Bani-Sadr and Rajavi quarrelled about the latter's decision to collaborate with Iraq in the Gulf War. By that time, however, the agency was apparently persuaded that Bani-Sadr did not have a constituency of his own.

The choice of a leader to head a united front of moderate forces fell upon Ali Amini, the octogenerian former premier who had been a close friend of the United States and well known to the agency for more than thirty years. Amini had a number of advantages. In 1981 he had been the only leader in exile to succeed in raising substantial funds among Iranians for an anti-Khomeini campaign. At that time he had hoped to bring together Madani, Hassan Nazih, Khomeini's oil director who had also fled into exile, and a number of other former critics of the shah, as well as some of the leading figures of the *ancien régime*. Amini's hopes had been dashed as a result of personal jealousies among the group[39] and he had once again faded into the background, spending most of his time at his lakeside home in Geneva. When encouraged to step forward again to launch his Front for the Salvation of Iran (FSI), Amini had to be reassured that Washington was genuine in its desire to help the Iranians get rid of Khomeini. The agent who established the initial contact was one S. D. Julp, who had known Amini for more than two decades.[40] He advised Amini to move closer to the monarchists as the only substantial force that remained on the right of exile Iranian politics.

The FSI therefore declared itself a supporter of the monarchist constitution of 1906. Amini believed that the United States had prepared a long-term plan for overthrowing Khomeini and that the FSI was only expected to prepare itself to form a provisional government. 'The green light has come from Washington,' Amini began to tell his visitors. Oveissi also had the same impression and soon joined Amini's FSI. Bakhtiar refused to join and stuck to his own National Resistance Movement (NRM). Nevertheless he agreed to sign a joint declaration with Amini stating that both wanted to see constitutional monarchy established in Iran.

The irony of the situation, however, was that the young shah himself refused to give his benediction to these new efforts which, were they to succeed, would benefit him more than anyone else. He could not forgive Bakhtiar for the latter's 'unacceptable links with Iraq', while he objected to Amini on the grounds that the old politician had a 'history of association with foreign powers'.[41] The new movement was a curious mixture. Its main driving force was Shahin Fatemi, a dynamic organizer and passionate campaigner for the monarchy. But Amini's closest political adviser was Islam Kazemieh, who had been an ardent Khomeini supporter and had strongly endorsed the seizure of the American embassy in Tehran in 1979. Kazemieh had also edited the weekly *Jombesh* (*Movement*) in Tehran until his flight into exile in 1981 and had built himself a reputation as anti-American. Further, he had been an unsuccessful parliamentary candidate on a list backed by the Mujahedeen. But once in Paris he readily admitted that he had been mistaken all along and that Iran could never be happy without a monarchy and friendly ties with the West.[42]

The group of 'businessmen with noble intentions' were in a position to spend something like $400,000 a month in Paris. The Amini, Bakhtiar and Oveissi groups received $100,000 each. The rest was spent on smaller groups as well as on 'babysitters' who exercised a distant and generally unobtrusive control over the ill-defined project. Bakhtiar was advised to spend his share on the military side of the operation only. This was supervised by Brigadier General Ali Shahrdar, who used two bases in Turkey. Bakhtiar was also told not to let the Iraqis, who continued to support him occasionally, know about his new source of finance.[43]

Most exiles believed that the Paris operation was no more than a smokescreen for more serious activities inside Iran. The Americans seemed to believe that the provision of a regular flow of money would on its own be translated into genuine political activity in Iran. They looked like people with money to throw away. The exiles, for their part, thought that all they had to do was posture while other, secret organizations run by the Americans would do the real job of overthrowing the ayatollah. As a result American money unwittingly neutralized the few groups that, had they been left to find their own way, might have put up something of a fight against the mullahs. The flow of easy money had one more unwelcome effect: it attracted a large number of adventurers and conmen who managed to siphon off the bulk of the estimated $30 million that the 'businessmen with noble intentions' spent on anti-Khomeini groups in Paris. Easy money caused still further trouble by encouraging in-fighting often provoked by greed. When the Iraqis learned about the new situation they cut off their contributions to all groups except the Mujahedeen.[44] The Saudis made a few more occasional contributions, all recommended by the USA, but also decided to let Washington spend its own money as much as possible.

The double misunderstanding under which the exiles and their American benefactors operated continued until 1985, when the 'businessmen with noble intentions' began to worry about a singular lack of return on their investment. The opposition had simply pocketed the money and done strictly nothing of any consequence. It is quite possible that, with budget-cutting coming into vogue in Washington, someone thought of taking a closer look at the accounts. The opposition for its part was surprised when the real work expected of the Americans failed to materialize and began to feel dispirited.

Rumours began to circulate that Washington had used the exiles only as a bargaining counter in secret negotiations with the mullahs of Tehran. As the Americans began to demand some concrete results, the various groups involved came up with a variety of daredevil plans and invented achievements. The Bakhtiar group suggested staging a military uprising in a north Iranian town not far from the Soviet border. The suggestion apparently sent a chill down the spines of the few people who believed the group capable of any such adventure.

A group of 'international professional killers' approached the Bakhtiar group with a set of suggestions ranging from a plan to murder Khomeini in his bedroom for $100 million to blowing the Islamic parliament up for half that price. In both cases the 'businessmen with noble intentions' reacted negatively and pointed out that US law did not permit planning to assassinate foreign politicians.[45] The Bakhtiar group managed what it thought was a scoop and contacted Hojat al-Islam Abdul-Majid Maadikhah, Khomeini's minister of Islamic Guidance, during a visit to Paris in 1983. The ambitious mullah appeared amenable to the idea of playing a role in the formation of a future 'moderate' government. But he was dismissed on his return to Tehran and never allowed to rebuild his political career.

Unable to shine in action, the exiled groups were gradually turned into additional means for gathering information about Iran. But here too their performance was less than bright. They had no skills for the task and, lacking the necessary contacts inside the country, had little access to much meaningful intelligence. As a result they began to supply a steady flow of rumours, tidbits, speculations and personal dreams presented as hard fact. Because they all belonged to the same microcosm, they succeeded in making their tales agree so as to prevent any useful cross-checking by their American friends.

Some lone adventurers went even further and claimed credit for anti-Khomeini acts committed inside Iran by local groups that were in no way connected with them. Thus a communist guerilla attack on Amol, a town north of Tehran, in 1984 was presented as a right-wing pro-American move and used as an excuse for demanding substantial sums of money from the 'businessmen with noble intentions'. Another example of cashing in on someone else's feats came in 1986 when a group of Mir-Lashari tribesmen seized control of Zahedan, the principal city in Baluchistan, for three days. Five Paris-based groups claimed this as their own 'triumph'.

Exile infighting was also rampant and in some cases may have permitted the ayatollah's secret service, reconstituted thanks to former agents of SAVAK, to infiltrate the opposition circles. The possibility of Soviet infiltration of these circles could not be excluded either as the supposedly clandestine organizations worked from expensive offices in the most fashionable parts of Paris and paid little or no attention to security. What is certain is that the ayatollah kept a close watch on the activities of his opponents in Paris. Vahid Gorji, a man identified by the French police as the linchpin of the Khomeinist intelligence network in Europe, bought a sumptuous apartment near a building where Ali Amini had his residence on Avenue Suffren. The Party of Allah, Khomeini's international terror organization, had offices in the same high-rise building that housed Bakhtiar's planning and propaganda units in southern Paris.

Had the ayatollah been a different person he might have dismissed the activities of his exiled opponents as largely irrelevant. But Khomeini was known for his vision of existence as the sum of conspiracies and was easily persuaded that Washington was plotting to overthrow him. He reacted in two ways: by hitting American targets in the Persian Gulf and Lebanon and by dispatching death squads to dispose of some of his better-known opponents.[46]

In the universe of intrigue, double cross and falsehood created by easy money and misperceptions of intentions all round, the emergence of internecine feuds was no surprise. By the spring of 1985 the FSI was split into three factions. The main faction, led by Amini, wanted to

broaden the base of the front and coordinate its activities with those of
the Bazargan group inside Iran. A meeting between Kazemieh and one
of Bazargan's associates in Frankfurt in November 1985 was to mark
the beginning of a new alliance.[47] The breakaway faction was led by
Shahin Fatemi, who rejected any deal with former members of the
Khomeini regime and insisted that all those who had cooperated with
the ayatollah should be tried for treason once the Khomeini regime
was overthrown. A third faction, led by Kambiz Mahmoudi, a former
vice-president of the Asian Broadcasting Union (ABU), controlled the
FSI's radio station, which transmitted from Cairo, and advocated a
straight return to monarchism. The situation was rendered more
difficult when the value of the dollar began to decline, and the front,
whose financial experts had speculated that the American currency
would continue its upward trend, reported huge losses. The split
became inevitable and the Fatemi faction left the front blaming
'American ineptitude and meddling' for most of their troubles.[48]

The split did not improve the work of the FSI. In the year that
followed the front reported only three major actions. It had printed
and distributed a million copies of a fake Iranian postal stamp
showing the faces of Amini and the young shah. It had also recruited
the son of a fairly influential ayatollah in Tehran, who arranged a
meeting between an FSI representative and Khomeini's grandson,
Hossein, in Switzerland.[49] Hossein, who had often criticized his
grandfather's harsh policies, was believed amenable to the idea of
improving Iran's ties with the United States. Finally the FSI had
recruited a French journalist, Hélène Cofi, and dispatched her to Iran,
together with a guide and a photographer on a month-long mission.
She entered Iran illegally across the Pakistani border and was expected
to 'bring with her valuable information'.[50]

Confidence in American ability to design and implement covert
operations without suffering leaks at some stage remained low
throughout the exile microcosm. It was generally believed that the
USA, because of its own domestic problems, would not be able to
operate as a major power beyond flexing its military muscle. 'America
cannot keep a secret' was the motto of many of those who worked
with the United States. This view was confirmed when several
American newspapers published reports in 1984 which came close to
exposing all the supposedly clandestine operations that the CIA was at
the time engaged in with regard to Iran.

Another factor that undermined confidence in Washington's ability
to have a serious impact on developments in Iran was the periodic
changes of policy which pointed to wayward planning or a lack of
tenacity. At times, for example, the 'businessmen with noble in-

tentions' showed a keen interest in military officers in exile, giving the impression that the men in uniform might be looked upon as future saviours of the country. At other times establishing contact with the mullahs would be advocated by the American babysitters as the surest means of helping Iran achieve a moderate government. The exiled groups would go along with every change of mood in Washington, regarding the American way of doing things with maximum cynicism. The Americans paid and had the right to set the tune. This view was at times translated into scenes of pure farce. Exiled mullahs who had left Iran for a variety of personal reasons were introduced to the 'businessmen with noble intentions' in supposedly ultra-secret meetings as 'close associates of Khomeini'.[51] And on at least one occasion one of the exiled groups employed a professional Iranian actor to play the role of a high-ranking ayatollah from Tehran at a secret meeting with two Americans in Frankfurt, which was often used for highly sensitive rendezvous.[52] The Americans were regarded as capricious children: there was no point in reasoning with them. All one had to do was to silence them with a bit of candy which they asked for every now and then.

By the end of 1985 the entire operation seemed to be in deep crisis. The FSI management was handed over to Manuchehr Ganji, a former minister of the shah, who immediately initiated a thorough purge, dismissed more than four fifths of the front's employees and established a new system of accounting that produced monthly financial reports.[53] Ganji later abolished the front altogether and created a new group called the Flag of Freedom Organization which offered a more militant monarchist platform. But by the time he had began operations in earnest the Irangate scandal had already hit the headlines, changing the context of American operations concerning Iran and pushing the Reagan administration in new and unknown directions.

At the end of 1986 budget-cutting measures in Washington led to a 50 per cent reduction in the sums made available to Bakhtiar.[54] The saving thus achieved was used to create a financial relationship with the Mujahedeen group's representatives in Paris. This, according to French intelligence sources, was done within the framework of cooperation against Khomeinist terrorist activities in Western Europe and the United States. In 1987 the Mujahedeen established their credentials as a serious source of intelligence with the DGSE, the French equivalent of the CIA, by providing information that led to the dismantling of a major Khomeinist terror network in France.[55] The Mujahedeen also established strong credentials inside the United States by helping the FBI track down Khomeinist activists in California, New York and the Washington DC area.[56] Regular contributions of between $50,000 and $100,000 a month were made to the Mujahedeen office in Paris from 'private' US sources, starting in October 1986.[57]

The absence of a well-coordinated policy towards Iran meant that the various agencies of the United States government pursued different policies and gave conflicting signals. The State Department was content to wait and see. All it was concerned about was limiting the scope of the Gulf War and leaving the rest to internal developments in Iran. Allies and friends were occasionally used for the purpose of sounding out the Iranians about an eventual *rapprochement* with Washington or to warn the mullahs against long-term Soviet designs in the region. The department's patient attitude was in sharp contrast with the NSC's activism, which became increasingly marked under Robert McFarlane. The NSC, unlike the State Department, which generally avoided the exile opposition kept in close touch with Amini, Bakhtiar, Rajavi and other leaders through Howard Teischer, its Middle East specialist. All three leaders mentioned held secret meetings with McFarlane and his successor, Admiral John Poindexter, either in Washington or in Paris between 1985 and 1986.

It was also the NSC that tried to create a broad anti-Khomeini front with the semi-secret Hojatieh Society as its main component. Hojatieh, a right-wing Muslim movement, had been created in the 1950s to combat Baha'ism in Iran, but by 1983 had turned into a focal point of opposition to Khomeini. Anxious to prevent the Hojatieh from emerging as an alternative source of religious authority, Khomeini asked its leaders to disband the society or face dire consequences. The Hojatieh leaders complied by formally announcing the suspension of the society's activities. But their nationwide network remained intact and continued as a semi-secret organization with a strong presence in Tehran, Shiraz and Isfahan. Two Hojatieh representatives travelled to Washington at the NSC's invitation in July 1985.[58] But by that time Khomeini had ordered a crackdown on the society and had thrown many of its more active members into prison. The NSC also leaned heavily on Egypt, Jordan and Saudi Arabia to intensify their activities against the ayatollah. But the Arabs as a whole remained deeply suspicious of Washington's motives and were afraid of repeating what they termed 'the Rome disaster'. This referred to a plan for a *coup d'état* in Tehran in 1982 in which Ghotbzadeh and a group of monarchist officers had come together with the blessings of Grand Ayatollah Shariatmadari. The Saudis had provided the financial support needed – some $25 million, paid into separate Swiss accounts on different occasions over several months. The Saudis had informed the NSC, which had asked to contact the group with a view to offering advice and support. The plotters, informed by the Saudis, dispatched one of their leaders to Rome for a meeting with an NSC official.[59] The meeting was leaked and the plot was discovered. The man who had met the NSC official in Rome was shot, together with Ghotbzadeh, for plotting to kill Khomeini.[60]

The CIA for its part tried to recruit some of Khomeini's ambassadors abroad. Attempts in that direction were made in the case of Khomeini's ambassador to the United Nations, Sa'eed Raja'i-Khorassani, in 1985 and 1986. Raja'i-Khorassani, a supporter of *rapprochement* between the Islamic Republic and Washington, was, however, later accused of having tried to steal a raincoat from Alexander's, a New York store. Khomeini's ambassador to the Vatican, Hadi Khosrowshahian, a mullah, was also targeted as a promising case and contacted on a number of occasions, notably through the agency's Iranian contacts in Rome.[61] Probably aware of the potential danger to his ambassador, Khomeini recalled Khosrowshahian to Tehran and gave him the job of coordinating the Qom-based organization for the worldwide Islamic campaign. Another target was Ali Shams-Ardakani, Khomeini's ambassador to Kuwait, who had spent years in the United States. Once again Khomeini reacted by recalling his ambassador. This led to the break-up of Ardakani's marriage as his Palestinian wife, Ghida, refused to live in Islamic Iran.[62]

One man the Americans very much wanted to lay their hands on was Hojat al-Islam Mohammad Mussavi-Khoiniha, the radical mullah who had led the students during the occupation of the US embassy in Tehran. In 1982, 1983 and 1984 Khoiniha, who then led Iranian pilgrims to Mecca, was arrested by Saudi police and questioned for several hours on each occasion after being accused of causing public disorder in the holy city. Tehran was convinced that Khoiniha's arrest had been suggested to the Saudis by Washington in a bid to discover the radical mullah's true identity. The CIA was convinced that Khoiniha was a trained and seasoned KGB agent and wanted to verify this theory through carefully devised questions that were put to him by the Saudi police during a total of some seventeen hours of interrogation.[63]

The Saudis also cooperated with the Bakhtiar group in the production of a Persian-language daily for distribution among Iranian pilgrims during the Haj season in Mecca and Medina. The enterprise proved exceptionally successful and scores of pilgrims, including members of the Revolutionary Guards, contacted the group that produced the paper, offering to help by providing information from inside Iran. In later years the task of producing the Persian-language daily for Iranian pilgrims was given to a former ambassador of the shah to Riyadh.

The belief that the USA was prepared to back virtually any outlandish idea about Iran encouraged many who regarded every international crisis as an opportunity for making a profit. The mythical wealth of the late shah meant that his son instantly became a point of attraction for such types. A former BBC television reporter travelled to Rabat, where the shah's son then lived, in 1982 with a fifteen-page plan to overthrow Khomeini and restore the monarchy in Iran. He estimated the cost of such a feat to be no more than $1.5 million. Two Israeli businessmen, Al Schwimmer and Yaacov Nimrodi, came up with a more elaborate plan in which an army of 12,000 former Iranian soldiers and officers would be trained in the Sudan for the eventual conquest of Iran. The plan would cost $50 million, including a cash gift for President Jaafar al-Nimeiry, then the Sudanese head of state. The plan was torpedoed by the Moroccans, who said they were ready to train any number of Iranian freedom fighters without charging the kind of money the two Israelis were asking for.[64] Schwimmer and Nimrodi were to become key figures in the events that led to Irangate.

The effect of conflicting signals from Washington was compounded as a result of private initiatives taken by a number of influential Americans. Former President Gerald Ford, for example, attended a working dinner with Bakhtiar and Amini at New York's Hotel Pierre in 1984. Also present was Ford's national security adviser, General Brent Scowcroft. The subject of the discussions was the reconstruction of Iran and the revival of its economy after Khomeini's fall. Some of the Iranians present gained the impression that the task of over-throwing Khomeini with US support was already well advanced.[65] That impression was strengthened when two representatives of Chrysler contacted exiled Iranian businessmen in Paris in 1985 to discuss 'agency rights in the post-Khomeini period'.

The exile groups pulled off their biggest coup in 1986 when they managed to pirate an unused television channel in Tehran and broadcast an eleven-minute programme against Khomeini. The programme also included a message from the young shah in which he appealed to the people to continue resisting the mullahs. The pirate programme was telecast thanks to a miniature transmitter designed and built by the French company Thomson to specifications given by a former deputy director of Iranian television under the shah. The broadcast came in the middle of highly sensitive and secret negotiations between Washington and Tehran's strongman, Hojat al-Islam Ali-Akbar Hashemi Rafsanjani, the speaker of the Islamic Majlis. The broadcast and the tremendous publicity it received in the American media was seen by the Rafsanjani faction as a sign that Washington was not sincere in its offers to work out a *modus vivendi* with the mullahs of Tehran. In a public speech Rafsanjani said that no one had seen the 'alleged broadcast' and concluded that the publicity about it was only intended to worsen relations between the two countries. Confusion in Tehran became even greater when Voice of America refused to include reports about the pirate broadcast in its Persian-language news bulletin.[66] Rafsanjani must have concluded that one faction in Washington backed the secret talks while another wanted to sabotage them. But this was, in fact, what was happening in Tehran.

9

MAKING HISTORY AT BAR ALEXANDRE

The Bar Alexandre in Paris, near the Champs-Elysées, has been a favourite haunt of exiled dignitaries from the Middle East since the late 1940s. There, fallen princes, deposed presidents and dismissed ministers spend long lazy afternoons sunk in thick leather armchairs, listening to soft music, smoking fat cigars and sipping Chivas Regal. Many of them also dream of regaining their lost power and prestige or, if that proved an unattainable goal, as it often did, of making the money needed for financing a golden exile. Given the realities of the Middle East, a region where wars, revolutions and *coups d'état* are fairly frequent occurrences, some of the exiles soon ended up as arms merchants, helping to satisfy a persistent and growing demand.[1]

Those Iranian exiles who turned the bar into their headquarters from 1979 onwards proved no exception. They began by trying to launch a counter-revolution. Their champion was General Bahram Aryana, whose friends called him the Persian Napoleon. A group of Iranian businessmen financed his efforts to assemble an army in Turkey for an invasion of the northwestern Iranian province of Azarbaijan in 1981. The Turkish generals used the so-called 'Aryana factor' as a bargaining counter with the mullahs of Tehran and secured a $1000 million contract to supply food and medicine to Iran. In exchange they asked Aryana to return to Paris. A former minister under the shah who had played a key role in raising funds for Aryana was convinced that the Turks had acted on advice from Washington. The Turkish generals, who had staged a coup with US support, would not have launched a policy of helping the mullahs without getting the green light from Washington.

The former minister, Jamshid Vatandoust,[2] concluded that the new Reagan administration in Washington did not, contrary to earlier expectations, wish to destabilize the Khomeini regime for fear of unleashing a Soviet takeover of Iran. Vatandoust began thinking of a new strategy: he would establish direct contact between the mullahs and the West as a first step towards 'bringing Iran back from the brink of Soviet slavery'.[3] He decided to use trade as a means of infiltrating the ranks of the new rulers of Iran. In 1981 he set up a trading company in Paris with headquarters on Avenue Marceau. He had two partners. One was a former high-ranking member of the French intelligence service who had resigned because he found the new socialist government 'too anxious to help the Iraqis while France's interests lie with an Iranian victory in the Gulf War.'[4] The second partner was Manuchehr Ghorbanifar, also known as Suzani, who had become a friend of Vatandoust during the latter's brief stay in Turkey. Ghorbanifar was a born activist. He could not conceive of spending the rest of his life haunting the Bar Alexandre. He burned with ambition and a keen desire to 'make history'.[5] Years later he was to say: 'When I fled from Iran in 1980 I had the sensation that I was granted a second life. Now I was ready to do anything and everything needed to make this second life exciting and profitable.'[6] The idea of 'leaving Iran's fantastic wealth to a bunch of stinking mullahs' made his 'heart bleed with rage'. Ghorbanifar, known to his friends as Gorba, sounded out his Israeli connections on the possibility of establishing a channel to Washington. His partners in a shipping concern which he had managed in Iran before the revolution were Yad-Allah Shahbazi, an Irano-British dual national, and three Israelis, Saul Retz, Aharaon Raviv and retired Colonel Haim Rosenblith. His former partners made inquiries and reported that the Reagan administration was not interested. The American people wanted to forget Iran as a bad dream, they claimed.

Back in 1980 Gorba had been approached by a CIA agent, presenting herself as 'Lucy', in London, who wanted to recruit him to obtain information on Aryana's plans. But Gorba refused to accept 'a menial position' and would settle for nothing short of dealing directly with the White House.[7]

The Reagan administration, however, was genuinely keen to keep the Iranian issue on the back burner, at least for a while. It kept itself informed about exile activities and at times helped some counter-revolutionary groups, but it did not wish to get more directly involved. The mullahs had tried to open their own channel to the Reagan White House but had failed on two occasions. The first was in October 1980, before the US presidential election. Hadi Ha'eri, an Irano-American dual national, had then been asked by Khomeini's son Ahmad to contact 'the future ruler' of the United States with a view to discussing a 'fresh start'.[8] Ha'eri contacted Robert McFarlane, who was to become a key member of the NSC after the election, and through him met Richard Allen and Lawrence J. Silberman, two of Reagan's principal advisers at the time, at the Embassy Row Hotel in Washington. At the meeting Ha'eri said that Khomeini would delay the release of the American hostages in Tehran until after the election so that Reagan would be 'sure of getting elected'. The two men responded by describing Khomeini's policy as 'criminal and crazy' and said they were not prepared to discuss the US election with outsiders. Ha'eri did not report this negative reaction to Tehran because he was sincerely interested in improving Irano-US relations.[9]

The second attempt at a dialogue with the Reagan administration was made in March 1981 when Sadeq Tabataba'i, Ahmad Khomeini's brother-in-law and a key figure in the negotiations that ended the hostage crisis, asked the West German authorities to draw Washington's attention to the necessity of 'a new beginning with Iran'. Once again the US response was negative. 'Some wounds take long to heal,' the Americans reportedly told the Germans regarding the Iranian proposal.[10]

In October 1980 all indications were that Reagan, if elected, would adopt an aggressive policy towards the Islamic Republic as a means of restoring part of the American prestige that had badly suffered during the hostage crisis. Ex-President Bani-Sadr was subsequently to confirm this view and recalled that the mullahs had been dismayed by the prospects of the Reagan administration moving against them. According to Bani-Sadr the mullahs decided to delay the release of the hostages until after the US presidential elections as a gesture of goodwill towards Reagan.

One power determined not to let Iraq win the Gulf War was Israel, who had, for over thirty years, maintained close ties with Iran. The Iranian lobby in Israel was led by Yaacov Nimrodi, a businessman, who had for years served as Israeli deputy military attaché in Tehran. Nimrodi, whose real name was Yaqub Nimroudi, was an Iranian Jew born in Hamadan, west of Tehran. He had emigrated to Israel in 1946 after a brief spell at the Iranian Ministry of the Imperial Court, where he worked as a Persian-English translator. Those who knew Nimrodi well claimed that, although a passionate Israeli patriot, he never ceased to consider Iran also as his homeland. The Iranian Jewish community in Hamadan dates back more than 2500 years and is one of the oldest in the world.[11] Nimrodi returned to Iran in 1959 to work at the Israeli mission. He became the architect of close military cooperation between the two countries against the 'common Arab enemy'. An enthusiastic supporter of the shah, Nimrodi retired from the army in 1976 and started a company specializing in building desalination plants. Iran gave him his first major contract.

As the revolution gathered strength Nimrodi advised his friends in the Iranian military to take with them as many of the army's documents as they could. Some of these documents were later used by a company set up by Nimrodi in London, with headquarters at Montrose Court, Kensington. With the help of his friend Al Schwimmer, the father of the Israeli aircraft industry, Nimrodi persuaded David Kimche, director-general of the Foreign Ministry in Jerusalem, that some critical spare parts and certain categories of weapons should be supplied to Iran. Kimche needed no convincing. He saw Iran as 'the eternal friend of the Jews' and recalled the fact that Cyrus the Great had liberated the Jews from bondage in Babylon as the start of an alliance that was only temporarily interrupted by the takeover of Tehran by the mullahs in 1979.[12] The Israeli defence minister, Ariel Sharon, raised the matter with Alexander Haig, US secretary of state at the time, in 1981. Haig agreed that Israel should supply materiel to Iran provided it did not tip the balance against Iraq in a dramatic way. Sharon gave the go-ahead for a first shipment of tyres and spare parts for Iran's F4 Phantom fighters. The flow of spare parts which continued throughout 1982 helped the Iranian Air Force, squeezed by the arms embargo imposed by President Carter, to remain airborne and play a crucial role in pushing the Iraqis out of Iran.[13]

According to some accounts, Nimrodi had meanwhile established his own supply route to Tehran and, in July 1981, shipped to Iran a number of Lance and Hawk missiles and Copperhead bazookas.[14] That the USA was not especially keen to continue the arms embargo against Iran became more evident when the Iranians opened an important arms procurement office near Victoria, in London, in walking distance of Nimrodi's headquarters.[15] The Iranian office employed a staff of 320 including some seventy-five army, navy and air force officers – the largest military mission in London after that of the United States.

The Iranian arms procurement mission was eventually closed in the summer of 1987 on orders from the British Government and in response to Iran's refusal to comply with a United Nations Security Council resolution calling for an end to the Gulf War. But the fact that it had operated without hindrance for so many years could not have escaped Washington's attention.

The mullahs remained in contact with Nimrodi and other Israelis through two former officers of the shah who were based in London. Both had been released from prison, after being sentenced to death, in order to help secure the arms Iran needed. Their wives and children remained in Iran as hostages so that the two officers would not dream of defecting.[16] Attempts by the Israelis to establish contact with the ruling mullahs and draw them into political talks failed. The Israelis pointed to the fact that their air force had destroyed the Iraqi nuclear capacity in September 1981, in the early stages of the Gulf War, as a sign of their goodwill towards Iran. 'Baghdad was about to produce a nuclear warhead which would have been used against Tehran,' they told the mullahs through intermediaries. The mullahs were apparently grateful but still considered Israel 'number two enemy after the United States'.

Nimrodi did not limit his activities to supplying Iran with some of the materiel it needed. He also tried to put together various scenarios aimed at overthrowing the mullahs in Tehran.[17] Through Colonel Rosenblith he came to know Ghorbanifar in 1983. The three discussed ways and means of infiltrating the new leadership in Tehran. Ghorbanifar had by then acquired an important asset in Iran in the person of one Abbas Kangarloo. This Kangarloo had served as a butler to Ghorbanifar in pre-revolutionary Tehran.[18] In 1980, however, he had been appointed a commander of the Revolutionary Guard before becoming deputy foreign minister a year later. In 1984 he was named deputy prime minister. Ghorbanifar was not sure that his former employee would now agree even to speak to him on the telephone. Nevertheless he decided to have a try. Over the telephone Kangarloo appeared as charming and happy to serve as ever. In order to test his former employee's current intentions, Ghorbanifar asked Kangarloo to help secure the release of several friends and relatives, among them Ghorbanifar's own sister, who was in prison on a charge of trying to overthrow Khomeini. The deputy premier obliged and thus also proved his own power and influence in Tehran.

Kangarloo soon took charge of security planning within the cabinet and it was in that capacity that he asked Ghorbanifar for a few services in return. Ghorbanifar was more than willing and soon came to know a number of other leading figures in the revolutionary regime, including some mullahs who came to Europe for medical treatment or on holiday. He scored a success when he persuaded Danish authorities not to arrest Ayatollah Mahmoud Aqda'i, who had been charged with having stolen a vase in a Copenhagen hotel during his stay there.[19] Still later he succeeded in having a high official of the Islamic embassy in Paris filmed during a moment of sexual indiscretion. The film was sent to Kangarloo in Tehran and may have been used to blackmail the official in question, who later became an assistant to the Islamic prime minister in charge of foreign affairs.[20]

By the spring of 1984 Ghorbanifar had built up an impressive number of contacts in Tehran. Included among them were such powerful figures as Ayatollah Mehdi Karrubi and Ayatollah Ali-Akbar Mohatashami.[21] It is likely that Ghorbanifar presented himself to the mullahs as a powerful and well-connected international intermediary with influence with both the British and the US governments.

The Israeli invasion of Lebanon in 1982 and the subsequent confrontation with Hezb-Allah (the Party of Allah) there, led to an interruption of the dialogue between Tehran and Jerusalem. Khomeini was outraged by Israel's move and saw the oppportunity to mobilize Lebanese Shi'ites for the creation of an Islamic republic in Beirut. Israel had for years worked with Lebanese Shi'ites against the PLO. But from 1983 onwards it was Tehran that represented the main influence among the more radical Shi'ite elements in Lebanon.[22] Khomeini endorsed a series of suicide attacks against Israeli military positions in southern Lebanon and dispatched some 1200 Revolutionary Guards to train Shi'ite guerrillas in the Beqa'a Valley as well as in camps set up in Syria. Israeli Prime Minister Menachem Begin retaliated by ordering all support for Iran to be halted.

A new phase of tension also began in relations between the Islamic Republic and the United States as a result of President Reagan's decision to send some 2000 Marines to take part in a multinational force invited by the Lebanese government to help restore peace to the country. Khomeini and his ally, Syria's President Hafez al-Assad, saw the scheme as a repeat of the 1958 scenario in which US Marines helped restore Maronite hegemony in Lebanon. Tehran and Damascus worked together in preparing a response to the Western move in Lebanon and organized suicide attacks against the US and British embassies in Beirut. The attack on the US embassy wiped out practically all the CIA's key agents in Lebanon plus a number of other agency operatives from Jordan and Syria. But the most dramatic attack came in November 1983 when suicide drivers drove two truckloads of explosives into the dormitories of American and French troops in Beirut, killing nearly three hundred soldiers in their sleep. President Reagan saw this as a declaration of war by Tehran and for a while toyed with the idea of taking some punitive action against the mullahs. But in the end he did nothing dramatic and soon ordered the withdrawal of the Marines. Khomeini felt that he had scored yet another victory over the Great Satan.[23]

In January 1984 Ghorbanifar and Vatandoust prepared a long paper addressed to Reagan. In it they underlined Iran's geopolitical importance and invited the president to think about Irano-American relations not in terms of 'these turbulent moments' but on a long-term basis.[24] They also offered to help establish a 'meaningful dialogue' between Tehran and Washington. The two could not have picked a worse moment, for it was exactly at that time that Reagan, persuaded by Secretary of State George Shultz and Defence Secretary Caspar Weinberger, both known for their belief that the United States should not risk losing its Arab friends by helping Iran in the Gulf War, had ordered the preparation of a new arms embargo against the Islamic Republic. This led to Operation Staunch, whose aim was to 'take Iran's teeth out' and force the mullahs to abandon their terrorist activities in the region and agree to an early end to the Gulf War.

The Reagan administration had become aware of Iranian involvement in anti-Western terrorist activities, including the taking of hostages in Beirut, as early as July 1982, but it was not until January 1984 that Secretary Shultz designated Iran as a sponsor of international terrorism and asked the United States' allies not to sell arms to Tehran.[25]

Operation Staunch succeeded in slowing down the flow of Western arms to Iran but did not greatly hamper the Iranian war effort. New suppliers such as China, North Korea, Brazil, Argentina and Sweden appeared on the scene, while Western intermediaries increased their activities as well as their prices, which at times were quadrupled.

One man determined to help Iran beat Operation Staunch was Adnan Khashoggi, a Saudi businessman of Turkish origin whose outlandish life-style and liberal manners had made him *persona non grata* in the ruling circles of Riyadh. Khashoggi believed that the Islamic Revolution in Iran was the 'single most important problem of the Muslim world today' and argued that if Iran were isolated she would, sooner or later, end up in the Soviet camp. 'And that would mean the end of everyone else also in this region,' he emphasized.[26]

He consulted his Israeli friends and was apparently told to go ahead cautiously. Within months Turkey had been turned into an important route for the supply of arms to Iran. A right-wing Turkish press baron known for his fundamentalist sympathies and a Turkish contractor close to the Libyan leader Moammar al-Gaddafi became partners in the new operation. The United States must have known about this but took no action to stop the flow of arms through Turkey. The Turkish premier, Turgut Ozal, used the new 'Tehran connection' to secure a greater share of the Iranian market for his country.[27] Word was spread that American opposition to the sale of arms to Iran was a matter of form only, calculated to satisfy Arab allies such as Egypt, Morocco and Saudi Arabia which backed Iraq in the war.

The fact that Turkey, a NATO member, was able to get a share of the Iranian cake without provoking Washington's anger encouraged other international arms dealers to enter the scene. Some even began to plan for the direct export of American arms to Iran and, in a few instances succeeded. An FBI probe in San Diego, California, produced evidence that some $20 million's worth of materiel stolen from the United States Navy stocks had been illegally shipped to Iran between 1981 and 1985. A far bigger operation was discovered in New York and Florida in 1985. This involved an attempt to export some $2000 million's worth of American-made arms, including Skyhawk missiles and F4 fighters, to the Islamic Republic. The operation was master-minded by Abraham Bar-Am, a retired Israeli general with a licence from the Israeli Defence Ministry to engage in the arms trade. His principal partner and contact man with Tehran was Cyrus Hashemi, the London-based arms merchant of Iranian origin. Hashemi was to die in mysterious circumstances a few months later.

By February 1984 relations between the United States and the Islamic Republic seemed to have reached a standstill that would last for as long as Khomeini was alive and pursued his provocative policies in the region. The State Department and the Pentagon seemed convinced that the USA was best advised to concentrate its efforts on isolating Iran and preventing her from winning the war against Iraq. The CIA was still hoping to reap some benefit from its investment in exiled opposition groups and was busy organizing special training courses for would-be militants introduced by Bakhtiar and Amini.[28] Congress as a whole had little interest in Iran and the White House did not wish to get involved with an issue that spelled only trouble.

The NSC was, therefore, the only organ of the US government which kept an open mind about developments in Iran. The West German foreign minister, Hans Dietrich Genscher, who was the first Western leader to visit Tehran since the revolution, tried to attract the State Department's attention to the possibility of sounding out some 'moderate elements' in the Islamic leadership as early as August 1984.[29] He did not succeed, but his views, passed on to the NSC, triggered a train of thought that led Robert McFarlane to order a fresh assessment of the situation in Iran, especially as far as the post-Khomeini era was concerned. Howard Teischer was in charge of the project, which was expanded into an inter-agency effort. The State Department, in a letter dated 19 October 1984, told the NSC that there was virtually nothing the USA could do at that moment to influence events inside Iran. The CIA, presumably reluctant to expose its own covert operations then in full swing, replied, in a letter dated 11 December 1984, that it had only a limited capability for making an impact on developments in the Islamic Republic.[30]

The negative attitude of the State Department and the CIA towards a rethinking of the strategy concerning Iran did not deter the NSC from pursuing its own contacts with various Iranian exile groups, including some that were indirectly connected with the mullahs in

Tehran. These contacts remained informal and served mainly as a means of obtaining information for the NSC.[31] Howard Teischer and Donald Fortier, who retained an interest in Iran and continued to maintain contact with Iranian elements, succeeded in pushing through an update of an earlier 'Special National Intelligence Estimate' (SNIE) on Iran in cooperation with CIA analysts. Dated 20 May 1985, the paper claimed that the Soviets were well positioned to take advantage of the chaos in Iran and that the United States was unable to influence events. It further suggested that the gap left by the absence of American influence should be at least in part filled by allies who could 'fill a military gap for Iran' as a means of countering Soviet influence. This was, clearly, intended to mean the lifting of the formal ban on arms supplies to the mullahs.[32]

The following month Teischer and Fortier came up with 'a draft presidential decision document' in which they took their suggestion that arms be shipped to Iran through allies a step further. Reaction to this paper underlined the sharp divisions that existed within the administration. Shultz and Weinberger strongly objected to the very idea of the USA encouraging arms sales to Iran. The CIA's director Casey on the other hand, strongly endorsed the paper's conclusions without specifically referring to the arms issue.

The mullahs for their part were equally divided about the future of relations with the United States. The idea that combating the USA in the Middle East should be postponed until Iraq was defeated was indirectly raised at the Islamic Majlis on a number of occasions in 1984. Foreign Minister Ali-Akbar Valayati was a strong supporter of what became known as the 'first things first' policy, meaning that the Islamic Republic should not try to fight the whole world all at once. It is possible that Genscher's lecturing, as well as the contact that he maintained with Sadeq Tabataba'i, one of few men with direct access to Khomeini, contributed to the debate among the mullahs. Unofficial emissaries tried to open a dialogue with the United States on at least three occasions between October 1984 and August 1985. Ayatollah Mohammad-Reza Mahdavi-Kani, the powerful leader of the Combatant Clergy in Tehran, tried to get Canada to act as an intermediary with the United States during a visit he made to Toronto and Ottawa in November 1984. By the time his wishes were communicated to higher authorities in the Canadian government the ayatollah was back in Europe en route to Tehran.[33] Before flying home he telephoned Vatandoust in Paris and told him: 'How do you want Iran to win this war? We need weapons and we need to be sure that the Americans do not come to Saddam Hussein's rescue.'[34]

Washington was undoubtedly informed of the desire of some

elements in the Islamic leadership to open a dialogue with the United States. But the signals which came from Tehran also included some that indicated no change in Khomeini's policy of regarding the USA as 'number one enemy of Islam'. American interests were attacked in Kuwait, Bahrain and Turkey by Islamic terrorists and the violent anti-American campaign launched in Lebanon in 1983 continued unabated.

In March 1984 a new and potentially very serious blow was dealt to the American presence in the Middle East when Hezb-Allah militants kidnapped William Buckley, the fifty-six-year-old CIA station chief in Beirut. Buckley's fate became a matter of grave concern in Washington for emotional and security reasons. Casey was personally attached to his agent and saw in Buckley's abduction a major blow to the CIA's morale, restored under Reagan. Buckley risked being tortured and forced to provide information on the entire CIA network in the region. The Beirut station chief knew the names of scores of agents and was also a mine of information on the agency's methods and techniques.

The USA put in motion an important effort to get Buckley released. But much of the effort was centred on Syria, who had somehow convinced the Americans that she alone could reason with the terrorists. The Syrians were asking for major concessions from the United States in regard to her Middle East policy in exchange for Buckley's safe release. The possibility of the United States going along with the Syrian proposals alarmed the Israelis, who began to try to convince Washington that only Khomeini and not the Syrian leader, Hafez al-Assad, could save Buckley's life. By July 1984 Buckley was transferred to Tehran, partly to prevent the Syrians from trading him in exchange for American concessions and financial support.

In the meantime Buckley was extensively interrogated by a team of Islamic experts headed by the minister for Revolutionary Guards, Mohsen Rafiqdust, at the Saleh-Abad military camp southwest of Tehran, probably in September and October 1984. According to reliable sources in Tehran, Buckley's 'trial' was recorded on more than forty hours of videotape. The Soviets later showed a keen interest in the tapes but failed to obtain copies.

The ayatollah's agents in Lebanon were to announce Buckley's death on 4 October 1985, less than a month after Casey had hoped to get his agent released thanks to the Israeli connection, which had by then been in operation for more than two months. Was Buckley killed or did he die under torture and because of heart failure? The question remains unanswered. Only Khomeini and his closest advisers know the answer. Buckley's capture did not lead to any immediate change in the American attitude towards the Islamic Republic and Washington continued to keep a low profile.

From the summer of 1984 the CIA began what looked like a major drive to recruit former members of SAVAK who had fled into exile in Western Europe and the United States. This was presumably a result of reports that the mullahs had reconstituted the counterespionage section of the shah's secret police with a view to monitoring Soviet activities in Iran. Since SAVAK had developed into a large clan over the years, it was presumed that those of its members now invited back to work by the mullahs would maintain private contacts with former colleagues in exile.

One man contacted by the CIA as part of the new drive was Brigadier General Manuchehr Hashemi, a former head of the counterespionage section of SAVAK. Hashemi had left Iran shortly after the revolution and had chosen London as his exile home. It was during a trip he made to Los Angeles in the second half of 1984 that an Iranian-born CIA agent, Nozar Razm-Ara, asked him to meet one Theodore Shackley, who had flown in from Washington to see the general.[35] Shackley introduced himself as a retired CIA employee and said that he acted as intelligence consultant for Vice-President George Bush and the NSC while running a commercial business in Washington. After a long lecture about the Soviet threat to Iran, Shackley asked Hashemi whether the USA could establish contact with high- or middle-ranking officials in the Islamic Republic. Hashemi agreed to help and in November 1984 telephoned Razm-Ara to ask Shackley to come to Hamburg for a meeting with Ghorbanifar, himself and another Iranian.[36] This turned out to be a lengthy session and covered a variety of issues ranging from supplying arms to Iran to joint action against the Soviet threat in the region. Hashemi did not see Shackley again. Two weeks after the Hamburg meeting Razm-Ara telephoned Hashemi to tell him that it was not possible to fix a second meeting because of the approaching elections in the United States.

Ghorbanifar was nevertheless able to show his Iranian friends that he was, indeed, capable of producing high-level American contacts. He recalled later that Shackley had introduced himself at the meeting as 'very close' to Vice-President Bush. Shackley also implied that he might be the next CIA director since Casey was unwell and could not cope with the burden of his work.[37] The Iranian contact had been impressed and on his return to Tehran asked Ghorbanifar to set up more meetings after the American election. Once again, however, the Americans simply disappeared, using the 'usual tactic' of changing all the telephone numbers they had given to Ghorbanifar.[38]

It was in some desperation that Ghorbanifar contacted Rear Admiral Mir-Kamaleddin Mir-Habib-Allahi, the last commander of the Iranian Navy under the shah, who was then in Washington, and asked him to arrange a meeting with 'responsible Americans'. Ghorbanifar had hoped that Mir-Habib-Allahi would put him in touch with the Pentagon or the NSC, but when a meeting was arranged in Frankfurt at the end of December the men who showed up turned out to be CIA agents. They thought Ghorbanifar had applied for a job as an informer and insisted that he take a lie-detector test. The CIA had already formed a low opinion of Ghorbanifar partly because of negative reports from French and British intelligence services, which had dealt with him previously.[39] Further, Shackley had reported back in November that all Ghorbanifar was interested in was discussing the release of the American hostages in Lebanon in exchange for a cash ransom, to be paid through him.[40] Ghorbanifar, however, rejected Shackley's accusations, which were, incidentally, not mentioned by General Hashemi either.

At any rate, Ghorbanifar took the lie-detector test demanded by the CIA and failed it. Later he was to claim that he had deliberately lied during the test because he had not wanted to get involved with the CIA after having been contacted by the vice-president. In addition, he saw no reason why he should supply sensitive information to people who appeared to be fairly low-level officials.[41]

News that the Americans had made contacts with Hashemi, Ghorbanifar and 'the man from Tehran' could not be kept a secret in the Iranian exile community, where everything ended up by becoming public. Bored exiles often boasted of 'high-level contacts' with most major capitals as a means of underlining their own importance. Some used such real or imaginary contacts as a means of winning commercial contracts in Tehran. Shackley's supposedly ultra-secret mission was revealed in an exile paper published in Hamburg in December 1984.[42]

But not all those who wished to create a dialogue between Tehran and Washington were prompted by mercenary motives. There were an estimated 30,000 people with dual Irano–US citizenship in 1985.[43] Many of them had become naturalized Americans long before the revolution. Others had fled to the United States after the seizure of power by Khomeini. Most were supporters of the former regime. But an appreciable number were interested in restoring friendly relations between Iran and the United States regardless of the type of regime in power in Tehran.

The Americans, however, showed a singular lack of interest, at times combined with unusual hostility, in meetings with intermediaries from Tehran. One intermediary, Mahmoud Alavi, recalled how he felt 'humiliated'. He had contacted a former counsellor of the Iranian embassy in Washington under the shah with a demand that he

be put in contact with 'responsible Americans'. The former counsellor had succeeded in fixing a meeting in Frankfurt after some three
weeks. When Alavi went to the hotel where he was to meet the
Americans, he was whisked into a top-floor suite and told that he
must take a lie-detector test. He protested that there might have been
a mistake and left.[44] Another intermediary was met in a Hamburg
hotel by 'two men wearing dark glasses and reeking of alcohol'.
'Well,' one of the men began without any initial cordialities, 'let us
have what you've got to say.' The encounter became distinctly
unfriendly when one of the Americans suggested that many Iranians
were 'phonies' and posed as intermediaries in order to secure visas to
enter the United States as illegal immigrants.[45]

By the spring of 1985 the talk at the Bar Alexandre focused on
ways and means of breaking through what looked like a lack of
interest on the part of Washington. It was recalled by Alavi that the
Americans had behaved quite differently when they had hostages in
Tehran. 'Then they would usher anyone who came from us or
claimed to come from us into the White House and the Oval Office,'
he said.[46] In other words, Washington would not change its attitude
towards the Islamic Revolution unless subjected to an adequate level
of pressure.

The pressure the Bar Alexandre philosophers dreamed about was
soon to be supplied by Mohsen Rafiqdust, minister for Islamic
Revolutionary Guards, who visited Damascus and Beirut in March
1985. He left behind in Beirut his 'chief of special operations',
Mohammad Khademi, who was to mastermind a new series of
hostage-holdings in Lebanon. On 14 June 1985 Khademi pulled off
his first 'wake-up blow to America' by hijacking an American
passenger aircraft with 135 US citizens aboard. The operation was
carried out by the Hamadei clan; it led to the murder of an American
passenger in a drama that dominated the news thanks to its
spectacular coverage by the American television networks. The
Islamic Revolution was once again under the limelight and the 'good
old days' of the Tehran hostages' crisis, when the mullahs felt they
were masters of the universe, seemed to have returned. The crisis
showed that Reagan, despite his talk of 'walking tall', was as
vulnerable to that type of terrorism as his predecessor had been.

Unlike 1979, however, the mullahs had no interest in a prolonged
confrontation with the United States over the hostages. They were
basically interested in two things: first, to force Washington to seek a
dialogue with them and, second, to show to the Lebanese Shi'ites that
only revolutionary Islam could produce results in a confrontation
with the big powers. The fact that Israel agreed to release more than

1000 Shi'ite prisoners in exchange for an end to the hijack drama enhanced Khomeini's position among Lebanese Shi'ites.

It was to underline the desire of at least some of the mullahs to use the hijack episode as an excuse for a new dialogue with Washington that Hojat al-Islam Ali-Akbar Rafsanjani, then considered to be Tehran's strongman, personally flew to Damascus to direct the release of the hostages.[47] But this did not seem to affect Washington's overall attitude towards the Islamic Revolution, although Iran was thanked for its positive role in ending the drama. The Reagan administration seemed prepared to live with the idea of American citizens being kidnapped for political reasons and determined not to repeat 'Carter's mistake' by negotiating with 'terrorists'.[48]

Almost at the same time that the hijack drama was in progress the Israelis were putting final touches to an update on Iran which showed a steep increase in Soviet activities. Shimon Peres was even prepared to single out Moscow's new activism in the Middle East, following the change of guard at the Kremlin, as the number-one threat to Western interests in the region. The NSC, which had habitually attached great importance to Israeli analyses, began to show some concern. The NSC staffers who believed that Iran was the emerging regional superpower were anxious to break the Iranian logjam and open a channel to Tehran. They found in Casey a powerful ally. The CIA director had never adopted a confrontationist position vis-à-vis the mullahs and his concern about Buckley's fate made him still more inclined to share the NSC's views.

The United States resumed its search for meaningful contacts with Tehran through both the CIA and the NSC. Aware of Israel's close relations with certain mullahs in Tehran, the NSC, encouraged by the CIA, decided to enlist Israeli support in securing an opening to the Islamic Republic. Casey's primary interest was the liberation of hostages rather than the establishment of a new strategic relationship with Tehran. That interest was keenly shared by President Reagan. The NSC, however, was more concerned about long-term geopolitical considerations. It was that concern that led to the NSC's decision to dispatch Michael Ledeen, a consultant on Iran, to Jerusalem where he met Premier Shimon Peres in May. Ledeen later presented his mission as one solely concerned with sounding out Israel about the possibility of cooperation with the United States in the field of intelligence on Iran.[49] But Israeli officials, including Peres himself, gained the impression that Washington was looking for an opening to Tehran.[50] Exchange of selective intelligence on Iran had, in any case, never stopped so far as Mossad and the CIA were concerned. Ledeen's mission would, therefore, have been superfluous had it been solely concerned with intelligence.

The Israelis moved fast to put together a new package to present to their American friends. Israel, which had been somewhat jealous of the close relations between Iran and the United States under the shah, was in 1985 anxious to bring the two countries closer together because of her own strategic interests in the region. The task of putting the package together was entrusted by Peres to David Kimche, the director general of the Foreign Ministry and then considered to be Israel's mastermind in international relations. He contacted Ghorbanifar through Schwimmer and Nimrodi and asked whether an urgent meeting could be set up with 'someone highly connected' in Tehran. Ghorbanifar said this could be arranged. Kimche, Schwimmer and Amiram Nir, Peres's specialist in counter-terrorist activities, flew to London, where they were joined by Ghorbanifar and Nimrodi towards the end of May. Ghorbanifar had established his *bona fides* seven weeks earlier by attending another meeting with Kimche and Nir in Hamburg. The meeting had been arranged by Khashoggi, who had told Ghorbanifar that others attending were American officials. At that meeting Ghorbanifar had telephoned Kangarloo and talked to him at some length to prove that he did, in fact, have high-level contacts in Tehran.[51] The Hamburg meeting brought together most of the many freelance diplomat-cum-arms-merchants interested in Iran in what began to look like a joint venture.

The Americans must have been aware of Khashoggi's activities through one of his business associates, Roy Furmark, who was also determined to contribute to an improvement in Iran–US ties and not for altruistic reasons alone.

The meeting in London in May convinced Kimche that Ghorbanifar held the key to a deal with Tehran. The Iranian adventurer produced two high-level mullahs from Tehran: Muhammed-Ali Hadi Najaf-Abadi, chairman of the Islamic Majlis Foreign Affairs Committee, and Hassan Karrubi, a close friend of Khomeini's son Ahmad. It is possible that Ghorbanifar had told the two men that they were to meet Americans and not Israeli officials and businessmen. But Najaf-Abadi, fluent in English after years spent in India and Pakistan before the revolution, would have been difficult to deceive. He may have accepted the meeting in the full knowledge that the people he encountered were Israelis in the hope of using Israel as a bridge to the United States.

At the end of June Kimche flew to Washington; he met McFarlane early in July. Kimche told the presidential adviser that Iranian high officials had conveyed to him an interest in a discourse with the United States and suggested that contact be maintained through an inter-mediary.[52] McFarlane briefed President Reagan, Secretaries Shultz and Weinberger and Director Casey on Kimche's ideas almost immediately after the meeting with the Israeli official. The president expressed interest and instructed his adviser to explore the matter further. McFarlane conveyed the president's decision to Kimche almost immediately.[53]

Israel was now convinced that it was acting on behalf of an ally and for the purpose of reducing tension between Iran and the United States. The foreign minister, Yitzhakh Shamir, also believed that his government was making a 'humanitarian move' in the hope of securing the release of American hostages.[54] He and Prime Minister Peres did not think at the time that Israel might later be accused of having tried to drag the Reagan administration into a new Iran adventure.

The Israelis set up a new meeting in London in which Schwimmer, Nir, Nimrodi and Ghorbanifar worked out a list of 'initial arms' requests' from Tehran for conveyance to Washington. All participants were under the impression that the United States had already approved a gradual lifting of the arms embargo imposed on Iran. The meeting suggested that the USA should agree to the sale of 100 TOW anti-tank missiles to Iran in exchange for the release of the American hostages in Beirut. The two moves were obviously intended to be symbolic and all the participants envisaged much broader relations between Tehran and Washington in future. The meeting's suggestions were put to McFarlane by Ledeen, who acted for Schwimmer, who said he represented Peres. McFarlane raised the subject with President Reagan and Secretary Shultz. Both agreed that 'a tentative show of interest' was in order. Shultz, however, suggested that McFarlane handle 'this probe' personally.[55]

The matter was raised again in August when Kimche met McFarlane in the White House. This time the Israeli diplomat was more specific: would the United States be prepared to sell arms to Iran as a means of improving relations? McFarlane replied that he thought not. Kimche then asked whether the United States would agree to replace arms that Israel might sell to Iran as part of a larger effort to support moderate elements within the Islamic regime? McFarlane said he would have to ask the president.

The issue was brought up in a series of meetings at the NSC, and McFarlane also discussed it with the president, the secretaries of state and of defence and the director of the CIA. The outcome of all these discussions was a positive response to Kimche's idea. The United States would not object if 'Israel chose to transfer arms to Iran, in modest amounts not enough to change the military balance and not including major weapon systems.'[56] The president also indicated that the United States was interested in a political meeting with the Iranians. The question of hostages was not included in the response that McFarlane conveyed to Kimche. But it was understood by all sides that the arms transfer ought to lead to the release of at least some of the seven American hostages then being held in Lebanon. Shultz, for example, was certain about the linkage and believed that four hostages would be set free in exchange for 100 TOW missiles supplied to Iran by Israel.[57] The Israelis told the Iranians that the United States was unable to get directly involved in arms transfers because of 'troubles with their system, their Congress'.[58] But it was understood that the Reagan administration was favourable towards exploring a radical change of policy on Iran. On 30 August Israel delivered 100 TOWs to Iran.

A second delivery, this time of 408 missiles, was made on 14 September, when two transport aircraft landed at Tabriz after overflying Cyprus and Turkey. Ghorbanifar was on one of the planes together with the Israeli crew, who had forged Argentine documents. Ghorbanifar was immediately arrested and escorted to Tehran under guard. He had been sentenced to death in absentia for his part in the Nowzheh coup attempt in 1980.[59] But once in Tehran he was met by Kangarloo, who put a bulletproof car with official number plates at his disposal. He spent four days in Tehran meeting his contacts, including Najaf-Abadi and Jalaleddin Farsi. That everything was going according to plan was emphasized by the fact that the Reverend Benjamin Weir, one of the American hostages, was released the day Ghorbanifar arrived in Tehran. Ghorbanifar had informed McFarlane of the impending release through Kimche a week earlier.

Ghorbanifar, an enthusiast with a super-active imagination, might have told his Tehran contacts almost anything concerning his 'miracle' in what he saw as a 'dramatic change in American policy.'[60] He claimed that he had America in 'his pocket'[61] and urged his contacts not to miss this golden opportunity to bring the United States over to the Iranian side in the Gulf War.

Ghorbanifar's operation accorded well with Tehran's policy at the time. The ayatollah was trying to improve ties with Saudi Arabia while preparing for a final offensive against Iraq. He wanted to make sure that neither the United States nor Saudi Arabia would rush in to prevent the fall of the Iraqi regime. Saudi involvement in the Ghorbanifar deal had not been limited to Khashoggi's role as a financier – he provided the down payment needed for the transfer of Israeli arms to Iran – but to a more than tacit approval of the venture by Riyadh. At the end of August Khashoggi had arranged for Ghorbanifar and an Iranian associate to meet with Prince Fadhel ben

Fahd, one of the sons of King Fahd of Saudi Arabia, in Geneva. The prince had indicated his father's support for 'any move that could help cool down things in Iran and persuade Khomeini that he can live in peace with us.'[62] Did that mean a change in Saudi's policy of support for Baghdad? The question interested Tehran beyond measure as it was well known that Saudi Arabia provided nearly half the money Iraq spent on its war against Iran.[63]

At the meeting with Prince Fadhel, Ghorbanifar presented some of the themes he was later to spell out in a letter destined for King Fahd. Two points were especially emphasized as basic objectives:

(a) a slow process of normalization between the two countries [Iran and the USA] to counterbalance expansion of Soviet influence in the region; and (b) a strengthening of those within the regime in Tehran who support normalization with the West and would stop the policy of exporting the revolution through subversion and terrorism and who seek, at the same time, an honourable end to the Gulf War.[64]

It was some time between September and December 1985 that Lieutenant Colonel Oliver North, the NSC's 'expert' on counter-terrorism among many other things, was informally put in charge of the Iran initiative, which was soon baptized Operation Recovery, presumably meaning a release of the hostages. North had not been a total stranger to the initiative and had led the team that debriefed Father Weir after his release. North and his immediate hierarchical superior, Vice-Admiral John Poindexter, had joined the NSC in 1981 and were thus among the longest-serving members of the *ad hoc* presidential body. According to Richard V. Allen, Reagan's senior national security adviser and the man who employed them both, North and Poindexter had been brought in to 'handle such routine duties as carrying the briefcase and some of the maps and charts'.[65] North was scheduled for a four-month temporary assignment and was not supposed to deal with classified material or get involved in secret activities. By the end of 1985, however, Poindexter was head of the NSC and North was his closest associate. The two men had distinguished themselves by handling the crisis caused by the hijacking of the Italian cruise ship *Achille Lauro* and the subsequent arrest of the hijackers by an airborne US commando in Italy.[66] North was also the main force behind the secret Project Democracy, which, among other things, aimed at leading a worldwide crusade against Soviet-backed communism. President Reagan knew and admired North; he was to describe him as a 'national hero' in the autumn of 1986. When North took over the leadership of the initiative on Iran there was little doubt among those concerned that President Reagan was himself intimately involved in the process. This view was later confirmed by more than seventy congressional testimonies as well as interviews with many of the Iranians, Saudis, Israelis and Americans involved, who were not, for the most part, invited to testify in Washington.

North organized what might have been the first staff meeting of those involved in the Iran initiative in his office in Washington on 8 October.[67] Ghorbanifar, using his Greek alias of Nicholas Keralis, was present, together with Nimrodi and Schwimmer. The Iranian intermediary gave a full account of his trip to Tehran and claimed that 'doors and hearts are all open' there.[68] He found North a 'very determined and tough man who spoke as if his every word would be engraved in history books'.[69] Ghorbanifar was to modify his view of North in later months when the two came to know each other better and spent some time together in London, Hamburg and Frankfurt. North was 'a maniacal patriot who would stiffen up as soon as he saw any sign of America: from their flag to Coca-Cola neon signs.'[70]

Everyone emerged satisfied from the meeting. Ghorbanifar was reassured about his future role. The two Israeli arms dealers began looking forward to a total lifting of the American ban on the transfer of arms to the Islamic Republic and may have started contemplating the profits they would later reap. North for his part thought that he had a genuine formula for securing the release of the American hostages, thus boosting the prestige of Reagan and driving a wedge between Iranian-sponsored terror groups on the one hand and those connected with the PLO on the other. Did he think even then of using the arms-for-Iran process as a means of making profits that could then be funnelled to dollar-starved 'freedom fighters' in Nicaragua? What mattered at the time was to pursue the dialogue which Washington believed it had started with Tehran. The question was: had a real dialogue been established?

10

THE SHARK, THE HE-CAT AND THE OWL

By the end of 1985 Lieutenant Colonel Oliver North, a soldier with virtually no diplomatic experience and a limited grasp of the major international issues, was, through his Operation Recovery, in effective control of the main stream of US policy concerning Iran. Considering the fact that Iran represented one of the four or five most crucial issues in US foreign policy in the 1980s, this was an extraordinary development. The State Department, the Pentagon, the NSC and the more than a dozen or so research institutes that advised the US government on international affairs were all aware of Iran's unique position both as a neighbour of the USSR and as the dominant power in the Persian Gulf. They were also fully cognizant of the effect the Islamic Revolution was having on political developments from Morocco to Indonesia.

Had US policymakers so wished, they could have obtained, within the United States itself, all the knowledge they required concerning the actual situation in revolutionary Iran. Surprisingly enough, they refused to look beyond information provided by exiles, arms merchants, foreign intelligence agencies, each promoting its own slant, and, worst of all, profiteers whose bad faith had been recognized even by people close to the administration. Iran policy was to be made by graduates of the Bar Alexandre and executed by amateurs in a great hurry. Diplomacy was too important to be left to diplomats as far as relations with Iran were concerned.

The emergence of this curious new method of conducting foreign relations was partly a product of the Reagan administration's extraordinary belief in the efficacy of covert operations and secret diplomacy. At the same time it reflected the abiding distrust that the administration felt towards Congress as well as the established institutions of American bureaucracy such as the State Department. In 1986, after Operation Recovery had already ended in disaster, President Reagan cited as the principal reason for his decision to support it a desire to counter Soviet moves in Iran and to pave the way for the normalization of relations with Tehran. But had he asked Congress and the State Department to help him achieve such objectives he would have received nothing but support. No one in mainstream America doubted the necessity of seeking an opening to Iran. Many people, including those within the State Department, in fact argued in favour of such a policy and to a certain degree even worked for it.[1] In other words, the so-called system or process of government would have lent itself quite adequately to the pursuit of such a policy. There was no need to circumvent it.

The most immediate and eventually the most damaging result of the decision to opt for covert methods, where none was needed, was the way that the North team began work on Iran at an exceptional level of ignorance. A paper prepared by Ghorbanifar and Nimrodi and presented to the venerable lieutenant colonel as a secret document in November 1985 described the 'three lines' that were supposedly competing for power in Iran at the time. It further claimed that Ghorbanifar's contacts in Tehran represented the more moderate line and should be strengthened through arms supplies from the USA.[2] Subsequent revelations proved that Operation Recovery was started without a precise definition of its goals and on the basis of inaccurate information. It was not even properly discussed by the key figures of the administration who devoted one session to it in September.[3] There were no discussion papers, no analyses and not even a full record of the session to guide North and his associates.[4]

Operation Recovery wanted to do too many things at once: it aimed at securing the release of the hostages, helping moderates win the power struggle in Tehran, countering Soviet moves in the Persian Gulf and also, as became apparent later, finding a new source of funds for the Nicaraguan contras. Only those who are unaware of the way diplomacy works could have hoped to take in so many complex issues in one single sweep of their imagination. The days of Nixon, Ford and Carter, when even details of US policy on Iran had to be brought to the attention of the president, or at least the secretary of state, were gone. Iran had become an *ad hoc* issue to be handled on the margin of the presidential agenda.

Ghorbanifar had persuaded North and others that his main contact in Tehran, Kangarloo, was a powerful man and could play a crucial role in post-Khomeini Iran. This was in fact not so. Kangarloo was one of several deputy premiers, with responsibility, mainly, for protecting the life of the prime minister and keeping an eye on people who might want to harm him. The title 'deputy premier' is misleading. A more exact translation of the Persian term would be 'auxiliary or assistant to the premier'. The holders of the posts headed no departments, did not have seats on the cabinet and did not have to be approved by parliament.[5] Not only did Kangarloo not have any real power to influence Tehran's basic foreign policy options in any meaningful way, but he could not even be sure about the future of his own boss – the prime minister. The holder of the post, Mir-Hossein Mussavi-Khameneh'i, an interior decorator by profession, was propelled into that position largely because of his hardline anti-Americanism in 1981. He claimed to have invented the slogan '*Marg bar Amrika*' ('Death to America') in 1979 to replace the less macabre one of 'Yankee go home' that was used from 1978, in early revolutionary phases, onwards.[6] Far from being a moderate, Mussavi belonged to one of several hardline factions fighting for power in Tehran.

The fact that Operation Recovery was based on contact with hardliners was clear to the Israelis right from the start. Nir was quite forthcoming in this respect when he told Vice-President Bush in Jerusalem in July 1986 that Israel and the USA were dealing with the radicals in the Islamic Republic.[7] This was not surprising: only hardliners would seize American hostages and would therefore also be in a position to release them if that suited a new strategy. In other words, the search for an end to the ordeal of the hostages within a short timespan was not compatible with the other avowed objective of Operation Recovery: the strengthening of moderate elements in Tehran.

More importantly, Lieutenant Colonel North did not know that there were in fact no moderates as such within the Islamic leadership and that the power struggle in Tehran did not take the classic form of faction-fighting developed in the more ideology-oriented revolutionary regimes. The one-liner stating that 'a moderate mullah is one who has run out of bullets' was not totally off the mark. But it was also possible to argue that almost all mullahs could be moderate provided they could dictate their own terms and secure from the United States, or anyone else for that matter, the things they needed for prolonging their stay in power.

Because the overwhelming majority of the new rulers of Iran were related to one another by blood or marriage, the tribal-style faction-fighting did not apply in their case either. Their quarrels were prompted by four categories of differences. And it often happened that two leaders who found themselves in one camp concerning one of these categories were on opposite sides in another.

The first category of differences concerned the exercise of power. The bureaucracy inherited from the shah had not been disbanded by the revolution and remained a serious pretender for power. Whoever happened to head the bureaucracy, as prime minister, was bound to end up supporting his own side in the power struggle. Thus Mussavi, a radical in social and economic policy, was a conservative in that he pleaded for government through the established bureaucracy. The institutions which emerged with the revolution had claims of their own. The president of the Republic, the Islamic Majlis, the Revolutionary Guards and, until the spring of 1987, the Islamic Republican Party were all united in their efforts to push the government machinery into the background but divided among themselves as to whom should have the lion's share in taking the key decisions. To cite just one example, Rafsanjani, a conservative in social and economic policy, was a radical when it came to the issue of exercising power by revolutionary institutions. Standing in a class of its own was the Imam's household, Khomeini's 'court', headed by his son Ahmad and overruling all other institutions whenever and wherever it so desired.

The second category of difference that divided the Islamic leadership concerned the objectives for which power was to be exercised. To many mullahs the very fact that the clergy were in power was sufficient for the regime to be presented as an expression of Allah's will. What was essential therefore was to devote all the energy needed to keep the *status quo* intact. Other mullahs, however, had been strongly influenced by pseudo-Marxist ideas and what could be described as 'Third Worldism'. They wanted to be more revolutionary than their rivals on the left. And to them anti-Americanism was the most immediately recognizable trait of a revolutionary movement.

Thirdly, the mullahs were divided about the attitude their revolution ought to adopt to the outside world, which also included the Westernized stratum of Iranian society itself. Major issues such as relations with the United States, the war against Iraq and attempts at imposing an Islamic republic on Lebanon all fell within this category.

Finally, the ruling mullahs were divided by their social and economic backgrounds. The Islamic Revolution was not a class revolution. Nor did it have to pass through long periods of struggle before it succeeded. This meant that the revolutionary process did not have enough time to shape its own hegemony. It swept to power widely different individuals: romantics, pragmatists, power-hungry rogues, opportunists and plain thieves. In the absence of a coherent ideology that might offer its own vision of the future and its own solutions to the problems of today, the revolution was bound to end up in violence and terror.

Trying to identify factions representing more or less durable alliances in this chaotic context was well nigh impossible. The best one could do was to look for powerful individuals likely to gather around them a sufficiently large number of other powerful people to affect policy. But here too alliances were often transitory and could break up at any moment. The result was paralysis on issues when positive decisions needed to be taken on the basis of compromise. After nearly nine years of power the mullahs had not yet succeeded, in 1988, in abolishing the laws in force under the shah and agreeing on legislation on such key issues as land ownership, foreign trade, labour and employment terms, and marriage and divorce. For Lieutenant Colonel North to succeed in his Machiavellian plan in such circumstances would have required a miracle. And there was to be none.

Three individuals dominated the politics of the Islamic Republic after 1981. The first of the three was, of course, Ayatollah Ruhollah Khomeini himself. The ayatollah claimed direct descent from the Prophet Muhammad and believed that the Shiite clergy should rule the entire Muslim world in the name of Ali, the first Imam of duodecimal Shi'ism.[8] The Shi'ites have added two principles to Islam's original three principles as enunciated by the prophet himself.[9] The two additions are the concept of *imamah*, which means that all governments of the world should be considered as illegitimate, unless they are led by a theologian, someone like Khomeini, for example, who bears the title of *sayyed* ('master'). The second addition is the concept of *'adl*, which means that Allah's justice must be done here on earth and that the rule of Islam must be spread to the whole world, by force if necessary. Khomeini's agenda was therefore crystal clear and constituted at the same time his very *raison d'être*. For him President Reagan and Lieutenant Colonel North were *kafirs* ('impious') who should either convert to Islam or be put to the sword. And if neither of these two options could be exercised at the moment, because of obvious difficulties, the Imam must continue to weaken the impious camp by all the means at his disposal. He could never become a friend of the impious and should not even dream of a give-and-take with them. For such an attitude would mean putting the impious and the true believers at the same level. Since ends justified the means in Khomeinism, it was possible for the Imam to lie, to cheat and to kill in order to achieve his noble aims. One of Allah's own titles is Khair al-Makereen, which means 'The Master Trickster'. There are no such things as intrinsic good or evil: whatever serves the cause of Islam is good and whatever prevents the Imam from becoming the ruler of the world is bad. If the Imam needed guns he ought to get them from wherever and whomever possible. And that, of course, included Lieutenant Colonel North. Because of his age and his physical features, as well as his own special brand of wisdom, Khomeini was often referred to as *Joghd*, which means 'the Owl' in Persian.

The second member of the Islamic troika of powerful individuals was Ayatollah Hossein-Ali Montazeri, commonly referred to in Tehran as *Gorbeh-Nareh* ('the He-Cat'). A simple man of God who sat on the floor and ate with his bare fingers, Montazeri was born in 1924. His father was a shepherd and he too spent his childhood looking after flocks belonging to local barons. He later attended theological school thanks to donations from relatives and village wellwishers. He spent some time studying under Khomeini in Qom. He had spent most of his life in remote villages and small towns where living conditions had barely changed since the twelfth century. Montazeri too believed that the whole world ought to be united under the banner of Islam. But here he had a basic theological quarrel with Khomeini and people like him. Montazeri believed that Islam should establish itself as the way of life for the whole of mankind only through the force of individual example. It is the true Muslim individual that can create the truly Islamic society. Montazeri believed that human beings everywhere, being basically good and wise, were bound to see that Islam offered them the best way of life. Khomeini, on the other hand, believed that men were weak, irrational and irresponsible and would more easily succumb to temptations to which they were exposed because of Satan's constant intriguing. Men should therefore be forced to be good, by the sword if necessary, against their own instincts, Khomeini contended.

Montazeri had been a pupil of Khomeini during the 1950s and had supported the exiled ayatollah in the 1960s. His support of Khomeini's cause had led to his imprisonment by SAVAK for a total of seven years between 1965 and 1979. In his writings and teachings, however, Montazeri had distanced himself from many of Khomeini's theological analyses. His magnum opus *Towzh al-Masayel* (*Explication of Issues*), published in Tehran in 1984, makes these differences amply clear: Montazeri puts the emphasis on individual initiative and example in promoting Islam while Khomeini argues that Islamic rules should be preserved and imposed by a strong government led by the clergy.

Montazeri spoke the language of the poor and also had a strong sense of humour, a characteristic lacking in Khomeini. Montazeri was no revolutionary in the sense that he did not like enforced change, violent measures and, above all, mass executions. And yet he had succeeded in becoming a power within a system that, on almost everything that mattered, operated against his wishes and convictions. He had been helped by two assets. First, he was the only senior cleric who stayed in Iran to fight the shah's Westernization programmes.

Secondly, he stayed away from official governmental power at a time when most ambitious mullahs were moving heaven and earth to become ministers, governors of provinces and directors of public companies. Montazeri devoted his energies to the creation of a nationwide network of preachers loyal to him. By 1986 he had an asset that few other mullahs could match: he controlled the vast majority of Friday prayer leaders throughout the country and could mobilize millions of people in the name of Islam. Thanks to his nationwide network of support, Montazeri won the majority of the seats in the Assembly of Experts, the body of mullahs charged with the task of choosing a successor to Khomeini.

In February 1986 Montazeri was formally named Khomeini's heir as Imam after the Assembly of Experts had approved his nomination in November 1985. That helped him emerge as a future saviour for all those who hoped that after Khomeini, Iran might one day return to the path of national reconciliation, economic development and peace. Montazeri, whose name can be translated as 'the man who waits', showed that he had mastered the art of patience in a society where undue haste could lead to death. Withdrawing to the holy city of Qom to be away from the excesses of the government in Tehran, Montazeri adopted the tactic of slowly distancing himself from Khomeini without antagonizing the ayatollah's still numerous followers.

A curious set of coincidences, however, persuaded the United States that Montazeri, the only leading personality of the Islamic Republic who could, by any stretch of imagination, be described as a moderate, was in fact the leader of the extremists and master of the terrorist network. In February 1986, when Ghorbanifar told North that the next stage in operations consisted of measures aimed at strengthening Montazeri's position in Tehran, the reaction he received was negative. North thought that Montazeri was 'the master terrorist' and recalled that he had read an article on the subject in the *Readers Digest*.[10] Teischer of the NSC was also persuaded that Montazeri was 'head of the hardliners'.[11]

The third personality in the troika was Hojat al-Islam Ali-Akbar Hashemi-Rafsanjani. His title of *hojat al-Islam* showed that he was a relatively junior cleric, a lieutenant colonel in terms of military hierarchy. But he was a specially powerful *hojat al-Islam* because he was leader of the Islamic Majlis and, far more importantly, enjoyed the confidence of Khomeini's son Ahmad. He was more of a politician in the generally accepted sense than either Khomeini or Montazeri. He was also wealthier than both of them combined.[12] His physical features as well as his known taste for profit had earned him the nickname of *Kusseh* ('the Shark') in Tehran. That the joke made him angry was illustrated by his decision to ban the marketing of a local brand of razorblades known as 'the Shark'. Intelligent and hard-working, the *hojat al-Islam* was a master of intrigue and a capable tactician. Aged only fifty-four in 1987, Rafsanjani was manifestly looking ahead to the time when his master and mentor, the eighty-five-year old Khomeini, would no longer be there.

Rafsanjani was spotted as a possible future strongman by West German and French intelligence as early as 1983. According to German sources, Washington was almost immediately advised to try to seek a dialogue with him.[13] At that time, however, the Reagan administration was still thinking in terms of confrontation rather than of accommodation regarding its future relations with the Islamic Republic. Rafsanjani himself sent several signals to Washington in the hope of starting a dialogue. The most important of these came in the shape of the *hojat al-Islam*'s personal intervention to secure the release of the passengers of a hijacked American aircraft in June 1985. He even went further and took the risk of calling for the normalization of relations with Washington in a number of speeches and interviews. But there was no response from Washington.

Why did Rafsanjani seek normalization with Washington? The first reason was that he was convinced that Iran was no longer capable of capturing Baghdad and deposing the Iraqi president, Saddam Hussein. That chance had come and gone in 1984. Rafsanjani was therefore determined to limit the damage the war might do to Iran. He was worried that the USA might throw its weight behind Iraq and enable Hussein's armies to regain the initiative in the war. The United States had already rendered invaluable service to Iraq by passing on to Baghdad information gathered by Saudi AWACs about Iranian troop movements. Further, Rafsanjani was convinced that the USA was behind the Saudi oil minister, Ahmad Zaki Yamani's policy of cheap oil which, in 1985–86, seemed specially designed to force the Islamic Republic into bankruptcy. By flooding the markets with Saudi oil, Yamani helped bring prices down to just over $5 a barrel at one point, from an average of $22 a few months earlier. Because Iran had to spend at least two extra dollars on oil trans-shipment to escape Iraqi air raids, as well as discounts designed to encourage customers to take the risk of trading in a war zone, the sharp drop in crude prices could only spell ruin for the Islamic Republic. The USA could help by joining Iran in persuading the Saudis to stop the price of oil from falling further, Rafsanjani thought. He also wanted the United States to release some of Iran's assets, frozen by President Carter in 1980. This point was of some importance when Iranian foreign currency reserves fell to less than $800 million in 1985, their lowest level in fifteen years.

The *hojat al-Islam* was convinced that, if there were to be any losers in a secret dialogue between Tehran and Washington, the Americans would be the likeliest candidates for that distinction. Iran could get from Washington the arms and the money it badly needed while driving a wedge between the USA and its Arab allies. And, if the secret link were to be exposed, he could always claim that he went along with it in order to divide the enemies of Islam. All he would give the USA in return would be freedom for a few hostages, knowing all along that more hostages could be taken in the future whenever necessary.[14]

The idea of establishing a dialogue with the United States was presented to Khomeini late in 1983. The proposal met with his approval. This did not mean that the ayatollah was prepared to abandon his strategic aim of forcing the Great Satan out of the Muslim world. He simply wanted to use the tactic of *tanfih* ('neutralizing one's enemy') which had been employed by the Prophet himself in his dealings with the Byzantine Empire in the seventh century. At an audience granted to the leading personalities of the republic in December 1983, Khomeini said he no longer objected to a dialogue with Washington provided two points were constantly borne in mind: that the USA remained the long-term enemy of Islam and that the Americans must not be allowed to divide the leadership in Tehran.[15] There was no disagreement about the first point: anti-Americanism remained one of the few principles that united almost all the rival personalities engaged in the power struggle in Tehran. Rafsanjani was able to reassure the ayatollah on the second point as well. He suggested that the Americans would 'never understand the way Islam works'.[16]

Later Rafsanjani was to put the point more precisely. In a speech at Tehran University he said: 'The Americans, despite their inquisitorial attitude [*sic*], their satellites, spies, the CIA and the rest, are so immensely uninformed about our region; how uninformed they are about our affairs. How many more half-baked analyses do they intend to make? They kept investing in trivial matters and issues in this country, believing that the leadership, the administration and the officials have risen against each other. Well, we have all seen that all that was in vain.'[17]

When Kangarloo began forging the Washington–Jerusalem connection through Ghorbanifar and his Israeli associates, Rafsanjani was the first to support it. He was determined to use this connection as a test of American intentions. If things developed in a favourable way, he could always step in and push aside both Kangarloo and his ineffective boss Mussavi. If, on the other hand, the path taken were to prove too hazardous, he could step aside and denounce his rivals for trying to surrender to the Great Satan. The least that Tehran could gain from the new connection would be the resumption and even the increase of Israeli arms supplies. The Israelis had always complained that their shipment of arms to Iran without the prior knowledge and approval of their principal ally, the United States, amounted to a big gamble for them.[18] Now that the United States itself was directly involved, the Israelis could be gradually pushed aside, thus minimizing the risk for the mullahs of being caught in the act of military cooperation with the 'Zionist enemy'. The point was of crucial importance since Khomeini had constantly claimed that the real aim of the Gulf War was to liberate first Iraq and then Jordan so that his armies could begin a war against Israel with the aim of bringing Jerusalem back to Islam. The ayatollah's 'volunteers for martyrdom' wore headbands marked with the legend: 'Pathfinder to Jerusalem!'

In their talks with the Americans on possible help for Iran in the Gulf War, the Israelis had often cited 'support for moderates' who might later oppose Khomeini as a major consideration. But Israeli thinking was certainly more sophisticated than that.[19] And it is possible that they used a simplified shorthand in their discussions with Washington because they were convinced that the USA was incapable of understanding the complicated situation in Tehran.

On 9 November 1985 Kimche held an extensive meeting with McFarlane and North in Washington, apparently to continue the process. He told them that Israel planned to provide some arms to moderates in Iran.[20] It was clear, at least to McFarlane, that the Israelis considered the earlier presidential authorization, issued in September, as 'an open charter for further arms shipments to Iran.'[21] The Israelis were confirmed in their view when their defence minister, Yitzhak Rabin, raised the matter again with McFarlane in Washington only a few days after the latter's meeting with Kimche.

Although McFarlane apparently told the Israelis that the president had approved shipments of Israeli arms to Iran only as part of a political agenda, Lieutenant Colonel North seemed to have seen the entire project as one primarily aimed at securing the release of the hostages. On 20 November North reported to Poindexter that a plan to bring out five of the hostages in exchange for eighty Hawk missiles supplied to Iran via Israel would be put into action in two days' time. On 19 November Israeli Defence Minister Yitzhak Rabin had contacted North to say that a problem had arisen in transporting the shipment to Iran.[22] North, true to his 'can do' reputation, authorized one of his friends, retired Major General Richard Secord, to proceed to 'a foreign country' to arrange the transport facilities required.[23] Secord acted swiftly and transport was assured that same day. But the local authorities refused landing rights to the Israeli aircraft bringing the Hawks. North tried to put pressure on the authorities in question through the CIA but failed. In the end the CIA referred Secord to a commercial carrier controlled by the agency and also arranged for landing rights in Cyprus and overflight in Turkish air space. When the aircraft landed in Tabriz the Iranians found out that there were only eighteen Hawks aboard. Worse still, they all bore Israeli army markings. No hostages were released and the Hawks were later returned.[24]

North was not deterred. On 4 December, a few days after Poindexter had succeeded McFarlane, who had resigned, North came up with a plan for the transfer of 3300 TOWs and fifty Hawks through Israel in exchange for the release of the hostages. The arms were to be delivered in five instalments, spread over a twenty-four-hour period. Each instalment was to be followed by the release of one or two hostages.[25] To allay suspicions that a secret deal between Tehran and Washington was the cause of the sudden release of so many American captives, it was agreed that at least one French hostage should also be set free.[26] The British mediator Terry Waite, the special envoy of the Archbishop of Canterbury, was to be used as 'the gift-wrapping' for the deal, allowing the kidnappers to claim that they had agreed to the releases because of 'religious and humanitarian concerns'.[27]

The decision to handle the problem of the hostages through secret channels and to link their fate to the question of arms shipments to Iran represented a dramatic reversal of US policy. It also gave the impression that all the hostages held were, as their captors claimed, indeed involved in espionage activities. Hojat al-Islam Ali Hassani Khameneh'i, president of the Islamic Republic, was to make this point in a direct way two years later. 'They say those people who are in the hand of our brethren in Lebanon are not spies,' he said. 'So why is it that the Great Satan was prepared to discuss their fate in secret negotiations? What was wrong with handling the whole thing openly if we were not dealing with spies who had gathered sensitive information on Islamic revolutionary organizations?'[28]

It might be argued that the tradition of secret negotiations in the hope of securing the release of the hostages had already been set by the Carter administration. But there were important differences between the 1979 drama in Tehran and the issue of the hostages seized in Beirut in the 1980s. In the first case the United States was dealing with a government which, although it had not initiated the act, accepted full legal responsibility for the seizure of the American embassy and the holding of the hostages. Concessions made to Tehran in secret negotiations concerning the embassy hostages would not, on their own, persuade the mullahs that holding innocent Westerners captive was the best means of furthering Khomeini's political aims. The seizure of the Tehran embassy was an act that could not be repeated if only because there were no more US diplomats to be held hostage in Iran. The situation in Beirut was different. Khomeini could order the seizure of Western hostages while denying all responsibility. The only way to discourage future capture of hostages was to make the act eminently costly or at least unprofitable. The North project, however, accepted the seizure of hostages as part of normal international practice in the region and showed that it could be eminently profitable as well. Subsequent relevations that profits from the shipment of illegal arms to Iran were to be used to finance the Nicaraguan contras showed that the whole matter was taken even further. The presence of American hostages in Lebanon was thus considered as a positive occurrence, a cover for pursuing one of Washington's most important hemispheric goals: the destabilization of the Sandinista regime in Nicaragua. In other words, if the hostages had not been there one would have had to invent them.

None of these points was brought up at a meeting, chaired by President Reagan, on 7 December 1985 and attended by Vice-President Bush, White House chief-of-staff Donald Regan, secretaries Shultz and Weinberger, Poindexter and the CIA deputy director, McMahon. McFarlane was also present to give an exposé of the programme. Testimonies offered by most of the participants showed that the meeting treated the North project rather casually. No troublesome questions were raised and, according to President Reagan, the meeting ended in a 'stalemate'.[29] Nevertheless, two days later, McFarlane kept a rendezvous with Ghorbanifar in London. North was also present at the meeting. McFarlane informed the Iranian that the United States, while interested in securing the release of the hostages and improving relations with Iran, was not prepared to achieve those goals by the shipment of arms to Iran.[30] Ghorbanifar said he would not pass on the message to Kangarloo because that might mean 'death for the hostages'. The Iranian did not gain the impression that the US position was final and thought McFarlane was 'just being difficult'.[31] Others present at the meeting, including Nir, seemed to share the impression. In any case North told Ghorbanifar and his friends that he would stay in touch. McFarlane reported the results of his London mission to President Reagan at the Oval Office on 10 December. Regan, Weinberger, Poindexter and CIA Director Casey were present. Once again no records were kept. McFarlane recommended that Ghorbanifar, whom he described as 'a devious character', be dropped.[32] Shultz, who was in Europe at that time and did not attend the meeting, was later informed of the decision by Poindexter. The secretary of state was later to testify that 'it was North who kept Ghorbanifar on the project after he had failed the polygraph'.[33]

The proceedings of the meeting at the Oval Office did not deter North, who lost no time in arranging a series of new meetings with Ghorbanifar and his associates in London and Frankfurt. The colonel was fully aware of what the Senate Intelligence Committee was to recognize as 'the deep personal concern on the part of the president for the welfare of US hostages'.[34] North gave every indication that he shared that concern. At every meeting with the Iranians and the Israelis he brought up the subject and referred to 'the sin of holding innocent people against their will'.[35]

In the new series of meetings North was accompanied by his friend Secord and the businessman Albert Hakim. Both were people with strong past links with Iran. Secord, a veteran of the war in Indo-China, had served in Iran between 1975 and 1979 as the commander of a 1200-strong US technical advisory team charged with the task of helping the shah's air force become the leading power in the skies of the Middle East. During that period he had been a valued adviser of the shah and his generals, who purchased thousands of millions of dollars worth of combat aircraft from the United States. Back in Washington in 1980, Secord was promoted major general and appointed deputy assistant secretary of defence in the first Reagan administration. It was in Washington in 1981 that Secord got to know North at the start of the latter's career at the NSC. The two of them managed the lobbying needed to win congressional approval for the sale of AWACs to Saudi Arabia. Secord's efforts won him the Distinguished Service Medal.

Secord's fall came at a time when everyone expected him to get his third star and become a lieutenant general. His personal relations with Edwin Wilson, a former CIA operative turned entrepreneur, got him into trouble when Wilson's illegal activities were exposed. No specific charges were pinned on Secord but in 1983 he was forced to apply for early retirement. Very soon he joined Hakim, a former associate of Wilson, who had been sentenced to a prison term, and together they created the Stanford Technology Trading Group International with headquarters in Vienna, Virginia.[36] Secord, although a close friend of Prince Bandar ben Sultan, the eldest son of the Saudi defence minister and his country's ambassador to Washington, failed to secure any major arms contracts in the Arab world. It was the advent of North's 'private aid to the contras' programme that helped Secord and Hakim save their company from going under.

Hakim's links with Iran were even stronger than his partner's. He had been born into an old Iranian Jewish family which boasted a history of several centuries. He had been sent to the USA from Iran to study agriculture or 'whatever he could' in the 1950s. But, instead of going to college, young Hakim began making money in a variety of ways. He became a naturalized American at the end of the 1950s and, when Iran began experiencing its oil boom, worked for various American companies as a Persian-English translator and interpreter.[37] In 1968 he was identified by SAVAK as someone 'connected with the CIA' and put under surveillance whenever he visited Tehran.[38]

Hakim was included in the North team largely because of his knowledge of Persian and what was perceived as his insight into the Iranian soul. He was supposed to decide which of the Iranians present at the meetings were trustworthy and which were not. That was a futile task because the club which had been formed had not come into being on the basis of the high moral standards of its members. Ghorbanifar and Hakim developed an almost instant dislike for each other. Ghorbanifar claimed that this was because his friends from the disbanded SAVAK told him that Hakim was 'a CIA man'.[39] Ghorbanifar pressed North to drop Hakim and the colonel obliged. In the later meetings he brought with him another Iranian-born American, Ebrahim Ebrahimian, who acted as interpreter. In the larger meetings Nimrodi also helped with the translation. In these meetings Nir, a journalist turned anti-terrorism expert, emerged as the strongman. His 'cool nerves, capacity to make complicated things appear simple and his piercing eyes' helped him dominate the proceedings.[40]

It was therefore not surprising that Nir almost took it upon himself to revive a project which everyone in the Reagan administration, with the important exception of North, had assumed to be dead and buried.[41] On 2 January 1986 Nir met Poindexter in Washington and presented a new plan. It consisted of two parts. First, Israel would supply 3000 TOWS to Tehran plus twenty Hezb-Allah prisoners held by Israel's allies in Lebanon. Second, Khomeini would order the release of five American hostages held by his men in Beirut. The proposal was brought up at a meeting at the Oval Office in the presence of the president. Bush, Shultz, Weinberger, Casey, Regan and Attorney-General Edwin Meese III were also at the meeting to hear Poindexter present Nir's project. Most of those present were later to testify that they had the impression that the president had approved the plan. In any case, a draft covert action finding had already been signed by President Reagan on 6 January, the day before the meeting at the Oval Office.[42] On 17 January the president signed a second draft finding after he had received a briefing from Poindexter. Bush, Regan and the NSC aide Donald Fortier had also attended the meeting. The president did not read the text that he signed but Poindexter must have informed him about the major policy change that the document envisaged. The new project effectively replaced the one that Nir had proposed; it suggested that the CIA purchase 4000 TOWs from the Pentagon and, after receiving full payment from Tehran, transfer them directly to the Islamic Republic. Israel's role would be limited to providing logistics support. On that day the president wrote in his diary: 'I agreed to sell TOWs to Iran'.[43]

It has been suggested that President Reagan approved the project because of urgings from Casey who had apparently not given up the hope of securing Buckley's release, despite persistent reports that the agent had died the previous autumn.[44] Whatever Casey's exact role in bringing the presidential decision about, the CIA became closely and directly involved in Operation Recovery from January 1986 onwards.

On 18 January Poindexter and North met with the CIA deputy-director of operations Clair George, the agency's general counsel Stanley Sporkin and another CIA official who had helped draft the original memorandum.[45] The first problem that was raised at the meeting concerned the polygraph test that had been administered to Ghorbanifar during the first week of January in Washington. The Iranian had once again failed the test and the CIA was unhappy about his continued involvement in the project. But North, supported by Casey, insisted that Ghorbanifar should remain on board and succeeded in making their view stick.[46]

On 24 January North, always meticulous about getting his initiatives approved by his superiors, sent a lengthy memorandum to Poindexter offering a notional timetable for Operation Recovery.[47] The plan was to begin that very same day, to be completed on 25 February with the transfer of arms and intelligence data to Iran. This last item was a new addition and had apparently been suggested by Nir as a further encouragement to the Iranian side. Under the plan Ghorbanifar was to transfer funds for the purchase of 1000 TOWs to an Israeli account at Crédit Suisse Bank in Geneva, Switzerland. The funds would then be transferred to another account in the same bank controlled by Secord. The retired general would then transfer $6 million to another account in the same bank, this one owned by the CIA. The agency, in turn, would then wire $6 million to a Pentagon account in the United States. The Pentagon would then transfer 1000 TOWs to the CIA without asking questions about end-users. The rest of the operation would be run by Secord and his associates. Khashoggi was to provide bridging finance for the operation.

The question of bridging finance was important because neither side trusted the other. The mullahs would not pay in advance and the Americans would not supply arms before receiving full payment. Thus Khashoggi was assigned the useful task with the promise of a 20 per cent profit plus personal expenses. Ghorbanifar expected to get 'at least $20 million' for himself and planned to 'keep half for myself and spend the rest supporting moderate elements in Tehran'.[48] He also thought that the first 1000 TOWS were meant to be a gesture of goodwill from the United States towards Tehran and not a means of ensuring the immediate release of any hostages.[49] Argument on that point was futile, for had the mullahs been sincere about wanting better relations with Washington, they would have arranged for the hostages to be released on their own initiative and as part of a broader political agenda. If, on the contrary, they were merely using the hostages as a bargaining counter with the USA they would certainly not give up all their assets in exchange for 1000 anti-tank missiles.

By the time the plan was put into motion Ghorbanifar's fertile imagination and Lieutenant Colonel North's strange credulity had blown the whole operation out of all proportions so far as its objectives were concerned. Ghorbanifar had persuaded the Americans that Khomeini would step down on 11 February, the anniversary of the Islamic Revolution, in favour of Montazeri. For some weeks prior to that Ghorbanifar had presented himself to the Americans as a key member of 'the Montazeri faction'. He had also claimed that his men controlled Tehran and would take over the government as soon as Montazeri became Supreme Guide. The faction would appoint Jalaleddin Farsi as the new prime minister, with Kangarloo taking over as commander of Revolutionary Guards and proceeding to arrest all leading 'Khomeinists opposed to a *rapprochement* with the West'.[50] That the Americans believed Ghorbanifar was evident from the fact that part of his scenario was included in the memorandum prepared by North and a CIA official for Poindexter and Casey.

Ghorbanifar had included in his purely imaginary scenario certain factual elements. Early in February the Assembly of Experts had convened to confirm Montazeri as heir to Khomeini. But this did not mean that the Imam was planning to retire. On the contrary, he was already thinking of promoting a five-man committee to succeed him, with his son Ahmad playing the role of strongman. The man Farsi, presented by Ghorbanifar as his choice for the premiership of the Islamic Republic, also existed. He was a Tehran member of the Islamic Majlis and was well known as a radical fundamentalist specially interested in exporting the Islamic Revolution to Lebanon. Farsi, born of an Afghan father and an Iranian mother in 1938, had been trained in PLO and Amal guerrilla camps in Lebanon in the 1970s and was generally considered to be a British 'influence agent' by SAVAK. He was the first candidate of the radicals in the first presidential election after Khomeini's seizure of power in Tehran. He was forced to withdraw his nomination after doubts were cast on his right to claim Iranian citizenship. His protector, Ayatollah Beheshti, was murdered in 1981 and Farsi began to draw closer to Montazeri. By 1984 he had accomplished a 180-degree change in his economic philosophy and become an enthusiastic advocate of an Iranian version of 'Reaganomics'. Was he signalling to Washington to recognize him as a potential friend?

By the end of 1985 Farsi had become the virtual boss of the Islamic Republican Party, the only political organization allowed to function legally in the country. A charismatic personality and a first-rate Persian orator despite his Afghan accent or perhaps because of it, Farsi was certainly an attractive ally. But it is doubtful that his links with Ghorbanifar went beyond the promises of support that the latter sent through Kangarloo and Ali-Beza Moayeri, another assistant to the prime minister, to Farsi.[51] Ghorbanifar claimed that his main objective in persuading the United States to develop an active policy towards Iran was to provide support for the moderates, led by Montazeri and Farsi, in their fight against allegedly pro-Soviet mullahs led by the Friday prayer leader of Qom, Ayatollah Ali-Akbar Meshkini, and his son-in-law, the security minister, Ayatollah Mohammad Rishahri.[52] Ghorbanifar also envisaged an alliance with 'the Rafsanjani faction' somewhere along the road, a theme which he also developed in a letter he sent to King Fahd through Prince Fadhel in the winter of 1987.

It is, of course, possible that Ghorbanifar sent messages to Montazeri expressing his support together with wishes for the ayatollah to become the next Supreme Guide. He may also have claimed to be in a position to secure American support for a future Montazeri government if and when a threat from Moscow took shape. Finally, it is also possible that Ghorbanifar promised financial support to groups backing Montazeri both in Iran and among the exile Iranians. But it is unlikely that the fast-speaking and highly imaginative wheeler-dealer ever put any of his own money where his mouth was in the case of Montazeri and Farsi. In 1987 Ghorbanifar was to claim that Operation Recovery had cost him more than $2 million. To back the claim he produced copies of travellers' cheques, used air-ticket coupons, hotel bills and a variety of other receipts. But there was nothing to show that any money reached the supporters of Montazeri and Farsi either in Iran or abroad.[53]

What is surprising is that the Americans made no effort to verify Ghorbanifar's sensational reports. The CIA was, apparently, reluctant even to consult its own operatives in the exile community – in elements of which the agency had invested more than $30 million in five years. That the Israelis were equally taken in showed that their claim to have access to sound information on Iran was based partly on wishful thinking.

The day of 11 February came and went without any of Ghorbanifar's predictions coming true. And yet North kept his part of the bargain. A week later the Americans delivered 500 TOWs to the Iranian port of Bandar Abbas and picked up the seventeen Israeli Hawks which the mullahs said they did not want. No hostages were released. Instead another meeting was arranged in Frankfurt for 24 February. North was accompanied by Secord and Hakim. Nir was also present. The CIA was represented by George Cave, the agency's deputy station chief in Tehran before the revolution. Cave had retired but continued to work for the agency as a contractual consultant. He was a fairly fluent Persian speaker and had much experience of working with Iranians. Once in Frankfurt, Ghorbanifar informed North that other meetings should be arranged with his Iranian contacts. He also insisted that Hakim be dropped. The second meeting, on 25 February, was much enlarged. Ghorbanifar brought with him two mullahs, Mohsen Khademi and Karim Lava'i. The Israeli side was strengthened by the presence of Kimche, Schwimmer and Nimrodi. Also present was John Shahin, a friend of Casey and business associate of Khashoggi. Ebrahimian acted as interpreter for the Americans.[54] Two days after that meeting, during which a variety of commercial, political and operational issues were discussed without much discipline, a further 500 TOWs were delivered to Iran.

While in Frankfurt Cave had tried to recruit Khademi, while Hakim wanted to forge a business relationship with him and was pressing for a separate meeting. The only tangible result of the Frankfurt meetings was an agreement to arrange a high-level encounter between the officials of the two sides. The NSC, through North, and the CIA, represented by an officer plus Cave, were to help organize the meeting, which would discuss all aspects of relations between Washington and Tehran.[55]

At least three other meetings followed in March and April in Paris, London and Frankfurt. North, Cave and a CIA official attended all three, together with Nir and Ghorbanifar. At the Paris meeting North and the CIA officer presented Ghorbanifar with intelligence supplied by Robert Gates, the CIA deputy-director, on what purported to be the build-up of Soviet troops in the Ashkabad and Yerevan regions on the Iranian frontier.

The mullahs had greatly appreciated earlier information supplied to them by the CIA and this helped Ghorbanifar bring his biggest rabbit yet out of his magician's hat. After meeting North in London on 6 May the Iranian intermediary informed the colonel that he could meet with a high-ranking mullah at the home of another 'trusted' Iranian. North took Cave with him. The man they met was Hassan Karrubi, a member of the Islamic parliament and a brother of Ayatollah Mehdi Karrubi who headed the Martyrs Foundation – a vast holding corporation that controlled over seven hundred different enterprises in the Islamic Republic. More importantly, from the Americans' point of view, the ayatollah was also the paymaster of the Party of Allah, the terrorist organisation that held the American hostages in Lebanon. Although Hassan Karrubi, also a mullah, had quarrelled with his more powerful brother a few months earlier, he assured his interlocutors that he spoke on behalf of the powerful chief of the Martyrs Foundation. He invited the Americans to make use of his good offices for the purpose of establishing useful contact with 'the healthy elements of government in Tehran'.

Karrubi was visibly 'moved and happy' to be meeting North, who was presented to him as 'the closest man to the American president' and a man 'considered by Reagan as his spiritual son'.[56] Cave was also similarly elevated and was introduced as 'the master of all secret activities of America'.[57] Ghorbanifar was later to justify his exaggerated introductions on the grounds that he had wished to impress the influential mullah so as to accelerate the release of the hostages.[58] Cave cracked some jokes with the mullah and the two men embraced at the end of the meeting with a profusion of cordialities both about their 'personal friendship' and the future friendship of the United States and the Islamic Republic. Later Cave was to commit a strange imprudence. He asked Nozar Razm-Ara, an Iranian-born CIA operative, to produce a handwritten letter to Karrubi thanking him for his kind attentions in London. The letter also included an invitation to Karrubi to ring Cave at the latter's home in the United States. The letter, which reached the mullah by post, drove Karrubi up the wall. 'Why are your friends so careless?' he cried out in a telephone call to Ghorbanifar in Paris.[59]

The idea of sending a high-level delegation to Tehran had been raised by Kimche as early as September 1985. The Israeli diplomat was convinced that the United States and the Islamic Republic could talk together and work out 'a framework for future cooperation' because they 'both need each other in this region'.[60] The idea was seized upon

by Ghorbanifar and North, who may have been excited by the
dramatic opportunities that it promised. North, a firm believer in
covert operations, was convinced that secret contacts, even though
ill-prepared, would, as if by magic, produce results which the more
routine methods of diplomacy would not.[61] The idea of the trip was
approved by Poindexter in April in response to a memorandum
prepared by North. The NSC head also asked McFarlane to lead the
American delegation to Tehran. But it was not until 22 May that
Ghorbanifar reported that his contacts in Tehran were ready to receive
the Americans.

Tehran and Washington had formed different ideas of the planned
visit. The mullahs were under the impression that the Americans were
sending a low-level delegation to prepare for another visit by more
senior officials. Rafsanjani was informed of the visit by Mussavi and
Kangarloo on 17 May and was told that the Americans were bringing
with them a further 1000 TOWs, weapons which Iran needed for a
new major incursion into Iraqi territory. This new operation was to
consolidate the victories Iran had scored in February by capturing a
good part of the Faw Peninsula in Iraq. The TOWs previously supplied
by the USA had played a crucial role in that campaign by neutralizing
Iraqi armoured divisions. Tehran was hoping for a repeat performance. The Americans had also rendered two more services to Iran in
February. First, they stopped the AWACs data on Iranian troop
movements which they had regularly supplied to Iraq, via Saudi
Arabia, for a crucial week, thus helping Tehran achieve the element of
surprise. More importantly, Washington, both by private 'advice' and
public pronouncements, led the Iraqis to believe that the next Iranian
offensive would occur in the Mandali region in the central sector of the
front, some 350 kilometres to the north of Faw.[62] Thus when the
Iranians invaded Faw the best-prepared Iraqi forces were far from the
actual scene of battle and Iraq suffered one of its worst defeats in the
war.

Rafsanjani reported to Khomeini about the planned American visit
a few days after consulting with Mussavi. The ayatollah was told that
the Americans were sending 'some technicians' for further talks about
a list of arms and spare parts which Kangarloo had passed on to North
through Ghorbanifar some weeks earlier. That list had contained
orders for 240 items of 'crucial importance for the progress of the
war'.[63] The ayatollah was also told that the Americans would bring
with them the TOWs promised. The ayatollah approved Rafsanjani's
suggestion that the visit should not be discussed at a full session of the
High Council of Defence. But the council's secretary, Kamal Kharazi,
was told that 'a group of arms merchants and American technicians'

was coming to Tehran to put the final touches to Iran's shopping list for material and weapons.

The mood in Tehran on the eve of the Americans' visit was good and the mullahs were for the first time in many years well disposed towards the Great Satan. Washington had in effect changed sides in the Gulf War by helping Iran confuse the enemy and also by providing the type of weapons the Iranian forces needed at that precise moment.

Preparations for the trip were completed by North and Secord around 23 May. North, in a memo to Poindexter, had suggested on 17 May that the planned trip be discussed with the president as well as Shultz, Weinberger and Casey. But Poindexter responded by noting that he did not want such a meeting. It is possible that North and Poindexter made the exchange of notes as part of their routine efforts to offer the president 'plausible deniability', a practice current in organizations dealing with covert operations.[64] But other evidence suggests that the president was fully briefed on the McFarlane mission to Tehran and approved it and its terms of reference.

The mission to Tehran was originally planned to include McFarlane, North, Teischer, Cave and a CIA official who was introduced to Ghorbanifer only as Bob. The Israelis insisted that Nir should also be included and, after a strong appeal from Premier Peres, McFarlane agreed to let the Israeli join the mission. A communications operator and a radio technician from the CIA were also included in the travelling party. Ghorbanifar, however, did not know exactly who was on the mission and certainly did not think that McFarlane was back. The Iranian had been handed a confidential report 'of a military nature likely to interest Tehran' in London the day before he left for Iran. He took this as one more sign of goodwill from Washington towards the mullahs.[65]

The delegation left Tel Aviv for Tehran on 25 May. It had with it a number of gifts for the mullahs: a key-shaped cake bought at a kosher bakery and intended to symbolize 'the new opening' between Tehran and Washington, eight Colt side guns destined for high-ranking mullahs, whose love of such dangerous toys was well known, and, more importantly, a pallet containing the Hawk spare parts urgently needed by Iran to cover its forces in Faw against almost hourly air attacks by the Iraqis. The leader of the delegation, McFarlane, was not told that the aircraft which took him and his associates to Tehran also carried military cargo.

11

THREE DAYS IN HELL

It was on a hot and dismal Sunday morning that the plane carrying McFarlane and members of his mission from Tel Aviv landed at Tehran's Mehrabad International Airport at the start of what was, in any event, a historic visit. For this was the first time in more than six years that an official American delegation was coming to wartorn revolutionary Iran at the start of what looked like a new beginning in relations between the two nations. The various members of the mission had different expectations concerning the outcome of the visit. McFarlane might have seen his mission as a repetition of his mentor Henry Kissinger's secret visit to Beijing that led to the establishment of formal diplomatic ties between the United Sates and the People's Republic.[1] North pursued the more modest, though no less laudable, goal of securing the release of the American hostages held by Khomeini's agents in Lebanon. Nir dreamed of the revival of the USA–Israeli–Iran alliance of the 1960s, an alliance which the shah's ties with Arabs in the 1970s had weakened and the Khomeinist revolution of 1979 had almost completely shattered.

The first impressions, however, did not encourage any of those thoughts. The plane landed an hour earlier than scheduled and there were no officials to greet the party at Mehrabad. The aircraft was instantly surrounded by bearded revolutionaries brandishing their Israeli-made Uzi machine guns. This is how McFarlane reported his first impressions to Poindexter the same evening:

> Delegation arrived Tehran Sunday morning. Absence of anyone to receive us for over an hour and recurrent evidence anxiety ineptitude in . . . even the most straightforward discourse makes it clear that we must take a step back from the history of the past 8 years and put our task in a different light.
>
> It may be best for us to try to picture what it would be like if after nuclear attack, a surviving Tatar became Secretary of State; and a bookie became the interlocutor for all discourse with foreign countries.[2]

The visitors were eventually greeted at the airport by Kangarloo and

Ghorbanifar and driven to the Independence Hotel (formerly the Royal Hilton) in two cars belonging to the prime minister's office. At the hotel they were housed on the top floor, which was isolated by a heavy security guard led by Kangarloo's younger brother Hamid. Lunch, consisting of boiled rice and grilled lamb and prepared under the direct supervision of Ghorbanifar's mother at her home, was delivered a few hours later. Another of Kangarloo's brothers assured the guard that no one would attempt to kill the visitors by poisoning their food.[3]

The first formal session of talks took place that same afternoon. McFarlane treated the whole thing in traditional diplomatic style, much to the dismay of his interlocutors who were more at ease with bazaar-style haggling. It was three days later, when the negotiations had already failed, that the American realized that he had been talking to individuals who were 'rug merchants'.[4] The Islamic team was led by Kangarloo and included another assistant to the premier, Ali Reza Moayeri, in charge of political affairs, and a junior foreign ministry aide. Ghorbanifar also attended although he was not an official of either government. The Khomeinists instantly made it clear that they were no more than messenger boys and were almost exclusively concerned with the spare parts that McFarlane had been expected to bring in his plane. McFarlane was nevertheless determined to play the role he had assigned himself and offered a fairly lengthy lecture on the benefits of improving relations and the necessity of countering Soviet mischiefmaking in the region.

The Khomeinist negotiators had been dispatched to the meeting after the ayatollah himself had been informed of McFarlane's arrival. Rafsanjani, Mussavi and Khamaneh'i were present together with Khomeini's son Ahmad and the ayatollah's special adviser, Mohammad Kaffash-Zadeh. As usual in all doubtful situations, the ayatollah placed the ball in the court of his aides. 'This has been your idea,' he said, 'and you must handle it yourselves. Go and see what the American has to say, receive the things he has brought and let him go in peace.'[5] Khomeini also remarked that the secret mission of the Americans was very much like the one dispatched to Prophet Muhammad by the Byzantine emperor Heraclitus. The Byzantines had also brought some arms with them but their main objective was to sow the seeds of dissension in the Muslim camp and to recruit spies.[6]

McFarlane played the classic number of blowing hot and cool, alternating gestures of friendship with demonstrations of pique. The Khomeinists, not familiar with the system of diplomatic signalling, did not read McFarlane's semiology until the very end, when it was too late. The former presidential adviser and the NSC's Teischer produced extensive records of the talks with the Khomeinists. These records portrayed a relationship of deep misunderstandings, attempts at mutual deception and an almost total failure to communicate. The cultural time gap that existed between the two sides was one reason for the failure. The Khomeinists' historical terms of reference were largely confined to the time of the prophet in the seventh century AD. At the same time they enjoyed no decision-making power, nor did their immediate bosses: the prime minister, the president and the speaker of the Islamic parliament. Every decision of consequence had in the end to be approved by Khomeini himself. The trouble was that it was Ramadan, the Muslim month of fasting, and Khomeini, who stayed awake all night long to perform special prayers, was asleep most of the day and could not be disturbed. Khomeini also did not like what was described to him by Mussavi as McFarlane's 'haughty, arrogant and insulting style'.[7] The ayatollah remembered that the Prophet would never allow 'cross-worshippers' and others 'still in the dark' to try to dictate to and humiliate 'the true believers'.[8]

After two futile sessions with the three officials from the premier's office, McFarlane insisted that he should meet someone more senior and suggested that a minister be sent. The demand, conveyed to Khomeini, was instantly rejected. But the ayatollah ordered the president, the speaker and the premier jointly to choose an emissaary to deal with the Americans. The man chosen was Muhammad-Ali Hadi Najaf-Abadi, chairman of the foreign relations committee of the Islamic Majlis. A former mullah, Najaf-Abadi had spent many years teaching at an Iranian primary school in Pakistan and spoke good English. He had begun his political career as a radical revolutionary in 1968 when, at the age of twenty-seven, he had joined a clandestine organization created by his boyhood friend Mohammad Montazeri, the son of ayatollah Montazeri.[9] The two men later spent some time in PLO camps in Lebanon and also travelled to Libya where they became personal friends of Colonel Moammar al-Gaddafi.

During the Islamic Revolution in Iran Najaf-Abadi, together with Mohammad Montazeri, was in charge of the revolt in Isfahan and organized a number of attacks on Bell Helicopter installations, where thousands of Americans worked. Najaf-Abadi had also led the mob that had tried to lynch a Bell employee after the latter had fired on a noisy crowd of Muslim revolutionaries in 1978.

After Mohammad Montazeri's death in a terrorist plot in 1981, Najaf-Abadi experienced what seemed a profound political change. Once recognized as one of the most radical of extremists, he began to advocate gradualism in enforcing the rules of Islam and supported a less virulent approach to foreign policy. In 1984 he was elected to the

Majlis from his dead friend's constituency and quickly emerged as a relative moderate. In 1986 he ran for the chairmanship of the foreign relations committee against the leading hardliner Ahmad Azizi, the man who had played a key role in the Tehran hostages crisis. Najaf-Abadi's success signalled a desire by the Majlis to bury the memory of that confrontation with the 'Great Satan'.

Najaf-Abadi's arrival on the scene of the Hilton negotiations was a distinct improvement. For one thing, unlike the three officials from the prime minister's bureau, Najaf-Abadi understood and spoke English. For another, he was able to telephone Rafsanjani directly, who in turn was able to contact Ahmad Khomeini. Another reason why Najaf-Abadi's arrival on the scene pleased the Americans was that he, unlike Kangarloo, who had led the Khomeinist side until then, was not an amateur of raw garlic. Cave had noted in his diary that Kangarloo's 'breath could curl a rhino's hide'.[10]

The new Khomeinist standardbearer in the talks was not, however, a moderate in the sense that Washington understood the term. He was conscious of the fact that the Islamic Revolution needed Washington's help at that precise moment and, reflecting the views of Khomeini, was determined to secure that help without offering any concessions in return apart from an agenda for a gradual release of the hostages. At first McFarlane, playing the 'I am hurt and angry' number, refused to talk to Najaf-Abadi, who patiently sat down to a marathon discussion with North and Nir. He found Nir 'reasonable' and appeared to like the Israeli counter-terrorist expert, one of the most wanted men in revolutionary Islam. Nir, introduced as an American named Miller, had made no effort to change his appearance before coming to Tehran despite the fact that an old photo of him had been published in the Tehran papers on a number of occasions with the caption: 'Number One Zionist Enemy'.

During the talk with Khomeini's new envoy, North concentrated on the problem of the hostages, using the prospect of further arms sales as an important bargaining counter. Najaf-Abadi played the game with good humour and, convinced that 'only money can make the Americans open their hearts', raised the possibility of a $2500 million order for arms from Iran.[11] North, who was already working on his 'neat idea' to spend part of the profits made on the sale of arms to Khomeini for the purpose of funding the Nicaraguan rebels, seemed to like both the new man and his big talk.

McFarlane, when he eventually agreed to have a one-on-one session with Najaf-Abadi, a session that lasted three hours, was also impressed by the man although he did not fail to discern the real purpose of the Khomeinist regime. In his report to Poindexter about

the talks McFarlane wrote: 'It was a useful meeting on the whole. . . . I
made clear that regarding Iran we sought a relationship based upon
mutual respect for each other's sovereignty, territorial integrity and
independence.'[12] The leader of the American delegation noted nonetheless that the Khomeinists 'appeared to us to be determined to
expand their influence through the spread of Islamic fundamentalism,
relying on the use of terrorism to achieve their purpose.'[13]

In his first two days at the Tehran Hilton McFarlane had learned all
that he needed to know in order to realize that his mission was
impossible. The mission was faulty in its choice of objectives, in its
design, in its timing and in its composition. In it a variety of issues,
ranging from the strategically vital to the politically trivial, were
mixed together. Nir and Cave were trying to persuade the Khomeinists
to allow a US-Israeli permanent communication team to be established in Tehran. The Khomeinists saw this suggestion as an attempt
by the 'Great Satan' to create an espionage nucleus. Cave also made
some noises about 'eight hours of material' that he had brought with
him on Soviet preparations to invade Iran with twenty-six divisions.
The Khomeinists took this as a crude attempt by the Americans to
disrupt relations between Tehran and Moscow. They kept coming
back to their complaint that the mission had not brought all the
materiel promised. The talks went in all directions as the two sides
drank endless cups of tea, ate watermelon, had fairly copious dinners,
followed by the special sweets of Ramadan, and failed even to work
out a proper agenda, which ought to have been prepared before the
mission left Tel Aviv for Tehran.

The Khomeinist negotiators continued to promise quick action on
the hostages and even claimed that a special emissary had already left
for Beirut to discuss the matter with Hezb-Allah. This was a
diplomatic lie and the matter of the hostages was not raised with
Khomeini until 5 a.m. on 28 May, a few hours before McFarlane
threatened to lead his mission out of Iran. It must have been clear to
McFarlane that even the highest of the Khomeinist officials, although
at times capable of ordering the capture of hostages in Lebanon,
would not be able to secure the release of a single hostage without the
agreement of the ayatollah himself.

At dawn on 28 May Khomeini agreed that the release of two
hostages, The Reverend Lawrence Jenco and David Jacobsen, should
be arranged with his agents in Beirut. The decision was passed on to
Rafsanjani by Ahmad Khomeini, and McFarlane was informed of it at
7.50 a.m. when Kangarloo arrived at the Hilton. The Americans
replied by saying, 'It is too late, we are leaving.' Ten minutes later
Najaf-Abadi arrived to offer the same promise, namely, to secure the

release of two hostages in the course of the day. He indicated that all the previously announced conditions for the release had been dropped as if by magic.[14] He also hinted that, if the mission agreed to prolong its stay by a day or two, during which time the rest of the materiel bought by Tehran would be delivered after the release of two hostages, a meeting would be arranged with 'one of our leaders' – presumably Rafsanjani. But McFarlane would not be moved; he would not promise that the materiel bought by Iran would be delivered two hours after the hostages' release in Beirut and was not prepared to spend one more day in Tehran. He gave the signal for departure and the mission, accompanied by the Khomeinist team and Ghorbanifar, left for the airport. Najaf-Abadi was constantly pleading with McFarlane in the car on the way to the airport: 'Please, don't leave. We are on the verge of getting results.' The Reagan envoy, however, was convinced that this was just a delaying tactic on the part of the Khomeinists. He felt that he had suffered enough humiliation and believed that he had to protect the prestige of the president by walking out. He might also have been concerned about the possibility of the entire mission or members of it being seized and held hostage by the more radical groups opposed to any dialogue with the 'Great Satan'. Kangarloo had hinted at such a possibility when he raised the problem of the American technician who had remained at the airport to guard the aircraft. 'That man could attract attention from certain elements,' Kangarloo told McFarlane, 'and that could lead to grave consequences.' That McFarlane was concerned about security was also indicated by his refusal to drive to Tajrish, north of Tehran and only a few minutes' drive from the hotel, to breathe some fresh air. The hotel's air-conditioning did not function properly and the city was, in any case, left without electricity for four to five hours each day in temperatures that rose to 38 degrees centigrade. Both the Americans and their Islamic hosts were also concerned about the possibility that their secret encounters might be exposed by political enemies. Indeed, it subsequently became known that agents of Mehdi Hashemi, who at the time headed the Office for Exporting the Islamic Revolution and was considered a rival and enemy of Rafsanjani, had photographed members of the McFarlane mission at the airport and tape recorded part of a conversation between North and Najaf-Abadi at the Hilton. The pictures and the tape were presented to Khomeini nearly a week after the Americans had left Tehran. Hashemi's men had not been able to identify the mysterious visitors and the purpose of their mission earlier. They also thought, quite naively, that Khomeini had not been informed of the presence of the American mission in Tehran.[15]

Was the mission on the verge of succeeding when McFarlane lost his temper and decided to leave? Members of the McFarlane mission carefully avoided giving a yes or no answer to that question. But their subsequent behaviour showed that they did not share McFarlane's belief that it was wise to leave. North pursued his efforts despite the failure of the mission. Cave exchanged private telephone numbers with the Khomeinists and began ringing them only two days later. Nir and Najaf-Abadi had embraced and professed 'everlasting friendship' at the airport. As for Ghorbanifar, he was convinced that 'a good deal was undone because McFarlane lost his nerve'.[16]

There was other evidence to support the suggestion that the mission might have succeeded in the end. Rafsanjani had ordered a complete ban on all anti-American propaganda by the state-owned radio and television networks a few days before the mission landed in Tehran[16] and attacks on Washington were appreciably toned down for six more months. The two hostages whose release had been approved by Khomeini on 28 May were, in the end, set free. Poindexter was to attribute at least one of the releases to McFarlane's efforts in Tehran. The Khomeinist leaders wanted the mission to succeed because they needed material urgently and also wished to woo the USA away from the Arabs. The fact that they continued their efforts in that direction after McFarlane had left Tehran underlined their genuine desire to seek a dialogue with Washington as a tactical move. The junior officials involved in the negotiations, together with Ghorbanifar, were also keenly interested in seeing the mission succeed because, as Cave put it in his diary, they could expect to make a lot of money.[18]

What McFarlane did not know is that almost all deals in oriental bazaars are clinched when the customer moves towards the door and appears to be leaving the shop.

North and Cave, who conducted a good part of the more sensitive negotiations, had a negative impact on the outcome. They behaved like pioneering Americans dealing with Red Indian chiefs in the Wild West of the nineteenth century. They offered the Khomeinists a mixture of bribes and threats. Instead of beads and booze, they offered Hawk missiles, satellite photos of Iraqi and Soviet military installations and even the possibility that the United States would help the Islamic Republic raise thousands of millions of dollars on the international credit market.[19]

The fact that not a single trained professional diplomat was present on either side complicated the situation further. The many objectives the two sides pursued were at no point put in order of priority. A discussion which began with Soviet geo-strategic designs would suddenly degenerate into an exchange about the need to refuel the mission's aircraft at Mehrabad. The traditional resources of diplomacy were not available to the mission, which could not make up its mind whether it wanted to secure the release of the hostages, find a new source of funding for the Nicaraguan contras, enlist Iran's support in the war against the Soviets in Afghanistan, create a US-Israeli intelligence capacity in Tehran, help the so-called moderates win power in the Islamic Republic, persuade Khomeini to forget about exporting his revolution through terrorism or, last but not least, help Ghorbanifar – affectionately referred to as Gorba by North and the others – make his $20 million.

In Israel, on the way home, McFarlane was clearly disappointed. North tried to cheer him by saying that 'the one bright spot is that the government can avail itself of part of the [Iranian] money for application to Central America.'[20] All participants in the mission, with the exception of Nir, blamed much of what had gone wrong on Ghorbanifar, who had obviously lied to both sides in order to make himself appear more influential and the deal he was brokering more important. The Iranian businessman was also accused of having forged letters to himself on US official notepaper in order to persuade the Iranians that he had obtained all that he had promised.[21] Nevertheless Ghorbanifar retained much of his influence in Tehran, where he stayed for two more days after the mission had left. He was taken to task because of the fact that the Americans had increased the prices of the items they had sold to Iran by as much as six times and, worse still, had refused to deliver part of the materiel that had already been paid for. Ghorbanifar found himself in a tight spot but managed to talk his way out of it with promises of bringing McFarlane back to Tehran. His former butler, at least, believed him and arranged for him to obtain an exit visa and fly back to Paris.

By the time McFarlane returned to Washington nearly a year had passed since the United States had first begun an informal relationship with the Islamic Republic with help from Israel. During that period the United States sold Iran 1508 TOW missiles, one Hawk missile, spare parts for the 240 Hawks which Iran already possessed and some radar equipment.[22] At the same time the USA provided Iran with intelligence on Iraqi war plans and Soviet military activity near the Iranian frontier. The relationship had led to the release of one American hostage in Lebanon, while another hostage, Buckley, had died in the same period, probably somewhere in Iran. The two sides had failed to develop mutual trust and the Iranians were especially unhappy about the fact that they had paid an inflated price for the TOWs purchased from the United States.

Ghorbanifar, the key contact man, was in a truly sad shape in June 1986. His creditors were threatening to purchase a contract on his life to benefit from a $20 million life insurance policy they had bought for him. His associate, Kangarloo, was in no more enviable circumstances and was told by his boss, Premier Mussavi-Khameneh'i, that he might be murdered by disappointed radicals for being 'cheated by the Americans and having lost a hostage without getting the Shi'ite prisoners out of Kuwait.'[23] So upset was Kangarloo that he continued to ring Cave in the hope of securing the items for which Iran had already paid. But Cave stalled. Later North decided that Kangarloo should be kept on hold and promised to help him escape from Iran and obtain political asylum in the United States if things went really wrong for him. Cave also told Kangarloo that the secret meetings in Tehran had been videotaped and that the USA might expose him at a moment of its choosing unless the Iranians made a move on the hostages. Fearing for his life and his money and facing what amounted to open blackmail, Kangarloo decided to do all he could to get another hostage out in the hope of keeping the process going. He apparently succeeded after convincing his superiors in Tehran that a new hostage release should be tried as a test. 'If this does not work,' he reportedly told his boss, 'all we have lost is a captive priest. And we can always order another American to be seized in his place.'[24]

The stalemate between Washington and Tehran had other consequences. Khashoggi had mobilized $15 million as a bridging loan to make the deal possible and was now under heavy pressure to return the money plus interest. He was specially harassed by three Canadian partners, who threatened legal action. But it was not until October that Khashoggi instructed his New York business partner Roy Furmark to contact Casey about the money. Furmark told Casey that there were rumours that the money in question, or at least part of it, had been funnelled to the contras. By that time, and before Casey could initiate any action, the whole operation was on the verge of being exposed. Meanwhile Khashoggi, no doubt under Israeli pressure, continued to finance a number of other shipments to Iran, including a batch of 1000 TOWs which passed through Spain, in the hope of keeping the new relationship with Khomeini afloat and at the same time getting his initial investment back. In the end he was to receive only part of the money he had put down.[25]

A surprising feature of the secret negotiations that went on between the mullahs on the one side and the USA and Israel on the other was the lack of attention paid to the possibility of accidental leaks or, worse still, Soviet discovery of the entire operation. The Americans and the Israelis tried to scare the mullahs by invoking the pervasive presence of Soviet agents, Moscow's devious methods of infiltration and other forms of aggression. And yet they seemed strangely relaxed about their game being discovered by the Russians. Ghorbanifar, who had just published in Persian a CIA-inspired book on the KGB, mentioned the KGB threat on one or two occasions. North was also aware of the possibility of a Soviet countermove, especially in view of the fact that a senior member of the prime minister's staff in Tehran was suspected of being a KGB mole.[26] The operation was extremely vulnerable. For one thing, too many people knew about it or at least some aspects of it. The total number of the people who knew came to a minimum of eighty-five Iranians, Americans, Israelis and Saudis and at least one French intelligence officer. The only ones systematically excluded from any knowledge of the operation were US congressional leaders. Khashoggi and Ghorbanifar, men who would miss no opportunity of demonstrating their real or imagined power in shaping the destiny of the world, might well have spoken about the operation in the hope of impressing their friends or hangers-on.

There is evidence to suggest that by the time McFarlane arrived in Tehran the Soviets had gained the impression that something was going on between Washington and Tehran. This impression, which did not crystallize into concrete intelligence, was reflected in Moscow Radio's Persian-language commentaries, which began to warn the Islamic Republic against 'deceptive acts by American imperialism'.[27] Iranian diplomats in Moscow were also fed information arranged to 'prove' American collusion with Iraq and spoke of 'plots by Washington to restore its former dominance in Iran'.[28]

The Russians might just have put two and two together in guessing that something was going on between the Reagan administration and the mullahs. They could not have failed to notice that the mullahs had suddenly toned down their anti-American propaganda. They must have also asked why it was that two American hostages were released in Beirut. They would certainly not have believed that the releases had been brought about simply by Terry Waite's spiritual intervention. Moscow must have also wondered how it was that hundreds of TOW missiles suddenly came into the possession of Iranian forces for use against Iraq. The KGB, active in Iraq since 1958, must have had enough sources in Baghdad to report that. The secret operation was not, in the end, discovered by the Russians, but it is not impossible to suggest that it might have been sooner or later had not someone else blown the whistle.

The point is worth making for a number of reasons. Operation Recovery was designed as covert action, but when it entered its implementation phase it was constantly put to the test in terms of ordinary diplomatic achievements. The two sides insisted on confidence building in the form of cessation of propaganda activity against each other. The mullahs even ceased attacking the 'Great Satan' at mosque gatherings. In exchange the Reagan administration stopped including the Islamic Republic in the list of nations sponsoring terrorism and even thanked Tehran for efforts that led to Weir's release. Such obvious signs that an attempt to patch up relations was being made could not have a place in the Machiavellian universe of truly covert action, which would have necessitated no moves on the hostages, at least for some time, plus a sharpening of the propaganda war in order to raise the smokescreen necessary.

The alternative to that curious game of amateur diplomacy conducted by self-styled experts in covert operations would have been good, classic, solid, and often boring, diplomacy conducted through one or more nations with friendly ties to both sides and with the knowledge of at least a few leading senators and congressmen. An attempt to discuss the problems which existed between Washington and Tehran might even have been made through the Hague machinery; after all, the two sides had been meeting there for more than six years. By attempting a dramatic shortcut and trying to prod history along by hook or by crook, the designers of Operation Recovery ignored the fact that some international problems could be solved only by the passage of time. Kissinger's coup in Beijing some twenty-two years after the rupture of Sino-American ties could not be repeated by McFarlane after only a six-year break between Tehran and Washington. Operation Recovery was a typical product of the 'can do' spirit on the part of adepts of the cult of action who prefer to act first and think afterwards. Had even a minute fraction of the discussion, debate and study devoted to Irangate after its exposure been invested in Operation Recovery before it was set in motion, the results achieved might have done more honour to its authors. But a more thoughtful approach would have almost certainly ruled against the very scheme put forward by Lieutenant Colonel North. American impatience, encouraged by the media constantly focusing on dramatic news, makes the practice of patient diplomacy far more difficult in the United States than in some other countries. In the United States advocating patient diplomacy as the best policy is often looked upon as either treason or lack of compassion. The issue of the hostages was one such. The American efforts to liberate their four hostages, by taking grave risks on issues of far greater importance, contrasted sharply with Britain's attitude towards the same problem. The Party of Allah had been holding four British hostages in Lebanon and two more in Iran and had murdered two more captive Britons. And yet the British government adamantly refused to negotiate for their release. The message was: let our people go for we will never link their fate to any other issue. Even the abduction of Terry Waite did not change that policy. The British policy did not succeed in securing freedom for the hostages, but at least it had the merit of consistency. It also recognized the dangerous fact that a hostage released could always be replaced by another one taken.[29]

A good part of the blame for the failure of the McFarlane mission to Tehran was put on Ghorbanifar, who was variously described as a 'compulsive liar', 'a fabricator' and 'a devious character'. But having recourse to falsehood was the very hallmark of the entire operation on all sides. The principal architect of the operation, Lieutenant Colonel North, admitted that he told lies even to his personal friend Secord to give the impression that President Reagan knew the details of what was going on. As for the other side, North was even more straight-forward: 'I lied to the Iranians every time I met them.'[30] Thus the aim of the operation could not have been the building of confidence on both sides so that Tehran and Washington could work for normal relations on the basis of mutual trust. He who lies must also take into account the possibility of being lied to. And Ghorbanifar was later to admit that he too had lied – to the CIA during the lie-detector tests, to North, to Nir, to Khashoggi and, of course, to the mullahs – because he too believed that he was working for a noble cause in whose service all means were justified.

McFarlane reported to the president on his mission on 2 June and was to hear no more of the secret efforts to release the hostages and help the moderates in Tehran until much later. In his report to Reagan, McFarlane advised against the use of further weapon sales to Iran and urged that the United States should work for a political agenda with the Islamic Republic.[31]

North, who did not believe in the virtues of patience, however, had a different view. Encouraged by Casey, who virtually acted as his case officer, he kept in touch with Kangarloo through Cave, thus by-passing Ghorbanifar, who had been branded 'an Israeli agent' by the CIA director. At the same time North revived the idea of trying to rescue the hostages through military action in Lebanon. On 6 June the president approved the use of force to release the hostages 'if current efforts failed'.[32] North set to work on the 'military option' the same day.

This was not the first time that the use of force to rescue the hostages was considered by the Reagan administration. The temptation to succeed where President Carter had failed, by using force for a cause likely to be almost unanimously endorsed by the American public, reached fever pitch within the administration early in 1985. Casey, determined to save Buckley or, failing that, to punish the abductors, persuaded the president to consider the option. He also chose North to supervise the operation. At that time, however, North did not yet have his own private network of 'can do' patriots and had to rely on CIA resources. The CIA succeeded in recruiting a force of eighty-five Druze fighters in Lebanon. Three of the force's commanders were brought to the United States where they received special training in North Carolina for five weeks.[33] A Lebanese Armenian, known by the codename of S. D. Arsham, acted as liaison officer. He succeeded in locating Peter Kilburn, one of the hostages, in a suburb of Beirut. But the action that followed, apparently undertaken by some of the Druze mercenaries, together with other soldiers of fortune, prompted by the prospect of $1 million in reward promised by S. D. Arsham, produced nothing.

Convinced that the CIA was not competent to handle such a delicate mission, North assumed direct control of the operation. In March 1985 the Druze hit team employed in Beirut decided to make up for its earlier failure by trying to kill two leaders of the Party of Allah, Sobhi Tufeili and Muhammad-Hussain Fadhlallah. The operation turned into a disaster when the hit team attacked the wrong block of flats in southern Beirut, killing seventy-seven innocent people, including women and children, and injuring a further hundred.[34] A shocked Casey was forced to stop the programme.

In June 1986 North, this time working through Secord and his private network, revived the Druze force, now with only forty of the original mercenaries. A few weeks later North informed Nir about the project and succeeded in securing Israeli support inside Lebanon. Israel, with its network of informers within the Shi'ite community, was seen as an essential element in securing the information needed for a rescue operation. It was also Nir who organized Secord's visit to Beirut to inspect the mercenary force. Secord reported that a rescue mission had only a 30 per cent chance of success.[35] Casey and North were once again forced to look for a negotiated solution to the problem.

Casey had pinned some of his hopes of obtaining accurate information on the structure of the Party of Allah and its underground network on Terry Waite. The special envoy of Dr Robert Runcie, the Archbishop of Canterbury, had established good contacts with Khomeinist leaders both in Tehran and in Beirut. But he had never thought of putting the knowledge he had gained about the Party of Allah at the disposal of any secret service. It was therefore in the guise of keeping Waite informed about US efforts on the hostages that North contacted the Archbishop's envoy. The two men met at least five times in England, West Germany and Switzerland. North must

have been aware of the dangers that such meetings would hold for
Waite. It was, in fact, to prove that he was not a CIA agent that Waite
decided to return to Beirut one last time in January 1987 after the
secret negotiations between Tehran and Washington had been
exposed. He was abducted and promptly accused of having worked
for the CIA. His supposedly secret meetings with North had been
reported to Tehran in 1985.[36]

The stalemate which followed McFarlane's trip to Tehran seemed
to come to an end in July, when Nir informed Cave that Jenco would
soon be set free as originally agreed in Tehran. Jenco was released on
26 July. The following day North met Ghorbanifar and Nir in
Frankfurt and had a long telephone conversation with Kangarloo in
Tehran. The Islamic deputy premier was anxious to continue the
arrangement under which Tehran would receive the arms it needed in
exchange for the hostages. North was also convinced that this was a
good channel, while Washington looked for a more direct dialogue
with Rafsanjani, who was, according to analyses prepared by the CIA
and the State Department, Tehran's strongman. Conscious of the fact
that Poindexter had doubts about the wisdom of pursuing the
Ghorbanifar–Kangarloo–Nir channel, North tried to twist his boss's
arm by warning that if Kangarloo did not receive 'something in
return', meaning the rest of the arms already sold to Tehran, one or
more of the hostages might die.[37]

Poindexter's reaction to that warning was not recorded, but he must
have believed the colonel for the NSC continued to seek a solution
through secret transfers of arms to the Islamic Republic. It is
important to note, however, that there was no chance of Khomeini
ordering the death of any of the hostages and North must have known
that. Buckley's death, no doubt under torture, had been an exception.
None of the other hostages were linked with American intelligence
and the ayatollah knew that. In fact, none of them were formally
accused of having been linked with the CIA. Khomeini also knew that
a dead hostage was no more than a corpse and far less interesting as a
bargaining counter. He was also aware of the Libyan experience. In
1985 the Libyan leader Colonel Moammar al-Gaddafi purchased two
British hostages from the Party of Allah for the sum of $1.2 million in
the hope of forcing London to reconsider its decision to sever
diplomatic ties with Tripoli. The ploy did not work and the two
hostages were put to death in Beirut. The double murder did not
achieve what blackmail had failed to achieve earlier.

Why, then, did Casey and North insist that the hostages were facing
death and that Khomeini should be given arms as a means of
preventing the murder of the captive Americans? One reason might

have been a desire to mobilize more money for the contras. But that was no longer urgently necessary in the summer of 1986, as the US Congress had lifted its total ban on aid to Nicaraguan freedom fighters. It is possible that Casey and North wanted the residual from arms sales to Iran to invest in other 'extramural' operations they were involved in or were thinking of starting in other parts of the world. It was less than a year later, in 1987, that North admitted that he and Casey had together started what was to become a 'privatized' CIA as a means of avoiding congressional headaches and the possibility of leaks.[38]

In August 1986 North reported to Poindexter that the Kangarloo channel was working so well that a new mission to Tehran was possible. He suggested that he should go to the Iranian capital accompanied by Cave and another CIA officer, who would stay in Tehran to set up a permanent communication system. North wrote: 'If you approve, we would use [false] documents (as we did in May) and go in via the Iran Air flight to/from Frankfurt. . . . We would plan to go over a weekend to reduce visible absence from DC.'[39] By that time, however, a new and potentially far more important channel was already in the making, one that ensured direct contact with Rafsanjani.

12

MULLAHS IN WASHINGTON

On 5 June 1986, just a week after the McFarlane mission had left Tehran in what resembled desperation, Ayatollah Khomeini received a delegation of clerics from the holy city of Qom at his Jamaran residence north of Tehran. Officially the delegation had come to convey to the Supreme Guide the holy city's greetings on the twenty-third anniversary of Khomeini's first revolt against the shah. Very quickly, however, it became clear that the thirty-five mullahs present did not wish to confine themselves to the ritual of flattering the Imam as 'the saviour of mankind' in front of television cameras. The leader of the delegation, Ayatollah Ibrahim Amini, asked the television crews to be withdrawn so that 'the men of God present here' could speak of 'matters of grave concern to our suffering nation'.[1]

Once Amini's wish was granted, he began presenting Khomeini with a bleak picture of life in the Islamic Republic. He blamed the 'tragic state of the country' on 'this endless war that has already plunged every town and every village in this country into mourning, taking away at least one child from every single family in this land.'[2] The Faw operation in February had enabled Iranian forces to capture parts of the southern Iraqi marshlands. But the price paid for that victory had been exceptionally heavy. Even Colonel Ali Sayyad-Shirazi, commander of the ground forces, had described the Faw operation as a 'disaster'.[3]

Khomeini, however, did not share these pessimistic views. With his gaze fixed on the pattern of the carpet on the floor, he replied in his usual strident tone that he would pursue the war 'until we pray at the al-Aqsa Mosque, in Jerusalem'. He went on: 'And if this joy is denied us, then our children or their children or the children of their children shall surely hoist the flag of Islam on top of the holy city, wiping out the Zionist state.' He concluded by saying: 'As long as I am alive, do not speak of peace. Leave that for after my death. Our youths are begging me to give them an opportunity to kill and to get killed and I am determined to give them every chance.'[4]

During his speech Khomeini also indirectly referred to McFarlane's visit to Tehran, which he saw as a sign that the United States was now prepared to acknowledge Iran's supremacy in the Persian Gulf. Two days earlier the main papers in Tehran had published large extracts of a *Washington Post* article which described the Islamic Republic as a 'regional superpower' and urged the Reagan administration to reconsider its policies towards Tehran. The article, written by a former NSC staffer, was believed in Tehran to have been inspired by people in the administration who wanted the United States to back the Islamic Republic in its war against Iraq.[5] Unable or unwilling to reveal McFarlane's secret mission to Tehran, the radical groups in Tehran seized upon the *Washington Post* article, which was extensively broadcast by the Persian programme of Voice of America, as a sure sign that the Great Satan was once again humbled and forced into admitting defeat. Khomeini was persuaded that, despite McFarlane's dramatic departure, which Ghorbanifar had described as largely the result of the former NSC chief's 'weak nerves', the United States was prepared to play ball according to rules set by him.[6]

A few days later the ayatollah presided over a session of the High Council of Defence, the body that decides all matters pertaining to the war against Iraq. Premier Mussavi offered a report on the abortive American mission to Tehran. Rafsanjani criticized the way in which the mission had been organized and accused Mussavi of taking 'unnecessary risks'. Khomeini concluded the discussions by ordering that the dialogue with the USA be pursued without, however, offering Washington any concessions apart from the occasional release of American hostages in Lebanon. The ayatollah also appointed a five-man commission, headed by his son Ahmad, to handle all future contacts with Washington. Kangarloo, Mussavi's deputy, could pursue his own efforts provided he reported regularly to the commission.[7]

The ayatollah's decision partially to lift the ban on secret contacts with the Great Satan resulted in competition among the mullahs for control of what they recognized would be an important and highly profitable relationship. Mussavi and the president, Khameneh'i, interpreted the ayatollah's latest orders as another victory for Rafsanjani in the power struggle which continued in Tehran. Rafsanjani had already secured control of almost all arms purchases through the Revolutionary Guards. The management of the dialogue with Washington would now give the Majlis speaker another important advantage over his rivals.

Ahmad Khomeini, although a tactical ally of Rafsanjani on some issues, was determined to open his own channel of communication with Washington. He instructed his brother-in-law, Sadeq Tabataba'i, who had negotiated the end of the Tehran hostage crisis in 1980, to reactivate his contacts in Washington. Tabataba'i immediately telephoned his cousin, Mohammad Alavi-Tabatab'i, in Geneva and told him to proceed to the United States and signal Tehran's desire to negotiate with Washington. Sadeq Tabataba'i had for long been Ahmad Khomeini's candidate for the premiership. Now Ahmad thought that success in Washington would improve the chances of his brother-in-law winning the post.

By mid-June three separate efforts were under way to renew the dialogue between Tehran and Washington. Unknowingly, the USA was being drawn into the Islamic power struggle in Tehran. The first of these efforts, by Kangarloo and Mussavi with help from Israel, was to continue for a few more weeks. It was eventually abandoned when the NSC, putting it on hold, decided to leave the Israelis out of the picture and pursue its own independent channel to Tehran.

The second effort was spearheaded by Mohammad Tabataba'i, who, leaving his mullah's gear in Geneva, flew to Washington, where he rented an office on K Street and began contacting people as 'an unofficial ambassador of Iran'. He stayed for three months and met North, Teischer, two CIA agents accompanied by an Iranian-born operative, several pro-Khomeini businessmen and Senator Jesse Helms (R. North Carolina). He also met some advisers to the shah's son and urged them to use their influence in Washington to persuade the United States to sell arms to the Islamic Republic. His message was straightforward: the faction led by Ahmad Khomeini was the most strongly anti-communist and should be supported in the power struggle in Tehran. The USA should do two things: give the mullahs the arms they required to defeat Iraq and commit herself to defending Iran against a Soviet threat of invasion.[8]

The third effort was led by Rafsanjani. His friend and close associate, Mohsen Rafiqdust, minister for Revolutionary Guards, first raised the possibility of a dialogue with Washington at a meeting with Eric Rouleau, a former journalist who had become an adviser to the French President François Mitterand. Rouleau, who was France's Ambassador to Tunisia at the time, secretly visited Tehran in the winter of 1986 and held extensive discussions with Rafiqdust, largely on the problem of French hostages.[9] Because Rouleau had helped with passing on messages during the Tehran hostages crisis, Rafiqdust and Rafsanjani thought he would be able to help again. Rafsanjani's tactic was to spread the word about his willingness to talk with the Americans and let the initiative come from Washington. That way he would always be able to claim that the Americans had begged him to talk to them and that he, the true Islamic revolutionary, would not have approached the Great Satan on his own initiative.

Rafsanjani also indicated his willingness to talk to Washington at meetings he had with the Turkish foreign minister, Vahit Halefoglu, and senior foreign ministry officials from Japan, France and Pakistan who visited Tehran in the weeks that followed the McFarlane mission. All the countries involved reported their impressions to Washington in separate and different analyses of the situation in the Islamic Republic. By the end of July a fairly coherent picture could be put together: the mullahs were concerned about the Soviet threat and worried that the Gulf War might not continue in their favour. They wished to normalize relations with Washington in the hope of receiving the arms they needed to defeat Iraq. The French, the Turks and maybe even the Japanese had become aware of McFarlane's visit early in June and knew much more about Washington's secret diplomacy than did the American Congress or even the State Department itself.

The first time Secretary of State Shultz learned of Rafsanjani's desire for a dialogue was on 2 July when his assistant, Michael Armacost, sent him a memo on the subject.[10] At least two other memos were sent some weeks later covering impressions gained by Japanese, Turkish and Pakistani officials who had visited Tehran. The Pakistani foreign minister, Sahabzadah Yaqub Khan, had told Washington as early as 20 June that Tehran was looking for a 'meaningful dialogue' with the United States.[11]

What is surprising is that Shultz seemed to have attached little or no importance to the kites flown by Rafsanjani. The Secretary of State appeared to have shut his mind to any possibility of changing relations with Iran as long as Khomeini was alive. This was a comfortable and apparently risk-free policy, but it left a large gap. The official CIA tried to fill part of that gap by supporting anti-Khomeini groups with money, training and logistical support in Pakistan, Turkey and some of the Gulf states. The unofficial CIA, led by Casey and North, wished to deepen the factional divisions in Tehran in the hope of making a deal with those who might come out on top. The crucial reports sent to Washington by at least five allied or friendly countries concerning Iran ended up on Lieutenant Colonel North's desk. And it was North who established contact with Rafsanjani, through Secord and Hakim. An important part of US foreign policy was 'privatized', so to speak. The signal to Tehran was clear: the USA is more comfortable with secret diplomacy.

Before contact was established between North and Rafsanjani, a fourth attempt at bringing Tehran and Washington together was made by a maverick group claiming to be connected with Khameneh'i, the president of the Islamic Republic. It was assumed in Tehran that it was open season so far as relations with the Great Satan were concerned and the chance to make political gains plus financial profits with Khomeini's blessings should not be missed. This new effort was led by Ayatollah Mahmoud Shahabadi, the man nominally in charge of orchestrating Iran's arms purchases. Shahabadi had made another attempt to reach out to Washington in 1985 when one of his cousins, Dr Ali Shahabadi, had contacted Khashoggi in London with a proposal to arrange large-scale arms purchases for Iran from the United States. Together with two Iranian-born businessmen, Ali Shoja'i and Mohammad Zahiri, both based in Houston, Texas, Shahabadi and Khashoggi had met Shackley in Cologne, West Germany. At the meeting Zahiri had telephoned Khameneh'i in Tehran who had asked Shackley to arrange for the sale of weapons to Iran in exchange for the return of American hostages in Lebanon. The meeting had ended in some disarray.[12] Later Khashoggi tried to merge the Shahabadi group with that of Kangarloo and Ghorbanifar, and Ayatollah Reza Karami was chosen by both sides to assure liaison. Ghorbanifar also opened personal accounts for Ayatollah Karami and Ayatollah Shahabadi in a Swiss bank with a promise that funds 'needed for the propagation of Islam in Western Europe' will be deposited in them.[13]

Karami had been involved in yet another attempt at trading hostages for arms. In June 1985 he had contacted Casey, through the CIA chief's personal friend, the financier John Shaheen, with a proposal for securing the release of all American passengers on a hijacked American jetliner in Beirut in exchange for the release of Khomeinists jailed in Kuwait. Karami's contact man, Cyrus Hashemi, had also suggested that the CIA should pay an unofficial ransom in cash to be divided between Karami and himself.[14]

In June 1986 Karami and Shahabadi had a presentiment that Ghorbanifar and Khashoggi had excluded them from future deals with Washington. They were determined to get their own share of what they believed would be a very large cake. Through an exiled mullah in London in July 1986 they met two CIA agents and an Iranian interpreter in Wiesbaden with a proposal for exchanging American hostages for weapons needed by Iran.[15] The mullah in question promptly informed both Rafsanjani and the Bakhtiar opposition group in Paris about the meeting.

All these comings and goings created the impression that the US government was as faction-ridden as the Islamic regime. They also made it clear that what interested Washington above all was not any geopolitical talk of the Soviet threat to the oil resources of the Persian

Gulf but a promise to secure the release of the American hostages in Lebanon. The United States appeared as a superpower incapable of developing a coherent policy on the Gulf and capable of being influenced through a mixture of threats and incentives offered within a framework of secret diplomacy. Various contenders for power in Tehran tried to strengthen their own hand by playing the American joker in a game that moved towards its denouement as an ailing Khomeini seemed to be fading out of the picture.

The American method of secret diplomacy destabilized the Islamic regime while also leading the Reagan administration on a dangerous path. The possibility of the whole thing running totally out of control was illustrated by a strange move by Reza Kaffashzadeh, a young mullah who served as Khomeini's private secretary. In July 1986, during a vist to Frankfurt, Kaffashzadeh contacted two exiled former officers of the shah and offered to sell them a list of suspected 'communists disguised as mullahs' in exchange for weapons from the USA. Kaffashzadeh was dismissed by Khomeini in July 1987 when the Frankfurt episode was exposed.

As different factions within the Islamic regime tried to beat one another in an undeclared race to solicit support from the United States, different parts of the Reagan administration pursued different and at times even contradictory policies towards the mullahs. Even the CIA was split on the issue. In January 1986, for example, Casey asked one of his assistants, Charles Allen, to meet a visiting mullah from Tehran. The visitor was none other than Ayatollah Sayyed Mohsen Khatami, who had been identified by two former Iranian officers working for the agency as one of the key figures in the Party of Allah, the group responsible for holding the American hostages.[16] Khatami was treated with great respect despite his known role in fomenting anti-American activities.

The mullahs who visited Washington were all issued with special visas arranged by the CIA so that their passports would not have to be stamped. Before boarding the aircraft for Washington they left their turbans and *abayahs* (mullah's capes) behind. Some of them also trimmed their beards into 'designer' stubbles so as not to attract too much attention. Each of the different sections of the administration in the end got the mullah they deserved. But the Americans could never get their act together and at times even bid against one another. The official CIA, for example, was much cooler towards both Karami and Khatami than were the private agents of Casey and North.

The task of establishing contact with Rafsanjani was left to the private network of Secord and Hakim. The decision, taken by Casey and North, appears surprising with hindsight. Rafsanjani had passed his messages to the State Department through normal political channels provided by friendly countries and must have expected a reply through the same channels. Nevertheless the USA seemed determined to complicate matters needlessly. The NSC, in agreement with the State Department, decided to reply to the Iranian message through Turkey. But instead of asking the Turks to pass a message to Rafsanjani, who had made the original move, the reply was to be delivered to the Islamic foreign minister, Ali-Akbar Valayati. And that was not all. Before the reply could be delivered, North dispatched Cave to Frankfurt to sound out Rafsanjani's brother Mahmoud. The meeting took place on 27 July at the home of Hojat al-Islam Mohammad Qomi, the son of a grand ayatollah of Mashhad.[17]

Mahmoud Rafsanjani, the brother of the powerful speaker of the Islamic Majlis, had served as ambassador to Belgium and Syria before being put in charge of supervising the international Islamic diplomatic network on behalf of his brother. A third Rafsanjani brother was head of the radio and television monopoly in Iran. Thus the three brothers could be seen as a powerful triumvirate. The Rafsanjanis had begun their conquest of Islamic diplomatic posts abroad by appointing one of their friends, Hojat al-Islam Mohammad Shahroudi, ambassador to West African countries, while another of their agents, Hojat al-Islam Saber Hamadani, acted as a roving ambassador in the eastern Mediterranean and supervised the progress of more than $3000 million's worth of Iranian imports that passed through Turkey each year. Exiled opponents of Khomeini suspected Hamadani of being a key figure in the Islamic secret police as well.

Rafsanjani had other attractive assets. He enjoyed the personal loyalty of some hundred members of the 271-member Islamic Majlis and was a key member of the High Council of Defence in Tehran. A close friendship linked Rafsanjani to Rafiqdust, the minister for Revolutionary Guards, who, in 1986, appeared to be winning the race for control of the 220,000-strong paramilitary force from Mohsen Reza'i, the commander of the Revolutionary Guards Corps. The fact that both Rafsanjani and Rafiqdust were involved in a wide variety of business activities and controlled sizable personal fortunes made them even more attractive, as future partners, in the eyes of the Americans.

The task of probing the new channel was given to Cave by North. The former CIA officer travelled to Frankfurt at the end of July and had a long meeting with Mahmoud Rafsanjani. The speaker's brother told Cave of Tehran's genuine desire for a new relationship with Washington. All that the United States needed to do was to recognize those capable of leading Iran in the future and preventing her from falling under Soviet influence. Mahmoud Rafsanjani was convinced that only his brother, with help from Ahmad Khomeini, could control Iran after the ayatollah's death. Most of the other contenders for power in Tehran were either 'immature kids' or 'communists in everything but name', Mahmoud Rafsanjani told Cave.

Back in Washington the CIA man succeeded in persuading North that the new channel was 'the real one' and that Kangarloo and Ghorbanifar ought to be put on hold. Cave shared the classic belief of all experts in covert operations that the fewer the number of loose ends in a project the greater will be its chances of success. Casey, informed of the opening of the 'second channel' by North, appeared enthusiastic. He also approved North's suggestion that the Israelis be kept in the dark about American contacts with Rafsanjani. The second channel was to be controlled by Secord on an *ad hoc* basis with virtually no intervention by the regular organs of the US government.

Secord, Hakim and Cave met Mahmoud Rafsanjani in Frankfurt early in August and were told that the speaker had been fully informed about the earlier session with Cave and had decided to pursue the contacts at a higher level. The Americans, Mahmoud Rafsanjani suggested, should travel to Brussels to meet the man who would be in · charge of the operation on the Iranian side.

Once in Brussels, Secord and his companions were introduced to a young man with Tatar features who represented himself as Mehdi Bahremani. The young man pretended that he was a son of yet another brother of the speaker. A former Iranian naval officer, working for Khomeini's secret police, SAVAMA, but also selling information to Secord, had told the general before the meeting that Bahremani was 'a favourite of Speaker Rafsanjani'. The young man, however, was not a nephew of the speaker, but his eldest son, although the Americans did not learn this until October. The Americans did not know that the speaker's true family name was Bahremani and that he had used the double-barrelled name Hashemi-Rafsanjani as a *nom de guerre* during the struggle against the shah. The Americans also did not know that the true name of the young man they met in Brussels was Mohsen and not Mehdi. He introduced himself as Mehdi, the name of one of his cousins, as a means of causing confusion in case of public exposure.

Rafsanjani's decision to transfer responsibility for secret negotiations with the Americans to his own son, who was only twenty-three years old at that time, was taken for a variety of personal and political reasons. 'Mehdi' had been dispatched to Belgium to attend university in 1981 while his uncle Mahmoud served as ambassador in Brussels. 'Mehdi' had not proved to be a brilliant scholar and showed more interest in his father's business activities. By 1986 the young Bahremani had abandoned his studies and presided over two companies handling his father's export-import business. One of the companies, registered in Luxemburg, handled most of Iran's pistachio exports to Europe and the United States. Bahremani had been involved in arms deals for Iran as well and, when he met the Secord group, he showed himself to be quite knowledgeable about Iranian military needs.

That Mehdi Bahremani held no official position was an advantage. The possible exposure of his secret negotiations would not concern the official authorities of the Islamic Republic. At the same time Bahremani found in his contacts with the Americans a good excuse for the fact that, unlike other young men in Iran, he had chosen to stay in Europe and thus avoided taking part in the war against Iraq. He could claim that, although far away from the actual battle front, he was still a soldier of Islam because he was procuring the American arms that Iran needed to fight the Iraqi enemy.

Another reason for Rafsanjani's decision to replace his brother Mahmoud in the negotiations was that Mahmoud had for some time been under close surveillance by the West German and Belgian police because of his contacts with radical Muslim groups during his tenure as ambassador to Brussels. The Syrians also apparently kept an eye on Mahmoud Rafsanjani, who had forged links with Muslim Brotherhood elements in West Germany who were planning to overthrow the regime of President Hafez al-Assad in Damascus.

The Secord team, accompanied by Secord's Iranian-born agent, spent more than eight hours with Rafsanjani's son in Brussels on 5 and 6 August. During the talks the young Bahremani was accompanied by Mehdi Rahnema, deputy director of the Intelligence Bureau of the Revolutionary Guards, and Iraj Va'ezi, identified by the CIA as a SAVAMA agent in London.[18] Secord and Hakim now felt they were really in charge of an operation which promised to lead to business deals worth billions of dollars. Bahremani constantly harped on the theme that Iran was forced to buy American-made weapons from more than thirty different countries because of Washington's policy of embargo. He said he would be able to spend a minimum of $3000 million on American-made weapons as long as the war with Iraq continued, and that meant for many more years to come.

Secord and Hakim had campaigned for the elimination of Kangarloo and Ghorbanifar from the process of *rapprochement* with Tehran. Their view now prevailed. Hakim had been especially angry with Ghorbanifar, who had objected to his presence at some of the sessions with officials from the Islamic Republic. Because of Ghorbanifar's objections, Hakim had been left out of the Iran project for several months. At one session Secord had nevertheless taken

Hakim with him after hiding his partner's balding head under a huge wig and covering his big black eyes with large sunglasses. Hakim, presented as a Turkish businessman wishing to provide bridging finance for arms purchases by Iran, had acted the part with great success.[19] Now, with the second channel firmly established, there was no longer any need to use such crude theatricals. This was illustrated by the fact that Secord and Hakim attended the Brussels meeting under their true identities.

Bahremani must have been impressed by whatever Secord and Hakim told him, for he flew to Tehran to report to his father only two days later. The day after his arrival the Islamic media, controlled by the speaker's brother, further toned down what little was left of their anti-American propaganda and instead began to intensify their attacks on Moscow because of Soviet involvement in Afghanistan.

Secord for his part was equally optimistic. On his return to Washington he reported to North: 'Meetings constituted comprehensive tour de force [sic] regarding Iran-Iraq war, Iranian views of US and other Western policies, Soviet activities, activities of nearly all important Iran government figures, hostage matters, activities in the Hague, and Iranian forces' equipment and material shortages.'[20]

Bahremani had told Secord that Senator Edward Kennedy (D. Massachusetts) and former Secretary of State Alexander Haig had separately tried to meet him but that he had refused to see them because he only wanted to deal with 'the president's men'.[21] Bahremani made it clear that he was aware of MacFarlane's supposedly secret visit to Tehran but promised not to sabotage Kangarloo's attempts to secure the release of more hostages in exchange for more weapons from the USA. His main interest was, he indicated, an overall improvement of relations with Washington, while Kangarloo was handling one specific problem. He promised to discuss the hostages with Rafsanjani in Tehran within ten days and then return to Brussels for further talks with the Americans. Finally, Bahremani said he would try to find out where the American hostages were being kept in Beirut so that the United States would have the information needed if and when a rescue mission became necessary. Secord was enthusiastic. Bahremani, he wrote, 'has been effectively recruited and wants to start dealing'.[22]

North shared Secord's optimism and in a long memo to Poindexter on 2 September he effectively suggested that both the Kangarloo channel and the diplomatic efforts started through Turkey, Japan and Pakistan should be put on the back burner in favour of the new channel. Even the fact that, in a meeting with the Turkish ambassador in Tehran, Rafsanjani had openly asked for F14 spare parts and

equipment for Iran's American-made helicopters did not seem important to North.[23] He preferred covert operations carried on outside
official diplomatic channels.

In his report to Poindexter, North wrote that Bahremani

> has returned to Tehran and has since informed us of a pending TOW sale
> through Madrid and further indicated that he is prepared to proceed with
> further discussions. He has further noted that the government in Tehran is
> very concerned over Soviet activities in the Gulf and is aware that a 'final
> victory' over Iraq will not be possible. There is considerable evidence that
> Bahremani is indeed a bona fide intermediary seeking to establish direct
> contact with the US government for Rafsanjani's faction within the
> government of Iran.[24]

North's reaction to Secord's report was that of the typical enthusiast. The colonel did not even take the trouble to check Secord's
impressions through other channels within the US government. Nor
did he deem it necessary to meet Bahremani in person to make his own
assessment of the young emissary. To pin Washington's hopes for
beating Moscow in the Persian Gulf, ending the Iran–Iraq war and
securing the release of American hostages on a twenty-three-year-old
man, who spoke no English and could not therefore communicate
directly with the colonel's passe-partout, Secord, did not appear to
North to be a risky venture.

The official CIA, only partly informed by North, was not keen on
putting so many eggs in Bahremani's basket and argued that the
Kangarloo–Ghorbanifar channel had so far proved the most effective
by ensuring the release of two hostages and organizing McFarlane's
trip to Tehran.[25] But North was not dissuaded. He was also impatient
with what he regarded as slow decision making on the part of
Poindexter. On the same day that he wrote to his boss, North also sent
a note to McFarlane in which he said he had asked Casey to urge
Poindexter to speed up the process of exchanging arms for hostages
with Iran. He wrote: 'The things one must do to get action. Am
hopeful Bill [i.e. Casey] can push hard enough to move on the
matter.'[26]

A week later North updated his memorandum to Poindexter to add
that his men had located a significant number of Hawk parts which
had previously been listed as unavailable. He added that he believed
that 'the total package will be sufficient to entice Iranians to proceed
with the sequential release of the hostages'. He also reported that
Kangarloo, in 'dozens of calls' to Secord, Hakim and Cave had asked
for a new meeting which had been approved by his boss, Prime
Minister Mussavi. Kangarloo had also made it clear that he knew
about the meeting with Bahremani in Brussels.[27] That meant that the

Israelis were also informed about the new channel. But North still refused to let Nir know about his new scheme. The CIA analysed Kangarloo's move to mean that Rafsanjani was moving to gain direct control of negotiations with Washington. Nevertheless the CIA continued to oppose the ending of contacts with Premier Mussavi through Kangarloo and the Israelis.

The complicated system of signalling between Tehran and Washington became still more confusing on 5 September when supporters of the shah's son managed to 'pirate' one unused television channel in Tehran to broadcast an eleven-minute anti-Khomeini programme. North wrote to Poindexter: 'this broadcast reportedly sparked protests in Tehran and elsewhere by supporters of the shah's family. Kangarloo, in one of his calls . . . asked pointedly how it was that we could profess to "accept the Iranian revolution as fact" and still sponsor such an event.'[28] The massive publicity given to the televison piracy by the American media convinced the mullahs that the United States had been behind the operation. Far from discouraging the mullahs in their quest for a new relationship with Washington, the illicit broadcast persuaded them that the sooner they normalized ties with the Great Satan the better for them.

Rafsanjani instructed his son to arrange for a fresh meeting with the Americans in Europe. Mahmoud Rafsanjani was to lead the Islamic delegation, apparently to give it some official weight. Poindexter had instructed North to meet the new contacts in person and to organize a new trip to Tehran. The purpose of this trip, to be undertaken by North and Cave only, was to meet Rafsanjani. It was understood that such a trip could take place only after a new arms shipment had been made to the Islamic Republic. Even at that early stage North was already thinking of arranging a secret meeting between Vice-President Bush and Rafsanjani.[29]

Rafsanjani seemed to be in something of a hurry. He had two reasons for not wanting to wait. First, he wished to launch a new major offensive against Iraq on 22 September to coincide with the anniversary of the Iraqi invasion of Iran. He wanted the Americans to believe that they had best bet on an Iranian victory. Secondly, he wanted to have something positive to report to Khomeini on contacts with Washington at the High Council of Defence session scheduled for the end of September. The new offensive against Iraq had to succeed not only so far as Iran's interests were concerned. Rafsanjani needed a new victory to save his own skin. He had supported the Revolutionary Guards against the regular army in February 1986 in launching the costly Faw operation. He wanted to efface the bitter part of Faw's memory with a new successful operation against Iraq. The Americans could help by once again supplying false information to the Iraqis concerning Iranian intentions and strength.

Convinced that the Americans' immediate interest was focused on the hostages in Lebanon, Rafsanjani instructed Bahremani to keep the subject alive in telephone conversations with Secord and Cave. He also worked on three other aspects of American political psychology which he believed were important. He portrayed himself as the most decidedly anti-communist leader involved in the struggle for power in Tehran. Between 2 September and 6 October he made a series of bitter attacks on Moscow in a number of public speeches. He also instructed Bahremani to tell the Americans that Rafsanjani was the only top leader in Tehran genuinely interested in ending the war with Iraq. The speaker had earlier tried the same line, with great success, with the Saudis.

Lastly, Rafsanjani presented himself as the most powerful man in Tehran after Khomeini. Bahremani went even further than that and claimed that his 'uncle' had been appointed head of the High Council of Defence.[30] This claim, totally untrue, was not checked by North, who also accepted Rafsanjani's other claims without demanding an analytical report on the speaker's actual status in Tehran and his delicate relationship with other players in the Islamic game. Rafsanjani wanted to mobilize Washington's resources for his own success in the Tehran power struggle and North appeared willing to oblige.

The first benefit that Rafsanjani derived from his link with North was that his agents were able to conclude contracts for the purchase of 1200 TOWs through an arms merchant in Lisbon, Portugal, without encountering any opposition from Washington. Secord talked to the merchant in question and quickly reported to North.[31] North and Secord also knew that Bahremani, using other names, was involved in the $16 million deal.[32]

The fact that the US government had for more than five years urged Portugal and other members of NATO to observe a ban on the sale of arms to the mullahs was conveniently ignored. Nor was much attention paid to the capture of a new American hostage, Frank Reed, in Beirut. Bahremani informed Hakim that Rafsanjani was not involved in the new hostage drama and North apparently fully believed him without checking the claim against independent information. The colonel was perhaps unaware that the mullahs controlled several different terrorist groups in Lebanon, each acting under a different label, as a means of denying responsibility whenever necessary. In any case, even if Reed had been abducted by agents of Gaddafi, the fact remained that the abduction took place in an area controlled by the agents of Khomeini in Lebanon.

Early in September Ahmad Khomeini convened a session of the special *ad hoc* committee set up by the ayatollah to handle relations with Washington. Foreign Minister Ali-Akbar Valayati, although not a member of the committee, was invited to attend the first part of the meeting in which Premier Mussavi-Khameneh'i presented a report on his contacts with both Israel and the United States. Valayati strongly approved the dialogue with the USA as a means of preventing Iraq from creating a diplomatic wall around Iran.[33] In the second, more restricted part of the meeting Rafsanjani, supported by Ahmad Khomeini, revealed his plans for the creation of a joint committee of Islamic and American officials which would act in secret until all the major problems between the two sides were resolved. The meeting agreed that Bahremani, accompanied by a Revolutionary Guards security officer, should be dispatched to Washington to establish direct contact with the White House. For the first time in nearly eight years the main factions within the Islamic leadership united in seeking an opening with the United States.

The unusual harmony in Tehran, which was to prove short-lived, was in sharp contrast with the absence of coordination which reigned in Washington. North was determined to keep the State Department out of the picture at least until some progress had been achieved. Responding to a suggestion that Shultz should be told about the operation, North wrote that the secretary of state 'would then talk to *** or *** who would in turn talk to *** – and that *** could well be the source of the Jack Anderson stuff we have seen periodically.'[34]

On 18 September Bahremani, accompanied by Va'ezi, flew from Istanbul to Washington aboard a jet chartered for the purpose by Secord. The two envoys of the mullahs insisted that negotiations be started immediately. North, Secord and Cave represented the United States government, but Bahremani was still insisting on assurances that the American trio were indeed representing President Reagan. One such assurance was provided when North arranged for Bahremani and his friend to go on a guided tour of the White House late at night. Another consisted of a commentary which North asked the Persian programme of Voice of America to broadcast after Bahremani had returned home. Finally, the two sides also agreed that Rafsanjani should send Reagan a copy of the Qur'an in exchange for a copy of the Bible from the president.

Bahremani brought up the idea of creating a joint commission and indicated that Kangarloo would be one of the Iranian members. He also said that there was no need to pursue the Tabataba'i channel since Ahmad Khomeini was now supporting Rafsanjani's bid for better relations with the USA. The young man also spoke of the mullahs' grave concern about possible KGB infiltration of their regime to the point that one of Kangarloo's senior aides was suspected of being a Soviet mole. He saw the future of bilateral relations in two phases. In the short run the United States had to show its good will towards the Islamic Revolution by supplying arms and materiel to Iran while helping Iran with intelligence on Soviet activities in the region. In exchange the mullahs would help bring about the release of the American hostages. In the long run, Bahremani noted, the USA could help bring an end to the Gulf War. This prospect provoked an enthusiastic reaction from North, who reported to Poindexter that the president 'can be instrumental in bringing about an end to Iran–Iraq war – à la Roosevelt with the Russo-Japanese war in 1904. Anybody for RR getting that same prize?'[35]

Rafsanjani's emissaries went even further than that. They used the four sessions of talks with the Americans on 18 and 19 September – a total of more than sixteen hours of negotiations – to give the impression that the speaker was determined to restore the United States to the position of pre-eminence it had once enjoyed in Iran. The USA, Bahremani said, should help with construction projects to rehouse Iran's more than two million war refugees while also playing a key role in restoring the nation's shattered oil industry and economy in general to its prerevolutionary levels of strength and achievement. Unlike Kangarloo, who had focused on limited shipments of arms in exchange for hostages, Bahremani wanted a strategic alliance that seemed to go far beyond anything that the late shah had ever been prepared to offer Washington.

An important feature of this new strategic alliance was to be the broad Islamic front that Bahremani said his 'uncle' was putting together with support from Saudi Arabia and the United Arab Emirates in order to combat the USSR in Afghanistan. He said that the Islamic oil minister, Gholam-Reza Aqazadeh, a close associate of Rafsanjani, had been dispatched to the Arab states of the Persian Gulf under the cover of discussing OPEC matters but with a brief to reach agreement on the anti-Moscow front.[36]

North was clearly impressed. He wrote to Poindexter that the new contact might well lead to 'a major foreign policy success for the president'.[37] Cave was equally enthusiastic and believed that the United States was now 'talking to someone at the political level, although the gentleman is very young'.[38] Nevertheless the Americans did not enter into the substance of the major issues raised by Bahremani. They fanned the fires of his anti-Sovietism and warned him that Moscow was preparing for military intervention in Iran.

They also told him that the United States was committed to supporting
the Afghan freedom fighters for as long as necessary. But most of all
the Americans focused on the problem of the hostages, which North
repeatedly described as an obstacle to any meaningful future relations
between the two sides. The Americans also asked for further signs
from Tehran and suggested that one such sign could come in the shape
of a Soviet-made T72 tank captured by the Iranians from the Iraqis.[39]

North was later to tell the joint congressional hearing in Washington in July 1987 that he lied to Iranians every time he met them, but
judging by his contemporaneous reports on his talks with Bahremani,
as well as accounts given by Cave and Secord, he was sincere in seeking
a genuine *rapprochement* with the mullahs beyond the problem of the
hostages. He must have recognized the role that large-scale systematic
Iranian support for the Afghan resistance could play in tipping the
scales against the Moscow-controlled government of Kabul. The
colonel was also sincere in trying to shape a major foreign policy
breakthrough for a president who singularly lacked one. Even Carter,
who could not have been one of North's favourites, had the Camp
David accords to wave as a spectacular foreign policy achievement.

The trouble was that North lacked the broader vision necessary to
put the issues raised into proper perspective. The United States, a
superpower with a variety of interests, some contradictory, in the
Middle East, had far less freedom of manoeuvre than did the Islamic
Republic, a regime capable of throwing everything to the wind at any
given moment and focusing on a single central, vital issue: its own
survival in a hostile climate. The mullahs were certainly prepared to
have the best of relations with Washington, including a united front
against Russia, provided the USA allowed them to pursue their other
objectives which included the exporting of their revolution to the
Arabian Peninsula and beyond. They were even prepared to offer the
USA advantages it had never had in that part of the world provided
Washington treated the Islamic Republic as a regional superpower
and recognized its interests in the Middle East.

On his return to Tehran Bahremani reported 'a dramatic change' in
US policies with regard to the Islamic Revolution. Rafsanjani took the
good news to Khomeini, who directed that the effort be pursued.[40]
The ayatollah must have seen the negotiations with the United States
as a modern version of another diplomatic experience in Islam's early
history. At that time the Prophet Muhammad had reached an
accommodation with the Byzantine Empire under which the emerging
Islamic state was allowed to extend its influence to the Christian Arab
principalities previously under Byzantine protection in exchange for
full respect for the regional interests of the emperor of Constantinople.

It may have been a coincidence that the Islamic radio began broadcasting a series of programmes about relations between early Islam and 'the satanic powers of the time' at exactly the time that Rafsanjani was conducting secret talks with Washington. What was surely not a coincidence was that Rafsanjani asked his brother Muhammad, as head of the radio and television networks, to cease broadcasting all items even remotely critical of the Great Satan.

What North was probably unaware of was that the mullahs were playing a similar game with Moscow. Between August 1985 and October 1986 the Islamic regime took a number of measures to improve its relations with the USSR. The objective was to woo Moscow away from Iraq by offering it prospects of larger gains from a closer friendship with the Iranian mullarchy. Death sentences pronounced against the entire leadership of the Moscow-sponsored Tudeh Party, who had been in prison since 1983, were suspended and the daily routine of anti-Soviet propaganda was reduced to a minimum. In the same period no fewer than seventy top officials or religious dignitaries visited the USSR, among them Foreign Minister Valayati, Oil Minister Aqazadeh and Ayatollah Sadeq Khalkhali, one of Khomeini's closest personal associates. The mullahs, who had at first announced they would boycott an Islamic conference organized in Baku, capital of Soviet Azarbaijan, changed their minds, and sent a delegation. The joint Irano-Soviet economic commission, created under the shah, was reactivated. In Moscow Aqazadeh offered the Soviets what they had failed to secure during nearly sixty years of their frustrating relationship with Iran: an oil concession in the Iranian part of the Caspian as well as in Iran's northern provinces. The minister also agreed to the creation of a commission to study an early resumption of Iranian natural gas exports to the USSR through a pipeline built under the shah but closed by the mullahs in 1979. But none of the projects Aqazadeh discussed in Moscow had been put into effect by the spring of 1988. It was evident that the main purpose of the exercise had been to reassure Moscow while telling Washington that the Islamic Republic could, at any moment, do what the Reagan administration feared most and tilt its foreign policy towards the USSR.

The Islamic personalities who visited Moscow put great emphasis on what they termed as 'the intrinsically anti-imperialist' aspects of Khomeini's revolution. In Washington they played the anti-Soviet tune. In Moscow they acted as the most dedicated enemies of 'earth-devouring America'. In Washington they gave North the idea of diverting the profits made from arms sales to Tehran to the Nicaraguan contras.[41] In Moscow they pointed to the aid they were channelling to the Sandinista regime in Managua in the form of cut-price crude oil, gifts of weapons, including mines and machine guns, and unspecified amounts of cash. The mullahs used all the lessons they had learned from Shaikh Sadduq and Mohammad-Baqer Majlisi, two of the great theoreticians of Shi'ism. Shaikh Sadduq had written in the thirteenth century: 'When negotiating with the heathen from a position of weakness, make them believe that you are a hundred times more heathen than they are. . . . Tell them what their ears like to hear but do not forget to sharpen your dagger in secret. For in the end you have to cut their throats.'[42] They made some Americans happy by repeating that they had no intention of closing the Strait of Hormuz, which they could not close without committing economic suicide in any case, while using the prospect of precisely such a move as part of their anti-imperialist credentials in talks with the Soviets. The mullahs must have laughed their beards off when reading comments by some American 'experts' that the fact that Khomeini had not ordered the closure of the strait was a sign of his 'growing moderation'.

The operation to charm the Soviets into putting more of their chips on the Iranian mullarchy was strengthened by Tehran's verbal and, when needed, financial backing for Russia's friends in the region – Libya, Syria and South Yemen. The mullahs adopted an anti-Israeli stance which made Abu Nidal look like a moderate. But at the same time they maintained close relations with Tel Aviv and even played host to Nir, who was number one on the PLO's hit list. Where the interests of Islam were at stake, principles of ordinary morality were not allowed to stand in the way.

If the attempt to take the sting out of the Great Satan by seducing it failed because of internal squabbles in Tehran as well as ineptitude in Washington, the similar campaign launched in Moscow's direction came unstuck because the Soviets were not prepared to play. From the very start of the Islamic Revolution in Iran the Soviets had been unable to achieve a consensus in their evaluation of the event and a fortiori the relations that might be forged with the new regime in Tehran. The Soviet Azarbaijan Communist Party recalled Lenin's famous dream of an alliance of the 'downtrodden of the earth' in the Orient with the forces of the proletarian revolution. Islam, the supporters of such an alliance argued, was an objective ally of the USSR because both shared the same aim objective: defeating Western imperialism. In the 1980s the principal defender of this school of thought within the Politburo was Haydar Aliev, who rose to become deputy prime minister before he was forced to resign in October 1987, ostensibly for health reasons.[13] The Central Asian communist parties, on the other hand, saw the revolution of the mullahs as the last and potentially the most violent somersault of 'dying feudalism' and recommended resolute opposition to it by all 'progressive forces'. They pointed to the fact that most of the CIA-financed and trained Mujahedeens who shot Soviet soldiers in Afghanistan were Khomeinists whose dream was the establishment of an Iranian-style Islamic republic. The Uzbek party chief, Din-Muhammad Kunaev, was, until his fall, a strong advocate of a tough policy against 'those reactionary mullahs'.[44] This latter view was largely shared by Andrei Gromyko, long-time Soviet foreign minister, who became president of the Supreme Soviet after Mikhail Gorbachev took over from Konstantin Chernenko. In more than half a dozen meetings with senior representatives of the Iranian mullarchy in Moscow, Gromyko went out of his way to criticize Tehran's policies especially with regard to the Gulf War. The Soviets did not succeed in working out a coherent and unified policy concerning the Islamic Revolution partly because the Andropov–Chernenko period was marked by inaction and lassitude and partly because Gorbachev focused his attention on two central objectives: reforming the economy and securing a new arms-limitation accord with Washington. In the meantime the KGB continued its infiltration of Iran while military measures were taken to deal with any eventuality in the region.

The Islamic Revolution confronted both superpowers with a new phenomenon they were not prepared for. There is now little doubt that one of the most important reasons for the Soviet military intervention in Afghanistan was Moscow's concern over the extension of the Khomeinist movement to the borders of Soviet Central Asia. Unable to analyse the new situation, the Soviets reacted in the way they knew best: the use of military force. The Americans also fell back on the means they best knew how to use: the offer of a package of arms and money and secret information in exchange for real or feigned friendship.

On balance it seemed in 1988 that the United States had committed more mistakes in its dealings with the mullahs than had the Soviets. One important point which the Soviets understood and the Americans apparently did not was that the mullahs respected superior force provided they were convinced it could be used against them. In August 1984 the Soviets asked Tehran to stop the Afghans from using the Tayebad–Herat roads for ferrying arms to the anti-Soviet guerrillas. Tehran chose to ignore the demand. The response came a few weeks later in the form of a strong attack on the Tayebad garrison in which over two hundred Islamic Revolutionary Guards were killed and most of their military installations there destroyed. That route was, with a few accidental exceptions, never again used by the guerrillas financed

and armed by the mullahs. In the spring of 1987, after a Soviet ship
was accidentally hit by the Iranians in the Persian Gulf, Moscow
dispatched the Cuban foreign minister, Isidore Malmierca, to Tehran
with a strong warning. The mullahs replied defiantly. Ten days later a
squadron of Soviet MiGs flew over northwestern Iran, breaking the
sound barrier above the border city of Astara and returning via
Caspian air space. Malmierca was contacted immediately and told
that his message was fully understood.[45] Another significant incident
came in July 1987 when a Soviet military aircraft, transporting some
hundred soldiers presumably to some point in western Afghanistan,
made an emergency landing in Zabol in eastern Iran. This was at first
greeted with some sabre-rattling by the Islamic media. But the aircraft
and its passengers, including a few suspected hijackers, were returned
to the Soviets within a few days. The reason was, once again, the
mullahs' firm conviction that the Soviets were not bluffing when it
came to the use of force.

Nevertheless the Russian threat, although a permanent feature of
the geopolitical habitat in which Iran has found itself since the close of
the eighteenth century, was not on the point of being actualized as the
Americans seemed to believe from 1981 onwards. The Americans no
doubt exaggerated the imminence and the extent of the Soviet threat as
a means of frightening the mullahs into adopting a less hostile policy
towards Washington. But at least some of them believed some of the
points they made about the 'Communist menace'. The State Department did not share the views of the CIA and the NSC that the Soviets
were already working on a secret plan for seizing power in Tehran
through surrogates. This view was strongly expressed in a paper by
Graham Fuller, the chairman of the umbrella National Intelligence
Council in a memorandum he wrote for the CIA in 1985. Fuller did
not modify his views even after North's efforts to woo the mullahs on
behalf of the West had come to grief.[46]

The various American officials and private entrepreneurs who
became involved in the dialogue with the mullahs made no secret of
the paucity and unreliability of the information the United States
could secure with regard to Iran. Poindexter was even to claim that
one of the original purposes of a presidential finding, signed by Reagan
in 1985, authorizing the sale of arms to Iran in exchange for the release
of the hostages, was to forge a new relationship that would help the
United States correct the deficiency in its intelligence-gathering work
inside the Islamic Republic.[47] One objective that Cave and Secord had
constantly in mind whenever they came into contact with Iranians was
to recruit them as informers or agents. Secord even considered the
possibility of employing Bahremani as 'an excellent source inside the

country'.[48] Although fully aware that they did not have the basic data and information needed for sound policy planning the Americans nevertheless agreed to run major risks in a number of blind dates.

13

FRIENDS IN FAITH

When he arrived in Frankfurt early in October 1986, Mohsen Rafsanjani, alias Mehdi Bahremani, was a very happy young man. A few days earlier he had marked his twenty-fourth birthday. And almost at the same time he had been put in effective charge of Iran's multi-billion-dollar arms purchases. Bahremani had avoided military service on the war front where some 700,000 of his compatriots had fallen on the battlefield while a further 500,000 had been injured or disabled for life. Now at last he was able to do his bit for the war by procuring the American arms and spare parts which Iran needed to achieve the victory that had eluded it for six years. Bahremani felt he was on the verge of entering history as a true soldier of Allah while enhancing the financial position of his powerful father, Hojat al-Islam Ali-Akbar Hashemi-Rafsanjani, at the same time.

The speaker of the Islamic Majlis had persuaded Khomeini to accept young Mohsen, known to the Americans as Mehdi, as coordinator of secret talks with the Great Satan with the argument that this would avoid 'confusion and mischief'.[1] At a meeting with Khomeini, Rafsanjani had recalled the fact that many millions of Iran's money had been siphoned away by less than scrupulous arms merchants. The fact that Kangarloo had bought TOW missiles from Lieutenant Colonel North for six times the real price was cited by the speaker as the latest example of threats to Islam's interests.

There were many other instances of overcharging, fraud and outright rip-off in the six-year-old saga of Iranian arms purchases. In one instance, in 1981, an arms dealer received $49 million from Iran in exchange for Hawk spare parts which he had supposedly shipped from Spain. When the cargo arrived at the Iranian port of Bandar-Abbas it contained nothing but cement blocks. Another middleman, a relative of Ayatollah Mohammad-Hossein Beheshti, Tehran's strong man until his murder by terrorists in 1981, had simply made away with $80 million on hearing the news of the ayatollah's death. When

Tehran sent him word that he would be murdered if he did not return the money, the middleman claimed that he had put the money in an account which Beheshti had opened in a Swiss bank for the purpose of 'helping propagate Islam in Latin America'. In the end only part of the money was traced to an account opened in the name of one of Beheshti's daughters in Vienna.[2]

Some of the arms that the middlemen sold to Iran turned out to be second hand or useless because they lacked essential parts. An Iranian arms procurement officer, the brother of a powerful member of the Majlis, had gone even further in 1983 by purchasing 300 American-made tanks from the Greek army in Athens. Needless to say, the Greeks did not know anything about such a deal and the middleman disappeared with the down payment of more than $70 million already made by Tehran.

The question of who should control Iran's arms purchases was of great political importance also. The mullahs were determined to prevent the regular army officers from playing a direct role in that regard. Army officers, for the most part Western-educated and secular in outlook, were likely, so the mullahs feared, to use contacts with foreign arms suppliers as a means of enhancing their own position with a view to staging a *coup d'état* after Khomeini's death. Khomeini's constant urging to the mullahs to learn about all aspects of public life, including military matters, helped the clergy extend its control to the realm of arms purchases from 1981 onwards. By 1983 the regular army played no direct role in the matter which was recognized as part of the responsibilities of the Revolutionary Guards. The fact that financial irregularities continued in that domain showed that certain Revolutionary Guards commanders as well as some influential mullahs were either unable to impose discipline or were taking part in what Khomeini himself once described as 'a shameless pillage'. 'Our poorest people,' the ayatollah had remarked, 'forego their daily bread so that we can buy arms. And yet there are individuals heartless enough to steal the money provided by the sweat and blood of the downtrodden.'

Now the young Bahremani was expected to put things right by negotiating a global and long-term agreement for arms purchases from the United States.

On 6 October Bahremani, accompanied by Rahnema and Va'ezi, met North, Secord, Cave and Hakim in Frankfurt. At the meeting Bahremani presented North with a copy of the Qur'an as a gift from Rafsanjani for President Reagan. North reciprocated by presenting a copy of the Bible, autographed by Reagan, to be presented to Khomeini. The president, in order to show that he was personally aware of the contacts and aproved of them, had also written in his own hand a brief passage from the New Testament inside the cover of the leatherbound bible.[3] 'We are both peoples of Faith,' the young emissary observed. 'And now we are bound together by our belief in the oneness of God.' He also repeated an earlier statement he had made during his Washington visit that President Reagan, being 'a true man of God', left the Islamic Republic with no reason to oppose him.

After exchanging these niceties, the two sides settled down to business. The Americans once again concentrated on the problem of the hostages. North told the Iranians that there could be no real progress in relations as long as the hostages issue was not resolved. Bahremani, however, was more interested in strategic matters and dwelt upon the necessity of arming Iran to withstand Soviet threats and to provide greater assistance to anti-Moscow rebels in Afghanistan. The talks soon entered a zone of turbulence, and North tried the tactic that McFarlane had used in Tehran and stormed out of the room, leaving Hakim in charge.

Hakim handled the situation in the style of rug merchants in a Persian bazaar. North wanted at least two hostages released before the US mid-term elections in November so that the president's party could improve its chances of retaining its majority in the Senate. What Hakim was prepared to promise in return for the release of two hostages was far from meagre. He pledged direct American military support for Iran in case the Soviets invaded the country and gave assurances that Washington would seek to organize the overthrow of the Iraqi president, Saddam Hussein, Khomeini's *bête noire*. Further, Hakim also promised a US plan to force Kuwait to release the seventeen convicted terrorists held in prison in the emirate. When he returned to the meeting, North was more than happy to approve the deal negotiated by Hakim.[4] As for future deliveries of arms to Iran, the matter seemed all but settled. A further shipment of 500 TOWs and the remainder of the Hawk missile spare parts already ordered by Kangarloo were delivered to Iran via Israel on the day the talks began.

During a follow-up meeting on the same day Cave provided the Iranians with a long exposé of Washington's view of the Gulf War. The exposé was designed in such a way as to discourage Tehran from launching a new 'final offensive' against Iraq,[5] but it included items of great interest to the military in Tehran, especially the section dealing with Kuwait's defence capabilities and the situation in the Khor Abdallah channel, which Iran now effectively controlled.[6] The two sides parted with a promise to meet again in Frankfurt before the

end of the month. 'We are now convinced that your president is a man of God,' Bahremani told North. 'We are also convinced that we will go a long way together.'[7]

The two teams met again in Frankfurt on 26 October. Bahremani informed North that David Jacobsen, one of the hostages, would be out on 2 November. He also said that there was a good chance that Terry Anderson would be home soon afterwards. During the meeting Bahremani talked on the telephone to his father in Tehran at some length, not knowing that the conversation was being taped both by West German counter-intelligence and by Rafsanjani's enemies in Tehran.[8] In that conversation Bahremani told his father that he was negotiating with 'Reagan's principal men for matters of the Middle East and military issues'. He also said that North had given him 'an important discount' on the price of TOWs compared to what Kangarloo had paid on earlier deliveries. Rafsanjani asked his young envoy to tell the Americans that 'by recognizing the reality of our revolution' they would 'have a real chance of stopping Russia'. 'The shah,' he said, 'could not have saved Iran from communism. But our revolution has already destroyed communism in this country and can destroy it in the rest of the Muslim world as well, provided our friends [i.e. the United States] are wise and act properly.' He also said: 'Tell them [i.e. the Americans] to walk with us [sic] and we shall give them more than the shah could ever offer.'[9]

The speaker also made a cryptic reference to 'arrangements about the corpse our friends are interested in'. This was presumably a reference to the remains of Buckley, the CIA agent who had died under torture in a camp near Tehran. Bahremani promised that the dead agent's body would be returned to the United States plus a 400-page transcript of Buckley's 'confessions' and an eight-hour videotape of his interrogation.[10] All these items were of special interest to Casey not merely as memorabilia of a rather macabre kind but as a means of assessing the damage that Buckley's revelations might have done to CIA operations in the Middle East.

The second Frankfurt meeting with the Americans convinced Rafsanjani that he had succeeded in persuading Washington to take a second look at the Islamic regime and perhaps to consider it as a potential ally against Moscow. The speaker was later to be accused of pro-Americanism by his rivals in Tehran but there is no evidence to support such claims. Rafsanjani was merely acting as a pragmatic politician more interested in power than in ideology. His calculation was simple: Iran must focus its attention on ending the war with Iraq in a way that it could claim as a victory. That would only be possible if Saddam Hussein were overthrown. Rafsanjani had already worked on that possibility with the Saudis and had been greatly encouraged by the demise of the Saudi oil minister, Shaikh Ahmad Zaki Yamani, earlier in the year.

Rafsanjani had partly exposed his real intentions in a speech to an open session of the Majlis in June 1986. Arguing that the revolution could not fight on all fronts at the same time, he said: 'We must learn to order our priorities. . . . We cannot bring down the Great Satan without first eliminating the little satans.'[11] He had added: 'We need arms and must procure them from wherever possible.'

It was also as part of his scheme for isolating Iraq and preventing her from uniting the main Western powers behind her that Rafsanjani had launched a new initiative aimed at improving relations with France in 1986. At the same time as he was arranging for the release of French hostages, also through Mehdi Bahremani, the speaker's agents in France were busy expanding a terrorist network they had created there in the early 1980s.[12] Rafsanjani was pursuing the Leninist tactic of one step backwards, two steps forwards. He was prepared to offer Western leaders the extra edge they often needed for winning elections, but his long-term objectives remained unchanged. Bahremani underlined Rafsanjani's contempt for Western politicians who seemed prepared to go to virtually any length to win votes when he told Cave during a meeting in Brussels that the French premier, Jacques Chirac, had 'nothing else in mind except becoming president'.[13]

The Americans could not have been totally unaware of the Islamic Republic's real agenda in seeking a *rapprochement* with Washington. Charles Allen of the CIA was nearest the mark when, in a memorandum, he cited the objectives of Tehran as follows: securing a continuing supply of weapons, achieving a favourable end to the war with Iraq, regaining Iran's 'rightful place' in the region, and the spread of Khomeinism.[14] And yet the prospects of a major breakthrough seemed too tempting to resist.

The possibility of the new secret relationship being leaked was always a major worry for North and his associates. As a result the operation was kept so secret that even the official CIA did not fully learn about it until it became public at the end of October. This ignorance meant that the agency did nothing to redesign the operations that it had been carrying out against the Islamic Republic for more than four years.

Far from asking its Iranian agents to slow down their campaign against the ayatollah in order to reflect the new relationship between the two countries, the agency encouraged greater militancy. It spent a great deal of money and effort on trying to turn four months of agitation by Iran's 14,000 physicians and dentists against the government into the nucleus of a nationwide revolt.[15] It also asked General Shahrdar to prepare an action plan for a possible military uprising in the southern province of Fars in October 1986.[16] The Islamic Revolutionary Guards retaliated by assassinating two of Shahrdar's most active aides, Colonel Aziz Moradi and Colonel Hamed Hassani, in Turkey. The agency also established links with the Kurdish Democratic Party of Iran and the Democratic National Front for the first time in nearly five years, mainly to make use of their information sources inside the country but also as part of what seemed to be a larger scheme for uniting most of Khomeini's opponents in a broad alliance. Working with the Mujahedeen urban guerrilla group, the agency seemed to be toying with the idea of a coalition on the same lines as the one that had brought the Cambodian resistance groups together with the once denigrated Khmer Rouge. Much of the official policy of the agency seemed geared to the possibility of Khomeini's imminent death, which, despite repeated reports, failed to materialize.

Rumours concerning Rafsanjani's secret links with Washington were first spread in the holy city of Qom, where an unsigned leaflet distributed in the bazaar in mid-September accused the speaker of having received a 'bribe from the Great Satan'. Qom had been full of rumours concerning Washington's intentions in Iran since April 1986 when the mullahs began to take the threat of an American military move against the Islamic Republic quite seriously. The American bombing raid on Libya that month was seen by many mullahs as the first stage of a vaster plan to bully the radical regimes of the region – a description that applied to both Iran and Syria as well as to Gaddafi's regime. Moscow Radio used what it termed 'American plots to use military force against Iran' as one of its main propaganda themes. It later elaborated on this theme by claiming that Casey had told a closed session of the Intelligence Committee of the US Senate that plans were being prepared for 'Grenada-style invasion of Iran'.[17] Other rumours, probably spread with KGB support, included one in which Rafsanjani was preparing to seize absolute power after an American attack on Iran's Persian Gulf bases followed by the murder of Ayatollah Khomeini at his Jamaran residence.

The speaker suspected his rivals of being in secret contact with Moscow, while the latter were convinced that Rafsanjani was trying to play the American card in the power struggle in Tehran. It is difficult to know exactly which of the many groups opposed to Rafsanjani were actually involved in the campaign of rumours. Kangarloo and Ghorbanifar certainly had an axe to grind against the speaker, although the deputy premier knew that he would be included in the 'joint commission' which Bahremani wanted to set up with North. Farsi's supporters also resented what they saw as Rafsanjani's ascendancy and tried to stop him. But the real blow finally came from Mehdi Hashemi, a man who had once been a close friend of Rafsanjani but who was now to become his mortal foe.

Mehdi Hashemi, an Islamic revolutionary, had been imprisoned under the shah for his part in the murder of Ayatollah Shams Abadi in Isfahan in 1975. After the revolution he declined an invitation to become defence minister and instead concentrated his energies on creating a network of semi-clandestine terror groups collectively known as Strugglers of the Islamic Revolution. By 1986 Hashemi had won control of the bulk of the regime's financial and organizational resources devoted to exporting the Khomeinist revolution. One jewel that his crown lacked, however, was Lebanon, where Hezb-Allah remained under the control of Khomeini himself through Sayyed Muhammad Hossein Fadhl-Allah, the Imam's personal representative in Beirut. Hashemi believed that Rafsanjani was preparing the ground to evict him from his post and put in his place Ayatollah Hadi Khosrow-Shahian, a known favourite of the speaker. Informed about Rafsanjani's negotiations with Washington – in which the hostages in Lebanon featured as the speaker's principal asset – Hashemi decided to kill several birds with one stone by revealing what he knew. Hashemi's supporters claim that he was aware of McFarlane's visit to Tehran before it took place and had even contemplated taking the American envoy and his companions hostage but had been dissuaded from pursuing the scheme after being told that Khomeini himself had wanted the visit to take place.[18]

Convinced that Hashemi would cause trouble somewhere along the road, Rafsanjani decided to strike hard. But before he could tackle such a powerful adversary the speaker had to neutralize some of his other rivals. He concluded a tactical alliance with the prime minister and with the minister of intelligence and security, Hojat al-Islam Mohammad Rishahri, by promising both of them representation on the forthcoming joint commission with the United States.[19] An isolated Hashemi was easily arrested and put into Evin Prison. Most of his close associates, a total of 167 people, were also thrown in gaol. The speaker asked Bahremani to mention the move against Hashemi as a sign that the Islamic Republic was distancing itself from violent activities. Two of Hashemi's close friends who had escaped the net because they happened to be abroad decided to retaliate by exposing Rafsanjani's American connection. They informed the Syrians, who directed them to a Beirut weekly supported by Damascus.[20] The magazine put out the story only days after Bahremani had what was to be his last meeting with Secord, Cave and Hakim in Brussels in October. Hashemi was tried at an Islamic court and sentenced to death. He was executed, together with forty-two of his close associates, in September 1987.

The Reagan administration, after a confused attempt to kill the story, came up with a partial version of events. And Rafsanjani, both directly and indirectly through Khomeini's ambassador to the United Nations, Sa'id Raja'i-Khorassani, at first fully corroborated the account given by the White House. The story might have been drowned in a sea of disinformation produced by both Tehran and Washington had it not been linked with the diversion of funds to the Nicaraguan contras. There were no pressure groups in Washington specifically opposed to a *rapprochement* with Tehran. This fact was best illustrated by the attempts made by senators Edward Kennedy and Jesse Helms and former Secretary of State Alexander Haig, each in his own separate way, to seek an Iranian contact. Even the sale of arms to Khomeini might not have raised a major storm. Altogether six arms shipments had been made to Iran with the approval of Washington and only one of these had involved direct transfer from the United States. The maximum value of all the weapons and spare parts shipped to Iran did not exceed $63 million, an insignificant figure compared to the thousands of millions that Tehran spent on arms each year. It was clear that the shipments could not have affected the outcome of the Gulf War in a way likely to antagonize Washington's Arab allies. Even Iraq did not wish to embarrass the Reagan administration over what she termed 'a minor issue'.[21]

What really brought the story to life as far as the American media and public were concerned was the revelation by Attorney-General Edwin Meese that some profit from arms shipments to Iran had been diverted to the Nicaraguan freedom fighters.[22] The Iran–contra scandal was fully launched. The reason was that strong and influential groups opposed to American support for the contras were now directly interested in a story which, in its purely Iranian aspect, might have been buried within a few weeks. The point is worth emphasizing because it underlines the importance that domestic political divisions in the United States have in determining the course of foreign policy. By any standards the issue of future relations with Iran was far more important to the United States than the future of either the contras or the Sandinistas in Nicaragua. But it was Nicaragua and not Iran that was treated as the key issue in US foreign policy, second only to relations with the USSR and disarmament. Another factor which contributed to the eventual proportions of the scandal was the resentment felt by the US Congress, always jealous of its role in shaping foreign policy, over the fact that it had been kept in total darkness about the secret talks with the mullahs. Once again, what was important was not the actual content of the efforts made towards the Khomeinist regime but the fact that it seemed to upset the post-Vietnam, post-Watergate balance which had been created between the presidency and Congress in regard to the making of foreign policy.

That contact with Iran was not the real issue was illustrated by Secretary Shultz, who quickly moved to take over the secret talks with Bahremani. He dispatched Charles Dunbar, one of his senior aides, to Europe to tell Bahremani that the format of the talks had to be changed, although the United States retained a strong interest in pursuing a dialogue with the Islamic Republic.[23]

Rafsanjani, however, quickly realized that a takeover by the State Department would mean an open relationship, for which he was not prepared. He stopped plans for releasing another American hostage and, once he became aware of his rivals' determination to brand him as an agent of the Great Satan, tried to appear more anti-American than anyone else around. He gave his approval to a series of new anti-American acts in the Middle East including the seizure of four more American hostages. In what looked like an exceptional loss of nerves, the *hojat al-Islam* began linking the fate of the American hostages with the unfreezing of Iranian assets controlled by arbitration teams in The Hague. For a while Rafsanjani was even afraid of being assassinated and kept a low profile as the scandal continued to grow. On 15 November the speaker became concerned about reports, partly provided by Syrian intelligence, that the Americans were trying to abduct his son and take him to the United States as a bargaining counter in negotiations for the release of their own hostages in Lebanon. The idea was not totally fanciful. President Reagan had approved a plan for kidnapping suspected terrorists or those believed to be in charge of terrorist organizations so that they could be put on trial in the United States. Colonel North had tried to do precisely that when he organized the interception of the aircraft carrying the *Achille Lauro* hijackers from Cairo to Tunis in 1985.[24] The idea of capturing terrorists so that they could be tried in US courts had been approved by a special committee on counter-terrorism headed by Vice-President Bush in 1986. It had provoked strong opposition from the then FBI director, William Webster. But Reagan himself had ended all debate by authorizing the kidnap plan in a secret finding at Casey's request. It was also Casey who asked North to pursue the idea.[25]

Early in the morning of 15 November, Rafsanjani telephoned his son in Brussels and asked him to go and 'rest in a quiet place'. He told Bahremani that 'jealous and ill-willed individuals are entertaining very evil thoughts about you'.[26] The speaker also instructed his son to hand over all future contacts with 'the new partners', meaning the Americans, to Rahnema in Brussels and Va'ezi in London. 'I do not want you to be involved in this any more,' he emphasized. The speaker did not know that his supposedly private telephone conversation with his son was being taped on the orders of the Intelligence and Security minister, Rishahri. The minister, who had forged a tactical alliance with the speaker earlier on, was apparently angered by the fact that Rafsanjani had kept many important details of negotiations with the Americans to himself. Copies of the taped telephone conversation were distributed in Tehran and Qom the following day. One member of the Islamic Majlis even took a copy of the tape to an open session of the parliament and began playing it on a tape-recorder when he was attacked and badly beaten by Revolutionary Guards. On 20 November the Islamic revolutionary prosecutor, Khoiniha, issued an edict calling on Mohsen Rafsanjani (Mehdi Bahremani) to return to Tehran to answer a number of 'serious charges'. But the young Bahremani had already fled Belgium in the opposite direction, to Canada, where he thought he would be safer because Washington was unlikely to try to kidnap him in a neighbouring and friendly country.

In a letter to the revolutionary prosecutor, posted in West Germany in December 1986, Bahremani wrote that he would return to face all charges 'at a better moment, when passions have cooled down'. He also claimed that he had to stay abroad in order to pass 'a number of examinations while also receiving treatment for maladies that have affected my health in the past few months'.[27]

In February 1987 Bahremani, true to his newly won reputation as the James Bond of Islam, tried to test American intentions towards himself in an original way. He dispatched his old friend and companion, Reza Askari, from Toronto to Los Angeles to perform a piece of pure theatre. Askari, using a passport that identified him as Mehdi Bahremani, checked in under that name at the Miramar-Sheraton Hotel in Santa Monica where he stayed a whole week in the hope that someone might get in touch with him either to resume the talks with Tehran or to manifest an intention to harm the speaker's 'beloved son'. But there was no contact. North had already been fired and had changed his telephone number. Hakim had gone underground and the telephone numbers provided by Cave and Secord had also been disconnected. Even the number that North had given for use only by the speaker himself, a number supposedly connected to the Oval Office, did not answer. On 27 February Askari pushed his audacity a stage further and organized a bizarre press conference at his hotel. In it he claimed that North had given him, meaning Bahremani,

$6 million as commission for future arms purchased by Iran. He offered to return $5.5 million of that to the United States keeping the rest to cover 'the expenses I have personally incurred'.[28]

Although convinced that the Americans were now in too much disarray to try either to renew talks with Iran or to kidnap him as a means of putting pressure on the Islamic Republic, Bahremani nevertheless remained underground, spending most of his time in Canada and Japan. He was now afraid of encountering professional criminals or hired killers dispatched by the political enemies of his father.

Meanwhile in Washington the dismissal of North and the forced resignation of Poindexter did not end the drama. In February McFarlane was taken to hospital after having taken an overdose of pills. Reports suggested that he might have wanted to end his life. A major reorganization at the White House brought in Frank Carlucci as the new head of the NSC and later Howard Baker as chief of the presidential staff, replacing Donald Regan. A special inquiry set up by the president under the chairmanship of former Senator John Tower heard over fifty witnesses, including Reagan himself, and produced a report. The Senate and the House of Representatives, at first separately and later jointly, pursued their own investigations. The president also appointed an independent prosecutor to investigate any possible violations of the US law in more than eighteen months of controversial covert operations.

In May Casey died after being taken ill with a brain tumor. The CIA director had flatly denied any prior knowledge of some of the most important aspects of the covert operations, but testimony by North and Poindexter in July 1987 showed that Casey had been a prime mover in the whole affair. Islamic propaganda, which had earlier claimed that Casey had attempted to kill himself, changed its story about the former CIA chief in May by claiming that Casey had been poisoned by 'those who really run America'.[29]

Revelations about secret talks with the Great Satan dealt a serious blow to Khomeini's prestige among fundamentalist militants both in Iran and abroad. The ayatollah tried to present the whole episode as a carefully planned coup on his part with the double aim of dividing the American leadership and undermining Washington's credibility with its allies. Khomeini dubbed the White House which he often compared to the 'palaces of the emperors of Rome', the 'Black House' and told his followers that Reagan was 'now in mourning because of the chastisement he has received at our hands'.[30] Rafsanjani also followed a similar line and tried to appear a true soldier of Islam whose sole intention in opening secret talks with the Americans had been to sow discord and confusion among the enemy. The tactic, however, did not work and, while Washington experienced the so-called Irangate trauma, Tehran became the scene of 'Americagate'.[31]

The Reagan administration, however, seemed no longer concerned with the once much-coveted prize of a dialogue with the mullahs. Its attention was now focused on the need to stop the further erosion of the president's power and prestige. With memories of Watergate haunting the American psyche, Reagan quickly moved to prove that he was no mullah lover and no lame-duck president. The kidnapping of four teachers at the American University College in Beirut and the brief detention of Gerlad Seib, an American reporter on a visit to Tehran, revived the anti-mullah sentiment which had marked the last year of the Carter presidency. Reagan, who had feebly tried to justify his secret contacts with the mullahs by appealing to long-term geopolitical considerations, including the countering of Soviet expansionism in the Persian Gulf region, rapidly moved towards a policy of direct confrontation with the Islamic Republic. Once again little time was spent on formulating a coherent alternative policy and major decisions were taken in exceptional haste. There was to be a 180-degree change in policy without allowing for a period of transition, which could have been used for reflection and the study of all the implications of a U turn. By July 1987 both the Nixon Doctrine and the Reagan Doctrine were thrown to the wind as the United States positioned itself to play the role of the gendarme of the Persian Gulf.

The dramatic shift in policy towards Iran was to some extent prompted by Shultz and Weinberger, who wished to reassure Arab allies of the United States that Irangate was a thing of the past. Shultz's personal humiliation by Casey and Poindexter, a fact to which he returned again and again during his appearances in front of the joint congressional hearings in Washington in July 1987, may have also played a part in encouraging the secretary to opt for what seemed a total reversal of the previous policy on Iran. Shultz revealed that on at least three occasions he had been on the verge of offering his resignation but had changed his mind at the last moment because he thought he should stay and help the president learn the truth. Accusing the CIA of virtually lying to the president, the secretary of state also claimed that Casey had once written to Reagan to ask the president to replace Shultz.

North's Operation Recovery was buried as Operation Staunch was revived. But fresh American efforts to prevent allies and friendly countries from selling arms to the Islamic Republic bore no fruit. Few people were convinced that the United States was capable of pursuing a policy for more than six months and consequently, saw no reason to

jeopardize their own lucrative arms sales to Tehran. China, approached by the United States with a plea to suspend arms deliveries to Iran in
February 1987, decided that her long-term interests pointed in the
opposite direction. She began speeding up her arms sales to Iran,
especially the supply of surface-to-surface Silkworm missiles which
the Islamic Republic needed to attack enemy ships in the Strait of
Hormuz. By the end of June 1987 the Chinese had installed more than
eighty such missiles near Bandar Abbas and Jask at the entrance to the
Persian Gulf.

14

A GULF OF BLOOD

It was on 4 July 1987 that a squadron of American fighter-bombers, taking off from the carrier *Constellation*, pierced the skies of the Persian Gulf in what was the first show of force of its kind in more than four decades. The jets were not, however, on combat mission: their task was to escort the disabled American frigate, *Stark*, through the Strait of Hormuz, on its long and dolorous journey home. On 17 May, *Stark* had been seriously damaged by an Exocet missile fired from an Iraqi Mirage in search of an easy target. The attack had claimed thirty-seven lives among the crew of the American ship which, despite its sophisticated weapon system, which theoretically gave it the power to cope with any attack from the air, had proved a sitting duck.

The arrival of the coffins, draped in the Stars and Stripes, under the glare of television flashlights, with President Ronald Reagan sombrely seeking to console the bereaved families, brought the Gulf War into every home in the United States. The distant and forgotten war, which had left more than a million people dead in Iraq and Iran, was no longer an abstract nightmare occasionally hinted at in the inside pages of some newspapers. Having largely ignored the Gulf War for nearly seven years, the United States government now began to consider it as a way out of the administration's humiliation over Irangate. The vital importance of the Persian Gulf as 'the jugular vein of the Free World' was rediscovered and emphasized as ample justification for a direct US role in bringing the war to an end while preventing the expansion of Soviet influence.[1]

The Reagan administration, which had played a singularly passive part in various international efforts to help arrange a ceasefire in the Gulf, was suddenly transformed into the prime mover on the subject. Within a few short weeks the United States had committed herself to reflagging Kuwaiti tankers, giving her own ships military escort in the Gulf and defending unidentified 'friendly Arab states' against possible attacks from Iran. The administration also turned the subject into one of the central themes of the summit of the seven most industrialized nations held in Venice in June and also launched an intensive diplomatic campaign to secure a UN Security Council resolution aimed at forcing Tehran and Baghdad to the negotiating table.

This outburst of activity which was characteristically not preceded by anything resembling adequate discussion and debate either within the administration or in Congress transformed the United States from a rather indifferent spectator of a deadly game into a major player. The Senate majority leader Robert C. Byrd (D. West Virginia) described the administration's new plans as 'half-baked, poorly developed'. Senator Robert Dole (R. Kansas) was no more accommodating. 'I don't think anyone knows quite what the policy is.'[2] But the administration did not wait to take notice of such doubts. The Pentagon launched a major information campaign about the Silk-worm missiles supplied to Iran by China and supposedly capable of wreaking havoc on Western shipping in the Strait of Hormuz. American warships in the Gulf were put on 'hair-trigger' alert and the US naval presence in the neighbouring Arabian Sea and the Indian Ocean was substantially increased. By speeding up legal procedures in an unusual way the administration ensured the registration of eleven Kuwaiti tankers in the state of Delaware so that they could pass as American ships under the American flag. Any attack on them would therefore be a direct attack on the United States.

Washington's new activism on the Gulf represented a victory for the State Department and the Pentagon, which had continued to pursue a policy more sympathetic to the Arab side in the Iran–Iraq war. But it was also possible that President Reagan wished to use the Gulf issue as a means of restoring his image as a strong leader capable of taking the initiative and imposing his solutions on important problems of the day. The United States was walking tall again, so Reagan's new policy in the Gulf implied. It seemed to matter little that even the CIA thought that America might be walking tall into a deadly trap.[3] The new policy, which amounted to strong US military and diplomatic support for Iraq, marked for Reagan a further step away from his original conservative constituency. That constituency had always considered Iraq to be a satellite of Moscow and urged the administration to back Iran as the likely winner of the war, despite the bitter memories of the embassy seige in Tehran. The pro-Iran conservatives urged the administration to ponder the possibility of turning the energy of the Islamic Revolution against the USSR.[4] The administration, however, seemed determined to side with Iraq almost openly and in contra-diction with a policy of neutrality announced by Carter in 1980 and endorsed by Reagan in 1981. Washington approved the resumption of military information supplies, notably from the AWACs flying over the Gulf, to Iraq in August 1987. A month later a package of food aid for Iraq worth more than $1000 million was approved by President Reagan.

The fact that the Venice summit refused to endorse Reagan's new belligerent policy in the Gulf did not seem to affect Washington's will to provoke Iran into a direct confrontation. Howard Baker, the White House chief-of-staff, went even so far as to invite Moscow to join the United States in ensuring freedom of navigation in the Persian Gulf. The statement was not only remarkable for the fact that it was made so casually and without any apparent consultation with the State Department or the US allies interested in the Gulf: what was more remarkable was that Washington seemed prepared to abandon a policy which the West had pursued in the Persian Gulf since the seventeenth century – the policy of denying Russia a direct presence in those warm waters, a presence that could threaten some of the most important shipping lanes in the world.[5]

The so-called tanker war had been initiated by Iraq in 1983 as a means of preventing Iran from getting her own oil to the market. Iran had retaliated by attacking tankers carrying Arab oil. At the same time, however, Iran repeatedly asked for the tanker war to be brought to an end and promised not to launch any attacks herself provided her own ships were not attacked by the Iraqis. Iran had every interest in keeping the Gulf open and safe for shipping so that she could export her oil and pay for the war. Iraq, however, had been shut out of the Gulf at the start of the war and made it a central feature of her strategy to disrupt Iran's oil exports. What Iraq wanted in effect was freedom to attack Iranian ships and tankers carrying Iranian oil while her own Arab backers would continue business as usual under big power protection. Iraq wanted to internationalize the war so that the big powers would mobilize their resources to bring it to an end, preventing Iran from achieving victory.

The Kuwaitis approached Britain first with a suggestion that the Royal Navy should protect the emirate's oil exports. After initial hesitation the British rejected the idea. London might have agreed to play a role had Iraq given a pledge to stop her own attacks on Iranian tankers. But the Iraqis were not prepared to abandon what was virtually their only means of putting military pressure on Iran. A few weeks later it was the turn of the United States to be invited by the Kuwaitis to join the Gulf War on the side of the Arabs. But Washington, then engaged in secret talks with Khomeini, refused the invitation. The Arabs turned to Moscow as a last resort.

The Soviets dispatched their deputy foreign minister, Yuli

Vorontsov, to Tehran to inform the mullahs about Moscow's decision to charter three tankers to Kuwait. Vorontsov justified the decision by referring to 'our common desire to keep the Americans out of the Gulf', according to sources in Tehran. The mullahs, while anxious to keep the United States out of the Gulf, had no wish to see the Soviets there either. They sent a diplomatic warning to Moscow by firing on a Soviet cargo ship and subjecting another Soviet vessel to a search in the Strait of Hormuz. Once again Tehran suggested that both sides should stop all attacks on shipping in the waterway. The Soviets put the idea to the Iraqis and were met by a firm refusal. Moscow decided to go ahead nonetheless because the Arab initiative gave the USSR the opportunity to become directly involved in policing the Gulf for the first time. A few weeks later Gromyko told the visiting Islamic foreign minister, Valayati, that Moscow was prepared to do 'a Tashkent' for Iran and Iraq, recalling an earlier Soviet success in bringing the Indo-Pakistani war to an end by inviting the leaders of the two belligerent states to a conference in the Central Asian city in 1965.

Up to July 1987, when the administration rediscovered the threat that the Gulf War posed to the free flow of oil to Japan and the West, a total of 275 ships, flying the flags of thirty-three countries, had been hit. Not one of the ships had been American and not a single American citizen had been killed or injured in the attacks carried out by Iran.[6] At no point had Iran even threatened any specific interests of the United States in the region. The last thing the mullahs wanted was for the superpowers to be drawn into the Gulf War. After 1982 the mullahs were in control of the war and knew that they could retain that control as long as the superpowers were not sucked into the region on the sides of the Arabs.

The administration's claim that Iran might want to stop the flow of oil through the Gulf was far from convincing. More than 95 per cent of Iran's foreign revenues came from oil exports, without which the Islamic Republic could not have pursued the war for more than a limited time. Nearly seven years of war had shown that the Iran–Iraq carnage had in no way affected the flow of oil. The OPEC ministers, in conference in Geneva in June 1987, were in fact concerned about overproduction as both Iran and Iraq exceeded the quotas assigned to them. The price of crude oil, which had reached $33 per barrel at the start of the war, had stabilized at around $18 in July 1987. None of the major industrial powers shared Washington's sudden concern for the future of oil supplies from the Gulf. It seemed as if the Reagan administration was entering the Gulf War solely in order to prevent an Iraqi defeat and to save the Iraqi leadership from paying the full price for mistakes they had made during nearly seven years.

The Iraqi regime could not be said to deserve support in terms of any of the declared objectives of the Reagan administration. Dominated by one man, Saddam Hussein al-Takriti, the Iraqi regime could hardly be described as a democracy. President Hussein and his ruling Arab Ba'ath Socialist Party had seized power in a *coup d'état* in 1968, toppling a pro-Western government.[7] Between 1968 and 1987 no fewer than 60,000 opponents of the regime were put to death, according to estimates by interntional organisations including Amnesty International. A further 800,000 Iraqis, out of a population of around 11 million, had fled into exile, while another 150,000 were in prison or held in concentration camps for their political or religious opinions. The same regime had concluded a treaty of friendship and cooperation with the Soviet Union – a treaty which in its clauses IV and V, provided for mutual assistance in the military domain. Moscow was established as the principal supplier of weapons to Iraq from 1970 onwards.[8] The USA, on the other hand, did not even have diplomatic relations with Iraq until 1984, when the US embassy in Baghdad was reopened after nearly sixteen years.

President Hussein had begun preparing for war against Iran in the autumn of 1978, when the rising tide of the Khomeinist revolution seemed to be getting the better of a vacillating shah. Hussein, who had not performed his military service, promoted himself field-marshal and began wearing a uniform adorned with as many decorations as he could get hold of. In 1979 he started projecting himself as a great military leader destined to achieve the first major Arab military victory in over a thousand years. He bought $5000 million's worth of weapons from the USSR and France and raised an army of 300,000. On 22 September 1980 he ordered his army to invade Iran at the start of what he declared would be 'the dismemberment of the remnants of the Persian Empire'.[9]

When Iraqi forces invaded Iran at three points on 22 September 1980 the general expectation was that they would have no more than a few weeks of fighting ahead of them. Iran's armed forces, decapitated and demoralized by the revolution, were believed to be in no fighting position. The Iraqis, on the other hand, were well equipped, better disciplined and clearly looking for a quick victory. Nevertheless the pattern of fighting soon changed, turning against Saddam Hussein's forces. There were several reasons for this. First, the Iraqi generals had used the textbook tactic of capturing territory after heavy artillery bombardment followed by tank and infantry advances. They did not realize that Iran, a country almost three times as large as Iraq, could lose a lot of territory before its morale became affected. Secondly, Saddam Hussein did not wish to take great risks, especially that of heavy casualties. As a result he did not commit enough troops to the crucial battles of Ahvaz and Abadan and failed to capture the Iranian stronghold of Dezful. Not wanting to lose thousands of men in the early stages of the war, he opted for a strategy that would lead to the loss of tens of thousands of men over nearly seven years of fighting. Content with the large chunks of Iranian territory he had conquered, he ordered his armies to stop so that peace talks could begin. He forgot that holding territory was no substitute for destroying the enemy's forces and overall fighting capabilities. The breather which Hussein allowed the Iranians gave the ayatollah time to mobilize tens of thousands of volunteers for martyrdom and dispatch them to the front. Hussein's third mistake was to keep his air force in reserve in bases on Jordanian territory, apparently because he was afraid that the Israelis, seizing the opportunity provided by the confusion of the war, might try to destroy Iraq's planes on the ground. As a result the Iranian Air Force, despite all the purges it had suffered, was able to control the skies of the region in the initial phases of the war.

The biggest mistake made by the Iraqis, however, was their indecision and confusion concerning the precise objectives of the war they had started. They at once pursued aims that could not be reconciled: they sought to annex parts of the province of Khuzestan while pursuing the larger goal of overthrowing the ayatollah's regime. Their whole strategy was based on negotiating territorial concessions from a regime which they wanted to overthrow. That would have been possible only if Iraq had had enough military, economic and demographic strength to conquer most of Iran and gain control of Tehran itself. In the absence of such strength, Iran's sheer physical size became her best defence.

Six months after the Iraqi invasion, Iran seized the initiative and launched a series of counter-attacks that broke the siege of Abadan and drove the Iraqis back on the central Khuzestan front as well. This was followed by three major Iranian offensives into Iraqi territory in 1982. The Iranians sent in tens of thousands of young volunteers in a series of human wave attacks supported by the regular army's heavy artillery and helicopter gunship units. In 1983 Iran launched five more offensives and captured large tracts of Iraqi territory, including some of the richest oilfields of Mesopotamia. By that time the Iraqis had lost all appetite for attack and were bogged down by a defensive mentality that prevented them from taking the initiative even at a local level. The on-again off-again war continued into 1985, when Iranian forces established themselves at a distance of some 100 kilometres from Baghdad and about 12 kilometres from Basra, Iraq's second largest city. In 1986 Iran captured parts of the Faw Peninsula thus taking the war to the borders of the emirate of Kuwait.

From 1983 onwards the Iraqis pinned their hopes on breaking Iran by preventing it from exporting its crude oil. The Iranian oil terminal at Kharg was attacked more than 180 times and was eventually used only as a secondary facility. The Iraqis continued to hit other Iranian oil terminals at Lavan, Sirri and Larak islands further down the Persian Gulf. They also attacked more than two hundred oil tankers belonging to more than thirty different countries carrying Iran's oil. Tehran's repeated demands for action by the United Nations to end attacks on tankers in the Gulf remained unheeded. Nevertheless Iran managed to export enough oil to pay for the war as well as the terrorist operations that the mullahs financed in more than thirty countries.

During the war the Iraqis used chemical weapons on at least fifteen different occasions. Once again the United Nations refused to act to prevent such violations of all international rules of war. It was also Iraq that initiated massive air attacks on civilian targets which killed thousands of people.

Throughout the war the USSR and France strongly supported Iraq. The French sold Iraq Exocet missiles and the latest models of their Mirage combat aircraft. In 1983 they even sent five of their own Super-Etendard heavy bombers to Iraq on 'loan'. The Iranians retaliated by ordering the seizure of French hostages in Lebanon and a series of terrorist attacks on French interests in the Middle East as well as on targets inside France itself.

Throughout the long war Khomeini too made a number of serious mistakes. His most important error was to seek a personal political victory by pinning his hopes on an anti-Baghdad uprising by the Shi'ites who formed the majority of the Iraqi population. The ayatollah did not want a purely military success in the war, an outcome that could have turned Iran's army and Revolutionary Guards into victorious heroes. He wanted the experience of Iran itself to be repeated, with Iraqi Shi'ites forcing Saddam Hussein's army to surrender and accept the creation of an Islamic republic led from Tehran. Khomeini even chose the first 'president' of the future Islamic Republic of Iraq. The man chosen was a forty-two-year-old mullah from Shiraz named Hojat al-Islam Mohammad-Baqer Hakim Tabataba'i. By the end of 1987 it had become clear that Iran could no longer lose the war while Iraq was unable to win it. A long stalemate seemed to be the likeliest prospect. By then the war had already claimed a million lives on both sides in addition to nearly twice as many injured. It had also made more than four million people homeless in Iran and Iraq. The economic damage done by the war was estimated to exceed $400,000 million on both sides, although Iran alone claimed that it had lost almost that much.[10]

The fall of the shah in 1979 had, for a while, given rise to Western fears that the USSR might be tempted to seize the opportunity provided by the Islamic Revolution to expand its influence in the Persian Gulf or even attempt to win control of the Strait of Hormuz. William Sullivan, the last American ambassador to Tehran before the break in diplomatic relations, had raised these fears in a number of high-level conversations with members of the Bazargan government. But he had been given full assurances that revolutionary Iran would not allow any outside power to gain a foothold in the Gulf. In the summer of 1979 Moscow sounded out Iranian views about the possibility of Soviet warships paying courtesy calls on Bandar Abbas and Khorramshahr. The Iranian answer was a firm refusal, despite the fact that Soviet warships had visited Iranian ports on a number of occasions during the shah's reign.

Another strong sign of Iran's determination to continue the shah's policy of keeping outside powers out of the Persian Gulf was the failure of an attempt by the PLO to win a few chips of its own in the revolutionary chaos that reigned in Tehran. In September 1979 the PLO suggested to Khomeini that Palestinian units be established on the two Iranian islands of Tunb and Abu-Mussa near the Strait of Hormuz ostensibly to prevent oil from being shipped to Israel. The Omanis, concerned about such a development, raised the matter with the United States.[11] But by the time the USA brought up the issue in Tehran Khomeini had already told the PLO to nurture no such dreams. To emphasize the point further, the ayatollah also ordered that the PLO 'ambassador' to Tehran, Hani al-Hassan, should not be allowed to travel to any point within 100 kilometres of Iran's Persian Gulf ports.

The only increase in Soviet activity in the Persian Gulf following the fall of the shah came in the form of more frequent visits by Soviet naval units to the Iraqi port of Um al-Qasar and a substantial rise in Soviet arms sales to Baghdad. By 1987 Um al-Qasar was a ghost port city totally cut off from the Gulf by Iranian forces. The claim made by members of the Reagan administration that the mullahs of Tehran were somehow likely to bring the Russians into the Persian Gulf could not be taken seriously in view of the abundant evidence to the contrary.

Nevertheless the Reagan administration, turning the USS *Stark*'s tragedy into a powerful emotional theme, continued to point to the Soviet threat as a tangible reality in the Gulf in the summer of 1987. At a memorial service for the victims of the Iraqi attack on *Stark*, the president said: 'Were a hostile power ever to dominate this strategic region and its resources, it would become a choke-point for freedom

–that of our allies and our own.'[12] Defence Secretary Weinberger was even more to the point: 'We simply cannot allow the Kremlin to have its will over this region. We will not be intimidated. We will not be driven from the Gulf.'[13] The secretary did not say exactly what was new in the situation in the Gulf to warrant such fears. The fact that a few days later the administration invited the Kremlin to help keep the peace in the waterway further illustrated the confusion that reigned in Washington. The United States had maintained a naval presence in the Gulf, in Bahrain's territorial waters, for more than forty years and also enjoyed naval and air force facilities on the Omani island of Massirah and the Omani port of Ras al-Hadd in the Arabian Sea within easy distance of the Strait of Hormuz.[14] At no point had the ayatollahs of Tehran threatened the US military presence in the region or even formally asked for it to be withdrawn. The only attack on an American target in the Gulf had come from the Iraqis, and yet the administration used this as an excuse for virtually entering the war on the side of Iraq. Commenting on the attack on *Stark* the president said that it was in fact Iran that was 'the villain in the piece'. The fact that, only thirty-six hours before *Stark* was hit by the Iraqis, a Soviet tanker, escorted by a Soviet frigate, had been damaged by an Iranian mine near Kuwait was ignored. Also ignored was the attack launched by an Iranian gunboat against a Soviet freighter a few days later, drawing an angry response from the Kremlin. More than six years after entering the White House President Reagan invoked the Carter Doctrine under which the Persian Gulf was declared a region of vital interest that would be defended militarily by the United States against incursions by the Soviet Union or any other hostile power. The only trouble with this was that there was no sign of an increased Soviet presence in the Gulf and no hostile action had been taken against the United States except for the lone Iraqi attack on *Stark*.

On 10 July Rafsanjani sent a special emissary to London and then to Washington to assure the Western powers that there would be no Iranian attacks on bona fide American ships provided the United States did not enter the war on the Arab side by escorting Kuwaiti oil tankers which brought a steady flow of cash to Baghdad.[15] Prior to that Tehran had on several occasions assured the United States, through the Swiss and the British governments, that no American targets would be hit in the Gulf. US Assistant Secretary of State Richard Murphy, revealing Iran's assurances at a press conference, also underlined the fact that no American ship had been attacked by Iran in the past.[16]

While drawing public attention to what it described as a growing Soviet threat in the Gulf, the Reagan administration dispatched its ambassador to the United Nations, Vernon Walters, to Moscow to enlist Soviet support for a resolution aimed at ending the Iran–Iraq war. It was difficult to see any logic in the many contradictory moves that were being made by the administration beyond an evident desire to re-establish US credibility with friendly Arab countries and to show that the Irangate episode was truly over and that Reagan no longer wanted to make friends with the ayatollah. Some American leaders continued to doubt the efficacy of the means chosen for that end. 'What are our goals? What is our strategy? What are the risks? And how much cost are we willing to pay?' asked Senate Republican leader Robert Dole.

The administration also raised the spectre of a new global oil shortage as a result of domination of the Gulf by hostile powers. But the fact was that no more than 3 per cent of total US oil consumption passed through the Persian Gulf, a percentage that could be easily met by other oil exporters, especially Mexico, Venezuela and Ecuador. The international oil market, however, knew better and showed no concern about developments in the Gulf.

Oil experts knew that the flow of black gold could be halted at the well heads and that the 'hostile powers' that President Reagan referred to did not necessarily need to attack tankers heading for Western ports. A pro-West regime in Iran lost control of that country's oil resources not because of any Soviet naval threat but because of a revolution that turned the oil taps off at the well heads. Revolutionary Iran, however, had no interest in stopping its own oil exports because, without oil revenues, it could not survive. Nor could the mullahs choose not to sell Iran's oil to the West and Japan. There were no other customers willing and able to pay for that oil. The mullahs were not determined to stop Arab oil exports either. The whole of Kuwait's production zone was within reach of Iranian artillery by the summer of 1987 and yet not a single attack was made on it. Militarily Iran was also capable of knocking out more than half the Saudi installations plus the whole of the United Arab Emirates' production capacity. But the mullahs knew that such attacks would lead to the break-up of OPEC and possibly military involvement by the superpowers. Tehran was not even prepared to go all out to stop Iraq's oil exports. The Iraqi pipeline carrying more than half that country's exports to the Mediterranean through Turkey was vulnerable to direct Iranian or pro-Iranian Kurdish attacks since 1983 and yet no attempt to cut it off was made. The reason was that the mullahs did not wish to antagonize Turkey through which more than half Iran's vital imports passed.

On 20 July the United Nations Security Council unanimously passed a resolution calling for a ceasefire in the Gulf War. To give the decision more weight, Secretary Shultz personally led the American delegation during the council's deliberations. The British, West German and French foreign ministers were also present to give the occasion a greater measure of solemnity. But, by an unfortunate coincidence, the passing of the resolution coincided almost exactly with the escorted passage of the first of the eleven Kuwaiti tankers sailing under the American flag through the Strait of Hormuz. Despite assurances by Shultz during the Security Council session that the USA remained neutral in the Gulf War, Tehran was convinced that Washington was now directly involved in the Arab war effort. After all, few people believed that Kuwait, which financed Iraq's war effort, was a neutral state. The secretary's assertions that Washington was doing exactly what Moscow had also done for the Kuwaitis did not sound convincing either. The Soviets had chartered three of their own tankers to Kuwait, whereas the USA was simply putting its own flag on Kuwaiti-owned tankers.

The much publicized Security Council resolution remained a dead letter so far as the Islamic Republic was concerned. Khomeini had on many occasions described the United Nations as 'a club for the heathen' and was not prepared to allow his policies to be dictated by 'satanic powers'. He used the resolution as well as the American decision to escort Kuwaiti tankers for his own propaganda purposes. Right from the start of the Gulf War Khomeini had claimed that his Islamic Republic was not only fighting Iraq, a small and unworthy adversary, but was, in fact, at war with the United States and France, which backed the Baghdad regime. The Security Council resolution, passed during a session chaired by the French foreign minister, Jean-Bernard Raimond, and the escorting of Kuwaiti tankers by the US Navy enabled the ayatollah to sustain his outlandish claims at least as far as his followers were concerned. He saw himself as Prophet Muhammad taking on the Byzantine and Sassanid empires, the superpowers of the ancient world. The mullahs refused to be drawn into a formal acceptance or rejection of the Security Council 598.

The Reagan administration's dramatic decision to abandon what had been a genuine policy of neutrality in the Gulf War had another consequence that should have easily been foreseen. The Soviet leader Mikhail Gorbachev, always ready to exploit every opportunity to portray the USSR as a reasonable and peace-loving power, wrote a letter to President Reagan proposing superpower talks about the future of the Gulf. Washington instantly rejected the offer. But Moscow had already scored a point by launching the idea of a superpower consortium to ensure freedom of navigation in the Persian Gulf, while insisting that all outside powers withdraw their military presence from the region. It was obvious that the United Nations would not be able to impose a ceasefire on Iran and Iraq without Soviet cooperation. This meant that the United States had set itself forward as the champion of a cause whose success or failure depended on Moscow's attitude. The Soviets were visibly engaged in a long-term, step-by-step game which would be only marginally affected by passing events. The USA, on the other hand, lived from headline to headline and moved from tanker to tanker, so to speak. It became identified with policies dictated by circumstances and likely to harm its long-term interests in a sensitive region.

In a speech on 15 July 1987 Rafsanjani in effect invited President Reagan to reconsider his strategy towards Iran. 'All the US can do against us in the Persian Gulf is to undertake bombing raids against targets in our territory,' the speaker said. 'But the United States is far far away and cannot sustain a long war against us. It has no bases in this part of the world and cannot commit the large numbers of troops needed to make a serious impression on us.'[17] In the same speech Rafsanjani compared what he saw as Washington's weakness in the region with the strength of the Soviet Union, which, being a neighbour of Iran, could mobilize huge forces for intervention in the region. Once again Rafsanjani tried to tell Washington that he, and maybe even Khomeini himself, considered Moscow as the principal source of danger for Iran and still hoped that the USA would be on Iran's side if and when 'the threat from the north' manifested itself in military terms.

The mullahs were not, however, prepared to sit back and watch while the United States put her military might on show on the side of the Arabs. Khomeini had never conceded even a tactical victory to the 'Great Satan' and was now not prepared to do so. The blow which the ayatollah had promised would be dealt against the US naval convoy came on 24 July when a floating mine, placed in the deep channel which led past the Iranian island of Farsi on the way to the head of the Gulf, holed the Kuwaiti supertanker, renamed *Bridgetown*, as the American warships watched helplessly. The commander of the naval convoy announced that he lacked the equipment needed for detecting and neutralizing such 'primitive mines'. As a precautionary measure he ordered his warships to move behind the Kuwaiti tanker, using the *Bridgetown* as a shield for themselves. The reason was that the Kuwaiti supertanker was better able to withstand an explosion because of her sheer bulk. It was a matter of pure chance that the floating mine that had disabled the *Bridgetown* had not hit one of the American escort ships. Such an accident might well have caused heavy casualties among American military personnel. The incident forced the United States to appeal to Saudi Arabia, Qatar, Kuwait and Bahrain for help in clearing the mines laid by the Iranians in the main shipping channels leading to the emirate. The US war machine itself was too sophisticated to meet the needs of the situation. The captain of one of the escort ships, USS Fox, complained that although he had full equipment for detecting submarine attacks his vessel was 'totally blind' when threatened by 'classical type mines'.[18]

The mishap suffered by the convoy was instantly presented in the Islamic Republic as another 'sign from Allah'. Mighty America was, once again, shown to be vulnerable. This was not the first time that the Great Satan had suffered a military setback in its moves against the forces of Islam. In 1980 a US military mission sent to rescue the Tehran hostages ended in disaster when desert sandstorms disabled helicopters needed to carry the commandos. In 1983 the USA was forced into a humiliating retreat when its Marines became objects of suicide and sniper attacks in Lebanon. The subsequent show of force ordered by President Reagan and involving the biggest armada ever assembled in front of Beirut had also ended in further humiliation for the Great Satan because of its failure to influence events in Lebanon in favour of the United States' local allies and clients. 'This is the third time that the Great Satan has tested its satanic power against the government of Allah,' Ayatollah Ali-Akbar Mohtashami, the Islamic interior minister, said in a radio interview. 'The rulers of Washington would do well to learn from a lesson that had been taught to them three times. Our Supreme Guide [i.e. Khomeini] is a descendant of Imam Ali and, as the proverb says: He who crosses swords with the children of Ali shall be annihilated.'[19]

A few weeks later, however, the American 'Great Satan', acting out of character as far as its relations with the Islamic revolution were concerned, decided to strike back albeit in a limited way. An Iranian ship, the Iran Ajr, allegedly caught laying mines in one of the Gulf's main channels, was seized by an American commando. Three members of the Ajr's crew were killed and the rest were captured by the Americans.

The attack on Ajr was followed by another American operation the following month in which four Iranian off-shore oil platforms were blown up and destroyed after Washington claimed that they had been identified as radar-bases used by the Islamic Revolutionary Guard. The operation claimed no casualties and was intended more as a warning to Tehran than a specific military action aimed at dealing with an immediate threat to shipping in the Gulf.

The US forces, indirectly supported by naval units from Britain, France and Italy, failed to make the waterway a safer place for shipping. Iraq continued its on-again off-again air raids on Iranian tankers and oil installations in the Persian Gulf despite a strong plea by Britain to observe an unannounced cease-fire. And Iran retaliated by hitting ships carrying Arab oil through the waterway. The average number of ships hit in any one week remained as high as at any time since 1983.

Washington had sent its armada into the Persian Gulf with the declared aim of ensuring the safety of international navigation. But it was obvious to the Islamic leaders in Tehran that the USA was pursuing larger objectives. The USA was clearly hoping to influence internal developments in Iran by exerting what geostrategists describe as 'close proximity pressure'. One theory raised both in Tehran and elsewhere was that the real purpose of the American naval presence in the Persian Gulf was to strengthen the hand of those in the Islamic leadership who argued for an end to the war and a gradual improvement of relations with the West.[20] It was also possible that the USA wished to have a strong military presence close to Iran's sensitive oil lanes so as to influence events in the aftermath of Khomeini's death. The immediate effect of the American presence, however, was a general weakening of those in Tehran who might have argued for a less hostile attitude by the Islamic Republic towards the West in general and Washington in particular. Even Rafsanjani, who had worked hard to bring about a step-by-step change in relations between the Islamic Republic and the United States, was left with no choice but to try and appear more anti-American than anyone else within the leadership. As late as May 1987 Rafsanjani had tried to resume talks with Washington.[21] But by November he had become the architect of a new wave of anti-Americanism in Iran.

The Reagan administration must have been aware of the strict and inevitable limits to the impact that American military power in the region could have on the larger course of developments in the Gulf War. The sheer size of the forces present on both the Iranian and the Iraqi side made it impossible for the United States, or any other outside power for that matter, to make much of an impression in the broader theatre of the conflict.[22] The USA could not, and did not wish to, help Iraq win the war but was, because of its military posture in the Gulf, seen by many Iranians, including some opponents of the ayatollah, as an objective ally of the Ba'athist regime in Baghdad. The Arabs, on the other hand, were not prepared to give the United States much credit for having come to their aid.

As the international press continued to speculate about possible American military action against Iran, few people stopped to ask whether or not the USA could, by using force, succeed where Iraq had failed for more than seven years. The USA was reported to be preparing raids on some 120 'sensitive targets' in Iran.[23] But most of these targets had already been hit by the Iraqi Air Force on many occasions since 1983. Iraq's indiscriminate attacks on Iran's economic nerve-centres had not forced Khomeini to abandon his plans for exporting his revolution. There was no reason to believe that the United States would secure different results by taking similar action against Iran.

The American military presence in the Gulf might have been expected to act as a morale booster for the Iraqi army. In October, however, the US Congress, in a report parts of which were duly leaked to the press, claimed that Iraqi morale was still fragile and that the Ba'athist army had shown no signs of any improvement in its fighting abilities. The report was so damning for the Iraqis that Tehran radio broadcast its basic points several times each day for a whole week.[24]

The actions taken by US forces against the Islamic Revolutionary Guards in the Persian Gulf persuaded Tehran that Washington was not simply trying to persuade the mullahs to accept Resolution 598. The actions in question, though militarily insignificant, were dramatic enough to appear as if they had been specifically designed to humiliate the ayatollah and undermine the myth of invincibility that he had patiently created around himself.

'The Security Council resolution is nothing but a pretext', Rafsanjani told the crowds in Tehran on 4 November 1987. 'What the Great Satan is aiming at is to harm our revolution. The Great Satan is trying to take revenge because of the humiliation it has suffered at the hand of our committed and martyrdom-seeking youths.[25]

The idea of 'punishing' Khomeini for his provocative acts had always had its supporters in the United States. After all, Ronald Reagan himself had spoken of bombing raids on Tehran and Qom during his first presidential campaign in 1979. And Carter's National Security Adviser Zbigniew Bzrezinski had revealed in 1982 that the USA had worked out a plan for a 'larger, punitive assault on Iran designed to salvage national prestige' during the hostage crisis.[26] The plan would presumably have been implemented had the Tabas rescue mission succeeded in securing the release of the hostages in April 1980.

The passage of years had not changed public attitude in the USA about the ayatollah, and the 'Iran-contra' scandal only fanned the fires of revenge in America. South Dakota Governor William Janklow expressed the views of many when he said that the only way the USA should deliver weapons to Iran was 'from a B–1 bomber from an altitude of 30,000 feet'.[27] And President Reagan, in a speech in which he called Iran a 'barbarian country', said that he wanted the mullahs to go to bed every night wondering what action the USA would take against them.[28]

With this background in mind the efforts of the United Nations Secretary General Javier Peres de Cuellar to salvage something of the resolution 598 often appeared futile and pathetic. The mullahs resented the fact that the resolution had been drafted, negotiated, amended and approved without anyone bothering to consult them or take their basic views into account. What had emerged from weeks of diplomatic activity in Washington, Moscow, London, Paris and Beijing looked more like a big power ultimatum than an invitation to negotiations. Resolution 598, which even stated details of an as yet unachieved cease-fire accord, seemed to have been deliberately designed in such a way that would make it difficult if not outright impossible for Tehran to accept. Nevertheless, de Cuellar would not be discouraged. He visited Tehran and Baghdad and continued to negotiate separately with both sides throughout the summer.

The diplomatic breathing space created by de Cuellar also gave Moscow an opportunity to cast itself in the role of a potential peacemaker. Soviet Deputy Foreign Minister Yuli Vrontsov became a regular visitor to Tehran and Baghdad, as well as some other Gulf capitals, and evoked the memories of Tashkent – the peace conference in which the USSR brought India and Pakistan together in 1965. In Baghdad and Kuwait, Vrontsov pledged support for sanctions against any party that refused a cease fire followed by peace talks. In Tehran, however, he expressed support for the objectives of the Islamic Revolution and branded the United States as 'trouble-maker' in the Persian Gulf.[29]

Once again, the absence of precise objectives meant that the United States found itself in a difficult situation in the pursuit of contradictory goals. The different objectives of ending the Gulf War, keeping the Soviets out of the Gulf, helping 'moderates' win power in Tehran, reassuring Arab allies, offering the angry public at home something to chew on and giving the United Nations a belated boost as a practical instrument for making peace competed with one another in the narrow context of a policy based essentially on an unconvincing and yet highly provocative show of force.

Washington must have known that its forces in the Gulf could not do more damage to Iran's war machine and fighting resolve than the Iraqis had done in more than seven years. In any case, inviting Khomeini to come to any negotiating table under open military pressure from the 'Great Satan' amounted to an invitation to political suicide as far as the Islamic regime was concerned. In other words, the US military presence in the Persian Gulf had, by the autumn of 1987,

become an additional hurdle on the road to peace between Iran and
Iraq.

Part of the US strategy in the Gulf seemed to have been based on the
assumption that Baghdad was fully committed to the cause of peace
and that all that remained to be done was to drag Tehran into a process
of negotiations. A closer examination of Iraqi policies and practices,
however, showed that President Hussein's government was not
prepared to offer Iran any meaningful concessions in exchange for a
cease fire followed by peace negotiations. Hussein had initiated the
war on 22 September 1980 but rejected suggestions from de Cuellar
that he should allow an international committee to identify 'the
aggressor' before a cease fire could be negotiated. Baghdad had also
declared the 1975 treaty that had fixed the common borders of Iran
and Iraq to be null and void. And yet resolution 598 spoke of a
withdrawal of forces behind the recognized borders of the two
neighbours. Logically, therefore, Iraq should have retracted its
cancellation of the 1975 treaty which Iran had always declared to be
valid. The Iraqis, however, refused to re-commit themselves to the
1975 treaty but insisted that Iran should withdraw its forces to
borders that Baghdad itself would not recognize as legitimate.

President Reagan had cited the need to support friendly Arab
regimes in the region as one reason for his decision to order the biggest
build-up of US forces in the Gulf since World War II. The American
show of force, at least in its initial stages, certainly reassured the pro-
West governments of several Arab countries. At the same time,
however, it gave some credence to claims by Khomeini that all Arab
regimes with the exception of Algeria, Libya, Syria and South Yemen,
were vassals of the United States. This is how Islamic propaganda
asked the Arabs to see the situation:

'Brother Muslims! You must ask yourselves why is it that the
American Great Statan has come to the Gulf and is ready to risk the
lives of its own soldiers in a war against Islam? Arab countries are
today nothing but protectorates of the United States with governments
put in place and kept in place by the Great Satan.'[30]

THE JOURNEY TO IRANGATE:
A CONCLUSION

When President Franklin D. Roosevelt decided, in 1943, to help Iran become a model of democratic development, the once glorious Persia of the Achaemenids was one of the poorest nations on earth. Roosevelt had pinned his hopes on Iran's ability to mobilize its vast natural resources in the service of economic growth sustained by social reform under an enlightened leadership determined to prepare the country for a more or less Western-style system of government.

Thirty-five years later, however, Iran found itself confronted with an Islamic revolution that wished to return it to a system of government developed in the seventh century in Arabia. Iran was farther away than ever from creating a Western-style democracy. In 1978 the United States embassy in Tehran noted with unusual brutality that none of Iran's basic political problems had been seriously tackled in the preceding four and a half decades. In its top-secret report the embassy said: 'If one examines Iran for political structures today, one is struck by the appearance of a wasteland. . . . The Iranian political system has proved unable to respond effectively to the surge of demands on it that has grown out of the myriad social and economic problems.'[1] The report concluded: 'Neither the people nor the state are yet prepared to accept the duties and responsibilities of a democratic political system.'[2] Almost exactly a year after that report was sent to Washington, where it was ignored, Ayatollah Khomeini was master of Iran and preparing for confrontation with the 'Great American Satan'.

During thirty-five years of close and varied relations with the United States, the leader of the free world and champion of Western democratic values, Iran not only failed to develop the political structures it needed to survive in the twentieth century but also gradually lost some of its own democratic traditions. The idea of a Western-style democracy had not come to Iran with the Americans. It had captured the imagination of the Persian intelligentsia from the

1820s onwards and dominated almost all mainstream political movements in the country until the 1950s.

In 1943, when Roosevelt adopted Iran in the same way as one adopts an orphan child, the country, although under foreign occupation, enjoyed a large measure of press freedom unknown in most parts of the world apart from the Western democracies. At that time in Iran there were no political prisoners, no censorship, no blacklists of books and films and no curbs on political activity. A variety of political parties, representing the entire political spectrum from fascist to communist, campaigned freely for public support. The reverse side of the coin, of course, was that 90 per cent of adult Iranians remained illiterate while more than half the population starved. Life expectancy did not exceed thirty-seven years in that 'abyss of beauty and misery'.[3]

The conventional wisdom, shared by successive US administrations was that economic development and, above all, the achievement of what W. W. Rostow described as 'take-off', a concept akin to that of orgasmic magic, was the *sine qua non* of genuine political development in Iran and throughout the so-called Third World. This crude crypto-Marxist concept was later even quantified to show that Third World nations would begin becoming democratic as soon as they achieved a $2000 gross national product per head per annum.[4] In 1978 Iran had completed its 'take-off' and passed the magical GNP figure. It was also one of the four countries with largest foreign currency reserves in the world.[5]

An embassy report noted:

> Until recently the steady and rapid growth of Iran's economy seemed able to assure material progress sufficient to override the ill effects of growing social problems. Now, however, the Iranian government and people are aware that the economic benefits already won are not well distributed, that future benefits will not come easily and that the overall quality of life may not be improving even in the areas where the economy has grown most quickly. Because the aspirations of virtually all classes have outpaced their material gains, moreover, the political impact of the economic situation has become much more troublesome.[6]

It was not enough to improve the material living conditions even of the majority of the people, for political development to follow automatically. The embassy report emphasized that the average Iranian certainly 'enjoyed a higher standard of living than in the past' without, however, feeling any gratitude towards the shah or being any more committed to the survival of his regime. It also noted that the shah had even failed to mobilize the middle class, who, strangely enough, seemed to want to listen more to the ayatollahs committed to the destruction of their way of life.

The economists of the 'take-off' school had also assumed that passing the $2000 threshold would be sufficient to reduce Islam's political role to that of an irrelevant relic of the past. The fact that literacy in Iran had risen to some 60 per cent of the adult population and that more than 300,000 young Iranians were at university at home and abroad should have weakened the position of the mullahs. But the opposite was the case. An embassy analysis noted that the mullahs had 'drawn renewed vigour from the literacy and education drives which have transformed so much of the Iranian population over the past four or five decades. Muslim leaders can call on educated Muslim youths, many of whom have learned western arts of propaganda and organization in their US or European schools and universities.'[7]

Another basic assumption of US policy in Iran was that strengthening the nation's defences was the surest means of countering the Soviet threat, which was assumed to be the main source of danger to Iran's relations with the West. By 1978 Iran was theoretically strong enough to withstand Soviet military pressure with help from the United States and had even moved onto the offensive in a campaign to push back Moscow's influence in Western Asia and the Horn of Africa. And yet, less than a year later, Iran's relations with the West were turned upside down without the Soviets firing a shot; the shah's mighty army simply collapsed.

Iran's experience showed that economic growth on its own was not necessarily a generator of political stability. On the contrary, it could provoke far deeper crises by saving large sections of the society from their enslavement by the problems of poverty. A poor, hungry and disheartened population is far less likely to revolt against authority than one which is reassured about the provision of its daily bread. Systems of government cannot simply purchase their legitimacy by offering material improvements in the lives of the people.

The Iranian experience also showed that economic development without corresponding political change could strengthen the most extreme strata in society. The battle against reactionary forces, whether religious or political – and the two often combine – must be fought in the political and cultural arenas and cannot be won on the basis of charts depicting economic growth.

Persistent demands for political change and social reform were one of the more important features of US policy in Iran during the 1940s and the first part of the 1960s. The Eisenhower administration put those demands on the back burner by emphasizing Iran's role as a link in the chain that Secretary of State Dulles wished to build around the USSR. Between 1968 and 1976 the Nixon and Ford administrations abandoned all pretension of forcing the Iranian regime into promoting reform. US policy in Iran was entirely restructured around almost unconditional support for the personal rule of the shah. And yet both administrations failed to study and understand the shah's deepest psychology, including his total inability to cope with a crisis situation. The United States was not even properly informed on the physical condition of the one man on whose fortunes it had pinned all its hopes in Iran. Less than a year before the shah died of cancer, an embassy report portrayed him as a man in 'good and strong health'.[8]

Roosevelt had committed the USA to Iran in the name of the basic values of the American way of life. But almost all those values were later quickly pushed aside in the name of fighting communism and profiting from Iran's oil boom. The United States presented itself as a champion of democracy and yet played a decisive role in preventing Iran's democratic development. As far as the American presence in Iran was concerned, a wide gap existed between the ideology that was proclaimed and the policy that was practised. The United States did not even defend the principle of private enterprise in Iran. In 1978 the Iranian economy was far more collectivized than that of, say, Poland or Hungary.

In the 1970s American interest in Iran was narrowed down to military and security issues and problems related to oil and foreign trade. The USA in effect abdicated the political role it had played in Iran for more than two decades. It even stopped monitoring the social and political impact of economic development on the traditional sectors of Iranian society which remained under the influence of the mullahs. It was not until less than five months before Khomeini seized power in Tehran that the embassy began preparing a report on the role of Shi'ism in Iran.[9]

The United States gradually lost its natural constituency in Iran – those sections of the society that believed in pluralism, free enterprise, limits on governmental power and respect for the individual. The shah, although a sincere ally of the United States on geopolitical matters, had little time for American ideals and ideas. He often mocked the American way of life and ridiculed the system of government by consent that gave every Johnny-come-lately on Capitol Hill the power to 'hold even the president to ransom, in the name of the people'.[10] He believed that he knew the American system well and was sure that he wanted no part of it for Iran. In later years he was even concerned that the many thousands of Iranians who studied in the United States might want to 'Americanize' Iran on their return home. The United States supported a government that was ideologically hostile to her and helped that very government repress forces which shared American political values even though they opposed Washington on specific issues. In supporting the shah, a tactical ally only, the United States abandoned its chances of seeking and finding its natural long-term allies within the Iranian society.

This situation was not unique to Iran. The United States was, in the 1980s, persisting with the same erroneous policy in several other Muslim countries. In a number of other countries, however, notably in Latin America as well as the Philippines and South Korea, the United States showed that it was not prepared to repeat its mistakes in Iran. In those countries the USA broke with tactical allies in power in order to help its strategic allies come out on top in struggles that might have led to revolutionary crises.

The term 'pragmatism', which gained wide currency in the United States from the 1960s onwards, was often used to justify a short-sighted and even mercenary attitude towards Iran. It was sufficient for Iran to be anti-communist and well disposed to Western interests for her to be considered a valuable friend. Some American policymakers, publicizing their dislike of ideology, forgot that such values as human rights, pluralism and free enterprise were typically ideological concepts that could not be defended by arms and money alone.

The conflict between ideological values and the practical policies that the United States pursued in Iran was only part of the problem. Washington was, at the same time, unable to develop and pursue long-term objectives. American policy was often short term, result-oriented and heavily geared to personalities. It suffered from the multiplicity of centres of decision making and of implementation. It was not rare for successive Iranian governments to incite one part of the US administration against another in order to obtain what had initially been denied Iran as a matter of principle. Further confusion was caused by the fact that frequent changes of personnel within the US machinery of state prevented the extension of the average span of attention to more than six months to a year. The American ambassadors in Tehran spent an average of less than thirty-three months in that post while their Soviet counterparts served an average of seventy-four months. None of the US ambassadors knew Persian and the number of Persian-speakers among other diplomats at the embassy was much lower than the average for other major powers represented in Tehran. There was, at the same time, very little contact between the US government and the many academic institutions that studied Iran. This contrasted sharply with the situation in both Britain and the Soviet Union where close links existed between the diplomatic apparatus and research centres.

Many of the Americans posted to Tehran seemed to want to discover Iran for themselves and had little time for the work done by

their predecessors. Between 1965 and 1976, for example, the embassy and the CIA produced four different biographies of Amir Abbas Hoveyda, the longest-serving prime minister in Iran's history and therefore no mystery man. The various biographies could not even agree on the premier's age. One said that his father was a tailor from Qazvin, while another reported that he was the son of a landlord in Shiraz. It was obvious that each new biography had been prepared by people who had not even read the preceding ones.

Covert action and secret diplomacy became important parts of US policy in Iran after the 1953 putsch that brought down the Mossadeq government. The shah, who was always critical of what he saw as excessive openness in public life in the United States, was more comfortable with secret talks where major issues could be discussed and decided quickly and, as he saw it, efficiently. It was the shah who initiated the tradition of one-on-one talks with Presidents Nixon and Ford. At some of these sessions the shah would insist that even note-takers should not be brought in. There are no records to show that these private talks were ever fully reported to the State Department or the Iranian Foreign Ministry. The net result of such encounters was a downgrading of the diplomatic apparatus. Excessive fear of leaks led both sides to make frequent use of unofficial emissaries for the purpose of transacting serious business. The first steps towards the 'privatiz-ation' of American relations with Iran were taken under President Nixon in 1969.

The Reagan administration was convinced of the overwhelming superiority of covert action compared to classical diplomacy right from the start. It wasted no time searching for a conventional framework within which the many problems it had with revolutionary Iran could be discussed and resolved. Some key members of the administration, notably CIA director Casey, manifested doubts about the loyalty of the traditional bureaucracy and some of its members. Even General Secord, for example, was not able to assure Casey that he was 'a true patriot' at the outset. Only six months after North had recruited Secord and used him on a number of secret missions, Casey noted that the general was to be 'trusted as a patriot'.[11]

The Reagan administration's recipe for success in international relations was simple if not simplistic: the United States would stand firm against the USSR on issues concerning Europe and disarmament while seeking to roll back Soviet influence in peripheral countries. In this latter domain covert operations were combined with the naked use of military force whenever feasible. The mixture came to be known as the Reagan Doctrine, although neither the president nor any of his key advisers ever actually used the term.

Ronald Reagan had entered the White House determined to rebuild American prestige, which he believed had been badly damaged by President Carter. Right from the start Ayatollah Khomeini figured prominently on the list of foreign leaders whom Reagan wished to cut down to size. This was why the administration ignored several attempts by the ayatollah to establish a dialogue with the White House from the very early days. Instead, the Reagan administration started organizing, financing and training a number of anti-Khomeini groups while launching Operation Staunch, which aimed at imposing an arms embargo on the Islamic Republic.

From 1983 onwards the Reagan administration had a choice of three options in its relations with the ayatollah. First, it could abandon all efforts to release the hostages through secret deals, which everyone agreed only encouraged further hostage taking. But this option would only have been effective if all the Western powers had acted in unison and, more importantly, had received support from the media. Second, the administration could adopt an openly bellicose policy towards the ayatollah and mobilize its allies and friends for the purpose of putting enough economic, diplomatic and military pressure on the Islamic Republic to force it into modifying its aggressive attitude. Third, the USA could try to appease the ayatollah by offering him the arms and intelligence he needed to fight his other enemies. Between 1983 and 1985 the administration tried the first two options and achieved little of consequence. The issue of the hostages did not simply go away, and united action on the part of the Western powers proved an elusive goal. In 1985 the administration began working on the third option, which suited its own taste for covert operations and secret diplomacy. From then on Congress, the State Department, the Pentagon and even the official CIA were left out of the picture as a handful of people tried to appease the ayatollah. The administration abandoned all pretences of playing a geostrategic game in Iran and the Persian Gulf and worked its way into a trap that was bound to snap shut sooner or later. The fact that covert operators despise grand strategy and prefer quick results that make them look good to their superiors meant that the entire Operation Recovery focused only on an exchange of arms for the hostages.

An American commentator summed up the situation in the summer of 1987 with a number of questions: 'Is there . . . a Western democracy that can coldly abandon its hostages, telling their families that it was their own fault if they wandered into dangerous lands? Can Western democracies delay taking action in a crisis until they build allied support? Can they resist a secret deal? Few have. To Iran they look weak, trapped by their hostages.'[12]

One of the most important mistakes that the Reagan administration and several other Western governments made in their analysis of the options open to them in seeking a dialogue with Tehran was their assumption that the ayatollah would work within the normal framework of the interests of the Iranian nation state. Seen from this angle there were few areas of importance where Iran and the United States might become involved in a clash of interests. There were no territorial disputes between the two countries; nor were they involved in a trade war. The two countries did not have a history of colonial hatred or memories of conflict behind them; they were in fact natural allies because of their mutual suspicions about Soviet intentions. Further, the United States should have welcomed access to Iran's markets, while Iran could have benefited from American technology in developing its agriculture and industry.

The Khomeini government, however, did not see the situation in such terms. It represented a universal messianic movement ready to sacrifice Iran's basic interests as a nation state in the service of the broader cause of conquering the world for Islam. In Qom in 1980 the ayatollah himself put the point succinctly in his first meeting with Islamic envoys whom he wanted to send abroad. He said: 'What is Iran? Iran is nothing but some mountains and plains, some earth and some water. A true Muslim cannot love a country – any country. For his love is reserved only for his Creator. We do not worship Iran, we worship Allah. For patriotism is another name for paganism. I say let this land burn. I say let this land go up in smoke, provided Islam emerges triumphant in the rest of the world.'[13] Between 1979 and 1987 the ayatollah had hundreds of his political opponents executed on a charge of 'patriotism', meaning that they had put the interests of Iran above the real or imaginary interests of Islam. To the mullahs Iran was little more than war booty and a stepping stone for future conquests. The agenda and interests of the Islamic Revolution did not always coincide with those of Iran as a classical nation-state. Such a contradiction between the state and revolution was not unique to Iran. France, Russia, China and other nations that went though major revolutions all experienced it in their own particular ways. The Iranian nation-state is a potential, almost natural, long-term ally of the West as it was between the seventeenth century until the fall of the shah in 1979. It needs Western support to counterbalance the overwhelming presence of Soviet power in the north. It also knows that it must seek its economic future in exporting crude oil, which only the West and Japan want and can pay for in substantial quantities, and in investing the proceeds in agricultural and industrial development which, in turn, would make access to Western technology desirable. The fact that more than eight years after the Islamic revolution more than 85 per cent of Iran's trade was still with the West and Japan reflected a reality the mullahs could not simply wish away.

Also, as a nation-state Iran had no interest in seeing the regional status quo modified in any significant way. During the past 150 years Iran lost territory and influence whenever such a change occurred, largely thanks to events beyond its control. From the 1820s onwards Iran was forced to adopt a conservative stance in the region and put stability and security high up on its agenda.

The Islamic Revolution, on the other hand, has quite different aims and interests. Some of these coincide with the long-term interests of the Iranian nation-state. But others are in direct contradiction of it. The revolution has a universal vocation. It hopes to unite all Muslim peoples under one flag and is fully aware that in order to achieve such a goal it has to change not only the regional status quo but also the existing political map of the world.

Iran's oldest and most important instinct is for survival. That instinct kept Iran on the map despite invasions by the Macedonians, the Romans, the Arabs, the Mongols and the Tatars over more than 2000 years of history. 'When there is a storm, bow your head until it blows over', says an old Persian proverb. Persian poetry praises life as the highest of values and urges man to be joyful and constructive. The Islamic Revolution, on the other hand, advocates a love of death as a means of 'an earlier return to the Creator'. Its highest value is martyrdom. It gives the impression of hating life because it fears that life might lead to compromise and corruption.

The American armada in the Persian Gulf witnessed the dual reality of revolutionary Iran first hand. Ships belonging to the regular Iranian Navy established warm and friendly radio communication with American vessels on a number of occasions. The Americans were surprised to see that the 'other side' also spoke English with an American accent, used precisely the same equipment and followed the same drills and routine manoeuvres learned at American naval academies. The military establishment of the old order survived with all its Western traditions alongside Khomeini's Revolutionary Guards who followed North Korean and Chinese models. Ships belonging to the regular Iranian Navy were given the task of detecting and destroying mines in the coastal waters of the United Arab Emirates and Oman in September 1987. At exactly the same time, however, ships belonging to the Islamic Revolutionary Guards continued with their mission of laying the very mines which the regular Navy would subsequently attempt to sweep off the seabed. The regular Iranian Navy invited Western TV teams to film its minesweeping efforts. The navy of the Islamic Revolutionary Guards, on the other hand, was caught redhanded, laying mines, on at least two occasions.

Another important fact that the Reagan administration and some other Western governments failed to understand was that Khomeini played his own game according to his own rules and paid no attention to international law, which he described as a 'Judeo-Christian plot'. All governments outside the realm of Islam belonged to the *dar al-harb* or 'the realm of war' and were therefore not covered by even the most elementary rules of moral conduct. An ideology that openly advocated murder in the service of the cause as a sacred duty would not hesitate to recommend lying and cheating as legitimate means of winning the diplomatic war against an enemy. Colonel North, who was visibly proud of himself as something of a Machiavelli, did not know that, compared to the mullahs of Tehran, he was not even a novice in the art of falsehood and duplicity.

The Khomeinist doctrine is put as follows by one of the saints of Islamic fundamentalism:

> We know of no absolute values besides total submission to the will of the Almighty. People say: 'Don't lie!' But the principle is different when we serve the will of Allah. He taught man to lie so that we can save ourselves at moments of difficulty and confuse our enemies. Should we remain truthful at the cost of defeat and danger to the Faith? We say not. People say: 'Don't kill!' But the Almighty Himself taught us how to kill. Without such a skill man would have been wiped out long ago by the beasts. So shall we not kill when it is necessary for the triumph of the Faith? . . . Deceit, trickery, conspiracy, cheating, stealing and killing are nothing but means. On their own they are neither good nor bad. For no deed is either good or bad, isolated from the intentions that motivated it.[14]

In the summer of 1987 the Islamic prime minister, Mussavi-Khameneh'i, ridiculed Washington's threats to attack Iranian military targets in the Persian Gulf. 'We are not a tree that trembles with that kind of wind,' he said.[15] He was not bluffing. Without the slightest feeling of remorse, his government had witnessed the destruction of five out of Iran's twenty-three provinces in a war that had made millions of people homeless and had wiped out an entire generation of young Iranians. Khomeini had said: 'Islam is a tree that needs the blood of martyrs to grow.'

By April 1988 the Gulf War seemed nowhere near an end, despite intensive efforts made by the United States through the U.N. Security Council. Resolution 598 remained a dead letter, whilst the conflict reached further tragic proportions when Iraq used chemical weapons against the civilian population of Halabcheh, an Iraqi Kurdish town captured by Iran in March. The attack on Halabcheh, in which more than 5000 people were killed by poisonous gas, followed weeks of missile attacks carried out by both sides on purely civilian targets. Attacks on oil tankers passing through the Persian Gulf also continued, underlying the impotence or the unwillingness of the major powers to impose even a partial cease-fire.

Through ill-designed covert operations the United States divided and weakened opposition to Khomeini, allowing the ayatollah to describe many of the leaders fighting his regime as agents of the CIA – a charge backed by frequent allegations to the same effect in the American media. Thus Khomeini, who had always been an enemy of Iranian nationalism, could make use of nationalistic feelings in Iran in order to cover his many failures. American patronage for anti-Khomeini parties, especially when coupled with cash donations, amounted to a kiss of death for several otherwise promising leaders. These leaders were no longer able to fight Khomeini on the battlefield of ideas, the very arena which the ayatollah dreaded most. They could simply be dismissed as hired agents, working in exchange for a stipend. As a result such ideas as democratic development, human rights, the rule of law and equality between men and women were, for the first time in nearly a century, left without known and respected defenders in Iran. The irony of the situation was that this vacuum in leadership coincided with the emergence of a genuine constituency for such ideas in many parts of urban Iran. The mullahs, who also forced confessions from Iran's top communist leaders that they had been Soviet spies, were able to claim that the two main ideologies of the modern world – democracy and communism – were foreign products designed only to advance the interests of the two superpowers in the Third World. For the first time in nearly a century the mullahs were unchallenged in their attempt to force the Muslim masses to unlearn all that they had learned from several generations of modernizing intellectuals.

The mullahs' fear of Western ideas – whether democratic or collectivist – can be illustrated by these words from Ayatollah Morteza Motahari, a chief theoretician of the Khomeinist movement until his death in 1979:

> The West represents the last attempt by Satan to destroy monotheism on earth. It tells man: God is dead and you are the master of the universe. Yes, the Western man can vote, can abolish divine laws, can even live without churches and without priests. He can devote all his time to pleasure and to debauchery and can stop work and go on holiday. Now it is difficult to find a man who would deliberately abandon the possibility of such a life in favour of a life of prayers, pilgrimages, penitence, poverty and unquestioning obedience to divine law. The satanic ideas of the West, which have their origins in pagan ancient Greece and Rome, have already finished off Christianity in all but name. Allow these ideas to reach the realm of

Islam, and the Faith of Muhammad will also be in danger. May Allah never allow that day to dawn.[16]

The typical fundamentalist, whether in Iran, Lebanon or in Malaysia is sincerely convinced that he is still fighting the Crusades against an aggressive 'cross-worshipping' West. Thus there can be no peace between Islam and the West; at best, only a truce could be arranged. And a truce is only acceptable where and when Islam finds itself in a position of weakness. Such a truce is only to be used as a brief respite in a struggle that must be resumed as soon as possible. It is no more than an opportunity for the forces of Islam to recuperate and prepare for the next attack.

This is how a leading Khomeinist theoretician sees international relations:

> Traitor historians [sic] claim that the Crusades ended centuries ago. But did they end? We look at the world and see that the opposite is true. The Crusades never stopped and the West conquered almost all Muslim countries. Even the Ottoman Empire was broken into pieces by the West and Egypt became a protectorate. Christians paid Hindus to massacre Muslims in the Indian subcontinent [sic] and tiny Holland, a ridiculous country made on a piece of swamp reclaimed from the sea, tried to convert Indonesia to Christianity. Iran did not become a colony but faced graver dangers. Its children began to learn about Western ways and defied the religious leaders. . . . Throughout the Muslim world, religious leaders, fully aware of Islam's military and political weakness, saved the situation by avoiding war but, at the same time, protected the masses by leading them into the protective shell of Islam so that they would not be contaminated by Western ideas propagated in the cities. That was not the end of the Crusades but a defensive withdrawal, a temporary retreat until Allah sent us our Great Leader, Khomeini the Smasher of Idols, who is going to end the Crusades for ever, with the victory of Islam.[17]

The mullahs' fear of the appeal that Western ideas might have for Muslim masses is illustrated by their frequent efforts to 'prove' that the West itself has acknowledged the superiority and justice of the Khomeinist cause as part of a process of moral surrender. An editorial in the London *Times* or the *New York Times* deemed to be remotely favourable to the cause of the ayatollah often receives massive publicity through the official media.

This is how one of Khomeini's closest associates in the spread of Islamic fundamentalism assessed some Western attitudes towards the Islamic Revolution in 1980:

> Every day people throng at our embassies in the West and beg for visas to come and see our Islamic Republic and our Islamic Revolution. Most of them are scholars and intellectuals and teachers at universities. They are envious of what we have achieved. For many of them spent years dreaming of a revolution that continued to elude them simply because their peoples

preferred to live comfortable lives and were reluctant to die for ideas. We had the good fortune that our young ones were anxious to die as quickly as possible. The thinking people in the West admire us and are full of envy. But those who seek domination and profit are afraid and prepare to fight us. Thinking people in the West know that their nations are guilty and doomed to destruction. They want to come here and apologize, ask to be forgiven by Islam. America's greatest law scientist Clark came here to ask the Imam to forgive America.[18] Other thinking Westerners are directly converting to Islam, before it is too late for them. Garaudy, the greatest French philosopher of this century,[19] has become a Muslim and wants to come here to pay his respects to our Imam. Yes, true believers, Islam is making a counter-attack for the first time in centuries. The new phase in the Crusades has just begun.[20]

The Khomeinist movement cannot be neutralized through its inclusion in the international system – a system it rejects as satanic. In this respect Khomeinism is no different from other messianic movements in recent times – most notably Nazism and fascism. But unlike these, Khomeinism cannot be eradicated through the use of force alone. For centuries the mullahs, not only in Iran but also in many other Muslim lands learned to refuse to acknowledge the consequences of military defeat suffered by Muslim governments at the hands of Western powers. Once again the tactic was simple: the poor and illiterate masses were to be kept out of the new system which had been imposed with direct or indirect Western participation. The protective shell began to operate immediately, cutting off rural Iran or Egypt or Turkey from mainstream politics dominated by Western ideas. Islamic fundamentalism has an established history of going underground only to emerge stronger many decades later. As long as Western ideas and ways of doing things are not adopted by the poorest masses, the fundamentalist has no fear of temporary defeat and military occupation by foreign powers.

Throughout the 1980s, however, the West confronted the Khomeinist movement on almost every battleground except the crucial one of ideas. While the United States flexed its military muscle in the Gulf and opposite Beirut harbour, it did not realize that its real strength in facing the challenge of Khomeinist obscurantism lay in its democratic traditions, advanced technology and the high standard of living that most of its people enjoyed. It also did not realize that there was at least one thing it could do that the ayatollah could not: wait for passions to cool down. It was the ayatollah who was riding the tiger in an increasingly dangerous world.

Appendix

WHAT WE FOUND WAS TRULY AMAZING

The following passages have been selected from introductions, written by the militant students who seized the US embassy in Tehran in 1979, to volumes containing documents found there:

In the name of Allah the Avenger

When our committed Islamic youths entered the Nest of Spies in Tehran for the first time they were not prepared to find what they found. They found a complicated structure for gathering information on all aspects of life about our land and its suffering Muslim people. [There] we found reports on key personalities involved in politics, commerce, industry, culture and all other aspects of life. We found electronic devices, computers, electric typewriters, shredding machines, telexes, cable facilities and other means required for the transmission of reports to Washington, the capital of the Great Satan.

The Nest of Spies had special personnel for finding out what is taking place in politics, in economics, in social areas and even in the military forces. These people wrote long, detailed and well-researched reports on the areas they covered. All members of the staff of the Nest of Spies were mercenaries with adequate training, each in a field assigned them by their leaders in Washington. They all had only one aim: to serve the filthy interests of earth-devouring America with no regard for the sufferings of the downtrodden nations of the earth. Their computer system was protected inside a steel safe which was larger than an apartment with several rooms and was protected by many electronically controlled gates. Worse still, much of the information they gathered was translated into code language which our committed youths could not easily decipher. This in itself is proof of their criminality since if these agents of the Great Satan had nothing to hide why did they have to put so many things into code language that nobody except themselves and their masters could understand? Some of the documents were quickly shredded or turned into powder by the mercenaries who had received specially adopted courses for the purpose. Their sole aim [in destroying the documents] was, we believe, to deprive the downtrodden nations of the world from getting wise to the Great Satan's secret schemes. As a result our suffering youths who have seized control of the Nest of Spies would have to spend months, maybe even years or decades, before they could decode all the documents and find out exactly what it was that the Great Satan wished to hide from believers in Allah.

In our search of the Nest of Spies we also found a veritable treasury of means of levity and of diversion. There were huge stocks of wines of all descriptions, alcohol, playing cards, chessboards, backgammon sets complete with ivory dice, film projection equipment with many films, musical instruments such as pianos, many different types of paintings, all things specially devised to lead believers astray and make them forget the need to devote one's entire attention to the worship of Allah. It is a matter of shame and of dishonour to admit that many people who professed to be Muslims, including some of those who had participated in the Islamic Revolution of our beloved Imam, had visited this Nest of Spies as guests and shared in the facilities available for levity and diversion in exchange for the information they furnished to the mercenaries of the Great Satan. These people we shall expose one by one so that their faces become black in the eyes of the true believers, so that they can no longer hide behind the hypocritical mask of support for our Imam, may Allah grant him long life.

Our rightly guided youths who conquered the embassy of the Great Satan in a magnificent operation that would have been impossible without the blessings of the Almighty also discovered many albums of photos in the houses occupied by American mercenary diplomats within the compound. These albums reveal the secrets of official parties held on many occasions, including every year on 4 July to mark the creation of the Great Satan as an independent country. We see individuals who claim to be Muslims facing the cameras with glasses, which are obviously filled with alcohol, in their hands and smiling as if no untoward event was being unfurled. We see men and women together, laughing and quite clearly in a state of relaxation assisted by the consumption of liquor, with not a moment to spare for the pains of suffering humanity in the downtrodden countries of the earth. Dressed in expensive clothing, these loose men and women can also be seen sitting at tables laden with huge amounts of expensive and elaborate food of the type no true believer can dream of consuming in this lowly world. Shrouded in an invisible whiff of corruption, we see these men and women, who have fogotten Allah altogether, caring about nothing but having a good time in this world and plotting against

Islam to the benefit of the Great Satan. Our revelations damn them in this world just as they are sure to burn in the raging flames of Hell in the next.

The conquest of the Nest of Spies represents a turning point in Islam's history. This is a splendid victory seldom matched during the fourteen centuries that followed the rising of the sun of Mohammad's golden message from Allah.

. . . America is an old, plotting and treacherous fox; it is none other than Satan, the enemy of Man. It is the enemy of Islam. It is perpetually plotting, making tricks and conspiring to pillage the property of weak nations and to continue its cruel and tyrannic domination of countries. In its plottings and trickery it has always made use of its scholars and experienced theoreticians who offer analyses and scientific views that are then used for the development of satanic policies.

But the case of America's plots against Islam was to be different because Allah had so willed. America has at its disposal some of the world's most experienced conspirators, some of the most talented tricksters history has ever witnessed. And yet, as we read in the holy Qur'an, Allah himself is the Supreme Conspirator and His trickery outwits the most talented of tricksters. This was why Allah the Great Conspirator led a group of our well-guided youths onto the path of conquest against the Great Satan and showed them the way to the seizure of the American embassy in Tehran which was a veritable Nest of Spies. It was Allah the Trickster who tricked the Great Satan by putting into the hands of our committed youths the keys to the Nest of Spies. . . .

Notes

1 Beautiful Americans

1. The country's name at that time was Persia as far as the outside world was concerned. The name Iran gained international currency from 1925 onwards.
2. Ali Naqdi, 'Americans in West Iran', research paper for Tabriz University, 1976, p. 19.
3. ibid., pp. 30 and 33.
4. The Turkish phase *Yengi-Dunya* ('New World') was used to describe the United States in Iran until the 1930s.
5. See Robert McDaniel, *The Shuster Mission and the Persian Constitutional Revolution*, Minneapolis, 1974.
6. Shuster was to write of his experience in Iran in his memoirs *The Strangling of Persia*, New York, 1912. The book was translated into Persian and served as an important item in the anti-colonial literature of the country.
7. It was to change its name to Anglo-Iranian Oil Company in 1926.
8. Abdul-Hossein Massoud Ansari's memoirs (in Persian), Tehran, 1968. The diplomat was a member of the Persian mission to Versailles and his father was head of that mission.
9. The term was used by General Shah-Bakhti who commanded Iran's defences in the southwest.
10. The Arabic-speaking tribes constituted a majority in those regions until the early 1950s according to the Iran Statistics Centre's analysis of the results of the 1338 (1959) census.
11. Mohammad Reza Shah Pahlavi, *Mission to My Country*, New York, 1961.
12. Roosevelt wrote to Secretary of State Hull that he was 'thrilled by the idea of using Iran as an example of what we could do by an unselfish American policy. We could not take on a more difficult nation than Iran. I should like, however, to have a try at it' (Cordell Hull, *Memoirs*, New York, 1948, vol. II, p. 1507.
13. Dr Jordan's college was later taken over by the Iranian Ministry of Education which renamed it Alborz High School.
14. According to Prince Firuz in private conversation in Paris in 1983.
15. Qavam made a brief comeback in 1952 when he served as prime minister for a few days. He was forced to resign as a result of street violence.
16. Donald Wilber, *Adventures in the Middle East*, Princeton, 1986, p. 133.
17. *New York Times* editorial of 17 November 1949.

18. Quoted by Barry Rubin, *Paved with Good Intentions*, London, 1980, p. 42.
19. The shah in private conversation in Tehran in November 1978.
20. Saleh is frequently mentioned in the secret documents seized at the US embassy in Tehran in 1979.
21. *Nowbahar (New Spring)* (Tehran), vol. 9 (1948).
22. In *At-Rafaseel (The Descriptions)*, for example, he wrote about California in 1948.

2 Satanic Liquid

1. Nassir Amini, who was at the time political correspondent for the daily *Kayhan* in Tehran, recalled in a private conversation with the author in London in 1986 that the whole episode had been 'stage-managed' by the US embassy in Tehran.
2. Grady is reported as saying: 'During my tenure as Ambassador to Iran I made at least half a dozen requests, all of which were ignored or flatly turned down by our government under British influence and assistance' (*New York Times*, 18 October, 1952).
3. The documents seized at the US embassy in Tehran show that with few exceptions the embassy was almost totally ignored by the State Department and later by the White House.
4. For more on this terrorist group see Amir Taheri, *Holy Terror: The Inside Story of Islamic Terrorism*, Hutchinson, London and Washington, 1987.
5. Cf. Mahmoud Mahmoud's *Hoquq – Begiran Englis dar Iran (England's Agents in Iran)*, Tehran 1968 and 1980.
6. Qiyam, a pro-Mossadeq paper, for example, claimed that the Fedayeen of Islam were in fact 'the *fedayeen* of Churchill' (*sic*) in its issue of 12 April 1951.
7. The full list of Tudeh officers was handed over to the authorities by a traitor among them, one Captain Abbassi. But a similar list of NCOs was destroyed by Tudeh members before their capture by the military police in 1953.
8. See Donald N. Wilber, *Adventures in the Middle East*, Princeton, 1986, p. 191.
9. Dehkhoda himself was not a communist and was, most probably, not even interested in seeking any political office.
10. According to Wilber, op. cit., the taskforce was headed by Kermit Roosevelt and had as members Wilber himself and Miles Copeland.
11. An editorial in the Tudeh organ *Besuy Ayandeh (Towards the Future)* on 22 July 1952 used the title 'Yankee, Go Home'. This was the first time that slogan was used in Iran and marked a change of tactics by Moscow as the Cold War intensified.
12. Documents seized at the US embassy in Tehran in 1979 (henceforth Documents), vol. 27, p. 150.
13. Interview with Shapour Dowlatshahi in 1980. Dowlatshahi was in charge of hiding Roosevelt and other CIA agents in Tehran.
14. For more details of 1963 uprising against the shah see Amir Taheri's *The Spirit of Allah: Khomeini and the Islamic Revolution*. Hutchinson, London and Washington 1985.

15. Conversation with Ardeshir Zahedi in Switzerland in 1985.
16. See Miles Copeland, *The Game of Nations*, London, 1976.
17. Wilber, op. cit., p. 192. Wilber also claims that Kermit Roosevelt exaggerated his own role in Operation Ajax (p. 187).
18. The figure is given by Kim Roosevelt, who offers his testimony in his *Countercoup: The Struggle for the Control of Iran*, New York, 1979. Much of the book has been 'sanitized' by CIA legal experts.
19. In a videotaped interview granted to Allan Hall of the BBC in 1977.
20. See *Defaiyat Dr Mossadeq* ('Dr Mossadeq's Defence at his Trial'), Dusseldorf, 1982.
21. Documents, vol. 4, p. 298.
22. Roy Melbourne, 'America and Iran in Perspective: 1953 and 1980', *Foreign Service Journal*, April 1980, p. 16.
23. The newsreels are owned by Paramount Pictures and are available at the National Film Archives both in Tehran and in Washington.
24. The term used to describe Communist Party moles in Iran.
25. Reza Amir-Khosravi, *'Enteqad as khish'* ('Self-criticism'), unpublished paper, Paris, 1985. The author, a former Tudeh leader reviews the party's 'errors' in 1953.
26. Conversation with Mohammad-Hossein Abbas-Mirza'i in Tehran in 1978. Abbas-Mirza'i was a leader of the workers at the cigarette factory in August 1953.
27. Bowie later joined the CIA and was its deputy director when Khomeini's revolution broke out in 1978.
28. Richard Cottam, the distinguished Iranologist known for his pro-Mossadeq sympathies, wrote: 'Regardless of foreign participation, Mossadegh [*sic*] could not have been overthrown if significant elements of the population had not lost faith in his leadership' (*Nationalism in Iran*, Pittsburgh, 1964, p. 229).
29. This charge was made in Persian broadcasts from Baku in Soviet Azarbaijan and from East Germany.
30. See Allen Dulles, *The Craft of Intelligence*, New York, 1963.
31. The term 'Ajax' was taken from the brand name of a washing powder manufactured in the United States. The idea was that the operation would 'wash the Communist Red' out of Iran.

3 *The Land where Happiness was Invented*

1. Barry Rubin in *'Paved With Good Intentions: The American Experience and Iran'*, London 1980, p. 97. See also Norman Hannah, letter, *Foreign Affairs*, vol. 52, no. 3 (April 1974) pp. 649–50. Raymond Hare, a former acting assistant secretary for Near Eastern Affairs, quoted John Foster Dulles as airing his objections to Iran's decision to join the Baghdad pact in following terms: 'It is too soon after their troubles.'
2. According to Abbas Aram, who served as the shah's foreign minister, in a conversation in Tehran in 1978. Aram related that the shah expressed 'resentment' at the fact that Dulles had opposed Iran's decision to join the Baghdad Pact.
3. The new alliance, the Central Treaty Organisation (CENTO) had Britain, Turkey, Iran and Pakistan as full-members. The USA became an

associate member and took part in the military committee of the alliance and never assumed a leading position.

4. A handful of KGB moles escaped the net at the time. One of them, General Moqarrabi, even became head of the army's counter intelligence section. He was exposed with CIA help in 1977 and executed by firing squad.

5. Needless to say, none of the authors mentioned received any royalties from Iran. The Iranian government refused to sign copyright conventions despite US pressure.

6. The play's director and main actor, Nosrat Vahdat, was himself forced to emigrate to the United States in 1979 when the new Islamic regime banned all comedy as 'the work of Satan'.

7. Documents, vol. 5, p. 92.

8. Among them were some of Mossadeq's prominent ministers such as Ali Shayegan who, after being accused by SAVAK of having had links with Moscow, faced numerous difficulties in obtaining a US visa. See Documents, vol. 9, p. 17.

9. The number of Iranians living in the United States was put, by unofficial estimates, at over one million, mostly in southern California.

10. The fact that the shah had close personal relations with the deposed King Farouk heightened tension between Tehran and Nasser's regime. Farouk's sister, Princess Fawziah, had been the shah's first wife and mother of his daughter Princess Shahnaz. The shah divorced Fawziah in 1948.

11. The coup leader, Abdul-Karim Qassem, was in fact an Arab nationalist and a very incompetent politician.

12. The powerful Wahabite shaikhs in Saudi Arabia did not consider Iranians, who are mostly Shi'ites, as true Muslims although a document recognizing Shi'ism as a form of Islam had been signed by the main leaders of Sunni Muslims in 1947.

13. Dulles' memorandum to Eisenhower, 28 June 1958. Also in Documents, vol. 9, p. 77.

14. Recalled by Abbas Aram, who served as the shah's foreign minister in the 1960s, in a private conversation in Tehran in 1978.

15. idem.

16. The bandit Dadshah, who was responsible for the double murder, was tricked and killed by gendarmes.

17. The Baha'i faith, created in Iran in the nineteenth century, represented the largest religious minority in the country but was not recognized as a bona fide religion by Iranian law.

18. In 1955-56, some Mossadeqist intellectuals and students visited Israel and came back impressed, among them Jalal Al-Ahmad and Abol-Hassan Bani-Sadr, who was to serve as president of the Republic under Khomeini between February 1980 and June 1981.

19. Documents, vol. 21, p. 163.

20. ibid., vol. 21, pp. 154 and 159.

21. ibid., vol. 23, p. 176.

22. ibid., vol. 21, p. 169, and vol. 23, p. 181.

23. According to a source in SAVAK interviewed in New York in 1987.

24. The cable was sent by Ali Shayegan, who had become a US resident in 1960.

25. The Confederation of Iranian Students Abroad was created in London in 1961 and immediately called for radical reforms and the holding of free elections in the country.
26. Documents, vol. 18, pp. 132 and 329.
27. Documents, vol. 18, p. 93.
28. The royal court was jubilant when Robert Kennedy was assassinated in 1968 (Documents, vol. 7, p. 130).
29. In August 1978 the shah told the author in Nowshahr, on the Caspian, that the Americans were again 'putting their old servant Amini into motion against us'.
30. See Wilber, op. cit., p. 221.
31. Documents, vol. 23, p. 180.
32. Bakhtiar spent some time in Switzerland before moving first to Beirut and then to Baghdad, where he was murdered by SAVAK agents in 1970.
33. For more on Khomeini's movement, see Amir Taheri, *Spirit of Allah*.
34. Hossein Mahdavi, one of the embassy's regular sources, told the political counsellor in 1963 that the mullahs were emerging as the real force of opposition to the shah and would, in time, force the Mossadeqists to rally to their cause (Document, vol. 7, p. 39). A CIA report, also found among the documents seized at the embassy in 1979, casts doubt on the efficiency of the shah's economic plans in 1964-65.
35. De Gaulle's crucial role in persuading the shah to mend his ties with Moscow was brought to my attention by Ahmad Mirfendereski, a former Iranian foreign minister who also served as ambassador to Moscow at the time (private conversation in Paris, 1987).
36. General Hassan Pakravan, who served as director of SAVAK in the 1960s, spoke of 'appreciable sums' spent on Nixon's behalf in both the 1960 and the 1968 presidential elections (in conversation with the author in Tehran in 1978).
37. Documents, vol. 11, p. 96.
38. idem
39. ibid., vol. 23, p. 22

4 Colossus with a Foot of Clay

1. In meeting with members of the organizing committee of the celebrations in Shiraz, 25 October 1970.
2. Nixon sent Vice-President Spiro T. Agnew instead. The president also telephoned the shah to offer his greetings and best wishes on the occasion.
3. Exaggerated figures, up to $1,000 million, were cited by anti-shah papers in the United States and Western Europe. Some figures took into account investment for roads, hotels, a new airport at Shiraz and other permanent facilities as part of the bill for the shah's party. The figure of $4 million was given by Minister of Imperial Court Assaduallah Alam and confirmed by Finance Ministry sources in 1972.
4. This was said in reference to the Indo-Pakistani war (related by Abbas Aram, who was foreign minister of Iran at the time, in a conversation in Tehran in 1978).
5. Documents, vol. 56, p. 19.
6. ibid., vol. 20, p. 17; also Abbas-Ali Khalatbari, then foreign minister of Iran, in private conversations in Tehran in 1977 and 1978.

7. Press conference at Tehran International Airport.

8. Private conversation in Tehran, October 1977.

9. The Pahlavi Foundation handled the shah's assets, which were estimated to be worth some $600 million in 1978.

10. Iran and Iraq were to go to war against each other in 1980 (see chapter 14).

11. No accords were signed with Kuwait and Iraq because the two Arab states could not first agree between themselves to demarcate their own continental-shelf lines.

12. All information concerning the Kurdish episode cited here came from Barzani in an exclusive interview he granted to me in Tehran in 1975. This was the mullah's last interview; he died of cancer in the United States in 1979.

13. The Afghans use the word *darri* ('courtly') to describe the Persian language.

14. Shafiq had established close links with Iran in the 1960s when, as his country's ambassador to Cairo, he also looked after Iranian interests during the period of rupture in relations between Iran and Egypt.

15. This was a republic only in the sense that the new ruler called himself 'president' instead of 'king'.

16. The two parties were Khalq (People) and Parcham (Banner). Moscow ordered their merger into one party in 1978.

17. The phrase *tout-azimut* ('in all directions') was coined by General de Gaulle and adopted by the shah to describe his new 'independent foreign policy'.

18. Documents, vol. 12, p. 100.

19. The islands were Greater Tunb, Lesser Tunb and Abu-Mousa.

20. He was replaced by his son Qabus.

21. The shah had agreed to one overflight only but the then deputy foreign minister, Ahmad Mirfendereski, told the Russians they could go as they pleased. He was later fired.

22. Interview with a former high-ranking official of SAVAK, Washington, 1987.

23. ibid.

24. For more on this see Amir Taheri, *Holy Terror*.

25. Official estimate in a confidential report from the Ministry of Foreign Affairs to the prime minister.

26. Interview with foreign minister Khalatbari, Tehran, 1975.

27. The contract provided for the sale of F4 and F5E fighter aircraft, C130 transport planes, helicopter gunships and the technical back-up needed.

28. Documents, vol. 12, p. 19.

29. Rahmat-Allah Moqadam-Maragheh, one of the shah's critics at the time, in an interview in Paris in 1981 (Also see Documents, vol. 36, p. 77).

30. Details of the alleged plot are given by Ali Davani in his *Nehzat Rouhaniyat dar Iran* (*The Movement of the Clergy in Iran*), vol. IV, pp. 132-4.

31. idem

32. On 30 May, 1972.

33. For example, the report cited in Documents, vol. 17, p. 22.

34. ibid., vol. 12, p. 101; supply of Howitzers to Morocco through Iran.

35. ibid., vol. 19. p. 47.

36. In private audience to Premier Amir Abbas Hoveyda in August 1974.

37. Quoted by Amir Abbas Hoveyda, then prime minister, in private conversation in Tehran.
38. idem.
39. idem.
40. According to private information Ambassador Richard Helms had 'recommended' the writing of the letter to Ford. Helms delivered the letter to the shah in person.
41. Amir Taheri, *The Spirit of Allah,* p. 168.
42. The contents of this report were communicated to the author by Ahmad Mirfendereski, then deputy foreign minister.
43. He was deputy premier at the time but later became President of Republic.
44. Interview with Gromyko in Moscow, August 1973.
45. The Soviet allies perceived to be threatened were Libya, Syria, Ethiopia, South Yemen, Iraq, India and Vietnam.
46. The Persian translation of the article was contained in *Bulltan Mahramaneh* (*Confidential Bulletin*) published by the Information Ministry for limited circulation.

5 Ugly Americans

1. There were no exact figures on the number of Americans in Iran and estimates varied between 35,000 and 75,000.
2. According to a confidential police report in 1977 the Mafia was involved in several casinos in the Tehran area and on the Caspian. The contents of the report was communicated to the author by Jaafar Sharif-Emami, who became prime minister in 1978 and ordered the closure of all gambling houses in Iran.
3. The nationals of more than twenty countries, ranging from Afghans and Pakistanis to Koreans and Japanese, also worked in Iran. The largest number of Westerners working in Iran were Americans, followed by Italians (11,000), West Germans (4500) and French (3500).
4. The phrase was used by Khomeinist propagandists as early as 1976.
5. To meet a shortage of doctors, for example, Iran imported some 3000 physicians from Pakistan, India and the Philippines between 1975 and 1978.
6. In a private audience in October 1976 the shah told the author: 'Our people are not warriors like their ancestors and we have to make sure that we have superiority in weapons in any war.' Asked whether that included a war with the USSR, the shah replied in the affirmative, adding 'at least until our allies come to our help'.
7. The US embassy was unaware of this and had heard only vague rumours about Kissinger and Heath coming to Tehran for what they believed would be a seminar sponsored by the Aspen Institute (see Documents, vol. 12, p. 115).
8. All figures in this paragraph are drawn from a confidential report by Ambassador Sullivan, reproduced in Documents, vol. 7, p. 90.
9. Documents, vol. 34, p.11.
10. ibid., vol. 34, p. 13.
11. ibid., vol. 34, p. 15.
12. Documents, vol. 22, pp. 86 and 88.

13. idem.
14. idem.
15. Private information supplied to the author at the time.
16. Michael J. Metrinko's diary of events in Tabriz is reproduced in Documents, vol. 6, pp. 59–63.
17. ibid., vol. 7, p. 140.
18. ibid., vol. 7, p. 98.
19. idem.
20. Documents, vol 7, p. 129.
21. ibid., vol. 7, p. 147.
22. ibid., vol. 7, p. 105.
23. Richard Helms in private conversation with the author in Tehran in 1976.
24. Hoveyda in private conversation with the author in Tehran in 1973.
25. The figure was supplied by the Information Ministry in Tehran in 1977.
26. According to a former high-ranking official of SAVAK in interview with the author in Washington, March 1987.
27. Statement by Cherik-hay Feday Khalq (People's Fedayeen Guerrillas) dated 20 February 1979, Tehran. Also Documents, vol. 9, p. 87.
28. The writer was Dr Mehdi Bahar and the book's title in Persian was *Miras-khar Estemar*.
29. Khomeini speech in Qom broadcast by Tehran Radio, 20 February 1979.
30. Khomeini in a taped sermon distributed in Isfahan in 1977.
31. The slogan 'Iran is the next Palestine [sic]' was designed to persuade people that American and other foreign colonies would be established throughout Iran just as Zionist pioneers had 'colonized' Palestine.
32. Documents, vol. 37, p. 22.
33. ibid., p. 108.
34. In an interview with the author in Tehran in 1975.
35. For Secord's role, see chapter 6.
36. Saeed Soltanpour, the poet, was executed on Khomeini's orders in 1981.
37. She resigned after press comment posed the question of clash of interests in view of Senator Javits's membership of the Senate Foreign Relations Committee.
38. The report was prepared by Sayyed Hossein Nasr, a distinguished Islamic scholar who became director of Empress Farah's private office.
39. Anderson's lands were confiscated without compensation by the Martyrs' Foundation after the Islamic Revolution.
40. David Rockefeller was Chase's chairman at the time.
41. In an exclusive interview granted to the author in October 1976 and published by the daily *Kayhan* on 29 October.
42. idem.
43. For a further discussion of this point see chapter 6.
44. Taheri, *The Spirit of Allah*, p. 213.
45. ibid., p. 212.
46. The letters did not reach Carter as SAVAK agents, posing as Iranian employees of the US embassy, collected all copies and destroyed them.
47. Leaflet by Cherik-hay Feday Khalq, published in Tehran. No date given.
48. Taheri, *The Spirit of Allah*, p. 213.
49. ibid., p. 212.

6 Fort Persepolis

1. In the turbulent years that followed these were replaced by iron fences.
2. See chapter 5.
3. Documents, vol. 23, p. 24.
4. ibid., vol. 4, p. 27.
5. Confidential report prepared for the minister of religious endowments in Tehran, 1978.
6. idem.
7. idem.
8. The politician in question was Rahmat-Allah Moqadam-Marageh (see Documents, vol. 23, pp. 111 and 112).
9. idem.
10. Afshar in private conversation with the author in London in 1985.
11. The Isfahan incident is reported in Documents, vol. 6, p. 103.
12. ibid., vol. 12, p. 109.
13. For example, Ebrahim Khajehnuri, who had worked with the embassy since the 1940s, told the political counsellor that the shah was finished in May 1978 (Document, vol. 22, p. 80).
14. ibid., vol. 12, p. 163.
15. Up to September 1978 there were no restrictions on the export of foreign currency from Iran. The Central Bank figures were for three months only. The flight of capital continued even after the government imposed a ban on the export of currency.
16. Documents, vol. 12, p. 145.
17. Author's private conversation with Sullivan, Tehran, September 1978.
18. Related to the author by General Gholam-Reza Azhari, then prime minister, in Tehran, November 1979.
19. ibid.
20. Documents, vol. 12, p. 52.
21. The two men in question were Nureddin Nabavi and Hedayat Eslaminia (Documents, vol. 27, p. 62).
22. Documents, vol. 27, p. 20.
23. ibid., vol. 27, p. 179.
24. idem.
25. ibid., vol. 27, p. 24.
26. ibid., vol. 27, p. 25.
27. ibid., vol. 27, pp. 44 and 47.
28. ibid., vol. 27, p. 70.
29. ibid., vol. 27, pp. 96–9.
30. ibid., vol. 27, p. 127.
31. ibid., vol. 27, p. 40.
32. ibid., vol. 27, pp. 56 and 57.
33. ibid., vol. 27, p. 78.
34. ibid., vol. 27, p. 151.
35. The belief that the United States had a plan to get rid of the shah still persists. Many Iranians believe that Washington brought Khomeini to power but later regretted this as a mistake.
36. Documents, vol. 37, p. 41.
37. idem.
38. Documents, vol. 19, p. 73.

39. ibid., vol. 11, p. 34.
40. The estate agent, a lady, did not get to see the shah. But she left her brochures and her sale offer at the embassy. These papers were later found by revolutionary students among the embassy's documents. The students concluded that the shah had bought the property and made much noise about it in their propaganda.
41. The political counsellor, George Lambrakis, began meeting Ayatollah Mohammad-Hossein Beheshti and Ayatollah Abdul-Karim Mussavi-Ardabili, two of Khomeini's principal aides in Iran, from the beginning of December 1978 or slightly earlier.
42. See Mohammad Reza Shah Pahlavi, *Answer to History*, London, 1980.
43. At an audience granted to the author at Niavaran Palace in Tehran.
44. Documents, vol. 7, p. 139.
45. ibid., vol. 7, p. 129.
46. ibid., vol. 7, p. 59.
47. ibid., vol. 7, p. 78.
48. ibid., vol. 17, p. 193.
49. ibid., vol. 7, p. 49.
50. ibid., vol. 19, p. 212.
51. ibid., vol. 19, p. 166.
52. ibid., vol. 19, p. 133.
53. Minutes of the meetings of the High Command of the Imperial Armed Forces, December 1978–February 1979, published in Tehran under the title *Methl barf ab khahim shod* (*We Shall Melt Like Snow*) in 1987, p. 53 (henceforth Minutes).
54. In *Bohran dar Iran* (*Crisis in Iran*), Paris, 1985, p. 77.
55. ibid., p. 102.
56. Minutes, p. 127.
57. The presidential decision said in part: 'Decisions on the acquisition of military equipment should be left to the government of Iran. If it has decided to buy certain equipment, the purchase of US equipment should be encouraged tactfully where appropriate and technical advice on the capabilities of the equipment in question should be provided' (Documents, vol. 34, p. 14).
58. This point was strongly raised by Donald Rumsfeld, who served as secretary for defence during Gerald Ford's presidency. Rumsfeld was overruled by Kissinger.
59. One example concerned the F18 L fighter which the Pentagon had not even fully studied. Defence Secretary Rumsfeld succeeded in stopping the project altogether.
60. General Yamin-Afshar in conversation with the author in Tehran, December, 1978.
61. Huyser later elevated the Soviet term to mean 'viceroy' and claimed that he was accused of having become the virtual ruler of Iran (see Robert C. Husyer, *Mission to Tehran*, London, 1986).
62. See Taheri, *The Spirit of Allah*, p. 244 (henceforth *Spirit*).
63. Badreh'i mentioned his plan to the author in December 1978.
64. *Spirit*, p. 248.
65. Documents, vol. 10, p. 5.
66. Minutes, p. 73.
67. Documents, vol. 10, p. 18.

68. The three were Reza Azimi, Gholam-Reza Azahari and Gholam-Ali Oweissi.
69. Documents, vol. 4, p. 103.
70. Minutes, p. 17.
71. The would-be minister was Mohammad-Ali Izadi. The embassy delayed his application for an immigrant's visa so long that the revolution changed his plans. Later he fled the country to settle in Canada.
72. Documents, vol. 5, p. 62.
73. ibid., vol. 5, p. 63.
74. ibid., vol. 14, p. 83.
75. ibid., vol. 14, p. 84.
76. ibid., vol. 14, p. 85.
77. ibid., vol. 14, p. 63.
78. ibid., vol. 14, p. 96.
79. Documents, vol. 5, p. 36.
80. Documents, vol. 4, p. 577.
81. Documents, vol. 6, p. 107.
82. ibid., vol. 6, p. 108.
83. ibid., vol. 5, p. 492.
84. Published in Navid, the Tudeh Party's organ, on 27 February 1979.
85. The Tudeh Party was to be disbanded on Khomeini's orders in 1983.
86. Documents, vol. 3, p. 19.
87. ibid., vol. 14, p. 12.
88. Saadati was later sentenced to death on a charge of espionage for Moscow and executed in 1981.
89. Ambassador Sullivan had retired a few weeks after the seizure of power by the mullahs.
90. Of the sums involved more than $4000 million had already been cancelled by Bakhtiar during his brief spell as prime minister.
91. Documents, vol. 3, p. 75.
92. ibid., vol. 2, p. 492.
93. Amir-Entezam in his trial in Tehran, 1980.
94. These conclusions are drawn from a number of cables sent from Washington to the embassy (see Documents, vols. 1–6).
95. Documents, vol. 10, p. 67. Cave's codename was Adelsick.
96. ibid., vol. 9, p. 48. The CIA officer's view of publishers is interesting. Noting that Bani-Sadr was then a publisher, the officer said in his report: 'Publishers often, according to years of experience, tend to be selfish and unreliable.'
97. Documents, vol. 7, p. 152
98. Documents, vol. 38, p. 112.
99. ibid., vol. 38, p. 115.
100. idem.
101. ibid. vol. 38, p. 117.
102. ibid., vol. 38, pp. 106–1120.
103. Documents, vol. 10, p. 17
104. Bazargan also defended his deputy against espionage charges. Amir-Entezam was sentenced to life imprisonment after Khomeini agreed to spare his life.
105. In 1983 Vladimir Kuzishkin, the KGB head in Tehran, defected to the

British and gave them a complete list of Soviet agents in Iran. The British handed the list to Khomeini as a gesture of goodwill. As a result eighteen Soviet diplomats were expelled and more than three hundred people arrested. Many were subsequently executed as Soviet spies.

106. Takht Jamshid is Persian for Persepolis. The name of the street where the embassy was situated was changed to Taleqani, after one of the mullahs who played a passing role in the early part of the disturbances soon after Khomeini seized power, but most people continued to use the street's old name.

7 The Longest Siege

1. The shah had suffered three attempts on his life and believed that foreign powers had been behind all of them.
2. Documents, vol. 7, p. 270.
3. ibid., vol. 7, p. 266.
4. idem.
5. The naval officer in question now lives in Houston, Texas. He related his experience in an interview with the author in Frankfurt, West Germany, in October 1986.
6. See Walter Laqueur's article in the *New Republic*, 8 December 1979.
7. Documents, vol. 51, p. 77.
8. ibid., vol. 10, p. 102.
9. idem.
10. ibid., vol. 10, p. 66.
11. ibid., vol. 10, p. 145.
12. ibid., vol. 10, p. 163. Farzami was later executed after his cover was blown as a result of the documents seized at the US embassy in Tehran in November 1979.
13. Documents, vol. 37, p. 63.
14. ibid., vol. 10, p. 13.
15. ibid., vol. 34, p. 218.,
16. ibid., vol. 34, p. 182.
17. ibid., vol. 34, p. 222.
18. ibid., vol. 34, p. 172.
19. ibid., vol. 34, p. 197.
20. ibid., vol. 34, p. 208.
21. The VOA Persian programme was the most-listened-to foreign broadcast between 1980 and 1984, according to a confidential study made by the Ministry of Islamic Guidance and leaked to opposition groups in Europe.
22. ibid., vol. 29, p. 73.
23. This figure was later reduced to $11,000 million in literature produced by the militant students.
24. The student group numbered around four hundred and at least thirty were communist militants. Many of them were later executed by Revolutionary Guards as part of the anti-left campaign.
25. For more on this, see *Spirit*, pp. 270 and 271.
26. This became the war cry of Khomeinists throughout Iran and later also in the Gulf states and Lebanon.
27. Documents (Introduction by students), vols. 1–6, p. 18.

28. For example, the sermon by Hojat al-Islam Ali Hassani-Khameneh'i at Tehran University on 2 Dcember 1979, broadcast by Tehran Radio.

29. Bani-Sadr, for example, claimed that the embassy had been the 'true government of this country' for twenty-five years.

30. Beheshti was not in Tehran at that time and two of his closest aides Khameneh'i and Hojat al-Islam Ali-Akbar Hashemi-Rafsanjani were on a Haj pilgrimage in Mecca when the embassy was seized. Rafsanjani, however, had made a vitriolic speech at a demonstration in front of the embassy in October shortly after the shah arrived in New York.

31. Information supplied to the author by a former Iranian diplomat who handled many of these contacts at the time, in interview in New York, 1987.

32. The tactic, known as the 'Rose Garden', was practised by Carter for a while and, according to some analysts, was a factor in his subsequent electoral defeat.

33. In December the aircraft carriers *Midway* and *Kittyhawk* were stationed in the Arabian Sea, some 100 miles from the Iranian coast. In January 1980 they were joined by aircraft carrier *Nimitz*, which stayed in the Indian Ocean.

34. The United States claimed the shah had left on his own accord. But the shah himself told his confidants in San Antonio, Texas, that he was asked by Lloyd Cutler, representing President Carter, to leave.

35. Sobh Azadehgan editorial, Tehran, 3 January 1980.

36. According to former Iranian diplomat (see note 31 above).

37. Wali Qanbari, a former associate of Ghotbzadeh, was in charge of protecting Waldheim. He supplied the information to the author in interview in Paris in April 1987.

38. The assertion that this was a KGB coup is not gratuitous. Babrak Karmal, who was installed as president of the republic, had been a KGB agent for some twenty-five years.

39. Beheshti said in June 1980: 'It is not our duty to get Carter re-elected' (in the daily *Jomhuri Eslami*, Tehran, 6 June 1980).

40. See Taheri, *Holy Terror*, for more information on the Khomeini editorial, Tehran, 3 January 1980.

41. Soviet opposition, for example, prevented the UN Security Council from considering sanctions against Iran in 1979.

42. A 500-page 'document' supposedly cataloguing 'USA's crimes against Islam' was published in Tehran in 1980 with an introduction by the then President Bani-Sadr. It contained photos of the 'show' put up at the Tehran Hilton by disabled people claiming to have suffered at the hands of 'American torturers'.

43. An account of the show was given at a meeting of the Islamic Majlis (parliament) in February 1981 by Hassan Ayat, one of the *metteurs en scéne*. He compared the show to passion plays in which actors play the roles of the martyrs of Shi'ism.

44. This was Bani-Sadr's version. Vance denied it.

45. Editorial in Bani-Sadr's paper *Enqelab Islami* (*Islamic Revolution*), Tehran, 12 March 1980.

46. See chapter 6 for details.

47. All the polls at the time showed that the majority of Americans supported stronger action and saw the president's previous response to the crisis as inadequate.

48. Most of them were married to Iranians or were children of mixed Irano-American marriages with dual citizenship.
49. These details were provided by the survivor, who was living in Texas in 1987. The author interviewed him in Washington in March 1987. The informant, an F4 pilot, flew his plane out of Iran and on to Cairo to escape from the Islamic Republic.
50. He was tried on a charge of having plotted to kill Khomeini and was executed in 1983.
51. See Hamilton Jordan, *Crisis*, New York, 1983.
52. An international tribunal was set up at The Hague to decide mutual claims case by case.

8 Businessmen with Noble Intentions

1. On 2 July 1980 one of the hostages, Richard Queen, who was suffering from multiple sclerosis was released. This brought the number of the hostages down to fifty-two.
2. Once the shah left the United States for Panama the Carter administration promptly announced that he would not be readmitted even for further medical treatment.
3. General Gholam-Ali Oveissi in interview with the author in New York in February 1981. The general said: 'I shall never forgive myself for having missed my shah's funeral. But I did it because our American allies advised it.'
4. His name was Sayf-Allah Nezhand.
5. Our account of the incident is based on interviews with Ameri, Qadessi, Suzani and other participants in the coup attempt (interviews conducted in Paris and London between 1981 and 1987).
6. Suzani is the same as Manuchehr Ghorbanifar of Irangate notoriety. We shall return to him later.
7. Suzani said in an interview: 'I knew nothing of the plot. All I did was to get foreign currency from one person and to hand over the same amount in Iranian currency to another contact' (interview with the author in Paris, May 1987).
8. Among those who escaped was Rear Admiral Ahmad Madani, once Khomeini's defence minister, who rallied to the opposition in 1980.
9. See note 5 above.
10. See Shapour Bakhtiar, *Ma Fidelité*, Paris, 1983.
11. According to a close associate of the general at the time.
12. Figure supplied by Princess Ashraf in private interview with the author in Paris in 1984.
13. ibid.
14. According to Taleb Shabib who was Iraq's ambassador to the United Nations at the time (cited by Fereidun Hoveyda at a conference in Paris in April 1987). Also Paul Balta, of the French daily *Le Monde*, related how Bakhtiar told him in August 1980, after a trip to Baghdad, that Khomeini would fall 'once a pair of hands are clapped from the outside' (in conversation with the author, Paris, April 1987).
15. According to several of Bakhtiar's closest advisers. Also the *Sunday Times* (London), 12 October 1980.
16. Oveissi in interview (see note 3 above). The general broke with Iraq the day Iraqi forces invaded Iran.

17. They had in fact increased their arms supplies to Iraq. At the same time it has been established that they warned Khomeini of an impending Iraqi attack (see *Spirit*).

18. This was conveyed by Lloyd Cutler, one of Carter's advisers, to one of the shah's former ministers in August 1980.

19. One scheme, for example, envisaged the seizure of the Vahdati air base near Dezful with a view to flying the fighters stationed there to Tehran for a bombing raid on Khomeini's residence.

20. Joseph Churba, an adviser of Reagan between 1980 and 1982, says: 'Iran was a dazzling triumph for the disinformation branch of the KGB, whose control of the events leading up to the ousting of the shah was, for all practical purposes, disregarded by everyone.' He adds: 'That Moscow was the principal catalyst in the Iranian hostage-taking was deliberately downplayed by the Carter administration' (*The American Retreat*, Chicago, 1984, pp. 15 and 21).

21. The account of the meeting was given to the author by two of the former ministers present.

22. idem.

23. According to Mehrdad Khonsari, a close Bakhtiar adviser between 1983 and 1987 in a private interview with the author, London, February 1987.

24. Hashemi in interview with the author in London, March 1984.

25. According to Mohsen Pezeshkpour, leader of the Pan-Iranist Party, who was a member of the coordination group (in a private interview with the author in Paris in 1983).

26. He had been a friend of Ghotbzadeh and an opponent of the shah in the 1960s but by 1975 he had become an ardent and active monarchist.

27. The term 'seed money' became an important part of the exiles' jargon.

28. Shariatmadari was stripped of his religious rank in 1983 and put under house arrest after being implicated in the Ghotbzadeh plot and accused of working for the CIA. He died in Tehran in 1986.

29. On the first day of the war he had sent a cable to the Iranian chief-of-staff declaring his desire to go and fight against the Iraqi 'enemy'.

30. According to two of Bakhtiar's closest advisers, who spoke on condition that their names should not be mentioned.

31. The name of the group, maintaining a semi-public existence inside Iran, cannot be given because it might endanger the lives of its leaders there.

32. According to Ali-Akbar Hallajpour, Madani's principal aide between 1979 and 1985 (in a interview with the author in London in 1985).

33. idem. This account has also been subtantially confirmed by Madani himself in a number of conversations with the author between 1982 and 1987.

34. This account of the opposition's activities is based on more than thirty interviews with various leading figures in the exile' movement between 1982 and 1987.

35. The radio programme was discontinued in 1982.

36. Louis is generally considered to be a KGB agent used for special missions to the West.

37. These details have been supplied to the author by several active members of the exile opposition who have asked to remain unidentified for obvious security reasons.

38. For more on Foster, see chapter 6.

39. Other politicians invited to join Amini's National Reconciliation Movement in February 1981 were Mohammad Derkhshesh, Rahmat-Allah Moqadam-Maragheh, Ahmad Bani-Ahmad and Mohsen Pezeshkpour. They all claimed that they refused because they did not wish to be identified with the USA. Derkhshesh and Moqadam-Maragheh later emigrated to the United States.

40. Documents, vol. 38, p. 118.

41. Quoted to the author by two aides of the young shah in 1983.

42. Kazemieh in conversation with the author in Paris, April 1984.

43. According to a senior Bakhtiar aide in conversation with the author in Paris in 1986.

44. The Mujahedeen's leader transferred his headquarters from Paris to Baghdad in June 1986.

45. See note 43 above.

46. Rear Admiral Shahriar Shafiq, a nephew of the shah, was murdered in Paris in 1980. A later attempt on Bakhtiar's life, also in Paris, failed. Oveissi was murdered, again in Paris, in 1984. Madani escaped an assassination attempt, also in the French capital, in 1986. Also in 1986 in Paris, Pezeshkpour escaped two attempts on his life. Between 1980 and 1987 a total of 25 opponents of the ayatollah were murdered in Turkey, Britain, Switzerland, France and the United States by death squads dispatched from Tehran.

47. In a confidential report (henceforth Report) prepared by Ali Amini in January 1986, p. 5. A copy of the report was made available to the author by a member of the FSI. The report also names two former ministers of the ayatollah as 'close contacts'.

48. Fatemi in conversation with the author in Wiesbaden, West Germany, in October 1985.

49. Report, p. 6. Hossein Khomeini is described as 'very influential among Muslim Iranian youth'.

50. Report, p. 4.

51. According to two exiled mullahs in conversations with the author in London in February 1987.

52. The actor in question now lives in southern California. He spoke on condition that his name should not be given.

53. Ganji in conversation with the author in Paris, May 1986.

54. This meant that the Bakhtiar group received only $50,000 a month after that. He complained to his confidants that the Americans had been indelicate enough to give him the bad news on New Year's Day (information supplied to the author by a Bakhtiar confidant).

55. More than three hundred people from twelve Muslim countries were involved in the network.

56. Information supplied to the author by intelligence sources in Paris.

57. Information supplied to the author by members of the Mujahedeen group in Europe, and the USA.

58. The names of the two are known to the author but cannot be given because both still live in Iran.

59. Information supplied to the author by intelligence sources in Paris.

60. The man in question was Hojat al-Islam Hossein Mahdavi-Kani, a dissident mullah.

61. Information supplied to the author by a dissident member of the Islamic embassy in Rome, 1986.

62. Information supplied to the author by a Lebanese personal friend of Ardakani and his wife in 1987.
63. Information supplied to the author by Arab sources in Paris, 1984 and 1985.
64. Information supplied to the author in 1986 by a former general of the shah who travelled to Israel at the invitation of Schwimmer and Nimrodi to discuss their plans in 1982.
65. Information supplied to the author by an adviser of Bakhtiar who was present at the dinner and acted as interpreter.
66. VOA eventually broadcast the news two days later, after having it confirmed by its own sources in Tehran.

9 Making History at Bar Alexandre

1. The Middle East imported an estimated $200,000 million in arms and military services between 1945 and 1987.
2. This is a codename. The minister in question agreed to make his information available on condition that his real name should not be used for fear of reprisals against his family in Tehran.
3. Vatandoust in conversation with the author in Paris, March and April 1987.
4. ibid.
5. Ghorbanifar in conversation with the author in Paris, April and May 1987.
6. ibid.
7. ibid.
8. Ha'eri in conversation with the author in Geneva, March 1987.
9. McFarlane said in April 1987 that he did not remember the name of the Iranian emissary but dismissed him as an adventurer. Allen and Silberman said in separate interviews, also in April 1987, that they rejected the Iranian's suggestion as irrelevant.
10. Information supplied to the author in Bonn, in October 1982, by two sources close to the Federal German Foreign Ministry.
11. The Jews came there when Hamadan, known as Ecbatana then, was the capital of the Persian Empire.
12. Kimche in conversation with the author in Vienna in May 1986 spoke of 'the objective community of interests between Iran and Israel'.
13. The arms embargo was the only one of the restrictions imposed by Carter which had not been removed after the release of the hostages in January 1981.
14. Iranian military sources supplied the information to the author, but this has not been confirmed by independent accounts.
15. Tehran also maintained an arms procurement office in Athens but closed it down in 1984.
16. The officers eventually managed to get their families out of Iran and applied for political asylum in Britain.
17. Ghorbanifar (see note 5 above).
18. ibid.
19. The ayatollah told the police that his teenage son had taken the vase 'by mistake'.
20. Ghorbanifar (see note 5 above).

21. idem.
22. For more on Khomeini's intervention in Lebanon, see Taheri, *Holy Terror*.
23. Hojat al-Islam Hashemi Rafsanjani recalled the murder of the US Marines in these terms: 'If the US Marines had to flee Lebanon and if a group of them even went to their graves under those circumstances, all this was part of the influence of the Islamic Revolution' (speech broadcast by Tehran Radio on 4 November 1986).
24. A copy of the paper entitled 'Iran and the United States: Towards a Future Friendship' was shown to the author by Vatandoust in May 1987 in Paris.
25. Also included in the list of 'nations sponsoring terrorism' were Cuba, Nicaragua, North Korea, Libya, Syria and South Yemen.
26. Khashoggi in conversation with the author in Istanbul in March 1984.
27. Turkish exports to Iran reached the $2000 million in 1985, a figure which represented more than 30 per cent of all Turkish exports.
28. These courses were organized in South Dakota and included instruction in using helium-propelled balloons for distributing leaflets over Iranian cities. Bakhtiar used two balloons to pour his own pictures on Tehran and Qom in March 1986.
29. Information supplied to the author by sources at the Federal German Foreign Ministry in Bonn, 1985.
30. The Tower Commission Report, Washington, 1987, p. 20 (henceforth Commission).
31. Vice-Admiral John Poindexter and Howard Teischer met several exiled leaders in 1984 and 1985.
32. Commission, p. 24.
33. Vatandoust in conversation with the author, June 1987.
34. idem.
35. Brigadier General Manuchehr Hashemi in letter to *Kayhan* (London), 23 April 1987.
36. idem. Hashemi does not give the other man's name, but he was Hassan Karrubi, an influential politician (see chapter 10).
37. Ghorbanifar in conversation with the author in Paris, May 1987.
38. idem.
39. Commission, p. 24.
40. idem.
41. See note 38.
42. The rag is named *Shahfaraz Aryan* and began irregular publication in 1981.
43. Estimate by the Concerned Iranians Association, Los Angeles, 1984.
44. The source is a businessman related to Khomeini by marriage.
45. The source is a former minister in one of Khomeini's cabinets.
46. Alavi in conversation with the author in Geneva in May 1987.
47. Rafsanjani cited the release of the hijack victims as a sign of his own goodwill towards the United States (speech at Tehran University, 4 November 1986).
48. The USA had even set up a special commission to combat international terrorism and urged allies to take stronger measures against the Islamic Republic.
49. Commission, p. 24.

50. Peres, in response to questions from the author in Jerusalem, November 1986.
51. Ghorbanifar (see note 37 above).
52. Commission, pp. 24-7.
53. idem.
54. Shamir, in response to questions from the author, Jerusalem, November 1986.
55. Commission, p. 26 (Also full text of testimonies by McFarlane, Donald Regan, who was White House chief-of-staff at the time, and Ledeen.)
56. Commission, p. 27.
57. idem.
58. Ghorbanifar (see note 37 above).
59. See chapter 7 for more on the coup attempt.
60. See note 37 above.
61. A Persian expression, used by Ghorbanifar on several occasions (see note 37 above).
62. An account of the meeting was given to the author by an Iranian personality who took part. He spoke on condition that his name was not mentioned.
63. By selling its own crude oil on account of Iraq.
64. A copy of the letter is in the posession of the author. The quotations are taken verbatim from the letter.
65. *Washington Post*, 11 March 1987.
66. During the terrorist control of the liner a paralysed American citizen was shot dead and pushed into the sea by Palestinian gunmen.
67. Lieutenant Colonel North's diary, cited in Commission, p. 31.
68. Ghorbanifar (see note 38 above).
69. idem.
70. idem.

10 The Shark, the He-Cat and the Owl

1. This was specially so in the framework of the joint Irano–US tribunal at The Hague, at least until the end of 1986.
2. A copy of the paper is in my possession, thanks to one of its original authors.
3. President Reagan, Vice-President Bush, Secretaries Shultz and Weinberger, Director Casey, McFarlane and Poindexter were among those present (see Commission, p. 31).
4. idem.
5. The 'deputy premier' trick was also used on the French when Ali-Reza Moayeri visited Paris and was given a red-carpet reception in 1986. He was received by President Mitterrand and Premier Chirac and treated as a high official rather than a fairly junior functionary.
6. The change from 'Yankee go home' to 'Death to America' also marked the decline of the pro-Moscow communists and the rise of anti-Americanism among the Khomeinists.
7. *Washington Post*, 8 February 1987.
8. 'Duodecimal' means 'twelve', the belief that Ali and eleven of his male descendants were the legitimate rulers of Islam. The sunnis, the vast majority of Muslims, reject that contention.

9. The three original principles of Islam were: monotheism, prophecy and the final judgement.

10. Ghorbanifar (see chapter 9, note 37, above).

11. According to Mehdrad Khonsari, Bakhtiar's contact with the NSC (in conversation with the author in London, February 1987).

12. Rafsanjani has emerged as the biggest exporter of Persian pistachios since the 1979 revolution. He is also majority shareholder in a number of private companies, including one he set up in 1982 with Khomeini's son Ahmad to import educational equipment and computers from Europe and Japan.

13. According to sources close to the Federal German Foreign Ministry in conversations with the author in 1985 and 1987.

14. In a number of public speeches Rafsanjani suggested that he would 'help' free the American hostages if the USA changed its policy on Iran.

15. An account of the meeting was given to the author by a member of the ayatollah's secretariat in a conversation in Frankfurt in 1986.

16. idem.

17. Speech broadcast by Tehran Radio, 19 December 1986.

18. The Americans, in fact, knew of Israeli arms shipments to Iran but did not take the matter to any official level until 1985 (see *Congressional Records* S2674, 3 March 1987).

19. This was made clear to the author in two long conversations with Kimche in Vienna in May 1986 and talks with Shamir and Peres in Jerusalem in November of the same year.

20. Commission, p. 31.

21. Testimony by John McMahon, deputy director of the CIA, cited in Commission, pp. 31–5.

22. ibid., p. 32.

23. The foreign country in question has not been named in the various hearings conducted in Washington, but it is generally assumed that it was Italy, which had been used by Israel as a supply route to Iran on previous occasions.

24. The Iranians used one of the Hawks in a test against Iraqi fighters in an attack on Kharg Island.

25. The American hostages in Lebanon at that time were in addition to Buckley, Peter Kilburn (61), librarian of the American University of Beirut (abducted on 3 December 1984), the Reverend Lawrence Jenco (50) (abducted on 8 January 1985), Terry Anderson (38), Associated Press Bureau chief in Beirut (abducted on 28 May 1985), David Jacobsen (54), director of the American Hospital in Beirut (abducted on 28 May 1985), and Thomas Sutherland (54), dean of the American University of Beirut (abducted on 9 June 1985). Buckley's death had been announced on 4 October 1985 before North's plan was conceived.

26. The French government was anxious to bring out one of its two captive diplomats, Marcel Carton, who was reported to be ill.

27. Hezb-Allah used the same tactic when it released other hostages after receiving cash ransoms or political and other advantages for the Islamic Republic in secret. In every case Waite was used to give the secret deals an acceptable appearance.

28. Speech broadcast by Tehran Radio, 5 June 1987.

29. Commission, p. 35.
30. ibid, p. 36.
31. Ghorbanifar in private conversation with the author in Paris, May 1987.
32. Commission, p. 36.
33. *Washington Post*, 8 February 1987.
34. idem.
35. Ghorbanifar (see note 31 above).
36. *Newsweek*, 11 May 1987.
37. An Iranian relative of Mr Hakim in conversation with the author in Geneva in 1987.
38. A former SAVAK director-general in conversation with the author in Washington, March 1987.
39. See note 31 above.
40. idem.
41. Casey 'had the idea that the president had not entirely given up on encouraging the Israelis to carry on with the Iranians.' He also noted that he suspected the president would 'be willing to run the risk and take the heat in the future if this will lead to springing the hostages' (Commission, p. 36).
42. ibid, p. 38.
43. idem.
44. *Time*, 22 December 1986.
45. The CIA official was head of the agency's Near Eastern section.
46. Commission, p. 40.
47. North said in his testimony at the congressional hearing on 7 July 1987: 'I sought authorization from my superiors for every one of my actions during my entire tenure at the NSC.'
48. See note 31 above.
49. Commission, p. 41.
50. See note 31 above.
51. Khomeini disbanded the Islamic Republican Party in June 1987, partly as a result of revelations concerning Farsi's alleged role in Irangate. But Farsi was untouched and continued to wield influence at the Majlis.
52. There was, of course, no evidence to support the allegations made against Meshkini and his relative.
53. See note 31 above. Ghorbanifar also sent copies of his documents to the congressional committees investigating the Iran-contra case in 1987.
54. See note 31 above.
55. Commission, p. 44.
56. See note 31 above.
57. idem.
58. idem.
59. Information supplied to the author by an associate of Karrubi in Paris, May 1987.
60. Kimche in conversation with the author, Vienna, May 1986 (a few days before the McFarlane mission arrived in Tehran).
61. See North's testimony at the congressional hearings in Washinern section.

11 Three Days in Hell

1. Shultz in Congressional testimony in Washington in February 1987. McFarlane, however, strongly denied suggestions that he had tried to imitate Kissinger.
2. Commission, p. 296.
3. According to Ghorbanifar in conversation with the author in Paris in May 1987.
4. Commission, p. 298.
5. Information supplied by a member of Khomeini's bureau in Tehran, during conversations with the author in Frankfurt in 1987.
6. idem.
7. idem.
8. idem.
9. Ayatollah Montazeri had not, however, approved any of his son's political options and in fact on one occasion called him 'an imbalanced young man'.
10. Commission, p. 334.
11. See note 3 above. Also mentioned in Cave's notes.
12. Commission, p. 320.
13. ibid., p. 321.
14. The conditions cited earlier by Najaf-Abadi merit being repeated: a full Israeli withdrawal from the Golan Heights, the release of seventeen Khomeinist terrorists imprisoned in Kuwait, the withdrawal of Christian forces from southern Lebanon and payment for 'expenses incurred in keeping the hostages'.
15. Qiyam Iran, 20 October 1987, Paris.
16. See note 3 above.
17. Rafsanjani's brother, Mohammad Hashemi, was head of the state-owned networks.
18. Commission, p. 330.
19. ibid., p. 311: 'Teischer summarized the Soviet military posture and threat around Iran. There are 26 divisions. The military districts in the Trans Caucasus have been reorganized and improved. Exercise activity has been intensified with respect to military action against Iran. . . .'
20. Commission, p. 337.
21. The charge was made during the talks at the Hilton in Tehran. Ghorbanifar, however, denies it.
22. This may have been an *ad hoc* deal involving other arms merchants working through Ghorbanifar. Iran wanted to buy twenty Hepar systems, but North, when in Tehran, advised the officials he met to repair those already stationed in the country instead of investing in new ones.
23. According to private sources in Tehran. The possibility of Kangarloo being assassinated was also raised in Cave's diary, which was handed over to the Tower Commission in 1987.
24. The mullahs released three hostages between their first contact with Washington and November 1986.
25. Figures cited vary between $3.6 million and $4.5 million.
26. Commission, p. 281.
27. 5 June 1987.

28. The daily *Jomhuri Islami* (*Islamic Republic*) (Tehran), 12 June 1987.
29. The French had a sad experience as well. As soon as they secured one release thanks to concessions, another of their nationals would be seized by the Khomeinists.
30. North in the congressional hearings, Washington, 8 July 1987.
31. Commission, p. 351.
32. ibid., p. 390.
33. Information obtained by the author from Lebanese sources in 1987.
34. idem. See also *Time*, 13 July 1987.
35. Commission, p. 352.
36. After Waite's abduction in Beirut, Tehran press reported that the archbishop's envoy's 'links with Washington' had been known all along.
37. Commission, p. 80.
38. North in the congressional hearings, 10 July 1987.
39. Commission, p. 391.

12 Mullahs in Washington

1. Details of the session were supplied to the author by one of the clerics present.
2. idem.
3. Shirazi was later dismissed from his command, but retained as a military adviser to the Ayatollah.
4. See note 1 above. Khomeini's pronouncements at the meeting were also quoted in a pamphlet published in Tehran by one of his former prime ministers, Mehdi Bazargan, in September 1986.
5. The article in question was published by *Washington Post* on 2 June 1986.
6. Information supplied to the author in July 1987 by a source close to Khomeini's cabinet.
7. The commission was to have as members Rafsanjani, Revolutionary Guards' Minister Mohsen Rafqidust, Defence Minister Colonel Mohammad-Hossein Jalali and High Council of Defence spokesman Kamaleddin Kharazi.
8. Tabatab'i in conversation with the author in Geneva, May 1987.
9. Rouleau in conversation with the author, Paris, July 1986.
10. Commission, p. 367.
11. Information supplied to the author by a high-ranking Pakistani diplomat.
12. Commission, p. 122.
13. Information supplied to the author by an associate of Karami.
14. Commission, p. 126. Shaheen was involved in extensive business relations with expatriate Iranians until his death in 1986.
15. Information supplied to the author by a source at Bakhtiar's office in Paris, January 1987.
16. Commission, p. 213.
17. ibid., p. 375.
18. ibid., p. 392.

19. Secord in the congressional hearings, May 1987.
20. Commission, p. 392.
21. idem.
22. idem.
23. Commission, p. 394.
24. idem.
25. Commission, p. 395.
26. ibid., p. 396.
27. ibid., p. 398.
28. idem.
29. North in the congressional hearing in Washington, 10 July 1987.
30. Commission, p. 403. The Islamic High Council of Defence is headed by the president of the Islamic Republic in accordance with the Islamic constitution.
31. Commission, p. 402.
32. Mehdi Bahremani used three different surnames in his dealings with arms merchants and foreign governments, including the Reagan administration.
33. Information obtained by the author from sources in Tehran. Also confirmed by Bahremani in his meetings with North in Washington (see Commission, p. 411).
34. Commission, p. 407. (Jack Anderson is an American columnist known for his sensational revelations.)
35. Commission, p. 408.
36. ibid., p. 413.
37. ibid., p. 414.
38. ibid., p. 413.
39. The tank was delivered to the Americans in Lisbon by Bahremani and Gholam-Reza Rahnema, according to information obtained by the author (see Commission, p. 542).
40. Commission, p. 414.
41. North told the joint congressional hearing in Washington on 10 July 1987 that the idea of diverting 'the residuals' to the contras first came from Ghorbanifar. Ghorbanifar, in private conversation with the author in July 1987 in Paris, said he brought up the possibility because he thought the Americans were doing it in any case.
42. Quoted by F. Akbari in *Tariq-e-Shohada* (*The Way of the Martyrs*), Tehran, 1979.
43. His name is often spelled Geidar in the western media.
44. From 1980 to 1987 the party papers in Uzebkistan, Tadzhikistan and Turkmenistan consistently criticized the mullahs.
45. Information supplied to the author by sources at the Islamic Foreign Ministry in Tehran. The illegal Soviet overflight was also reported by the bi-monthly *Ara* in its issue of 6 July 1987.
46. In a conference in Philadelphia on 11 December 1986, Fuller suggested that Khomeini's death might trigger 'immense chaos' in Iran 'allowing pro-Soviet radicals to seize power and ask for help from Moscow.'
47. Admiral Poindexter in the joint congressional hearing in Washington, 15 July 1987.
48. Commission, p. 543.

13 *Friends in Faith*

1. Information supplied to the author in Paris in July 1987 by an adviser of Rafsanjani.
2. Beheshti was killed in a bomb explosion in 1981 and his daughter denied any contact with the arms dealer, one Ahmad Haydari, who became a political refugee in France.
3. The passage was: 'And the Scriptures, foreseeing that God would justify the Gentiles by faith, preached the gospel beforehand to Abraham, saying: "All nations shall be blessed by you"' (Galatians, 3, 8).
4. Hakim at the joint congressional hearings, Washington, June 1987. At the hearing the congressional counsel asked Hakim how he felt about having played the role of secretary of state for the day. Hakim replied: 'I had it better than the secretary . . . I achieved more.' Senate Committee chairman Daniel Inouye expressed resentment that Hakim had had access to information and material that had been denied to Congress. He described as 'just unbelievable' Hakim's pledge of US military intervention against the USSR in defence of Iran.
5. Commission, p. 427.
6. Information supplied to the author by military sources in Tehran.
7. Information supplied to the author by political sources in Tehran.
8. A transcript of the telephone conversation was made available to the author through a member of the Islamic Majlis in July 1987.
9. idem.
10. Commission, p. 546.
11. Broadcast by Tehran Radio on 7 June 1986.
12. Four French hostages were released in exchange for some $200 million worth of material bought by Iran but frozen by the French government.
13. Commission, p. 416.
14. ibid., p. 538.
15. The agitation ended with the imprisonment of seven hundred doctors and the banishment of the leaders of the Iran Medical Association.
16. Information supplied to the author by a member of Bakhtiar's group of advisers.
17. Moscow Radio's Persian programme, 23 November 1986.
18. Information supplied to the author from sources in Tehran.
19. idem.
20. The magazine *Ash-Shira'* (*The Sail*) reportedly also received subsidies from Tehran.
21. Tareq Aziz, the Iraqi foreign minister, addressing the National Assembly in Baghdad on 14 November 1986.
22. Meese claimed that as much as $30 million was diverted, but the total sum available for diversion was no more than $19.8 million. Inquiries completed up to the end of 1987 showed that no more than $3.2 million of that sum might have actually reached the contras. Some $12 million remained unaccounted for.
23. According to Tehran media, largely confirmed by the State Department in Washington.
24. The hijackers' aircraft was forced to land in Italy and the terrorists were handed over to Italian justice, which put all of them, except their leader Abu Abbas, on trial.

25. *Time*, 2 March 1987.
26. A transcript of the conversation was made available to the author by a member of the Islamic Majlis.
27. Parts of the letter, leaked by Khoiniha's office, were published by anti-Rafsanjani mullahs in Qom.
28. *Los Angeles Times*, 28 February 1987.
29. Tehran Radio, 30 May 1987.
30. In speech broadcast by Tehran radio on 4 November 1986.
31. Term used by Rafsanjani's opponents.

14 A Gulf of Blood

1. The phrase was coined in 1971 by Amir Abbas Hoveyda, who served as the shah's prime minister for thirteen years.
2. *Time*, 29 June 1987.
3. The CIA reported that the risk of American ships being hit was 'quite high' (*Time*, 29 June 1987).
4. Dr Joseph Churba, once a Reagan adviser on the Middle East, wrote in a paper in March 1987: 'A victorious Iran will compete with the Soviet Union in their separate designs against Afghanistan, Pakistan and even Turkey. . . . Is it too much to say that having digested its victory, Tehran's gaze might turn to the subject Muslim population of the Soviet Union?'
5. Soviet warships began visiting the Gulf only in the late 1960s, at the invitation of Iraq.
6. The attack on the USS *Stark* and her casualties are not included in these figures.
7. That government, led by General Abdul-Rahman Muhammed Aref, had begun a discreet dialogue with the United States.
8. Moscow's share was around 70 per cent, while France supplied 25 per cent of Iraq's weapons, with the rest coming from Brazil, China, North Korea and others.
9. President Hussein's statement on 22 September 1980, broadcast by Baghdad Radio.
10. Figures compiled from statistics published by the government of Iran and of Iraq up to July 1987.
11. Documents, vol. 42, p. 75.
12. *Time*, 1 June 1987.
13. idem.
14. On Massirah the USA shared facilities with Britain.
15. The special envoy in telephone conversation with the author on 19 July 1987. He asked not to be identified.
16. *Time*, 1 June 1987.
17. Broadcast by Tehran Radio on 16 July 1987.
18. Interview with BBC World Service, broadcast on 25 July 1987.
19. Broadcast by Tehran Radio on 27 July 1987.
20. This view was reflected in exile opposition publications and also in Soviet comments on the American presence in the Gulf. Cf. *Irangate*, Novosti Press Agency Publishing House, Moscow, July 1987.
21. Kuwait News Agency (KUNA) report, date-lined Abu-Dhabi, 25 May 1987. The report claimed that the US Assistant Secretary of State for

Near Eastern Affairs Richard Murphy had met the Islamic Deputy
Foreign Minister Mohammad-Ali Besharati in Abu-Dhabi in May 1987.
22. Some figures could be instructive: Iraq had 1·5 million men (including
reservists) in its ground forces while Iran could field more than a million
men. Iraq had 5000 tanks compared to Iran's 7000. The Iranian Air
Force had 135 fighters and interceptors plus 95 transport aircraft and
150 helicopters. Iraq had a total of 615 military aircraft of all types
(excluding transport). (Source: *The Middle East Military Balance* cited
by Telex Confidential, no.475. 8 September 1986, Paris).
23. E.g. in al-Sharq al-Owsat, London, 27 October, 1987.
24. Tehran Radio took the unusual step of broadcasting a taped report
prepared for the Persian-language service of the *Voice of America* on the
subject.
25. Speech broadcast by Tehran radio on 5 November 1987.
26. In *The Failed Mission,* New York Times Magazine, 20 April, 1982.
27. *Washington Post,* 22 December 1986.
28. In response to questions by American TV reporters on 27 May 1987.
29. Press conference in Tehran, 30 October 1987 reported by Islamic
Republic News Agency (IRNA) English-language service.
30. Tehran radio broadcast in Arabic, 5 November 1987.

15 *The Journey to Irangate: A Conclusion*

1. Documents, vol. 12, p. 43.
2. idem.
3. This is how British journalist Kingsley Martin described Iran after a visit
in the 1960s.
4. Many of the technocrats who worked with the shah believed this theory
and cited it as justification for the lack of political development. Iran had
to wait for the magic $2000 figure before it could democratize, they
claimed.
5. See Documents, vol. 12, p. 112. The embassy estimated Iran's reserves in
1978 at over $19,000 million.
6. Documents, vol. 12, pp. 99 and 100.
7. ibid., p. 29.
8. ibid., p. 125.
9. ibid., p. 28.
10. In private conversation with the author in Tehran, October 1977.
11. North in testimony at the joint congressional hearing, Washington, July
1987.
12. *Wall Street Journal,* 24 July 1987.
13. *Gozideh sokhan-ranihay Imam (A Selection of the Imam's Speeches),*
Tehran, 1981, vol. III, p. 109.
14. Quoted Taheri, *Holy Terror,* p. 24.
15. Speech broadcast by Tehran Radio on 23 July 1987.
16. *Sayri dar Afkar Ayatollah Motahari (A Journey into the Thoughts of
Ayatollah Motahari),* Tehran, 1984, p. 39.
17. *Yadnameh Ayatollah Mahalati (Homage to Ayatollah Mahalati),*
Tehran, 1986, p. 79.
18. Presumably a reference to Ramsey Clark, a former US attorney-general
who attended a congress in Tehran on 'America's Crimes against Islam'.

19. A reference to Roger Garaudy, a former member of the French Communist Party, who converted to Islam at a mosque in Geneva, Switzerland.
20. *Yadnameh Ayatolah Mahalati*, p. 65.

Selected Bibliography

Ervand Abrahamian, *Iran between Two Revolutions*, Princeton, 1982.
Dean Acheson, *Present at the Creation: My Years in the State Department*, New York, 1969.
Abbas Amirie (ed.), *Iran in the 1980s*, Tehran and Washington, 1978.
Hossein Amirsadeghi, *Twentieth-Century Iran*, London, 1977.
Shapour Bakhtiar, *Ma Fidelité*, Paris, 1983.
Paul Balta, *Iran-Irak: Une Guerre de 5000 Ans*, Paris, 1987.
Abol-Hassan Bani-Sadr, *L'Espoir Trahi*, Paris, 1983.
E. A. Bayne, *Persian Kingship in Transition*, New York, 1968.
Mehdi Bazargan, *Enqelab Iran dar do harekat* (*Iranian Revolution in Two Moves*), Tehran, 1984.
Zbigniew Brzezinski, *Power and Principle: Memoirs of the National Security Adviser 1977–1981*, New York, 1983.
Jimmy Carter, *Keeping Faith*, New York, 1982.
Shahram Chubin and Sepehr Zabih, *The Foreign Relations of Iran: A Developing State in a Zone of Great-Power Conflict*, Berkeley and Los Angeles, 1974.
Richard Cottam, *Nationalism in Iran*, Pittsburgh, 1964.
Ali Davani, *Nehzat Ruhaniyat dar Iran* (*The Movement of the Clergy in Iran*), 11 volumes, Tehran, 1980–83.
Allen Dulles, *The Craft of Intelligence*, New York, 1963.
Mahmoud Ebtekar, *Jang ma ba Amrika* (*Our War on America*), Rome, 1984.
Anthony Eden, *The Reckoning*, London, 1964.
Dwight D. Eisenhower, *Mandate for Change, 1953–1956: The White House Years*, New York, 1963.
Hamid Ejtehadi, *Dar Nabard ba Shaytan Bozorg* (*Fighting the Great Satan*), Tehran, 1986.
Laurence P. Elwell-Sutton, *Persian Oil: A Study in Power Politics*, Westport, 1976.
Mozaffar Firouz, *L'Iran Face á l'Imposture de l'Histoire*, Paris, 1971.
William H. Forbis, *Fall of the Peacock Throne*, New York, 1981.
Richard Frye and Thomas Lewis, *United States and Turkey and Iran*, Cambridge, Massachusetts, 1952.
Richard Frye, *Iran*, London, 1960.
Abbas-Karim Gharabaghi, *Haqayeqi dar bareh bohran Iran* (*Facts about the Crisis in Iran*), Paris, 1984.
Robert Graham, *Iran: The Illusion of Power*, London, 1980.
Fred Halliday, *Iran: Dictatorship and Development*, London, 1978.
Nasser Hariri, *Mosahebeh ba tarikh-sazan Iran* (Interview with the *Makers of Iran's History*), Tehran, 1979.

W. Averell Harriman and Abel Ellie, *Special Envoy to Churchill and Stalin, 1941–1946*, New York, 1975.

Mohammad H. Haykal, *The Return of the Ayatollah*, London, 1982.

Mehdi Heravi, *Iranian-American Diplomacy*, New York, 1969.

Fereydoun Hoveyda, *The Fall of the Shah*, London, 1980.

J. C. Hurewitz, *Middle East Politics: The Military Dimension*, New York, 1969.

Asaf Hussein, *Political Perspectives on the Muslim World*, New York, 1985.

Sorush Irfani, *Revolutionary Islam in Iran*, London, 1982.

Charles Issawi, *The Economic History of Iran (1800–1914)*, Chicago, 1971.

Bizhan Jazani, *Capitalism and Revolution in Iran*, London, 1980.

Hamilton Jordan, *Crisis*, New York, 1983.

Ronald Kesseler, *Khashoggi: The Story of the Richest Man in the World*, New York, 1987.

Henry Kissinger, *White House Years*, Boston, 1979.

Martin Kramer, *Political Islam*, Los Angeles, 1980.

Bruce Kuniholm, *The Origins of the Cold War in the Middle East: Great Power Conflict and Diplomacy in Iran, Turkey and Greece*, Princeton, 1979.

George Lenczowski, *Iran under the Pahlavis*, Stanford, 1978.

Mahmoud Marandi, *Iran va Araq (Iran and Iraq)*, Tehran, 1985.

Robert McDaniel, *The Shuster Mission and the Persian Constitutional Revolution*, Minneapolis, 1974.

Arthur Millspaugh, *Americans in Persia*, Washington DC, 1946.

Houchang Nahavandi, *L'Anatomie d'une Révolution*, Paris, 1982.

Robert Paalberg, 'The Advantageous Alliance: US Relations with Iran 1920–1975', in *Diplomatic Disputes: US Relations with Iran, Japan and Mexico*, Massachusetts, 1978.

Mohammad Reza Shah Pahlavi, *Mission for My Country*, London, 1961.

Mohammad Reza Shah Pahlavi, *Réponse à l'Histoire*, Paris, 1979.

Thomas Powers, *The Man Who Kept the Secrets: Richard Helms and the CIA*, New York, 1979.

Jalaleddin Qorbani, *Khomeini bedoun Neqab (Khomeini without the Mask)*, Düsseldorf, 1979.

Ahmad Rabi'i, *Estemar Kohan, Estemar Now (Old Colonialism, New Colonialism)*, Tehran, 1986.

R. K. Ramazani, *Revolutionary Iran: Challenge and Response in the Middle East*, Washington DC, 1987.

Wafik Raouf, *Irak–Iran: Des Verités Inavouées*, Paris, 1985.

Kermit Roosevelt, *Countercoup: The Struggle for the Control of Iran*, New York, 1979.

Barry Rubin, *Paved with Good Intentions: The American Experience and Iran*, London, 1980.

Amin Saikal, *The Rise and Fall of the Shah*, Princeton, 1980.

Ali Pasha Saleh, *Cultural Ties between Iran and the United States*, Tehran, 1976.

Sa'id Simjur, *Ayandeh Lobnan (The Future of Lebanon)*, Tehran, 1987.

Dariyoush Shayegan, *Qu'Est Q'une Révolution Religieuse?* Paris, 1983.

Michael Sheehan, *Iran: The Impact of United States Interests and Policies 1941–1954*, New York, 1968.

Yadollah Shirazi, *Chera ba Amrika Mijangim?* (*Why Do We Fight America?*), Tehran, 1980.

Morgan W. Shuster, *The Strangling of Persia*, New York, 1912.

Robert Sole, *Le Défi Terroriste*, Paris, 1980.

John D. Stemple, *Inside the Iranian Revolution*, Bloomington, 1981.

William Sullivan, *Mission to Iran*, New York, 1981.

Amir Taheri, *The Spirit of Allah: Khomeini and the Islamic Revolution*, London, 1985.

Amir Taheri, *Holy Terror: The Inside Story of Islamic Terrorism*, London, 1987.

Abdel-Majid Tarab-Zamzami, *La Guerre Iran-Irak*, Paris, 1985.

John Tower *et al.*, *The Tower Commission Report: The Full Text of the Presidential Review Board*, New York, 1987.

Ghassan Tueni, *La Guerre pour les Autres*, Paris, 1985.

John Upton, *The History of Modern Iran: An Interpretation*, Cambridge, Massachusetts, 1961.

Cyrus Vance, *Hard Choices: Critical Years in America's Foreign Policy*, New York, 1983.

Vernon Walters, *Silent Missions*, New York, 1978.

C. W. Woodehouse, *Something Ventured*, London, 1982.

Robin Wright, *Sacred Rage*, New York, 1985.

Ibrahim Yazdi, *Akharin talsh-ha dar akharin ruz-ha* (*Last Efforts on Last Days*), Tehran, 1984.

Abraham Yeselson, *United States–Persian Diplomatic Relations 1883–1921*, New Brunswick, 1956.

INDEX